LIKE
Lambs
TO THE
SLAUGHTER

Johanna Michaelsen

HARVEST HOUSE PUBLISHERS
Eugene, Oregon 97402

LIKE LAMBS TO THE SLAUGHTER

Copyright © 1989 by Johanna Michaelsen
Published by Harvest House Publishers
Eugene, Oregon 97402

Library of Congress Catalog Card No. 87-061511
ISBN 0-89081-617-4 (Trade Edition)
ISBN 0-89081-795-2 (Cloth Edition)

Printed in the United States of America.

*In memory of
Joey, Carly, and Lindy—
three little ones who are now safe
in the arms of Jesus.*

This book would have never been completed—or even begun, for that matter—were it not for the fact that God has blessed me with faithful and long-suffering friends who took it upon themselves to help me. Two of them in particular—Debbie Smith and Sally Garrett—have spent the last three years or so of their lives cheerfully helping organize thousands of files and endlessly hopscotching all over Los Angeles scouting for research material. I'm grateful to them for their never-failing willingness to be of help and for the insights they provided.

I want to express my heartfelt thanks to Pat and Ben Jackson for donating the computer on which the book was written and for their continued friendship, support, and encouragement.

There are countless others across the country to whom I owe a debt of gratitude—parents, teachers, researchers, ministries, and even computer experts—faithful servants who must, for any number of reasons, remain nameless but to whom I shall always be deeply thankful.

I also want to extend special thanks to my editor and friend, Eileen Mason, for believing in this project all these years and for her invaluable insights and contributions to this book.

Most of all, I'm thankful for my husband, Randolph. He has borne with joy and godly patience what few husbands would have endured for the sake of this work. This book would never have been written were it not for his continued encouragement and love. It is an honor to be the wife of such a man.

FOREWORD

♦

Like Lambs to the Slaughter is an epic book. It is *must* reading
for every responsible parent and concerned educator. Most
Americans have no idea of the extent to which the New Age
occult evangelists have infiltrated our public school systems,
the media (particularly programming aimed at children),
books, films, toys and games, and even cartoons. Johanna not
only unveils this, but documents it.

This book will enable you not only to understand these
subtle religious programs, but also to spot the symptoms
which indicate when a child is being brought under their
dangerous influence. It will also prove that these programs
which are being masqueraded in our public schools as harmless personal development techniques are, in fact, ancient
occultic practices which should be labeled for what they are—
"a dangerous religion!"

Most importantly, Johanna, drawing upon her own unique
understanding of the occult, spells out how to help children
(or adults) who have fallen prey to these seductive philosophies.

Johanna's wit and writing style make a difficult subject
easy to read and understand. I will keep *Like Lambs to the
Slaughter* by my desk for constant reference.

—Hal Lindsey
June 23, 1989

CONTENTS

Chapter 1

The Beautiful Side of Evil

◆

New Year's Eve, 1983. I was sitting in the wings of Trinity Broadcasting Network wondering what on earth I was going to say. Hal Lindsey was hosting the New Year's television special and had asked me to discuss the most significant developments in the occult during the past year. Actually it had been a fairly quiet year on the occult scene. And yet I had the feeling that there was something tremendously important that I was supposed to say that night about the occult. I just had no idea *what*. "Please, Lord," I fervently prayed, "what is it that You want me to talk about?" A few moments of silence . . . and then I heard it—a still, small voice that said, "Look what they're doing to my children." And then again, *"Look what they're doing to my children!"*

As Hal and I discussed the occult, I pulled out some material I had with me—the now so-called "Diana letters" that a friend of mine had found left behind in a print shop's Xerox machine. These letters, in-house memos to a very large coven in Southern California, bragged about how many children in the area were choosing the "Pagan way." "Remember," the memo emphasized, "Each One Reach One!" Next, I talked about a Smurfs' cartoon I had watched a few weeks before in which the evil Gargamel had been given directions to "draw a circle in the ground, and in that circle draw a pentagram . . ."—thereby teaching millions of tiny fans the basics of ritual magic. And I mentioned that schools across the country were being inundated with occult books, assignments, and manuals.

After the program I was told that the phone lines of TBN were jammed for several hours with parents wanting to know more about how their kids were being lured and programmed into the occult and what they could do to counteract the trend. I knew the problem was extensive, for even before the publication of my book *The Beautiful Side of Evil* I had been gathering information on some of the more blatant occult influences that children were encountering.

It really should not come as any surprise to find our children being drawn into the occult. Since the early 1960's there has been an unprecedented worldwide outpouring of interest and participation in occultism. What was once kept hidden and secret by the initiated few is now paraded in the open and bragged about by those who have been lured by the appealing—even beautiful—aspects of the occult. Literally millions of people are involved in a desperate search for spiritual reality, and it seems that most of them don't much care what the source of it is or where they find it just so long as it's "real." They are sick to death of the dry and empty ritual, the unspeakable hypocrisy, and the suffocating legalism that characterizes so many of our churches today. And yet something deep within them yearns to be filled with the presence of God—not the God of the Bible, whom they have learned to despise and ridicule, but a God more to their own liking and understanding, a God who would just as soon be called "Goddess" or "The Universal Energy," and who promises them unlimited knowledge, power, and even the ultimate fulfillment of personal divinity.

New Age Voices Everywhere

Western occultism and Humanism have embraced Eastern mysticism to their bosom, and the bizarre offspring of this union has been christened the New Age Movement. What was once the squalling infant of the hippie era is growing up fast. The New Age Movement is spreading its roots into every facet of our society. Housewives can't even get out of their local supermarkets without running the gauntlet of magazines and weekly periodicals heralding the latest information on channelers, psychic healers, gurus, astrologers, etc.

It's the rare individual today who has not heard the term "New Age." Nevertheless, trying to give a precise or cohesive definition of the New Age is like trying to nail macrobiotic rice pudding to the wall. Everybody has his or her own way of looking at the thing. What is "definitely" an integral part of the New Age to one person is sneered at by another. Some cling to pyramids, crystals, channelers, goddess-worship, meditation, and guided imagery. Other New Agers are into the political aspects of globalism, saving the environment, "human potential," or any combination of the above. All, however, would agree that "dogma" and "decalogues" are out. Still, as long as you don't believe in sin or the basic sin-nature of man, Satan, the virgin birth, the exclusive deity of Christ, heaven or hell, or anything that smacks of Fundamentalism, it's even okay to be a "Christian." The New Age is the ultimate eclectic religion of self: Whatever *you* decide is right for you is what's right, as long as you don't get narrow-minded and exclusive about it.

It is truly ironic that our space-age, technological civilization whose god has been science, progress, rationalism, and cold-blooded empiricism has seen a mass stampede in the direction of Eastern mysticism and occultism that constitutes the backbone of this New Age Religion.

The statistics are staggering. According to a poll conducted by George Gallup, Jr., at least one out of every four Americans now believes in reincarnation.[1] In a recent poll by the University of Chicago's National Opinion Research Council (NORC), two million Americans report that they've had out-of-body experiences or near-death experiences.[2] Over 20 million are tuning into psychics and channelers, and a good number of these, tired of having to rely on a middle person, are now learning how to become channelers themselves. Almost half of American adults (42 percent) now believe they've been in contact with someone who has died. And at least two-thirds of these adults report having experienced ESP. An insightful article on the subject through the *New York Times* News Service recently reported that "a mounting tide of fascination with the supernatural is engulfing businessmen, housewives, military officers and artists of East and West. It's either plain old gullibility or the dawning of the NEW AGE OF AQUARIUS."[3]

Programming Kids into the Occult

The children have by no means been left untouched or ignored by the spiritual "transformation" of their elders. The question of how occultism is affecting the children of this country is no longer one that parents can afford to ignore. The children, in fact, are the key targets. It is, after all, the little ones who will be the leaders, teachers, politicians, lawmakers, and parents of tomorrow. What they are taught today as young children about who or what God is and about who they are, what the nature of reality is, what happens to a person after death, and what morality and ethics are based on must necessarily have a tremendous impact on the direction the society of the future will take. It is staggering to realize to what extent the answers they are developing to these crucial questions are firmly entrenched in occult philosophy.

In 1982 Michael London of the *Los Angeles Times* gathered together a group of eight people experienced in UFO and extraterrestrial encounters for a special screening of Steven Spielberg's movie *E.T.* London noted the following reactions of the group to the movie in an interview published in the June 27, 1982, edition of the *Times*:

"This is a true movie, not a romance. It's part of a conditioning process to prepare us for the arrival of alien beings."

"The movie is a vehicle," said F— who's employed as a marketing research analyst at Mission Insurance Co. "A lot of it is hokey, but it also invites the audience to be less afraid of the so-called paranormal. *And what better place to start than with the children.*"

... The other participants agreed that the film was primarily aimed at children—but that's all part of the plan, they said. "They're the ones who are going to have to deal with extraterrestrial visitation on a much greater scale."

"Everything's being done through the children. ... If E.T. would have approached the mother first, there would have been no movie."

Even so, the key manipulators of the New Age know that unless you train up and harness the spiritual direction of the children, there will be no New Age. At every level the child's worldview—that is, what he unquestioningly assumes to be true about himself and the world around him—is carefully being molded and programmed.

Saturday-morning cartoons are proving to toddlers that "I AM THE POWER!" They are told that there are "good" sorceresses and Witches and shamans and wizards who have access to untold power, and that telepathy and telekinesis (and those words are the exact ones used) are normal and useful abilities to cultivate.

In growing numbers of schools around the country, the children are being taught how to contact their spirit guides (euphemistically called their "Higher Self" or their "Inner Wisdom") to help them solve problems.

They are being sent home with assignments to research their astrological sign or to draw a *mandala* for art class or to practice the exciting rituals which little Elizabeth and Jennifer and Amanda do in some very popular children's books in order to become initiated into Witchcraft, just as they were.

In Gifted-and-Talented programs children are given projects dealing with Ouija boards—how to build them and use them, how to read palms, and how to be like the "amazing Mrs. Hughes," who helps policemen find missing bodies. They are being taught Yoga and meditation and techniques of guided imagery/visualization long used by shamans, mediums, and other occultists in the practice of their religion.

Despite overwhelming documentation of suicides and murders associated with it, Dungeons and Dragons now has a special edition of their "game" especially designed for use in school.

At the movies children are learning that "God" is a "Force" that they can tap into and manipulate for "good" or "evil" depending on their mood. They are learning to control and harness that awesome power through ancient Eastern techniques of mind control. They see that even though ". . . They're ba-a-ck," the evil poltergeists can be defeated through the techniques, chants, and powers of the shaman or the medium.

To some people these examples may seem thoroughly harmless. "After all," someone said to me once, "I've been watching 'Casper the Friendly Ghost' and 'Bewitched' for years and it never did anything awful to me!" Maybe not, although I believe that such a conclusion is debatable. However, taken in the context of the development and rapid expansion of the New Age Movement, He-Man and the Smurfs suddenly take on a whole new ominous significance.

Ushering in a One-World Ruler

To those familiar with biblical prophecy, the ever-increasing fascination with mysticism and the occult today will not come as any major surprise. Jesus Himself warned us that there would be worldwide religious deception on an unprecedented scale immediately prior to His return.

I believe we are living in the end times. I believe this generation may well be the one to witness the physical return of Jesus to this world. If so, then the one whom the Scriptures call the "lawless one," the "one whose coming is in accord with the activity of Satan, with all power and signs and false wonders" (2 Thessalonians 2:9), is in the world today. He is alive somewhere on the face of the earth waiting for the appointed time to reveal himself as God and Savior of mankind. He will not be dropping into a spiritual vacuum. For years now the world has been carefully prepared to receive him. One step at a time we and our children are being conditioned to accept the demonic signs and wonders and miracles that he will present as proof that he is God. It will make perfect sense to many people that this man is "God." After all, people have learned to believe that about themselves. He will just be "Goddier" than the rest of humanity, and therefore deserving of worldwide allegiance and worship.

We are raising a generation of children to be psychics, shamans, mediums, and occultists—a generation of children for whom there are no absolutes, no right or wrong, no morals, no allegiance to government or family. This generation of children is carefully being groomed to believe that Christianity is a dead, empty, irrelevant religion that is bigoted and narrow-minded; a religion to be feared and despised, for it stands in the way of the ushering in of the great New Age of "harmony" and "unity" and "peace." We have a generation of children carefully being programmed to understand the imperative for a one-world government, a one-world ruler, and a one-world religion. These children, soon to be adults, will at the right time "intuitively" grasp the importance of taking the final Luciferic Initiation[4] in order to enter the "New Age."

It's not too late to protect your child from what is already upon us. That protection begins by understanding how we arrived at where we are today.

Chapter 2

The Humanist Conspiracy

◆

The precarious position in which we find our children and our society did not spring up overnight. Long before the term "New Age" ever appeared on the scene, attempts were being made to turn society away from Christianity and traditional values through control of the public school system. Why? Because no other institution in this country offers the same potential for the intensive and long-term mass indoctrination of such open, pliable, and available subjects—namely, 43 million public school students. Humanists have worked long and hard for over 150 years to insure their domination of the public school system. They see their philosophies as the salvation of the world—the solution to all our social ills. The only serious obstacle in the way of their Utopia is Christianity. And it is an obstacle they have long been determined to remove.

C.F. Potter, author of *Humanism, A New Religion* (1930), said this: "Education is thus a most powerful ally of Humanism and every American public school is a school of Humanism. What can the theistic Sunday schools, meeting for an hour once a week, and teaching only a fraction of the children, do to stem the tide of a five-day program of humanistic teaching?"[1]

For decades now the Humanists have used the classrooms of this country as their personal pulpits and seminaries for the propagation of their atheistic, socialistic beliefs. In the 1960's especially there was an influx of humanistic programs presented as "alternatives" to the "oppressive" educational system of the day (i.e., reading, writing, and arithmetic are *such* a bore!).

So, bolstered by the "findings" of humanistic psychology, innovative educators "developed techniques to help people validate themselves, to communicate more effectively with others, to enhance their self-concepts, to ask directly for what they want, to clarify their values, to express their feelings, to celebrate their bodies, to use their will, and to take responsibility for their lives."[2] These techniques include role playing, global education, journaling, transactional analysis, sex education, death education, various forms of psychological testing and, of course, situation ethics and values clarification.

As a result, many of our children now know all about how corpses are embalmed, and many have written their own obituaries or suicide notes as class assignments. They have pooled their collective ignorance on "relevant" subjects ranging from nuclear war to homosexuality, euthanasia to birth control—all in the name of "clarifying" their values and morals. They have participated in survival games, in which the children must decide from a list of qualifications who in their midst should be allowed to survive in the lifeboat (or spaceship, or fallout shelter, or whatever). They know all about being "planetary citizens" and about the importance of redistribution of wealth in the world. They've learned all about sexuality and pornography in their sex ed. classes. They know about the occult and Witches, werewolves, astrology, Ouija boards, the Great Spirit, and Mother Goddess. They know that to mention the Bible, God, and especially Jesus of Nazareth on a public school campus is to risk being sued by the ACLU.

According to the statistics, what all too many of our children *don't* know is how to read, how to write, or how to add two and two so it comes out to four. They *don't* know geography or the facts of American history. They *don't* know what our system of government has meant to the preservation of freedom in the Western world.

The results of these "innovative humanist programs" in our classrooms are something which every Humanist can truly be proud of.

Back in the '40's, before everybody got "validated," about the worst disciplinary problems in the classroom were chewing gum, running in the halls, talking, getting out of line, and not throwing wastepaper into the basket.[3] Now that their values have been "clarified," however, the children are coming to understand what Sidney Simon and the other developers of "Values Clarification" have desperately wanted them to learn: that the values, moral codes, and beliefs of their parents and church are outmoded and irrelevant, and that neither parents nor church has the right to impose those values on them; that *any* value they choose for themselves is the right one, whether it be deciding to engage in premarital sex or deciding they are homosexual at the age of 11 or that they have the right to get an abortion or to take drugs. As long as they have "freely chosen" their "value" and behavior *themselves*, it's the right one, for there is no such thing as right or wrong, black or white. It would seem that we have "validated" an entire generation right into anarchy.

Dr. Brock Chisholm, head of the World Health Organization of the United Nations, said that "morality's a harmful perversion" and advocated that "the concepts of right and wrong should be done away with."[4] (It may be interesting to note that the inability to distinguish right from wrong still constitutes the legal definition of insanity in our courts.) Sidney Simon frequently tells teachers that they have to get all that "moralizing crap"[5] out of the classroom. So a lot of them did. And now we have an unprecedented epidemic of teen pregnancies, our classrooms have become frontline battle fields, and the drug and suicide rate among our young people has skyrocketed. After two generations of "clarified" children, we are now reaping the moral chaos that the Humanists have so diligently nurtured for us.

America Loses Its Moral Bearings

The eighteenth- and nineteenth-century forerunners of the

Humanists (the Unitarians, the Universalists, the Owenites, the Transcendentalists, and the Fabian Socialists) had firmly established their morally relative, atheistic grip on the educational system of this country by the 1800's.

The Owenites, founded by the father of modern socialism, Robert Owen, recognized that "proper education" was a prerequisite for the establishment of socialism. He and his followers were certain that if they could just educate the children of the country in their principles, they would eventually be able to establish a socialist state. To do that, however, they had to liberate the people in general, and the children in particular, from the tyranny of Christianity and other outmoded beliefs.

A crucial turning point came in 1805, when the Unitarians took control of Harvard University away from the Calvinists, from there sending out teachers whom they had carefully trained in their anti-Christian perspectives.[6]

According to one Universalist/Owenite, Orestes A. Brownson (1803-1876):

> *The great object was to get rid of Christianity* and to convert our churches into halls of science. The plan was not to make open attacks on religion . . . but to establish a system of state schools . . . from which all religion was to be excluded, in which nothing was to be taught but such knowledge as is verifiable by the senses, and to which all parents were to be compelled by law to send their children. . . .[7]

Their goal, it would seem, has been achieved. A little at a time they prepared the way, until finally, in 1963, with the government ruling against school prayers and Bible reading, God was ignominiously booted off the campus, along with the moral code He established. Instead the children are now taught that man is the measure of all things. They are taught that there are no such things as absolutes in *any* area of life, especially morals. Morals and ethics are "situational" and "relative."

These lessons have been carefully absorbed by our entire

society to the point where it has caused genuine alarm in some circles. *Time* magazine's cover article on May 25, 1987, screamed: "WHATEVER HAPPENED TO ETHICS?. . . Assaulted by sleaze, scandals and hypocrisy, America searches for its moral bearings."

Let us hope that America doesn't bother searching for those "moral bearings" in its classrooms. They're just not there, and haven't been for years.

At Harvard University's 327th commencement exercises in June of 1978, Aleksandr Solzhenitsyn, survivor of Stalin's prison camps and defiant critic of the Soviet regime, set his entire audience on its collective ear with a scathing indictment—not of the Soviet Union, as one would have expected, but of the West. On the campus of one of the institutions most responsible for the deliberate destruction of the Judeo-Christian basis for our society, schools, and ethics, he said:

> . . . in the West the idea of freedom stems from the humanistic idea that man does not bear any evil in himself. Life's defects are supposedly caused by a misguided social system. As a result, crime is now more prevalent in Western nations than in the lawless Soviet society. The cause of this moral poverty . . . can be traced to . . . a rejection of Christianity with its sense of responsibility to God and society.[8]

As far as I know, Harvard has not invited him back to speak since.

Psyched Out by the NEA

The last 20 years or so has witnessed an intriguing and escalating transformation. What used to be a classroom in which children were taught basic skills such as reading, writing, and arithmetic has now metamorphosed into a laboratory for teachers who are being encouraged to "experiment" with techniques designed to produce what the behaviorists call a Total Attitudinal Change in the child.

The basic goal of education is change... human change in desirable directions.... This issue... focuses attention upon the school as a change-agent... and the specific focus is on changing people.[9]

You will notice that the stated goal of education is to *change* people, not *educate* people. The two are not the same at all, as the National Educators' Association (NEA) knows very well. Education has not been a particularly high priority on their agenda for years, as even *Reader's Digest* pointed out in an article called "Guess Who Spells Disaster for Education?":

... None other than the powerful National Education Association, as it plays politics and fights to block much-needed reform in our nation's schools.[10]

NEA president Mary Futrell points out that "instruction and professional development have been on the back burner to us compared with political action." That political-action agenda embraces "radical socialism, World Government, abortion on demand, gun control, decriminalization of marijuana, sex education in the schools, nuclear disarmament," according to Dr. Samuel Blumenfeld, author of *NEA: Trojan Horse in American Education*.[11] The NEA, in existence since 1857, is now the most powerful labor union in this country: It controls 71 percent of America's public school teachers, has a membership of 1.6 million, and is working hard to bring the rest under its "care" whether they like it or not.

Vanderbilt University Professor Chester E. Finn, Jr., analyzed the NEA's materials and found them "pervaded by a cohesive radical strategy.... It includes the delegitimizing of all authority, save that of the state, the degradation of traditional morality, and the encouragement of citizens in general and children in particular to despise the rules and customs that make their society a functional democracy. The NEA is drifting into exceedingly dangerous waters, and probably carrying more than a few teachers and pupils with it."[12]

We spend over *308 billion dollars* annually on education.[13] That's more than the national budget for defense! And what do we have to show for it? About 60 million functional illiterates. Bill Bennett, now ex-Secretary of Education, said that he was sick and tired of "schools that gobble tax money while graduating students who can't read or write." He also thoroughly and accurately stomped the NEA for being "more interested in power, perks, and protection than in teaching the young."[14] Nevertheless, the NEA still wants more money for their programs, telling us that is what will solve the problem.

As William Bowen points out in *Globalism: America's Demise*, "It does not take a lot of time and money to educate children. It does take a lot of time and money to indoctrinate and modify their values."[15]

In order to change and modify the children, contemporary educational theories supported by the NEA encourage educators to use psychotherapeutic techniques such as role-playing, role reversal, psychodrama, encounter group sessions, journaling, sensitivity training (sometimes called "T groups" or "encounter groups"), "magic circles," psychological testing, "games," and questionnaires with open-ended questions designed to delve into the most private thoughts and beliefs of the child and his family.

These techniques were originally developed by psychiatrists to be used in their work with seriously disturbed patients in mental hospitals. Some of the techniques, such as role-playing are so sensitive and potentially dangerous that even experienced mental health workers hesitate to use them undiscerningly. Yet teachers around the country are being instructed to use them on their students. As applied in the classroom, these techniques are specifically designed to gain access to the inner workings of the child in order to release him from the "outmoded" values and beliefs of his parents and to "improve" him with the "new" and "desirable" Humanist beliefs appropriate to the "global citizen" they expect him to become.

The children, you see, don't need *educating*, in the view of these "educators"; what they need is *therapy*. Why? Because most Humanist educators believe that our children are mentally imbalanced and emotionally disturbed. According to

Dr. Chester Pierce in an address given to 2000 teachers in Denver in 1973:

> Every child in America who enters school at the age of five is mentally ill, because he comes to school with allegiance toward our elected officials, toward our founding fathers, toward our institutions, toward this form of government we have . . . patriotism, nationalism, sovereignty. . . . All of this proves the children are sick, because the truly well individual is one who has rejected all of those things and is what I would call the true international child of the future.[16]

If a child is brought up to love this country and all it has traditionally stood for, he is said to be mentally ill! Paul Brandwein asserts:

> Any child who believes in God is mentally ill.[17]

Not only that, but:

> The American family structure produces mentally ill children.[18]

The NEA seems to be 100 percent behind the idea that all the children of this country are in need of therapy. In their report "Education for the 70's" they state that "schools will become clinics whose purpose is to provide individualized, psycho-social treatment for the student, and teachers must become psycho-social therapists."[19]

The Cloning of Future Generations

The basic beliefs of Humanism that are spawning these outrageous teachings and statements we are hearing from our educators and policymakers are clearly spelled out for us in the First Humanist Manifesto, written in 1933 by John Dewey, the "father of progressive education." It was later updated by Paul Kurtz in the Second Humanist Manifesto in

1973. It is well worth taking the time to list some of the tenets of these manifestos, since the documents were signed primarily by educators and policymakers,[20] and since much of our educational system of today is based on these tenets. The NEA, in fact, has been working diligently to bring education into full compliance with the blueprint presented in the Humanist Manifesto.

Here is the vision of the future set forth in the introduction to the Second Manifesto:

> We stand at the dawn of a new age.... Using technology wisely, we can control our environment, conquer poverty, markedly reduce disease, extend our life-span significantly, modify our behavior, alter the course of human evolution and cultural development, unlock vast new powers.... The ultimate goal should be the fulfillment of the potential for growth in each human personality—not for the favored few, but for all of humankind. Only a shared world and global measure will suffice.

In order to accomplish these thoroughly New Age goals, the Humanists intend to break down the fundamental belief systems that are the basis of our society and the Christian faith. These tenets of Humanism provide one of the most diabolical pieces of propaganda ever conceived. Let me give you a sample from the 17 tenets they present in the Second Humanist Manifesto.

FIRST

> We believe... that traditional dogmatic or authoritarian religions that place revelation, God, ritual, or creed above human needs and experience do a disservice to the human species... We find insufficient evidence for belief in the existence of a supernatural... as non-theists, we begin with humans, not God, nature, not deity.... No deity will save us; we must save ourselves.

SECOND

Promises of immortal salvation or fear of eternal damnation are both illusory and harmful. They distract humans from present concerns, from self-actualization, and from rectifying social injustices.

THIRD

Ethics is autonomous and situational, needing no theological or ideological sanction. . . . We strive for the good life here and now.

SIXTH

In the area of sexuality, we believe that intolerant attitudes, often cultivated by orthodox religions and puritanical cultures, unduly repress sexual conduct. The right to birth control, abortion and divorce should be recognized. . . . The many varieties of sexual exploration should not in themselves be considered "evil" . . . individuals should be permitted to express their sexual proclivities and pursue their life-styles as they desire.

SEVENTH

To enhance freedom and dignity the individual must experience a full range of civil liberties in all societies. This includes . . . a recognition of an individual's right to die with dignity, euthanasia, and the right to suicide.

NINTH

The separation of church and state and the separation of ideology and state are imperatives. The state should encourage maximum freedom for different moral, political, religious bodies through the use of public monies, not espouse a single ideology and function thereby as an instrument of propaganda or oppression, particularly against dissenters.

TENTH

Humane societies should evaluate economic systems not by rhetoric or ideology . . . the door is open to alternative economic systems.

ELEVENTH

. . . Innovative and experimental forms of education are to be welcomed.

TWELFTH

We deplore the division of humankind on nationalistic grounds. We have reached a turning point in human history where the best option is to transcend the limits of national sovereignty and to move toward the building of a world community in which all sectors of the human family can participate. Thus we look to the development of a system of world law and a world order based upon transnational federal government. . . . We thus reaffirm a commitment to the building of world community, at the same time recognizing that this commits us to some hard choices.

THIRTEENTH

This world community must renounce the resort to violence and force as a method of solving international disputes. . . . War is obsolete. So is the use of nuclear, biological, and chemical weapons. It is a planetary imperative to reduce the level of military expenditures and turn these savings to peaceful and people-oriented uses.

FIFTEENTH

"... Hence extreme disproportions in wealth, income, and economic growth should be reduced on a worldwide basis.

The above tenets sound eerily familiar to what the children are being taught in most schools today. They will also sound familiar to any of you acquainted with the basic teachings of Naziism, socialism, and the philosophy of the New Agers, or "globalists," for that is exactly what these manifestos call for: the establishment of a socialist global order. Read the twelfth and fifteenth tenet again carefully. They "deplore the division of humankind on nationalistic grounds." While they do admit that building their "world community"... "commits us to some hard choices," what they don't tell you in the midst of their noble sounding proclamations, is that those "hard choices" include forfeiting the freedom of our American way of life in exchange for the glories of a system so poignantly typified by other governments based on their principles; the Soviet Union and Red China, for instance.

It would seem that what the Humanists are hoping to produce in our schools are atheistic, sociopathic, globalist clones whose only allegiance is to themselves and the "global" values with which they have been programmed. The Humanists hope to be able to program the child *before* the parents have a chance to infect him with their middle-class diseased beliefs in God, morality, and allegiance to this country. Through child-advocacy legislation (supported by the American Federation of Teachers and the NEA), they hope to eventually be able to mandate *compulsory* education for children beginning at age three! The younger, the better.

A Religion By Any Other Name...

John Dewey and the disciples that followed him have

worked diligently to expel traditional religion and values from the public schools.[21] They seem to have systematically and deliberately censored the facts not only about basic American history but also about the historical role that religion and Christianity have played in the forming of this nation.

For well over 20 years now, people like Mel and Norma Gabler have been documenting and protesting the deliberate and unmistakable Humanist bias and twisting of our history in our textbooks and curricula. A study by the U.S. Department of Education on "Religion and Traditional Values in Public School Textbooks" substantiates their findings:

> Those responsible for these books appear to have a deep-seated fear of any form of active contemporary Christianity.... This fear has led the authors to deny and repress the importance of this kind of religion in American life . . . this taboo extends to "Christ" and "Jesus." . . . Sometimes the censorship becomes especially offensive. It is common in these books to treat Thanksgiving without explaining to whom the Pilgrims gave thanks . . . no mention is made of God, to whom the thanks was given. The Pueblo can pray to Mother Earth, but Pilgrims can't be described as praying to God . . . and never are Christians described as praying to Jesus either in the United States or elsewhere, in the present or even in the past. . . .[22]

And yet Humanist Norman Lear, founder of People for the American Way, has the unmitigated gall and hypocrisy to inform us that "textbooks and curricula have deteriorated largely as a result of pressure by the religious right and other groups to avoid mention of controversial subjects."[23]

Every so often a judge in our land is courageous and honest enough, like Alabama's U.S. District Judge W. Brevard Hand, to officially recognize and deal with the persistent and pervasive influence of humanistic philosophies in our textbooks. (Not surprisingly, his ruling was ignominiously overturned.) In a 172-page ruling handed down on March 4, 1987, in

Mobile, Alabama, he reiterated the fact that Secular Humanism is a religion and that much of the government's school curriculum has been based on the tenets of that religion, in express violation of the Constitution of the United States. However, Judge Hand's court is by no means the first to declare that Humanism is a religion: The Supreme Court has recognized "Secular Humanism as a religion, defining it as 'a sincere and meaningful belief which occupies in the life of the possessor a place parallel to that filled by the God of those . . . [believing in God].' "[24]

It is by no means necessary for a belief system to believe in *God* in order to qualify as a religion. *Webster's New International Dictionary* defines Humanism as "a contemporary cult or belief calling itself religious but substituting faith in man for faith in God . . . [or] faith in the supreme value and self-perfectibility of human personality." Any system that seriously seeks to deal with questions concerning the nature of man and the goal or purpose for his existence as well as the nature of ultimate reality, and the relationship between the two, is absolutely religious in nature.

Humanism *is* a religion, despite the fact that today many Humanists are backpedaling on this issue as fast as they can. Articles in *The Humanist* magazine, as well as in numerous other Humanist publications, from time to time openly admit that Humanism is indeed religious. In an award-winning essay published in the January/February 1983 edition of *The Humanist*, John Dunphy proclaims:

> I am convinced that the battle for humankind's future must be waged and won in the public school classroom by teachers who correctly perceive their role as the proselytizers of *a new faith* . . . these teachers must embody the same selfless dedication as the most rabid fundamentalist preachers, for they will be ministers of another sort, utilizing a classroom instead of a pulpit to convey humanist values in whatever subject they teach. . . . The classroom must and will become an arena of conflict between the

old and the new, the rotting corpse of Christianity, together with all its adjacent evils and misery, and the new faith of humanism, resplendent in its promise of a world in which the never-realized Christian ideal of "love thy neighbor" will finally be achieved.

Despite the fact that the fire of Dunphy's rhetoric has proved embarrassing to some Humanists (who have since written articles of their own downplaying his influence), he has nevertheless accurately voiced the passionate zeal and determination that is the driving force behind many Humanists today. What he said about their perspective is true.

Paul Kurtz repeatedly asserts the religious nature of Humanism in the preface of the First and Second Humanist Manifestos:

> Humanism is a philosophical, religious, and moral point of view as old as human civilization itself. . . . In 1933 a group of thirty-four liberal humanists in the United States defined and enunciated the philosophical and religious principles that seemed to them fundamental. . . . To establish such a *religion* is a major necessity of the present.[25]

Yet when asked to testify in the Alabama textbook hearings about the nature of Humanism, this same Paul Kurtz said that the term "refers to humanistic development and is non-religious. . . . It uses science, reason, and evidence to test theory."[26] One must conclude it has been a while since he read through the Manifesto he helped draft and edit.[27]

Why are Humanists intent on all this current public disavowal of the religious nature of Humanism? Because they now realize that if Humanism becomes widely recognized as religious, it will become much harder for them to maintain and promote their doctrines in our public schools.

Some Humanists have even gone so far as to claim that Secular Humanism doesn't even exist—the Fundamentalists have made it all up in order to have a basis for sneaking their own agenda into the schools! The NEA is in this camp.[28] Others incorrectly try to equate "Humanism" with "humaneness," as in "humanitarian and deeply concerned for the welfare of humanity." In fact, one professor who was sued for implementing Humanism in a Kansas City public school in August 1979 defended himself by quoting the *Webster's New World Dictionary* definition of *humane*: "having what are considered the best qualities of [hu]mankind: kind, tender, merciful, sympathetic." "When my case was tried in court, the above definition was accepted as the philosophy that I was implementing in the public schools. I was allowed to continue teaching and promoting Humanism."[29]

Elementary, My Dear Watson!

Paul Kurtz in his book *In Defense of Secular Humanism* argues that it is untrue to say that the schools are dominated by Secular Humanists, because "while there are at least three million teachers in the United States, there are only ten thousand members of Humanist organizations. Surely, they do not dominate the schools."[30] But his point totally begs the question. A teacher doesn't need to carry an official Humanist Association membership card to ascribe to their philosophy and principles and to implement it in the schools!

A criminal doesn't need to leave his official calling card at the scene of the crime in order to be identified. All Sherlock Holmes needs in order to find the perpetrator is some kind of clue that will tie the suspect to the scene of the crime. The Humanists have left their fingerprints all over the school system's books and curricula. Text after text, program after program echoes the philosophy of Humanism as stated in their manifestos. Their own writings have consistently and continuously heralded their intent. They have been implementing their plan, and we have the casualties to prove it. Even Watson could put that one together!

Once the religious philosophy of Humanism became firmly entrenched in our society, the stage was set for the next logical step: the introduction of a *cosmic* Humanism which today we know as the New Age Movement.

Chapter 3

Your Teacher
the Occultist?

✦

For too long schools have been containers: holding
places for keeping the young off the streets and out
of the labor market. In the New Age, they shall, I
hope, be temples, where human beings are nurtured into the recognition and application of their
divinity.

—Walene James
Handbook for Educating in the New Age

Imagine, if you will, a place where you can learn astrology,
Yoga, numerology, the basics of color healing, and ESP; a
place where you are led into guided-imagery fantasy trips and
visualization techniques that help you contact your "Higher
Self" and your spirit guide; a place where meditation sessions
are regularly conducted to teach you to "look within yourself" for the solution to all problems; a place where you learn
chants and affirmations which assure you that "you are a
perfect person and student." Imagine a setting where you can
learn how to open your chakras and raise the Kundalini force,
or how to draw mandalas, interpret your dreams, and astral
project.

No, you have not been reading a syllabus for a seminar at your local ashram or occult center. These practices,
along with endless variations on the theme, were indeed once
relegated to the misty abodes of shamans, Yogis, wizards,
witches, magicians, mediums, witch doctors, and other assorted occultists. Today, however, in more "enlightened"

times, they have become the raging vogue in public schools in every state and in virtually every community around the country.

The news shouldn't come as any major shock, since these practices have been going on for the last 15 or 20 years now. All the teachers are doing is applying the latest innovations in the field of psychology to their classrooms.

I believe that the majority of the teachers who are using these "latest" psychological as well as Eastern/occultic techniques in their classrooms are doing so in ignorance of what they are actually involved with. Many of them find themselves unexpectedly exposed to the occult through the "psychological methodologies" used during in-service training sessions. One distraught Christian public-schoolteacher from California wrote and told me that in a recent Left Brain/Right Brain in-service session in Pasadena they were presented with material on Yoga, meditation, holistic education, centering, altered states of consciousness, wise persons, spirit guides, etc. This is rapidly becoming the norm.

The Compassionate Teacher

Not long ago a young teacher in Portland, Oregon, was one of 13 educators specially selected to go on a three-day seminar called "School Within a School." After arriving at the seminar grounds, she discovered that the program was designed to "help them become better teachers" by showing them how to lead the children on guided imagery/visualization trips, how to build a "psychic room," how to contact their spirit guides, how to read auras, and how to conduct out-of-body experiences. Of course, the teachers were led in these techniques themselves so they could experience firsthand the wonders into which they would be leading their children. Fortunately, this teacher, a committed and knowledgeable Christian, was familiar with the occultic/religious nature of these activities and she refused to participate in them.

Education courses in a growing number of universities around the country are offering young teachers courses with titles such as "Imagineering: Tools For Unlocking Potential."

This course, offered at California State University at Long Beach in the spring of 1984, was advertised this way: "Learn to use Imagineering Skills [visualization and guided imagery] in your classroom to accelerate achievement and facilitate learning. These tools can help you unlock creativity, solve problems, identify behavioral patterns and expand student potential. This experiential workshop is designed to enable you to lead others in new and dramatic ways. Imagineering Skills can become a most valuable resource in your Effective Learning Tool Kit!" What young or burned-out teacher could resist that!

Western Washington University, like so many other universities, has become quite open about its commitment to indoctrinating the future teachers of this country in the New Age globalist/socialist and Eastern mystical perspective. Professor Philip Vader Velde's course entitled "Foundations of Education" is a globalist/New Age classic. His key textbooks are *Global Mandate: Pedagogy for Peace*, edited by himself and Kyung-chan Kim, and a book by physicist and New Ager Fritjof Capra entitled *The Turning Point*. Capra's book tells apprentice teachers that "the crusades of Christian fundamentalists" are "promoting medieval notions of reality."[1] He would prefer to see our society's "cultural values and attitudes" based on the "framework that is developed in great detail in the I Ching . . . that lies at the very basis of Chinese thought."[2] The I Ching, by the way, is an ancient system of divination. He is also sympathetic to the cause of "feminist spirituality" and "worship of the Goddess,"[3] (i.e., Witchcraft).

A great deal of effort is going into luring teachers into the New Age perspective—what prominent New Age author Marilyn Ferguson calls "personal transformation."[4] Ferguson points out that "tens of thousands of classroom teachers, educational consultants and psychologists, counselors, administrators, researchers, and faculty members in colleges of education have been among the millions engaged in personal transformation."[5] She boasts that "of the Aquarian Conspirators surveyed, more were involved in education than in any other single category of work."[6] Transformation, by the way, literally means "a forming over, a restructuring."[7] Another term for it might be "conversion." Ferguson is quite correct when she points out that "a gifted teacher can infect generations with excitement about ideas, can launch careers—even revolutions."[8]

Personally, I find what these teachers are "infecting" our generations with to be profoundly disturbing.

The truly "Compassionate Teacher"[9] is increasingly being defined as one who uses these innovative techniques in the classroom. Those who refuse to go along with the program will eventually find themselves "phased out." As the NEA has pointed out:

> ... teachers who conform to the traditional institutional mode are out of place. They might find fulfillment as tap-dance instructors, or guards in maximum security prisons or proprietors of reducing salons, or agents of the Federal Bureau of Investigation ... but they damage teaching, children, and themselves by staying in the classroom. [10]

The Transpersonal Connection

Modern education has always been closely tied to psychology. Trends set by psychologists invariably find their way into the schools.

Psychology is indeed a funny thing. Certified neurotics (Freud) and occultists (Jung) sit around and formulate totally unprovable theories about man and his unconscious, the source of his problems, and how to solve them. Then, admittedly with great brilliance and authority, they present their speculations as virtual scientific fact, and sure enough, almost everyone believes them. Until, that is, someone else comes up with a different theory, which is then, in turn, adopted and venerated as "scientific fact."

First, Sigmund Freud (1856-1939) told us that man is programmed by the accidents of biology and by the first five years of his life. Buried deep in his unconscious mind are all the repressed horrors of the moral dogmas that his parents imposed on him, which must by force control his life (psychic determinism). And, unless he spends a good part of his life in psychoanalysis, he will never be set free from all the ghastly effects of botched potty training, repressed sexuality, and fear of death. This theory didn't cure Freud's own deep-seated neuroses, of course, but lots of very intelligent people nonetheless assumed that it would work on theirs. According to Thomas Bradford Roberts, "Freudian psychology bene-fited education by pointing out the role of emotions and the unconscious in human development and learning."[11] His psychoanalytic approach is known as "First Force" psychol-ogy.

Meanwhile C.G. Jung (1875-1961), onetime heir apparent of Freud, said No, sex and death don't have all that much to do with it. Man is basically good, and the unconscious is not just the mind's sunken sewage dump; Jung called this part the "personal unconscious." Beyond the personal unconscious, he speculated, is a universal and inherited[12] source of all knowledge and wisdom, the vast repository of the conscious-ness of the entire universe. What man needs to do is learn to tap into this "collective unconscious," which lies at the heart of all religious and mystical experiences.

Jung came from a deeply occultic background and had numerous spirit guides, among them an ancient Gnostic named Philemon. Philemon, who appeared to Jung as a wise old man "with a long white beard, the horns of a bull, and the wings of a kingfisher,"[13] gave him all kinds of insights con-cerning the "collective unconscious" and other mysteries, which should serve to give *us* some sort of insight as to the source of Jung's theories. Jung wasn't as popular as Freud for many years. It seems that the idea of spirit guides and the collective unconscious freaked out a lot of psychiatrists. This is changing today.

Then in the 1950's to mid-60's the Behaviorists ruled su-preme. Their programs of behavior modification (in the form of psychological testing and values clarification, for example) are still very much in use in the schools today. Their best-known exponent is B.F. Skinner, who took Freud one further and said, in essence, that man was nothing but a machine to be controlled and programmed by the rat mazers; man had no choice. He is beyond freedom and dignity, and, for all intents and purposes, beyond humanity.

Psychologists worked that one over as long as they could, but something kept nagging at a few of them; deep down some of these great thinkers had an inkling that something very like a soul and maybe even a spirit was down in there somewhere. That "God-shaped vacuum" (although most of them certainly didn't call it *that*) in them rebelled at the thought of being a mere machine or just a sophisticated, superbright, overqualified, and trainable monkey.

So when Abraham Maslow, Carl Rogers, etc., proposed that man was autonomous and had *infinite* human potential, and that through focusing on himself and his feelings and his experiences he himself could become "self-actualized" (i.e., "completely fulfilled" or "fully human"), a lot of people went for it. So developed what has been called "the cult of self-worship,"[14] or the "human potential" movement.

The Fourth Force

With that foundation, the development of the "Fourth Force" in psychology was inevitable: Psychology hooked up with Eastern mysticism and the occult and became "transpersonal." Maslow in his later writings included *self-transcendence* as the final peak experience of self-actualization.[15] He realized that a lot of those who had "self-actualized" would think that those who went on to "transcend" themselves had flipped their lids, but he nevertheless believed that it was an important and valid stage in man's evolution:

> I should say that I consider Humanistic, Third Force Psychology to be transitional, a preparation for a still "higher" Fourth Psychology, transpersonal, transhuman, centered in the cosmos rather than in

human needs and interest, going beyond human-
ness, identity, self-actualization and the like.[16]

Transpersonal psychology is firmly rooted in humanistic
psychology, with its emphasis on self and experience. But it
goes a step further by focusing on personal "transformation"
and "transcendence"—that is, the *experience* of *"becoming one
with all reality"* as *essential* to man's education, evolution, and
very survival on the planet. It's what the New Age is all about.

> Transpersonal psychology is both philosophically
> very old and psychologically very new. It is old in
> the sense that many of the topics it investigates have
> intrigued humans for thousands of years . . . altered
> states of consciousness (such as meditation and
> dreams), man's impulse toward higher states of being
> (such as peak experiences, self-transcendence, and
> spiritual growth), and psychic phenomena, includ-
> ing parapsychology. . . . Transpersonal psychology
> is studying their psychological aspects scientifi-
> cally, rather than relegating them to the realms of
> religion, mysticism, or the occult. . . . *It will lead
> to new educational understandings and practices* says
> [Thomas Bradford] Roberts.[17]

He couldn't have been more correct! Many educators have
assumed that since science and psychology have undertaken
to officially investigate the occult, it must therefore be real.
And, if it is real, then it is *valid*. And, if it is valid, then it is
good. So they mentally award occultism the Good Housekeep-
ing Seal of Approval and proceed to introduce it into their
classrooms under the cover of the "latest scientific and educational research."

Marilyn Ferguson heralds the arrival of Transpersonal
education (also known as "Integrative," "holistic," or "consciousness" education) as the "emergent paradigm" which,
"unlike most educational reform in the past . . . *is imbedded in
sound science*: systems theory, an understanding of the integration of mind and body, knowledge of the two major modes

of consciousness and how they interact, the potential of altered and expanded states of consciousness."[18] She calls it education's "Middle Way" because it "promotes friendly environments for hard tasks . . . celebrates the individual and society, freedom and responsibility, uniqueness and interdependence, mystery and clarity, tradition and innovation. It is complementary, paradoxical, dynamic."[19]

She neglected to mention that it is also *religious* to the core!

Disguised Religion

Among themselves, psychologists openly admit to the religious underpinnings of transpersonal psychology.[20] In the classroom, however, its religious nature is usually disguised, glossed over, and even deliberately lied about, as we will see, in order to insure its acceptance by parents, students, and others who might conceivably protest the use of religious indoctrination in the classroom.

The purpose of Transpersonal education is to present ancient occult techniques to students in order to open them up to the experience of "self-transcendence." What is that experience? It is the experience of "enlightenment" of Eastern mysticism, the ecstatic experience of unity with "Ultimate Reality" that produces, often in a burst of blinding light, the realization that All is One, One is All, therefore *everything* is God, including you!

It's enough to make Freud roll over in his grave. Here the man who founded psychoanalysis said that anyone who even *believed* in God was borderline insane, and now you've got a good number of his colleagues out there saying they *are* God!

All good and well. In this free country of ours they are still entitled to the delusion of their choice. What they and the educators who follow their lead should *not* be entitled to, however, is the outrage of smuggling their thoroughly religious "psychology of becoming" into our public schools in the name of "sound science," "self-esteem," and "educational progress." And yet that is exactly what is happening. Not only that, but your tax dollars are paying for it!

Transpersonal (New Age) educators are feverishly developing and testing curricula which they hope will prove acceptable to school districts around the country. The new curricula are, to be sure, being designed to meet some very real needs. After all, they can't just show up one morning and announce to the school board that they intend to convert the entire campus into a spiritual New Age occult training center. However, if they talk about brain research and "scientific" techniques to develop creativity and enhance the learning capacity of the children, and if they can present activities to help the children manage stress, solve problems, and improve their self-esteem (thereby supposedly reducing crime, vandalism, drug abuse, and teen pregnancies), then the vast majority of schools would welcome them with open arms. Many already have.

Tempus Fugit

As far back as 1947, the high priestess of the New Age Movement, Alice Bailey, wrote a book entitled *Education in the New Age*, which tells us that "enlightenment is the major goal of education."[21] Actually, the book was channeled through her by a demon who calls himself "the Tibetan, Djwal Khul," or "D.K." for short. The entire book is a blueprint and clarion call for the occult "transformation" (a euphemism for progressive demonization) of schools and teachers, and her occult influence is considerably more pervasive in our classrooms than many people would suspect. It should come as no surprise that it is presented under the dignified garb of "psychology."

For example, Dr. Roberto Assagioli (1888-1979), well-known Italian psychiatrist and developer of psychosynthesis, a "comprehensive psychology that sees as its goal helping one strengthen contact with the self . . . our true nature,"[22] is credited as a major influence in Transpersonal education through the "development of activities for training children's imagination for the primary goal of self-development. Assagioli has argued that the guided use of imagination is a powerful tool for personal change. . . ."[23]

Progressive New Age educators Jack Canfield and Paul Klimek inform us that "the theoretical model that we have found to be most useful in providing guidance for New Age approaches to education is derived from the work of Roberto Assagioli. . . ."[24]

Since his material is becoming increasingly popular in our schools, thanks to the influx of Transpersonal education, it is of interest to know something of Dr. Assagioli's background and perspective. That clue is to be found in Alice Bailey's book (written over a period of years before her death in 1949) entitled *The Unfinished Autobiography*:

> It was there [in Ascona, Italy] for the first time that we met Dr. Robert Assagioli, who had been our representative in Italy for several years, and our contact with him and the many years of work with him constitute one of the outstanding happy factors in our lives. He was at one time a leading brain specialist in Rome and when we first knew him was regarded as an outstanding European psychologist.[25]

Dr. Assagioli was unquestionably intimately acquainted with Bailey's occult teachings, and he acted as her interpreter during her lectures in Italy.[26] He was as concerned as Alice Bailey about reaching as many children as possible with the New Age doctrine and techniques laid down by the "Master" D.K., and he admonished at least one of his many disciples, a Northern California public elementary schoolteacher named Eva Fugitt, to "take it back to the children."[27] So, in evident fulfillment of that commission, Eva Fugitt eventually wrote a book called *He Hit Me Back First! Creative Visualization Activities for Parenting and Teaching* to help her pupils contact what she calls "The Wise Part" within themselves. One enthusiastic New Age reviewer of her book observed:

> Several decades ago, the Tibetan teacher, D.K., gave us, through Alice Bailey, an important book on *Education in the New Age*. It is most encouraging to see that now some teachers are applying those New Age educational principles, in a most practical way,

in their teaching of children right in our public schools.[28]

The review, written by a man who was a Methodist minister for over 50 years, goes on to praise Eva Fugitt as "an outstanding example of this." The book, which has sold thousands of copies, also carries enthusiastic endorsements on its back cover from Jean Houston, Marilyn Ferguson, and Beverly-Colleene Galyean.

Caution! Change Agents at Work!

Many of the teachers who are using occultic practices in their classrooms are undoubtedly doing so in ignorance. I'm convinced that the majority of them do not realize the source or the implications of what they are exposing the children to. Those who have developed the programs and who set the policies and trends, however, are in a different category. There is clear and abundant evidence *from their own writings* that they know exactly what they are doing and why they are doing it. A growing number of their teachers are indeed very deliberately acting as "change agents" among the children. In her excellent book entitled *Change Agents in the School*, Barbara Morris defines a "Change Agent" as—

> ... a person, organization, or institution that changes or helps to change the beliefs, values, attitudes, or behavior of people without their knowledge or consent ... to replace them with new beliefs and behaviors that will render the child susceptible to manipulation, coercion, control and corruption for the rest of his life.[29]

Change agents have been at it in the schools for a long time now. In recent years, however, change agents are gathering around the country to discuss the best methods available to them for smuggling occult techniques and philosophies into the classroom. Their goal, as stated by one teacher at a recent New Age seminar I attended: "To help the children get in touch with their divinity. These things are crucial to our evolution."

At last! A refreshingly honest, if unexpected, public admission of the true purpose behind exposing schoolchildren to the occult!

Transformation... Like It or Not

The seminar just referred to took place on the weekend of June 19-21, 1987. The conference was entitled "Through Crisis to Transformation" and was sponsored by a New Age group that now calls itself Unity-and-Diversity World Organization. Unity-and-Diversity is a coordinating network of hundreds of educational, scientific, religious, cultural, philosophic, esoteric, and occultic organizations from around the world dedicated to promoting the New Age.

The organization, originally founded by Leland Steward in 1973, is committed to "evolution of the United Nations into a world government," "changing human nature" for "the New Age," and "the emergence of the New Universal Man."[30]

Unity-and-Diversity has always harbored a special interest in education. The printed program for the portion of the seminar dedicated to education featured lectures with such titles as "Personal Transformation Through Education—practical applications in today's educational establishments"; "Stress Management is Elementary," in which the speaker shared his personal experiences in biofeedback training in a classroom setting; and "Social Transformation Through Education," which featured (among others) Maria Monetta, a teacher at a local public high school.

It was Ms. Monetta's lecture that captured my interest. It was billed this way: *"Parapsychology and Traditional Education. Maria Monetta will share her extensive experience in integrating various studies of parapsychology into a public high school curriculum. Open discussion will follow."*

Ms. Monetta, an unassuming, down-to-earth woman, was introduced as a teacher who was "doing a wonderful work within the framework of the current system." She described herself as a "kid of the 60's—I guess you could say I was into the whole hippie thing."

She has been teaching for some 20 years now, she said, and somewhere down the line realized that "teachers have incredible potential for revolution," but she was always careful in her "civil disobedience" not to get arrested for a felony.

She has had to be patient in her work. Fifteen years ago she wanted to teach a course in "nonviolence," but because of the Vietnam situation she "met with great opposition from the administration." Now, however, with the dreadful interracial violence between the Latino and white kids in her district, the administration was desperate for anything to help deal with the situation. She proposed what was in essence *exactly* the same course she had wanted to teach years before. It was a perfect platform for introducing her passivist, political views. She brings in speakers (ex-druggies, ex-felons, maybe a priest) to tell the kids about violence in Nicaragua and El Salvador, etc., and this priest tells them, "Hey, if you guys join the armed forces they're going to be sending you down to one of these places. You're going to be killing Catholics, Latinos just like you . . . maybe even one of your relatives." Her goal: "Little by little those kids are going to be out protesting our involvement in those countries."

Ms. Monetta teaches a lot of different classes at her school: history (which she hates), health classes, and psychology (her favorite). She found that calling her class "psychology" was the perfect vehicle for bringing in some *really* exciting material which she first learned about when she was at UCLA years ago.

Ms. Monetta here referred us to a folder which she had handed out to us at the beginning of her talk. I pulled out a copy of the flier which she said she had posted around the school advertising her class, which is an elective.

"PSYCHOLOGY . . . A COURSE ABOUT YOU!" proclaimed the bold, black letters across the top of the page. "This class is REAL and it's about RISK. Expand your mind, develop your spirit, explore your soul, touch your power, release your love . . . CREATE YOUR LIFE EXPERIENCE . . . AS YOU WANT IT TO BE. AFFIRM YOURSELF . . . YOU ARE INVALUABLE."

The rest of the flier was covered with questions such as "What's happening with you? What scares you? What do you think of yourself?"

The questions on the back of the flier were even more intriguing:

PARA-PSYCHOLOGY . . . ONE STEP BEYOND

- What do you think it's like to die? . . . How do you view the "death experience"? . . .

- What "psychic" (strange, unexplainable) experience have you had, and perhaps never before revealed to anyone? . . .

- How "close" have you gotten with another person . . . (ESP/Extrasensory perception) and with your self (intuition/inner voice)? . . .

- Have you ever "left your body" (astral projection)? . . .

- Have you "seen"/"heard"/"felt" another from the "spirit world" (ghost)?

Ms. Monetta said the kids really love the class and get a lot out of it. She spices it up by bringing in special speakers, occultists who are experts in their fields, and always instructs her speakers to be sure to "give the kids an experience with these things, not just lecture at them." (She even included their names and phone numbers for us in the material she gave us.)

"We do some pretty amazing things," continued Ms. Monetta: "psychic healing, shamanism, crystals, Witchcraft— hold ceremonies and stuff, creative visualization, Progoff— intensive journal-keeping, meditation in class, either guided or open, and then they write about it. We do much work around self-affirmation. . . . We burn candles and hold a full-moon ceremony once a month. On Valentine's Day we hold a love-relationship ceremony. We hold 'readings' sometimes. The kids bring things in . . . they really enjoy it."

In her closing statements Ms. Monetta put it all into perspective for us:

> I must have a divine light around me, because I've had no flack from anyone. I've never had anything but positive feedback from the parents. One time, though, I was conducting a spring equinox celebration for the kids. I mean I had the altar all set up—flowers, the candles were lit on the altar—and the principal walked in! Fortunately, he was a new principal and he was thrilled with what we were doing. The focus was on self-affirmations. I was lucky . . . I have to walk a fine line on the religious issue. Some might say I've crossed it. . . .

Wake Up, Crazies!

Educators like these have long depended on the ignorance and apathy of the "crazies"[31] (Fundamentalist Christians) to give them the time and space needed to bring about the transformation of our children. Tragically for our children and our country, that dependence has for the most part been well-rewarded. Most of us haven't got a clue about what's going on out there, despite the fact that it's been going on for years now.

In March of 1982 the U.S. Department of Education held seven hearings around the country on the proposed regulations for the Protection of Pupil Rights Amendment.[32] These hearings were attended by hundreds of parents who testified concerning the subjection of their children to such practices as Yoga, Transcendental Meditation, hypnosis, guided imagery and visualization sessions, parapsychology, sensitivity training, psychiatric exercises, and other practices designed to change the thinking, values, beliefs, and behavior of the children (all in the name of "education," of course). Phyllis Schlafly edited the more than 13,000 pages of testimony into a book entitled *Child Abuse in the Classroom*. If you have not read this book yet, I suggest that you do so.

The whole purpose of the "transpersonal" techniques is to develop the spiritual side of the child. And given the current trends in educational philosophy and literature, any teacher serious about following the program will be fully equipped to convert your child into a proper little Transpersonal Hindu occultist. As educator and author Gay Hendricks tells us:

> As teachers, we want our students to appreciate the full range of human experience. The transpersonal realm, although it goes far beyond what is usually considered traditional in education, is something for which most of us feel a deep yearning. We want to experience completion, wholeness, union, divinity, to feel what is sacred within us and around us.[33]

Mr. Hendricks is, of course, welcome to experience whatever divinity he may choose in his personal life. And it is certainly understandable why he would want to share his exciting occult/religious experiences with the children in his care. Nevertheless, in a country where Christian teachers are banned from mentioning the name of "Jesus Christ" in their classrooms on pain of dismissal, and where an 8-year-old girl can find herself in court for handing out Christmas cards to her classmates that actually dare to acknowledge that Jesus has something to do with Christmas,[34] one finds the raw hypocrisy of "Transpersonal education" more than a little difficult to swallow!

Chapter 4

Gifted, Talented, and Other Hazards

✦

If children in general are a target for New Age "transformation," you can be sure that those who are the gifted and talented among them are of special interest. After all, it is the gifted and talented who will be the leaders, trendsetters, lawmakers, doctors, presidents, and teachers of the future. They are the ones who are expected to be the leaders of the New Age, and as such they *must* receive special attention and indoctrination from the social engineers.

A recent article in the *Gifted Children Monthly* observed the importance of recognizing these intelligent and imaginative children as early as possible and presented some of the early signs of leadership quality, such as problem-solving ability, being a good communicator, having a "hearty and healthy self-concept," and having a high degree of motivation. It offered creative suggestions to the parents and teachers for helping the child develop his leadership qualities. This all sounds good, but then comes the punch line in the last third of the article under the headline "TRAINING THE THIRD EYE."

Dr. Dorothy Sisk, author of the article, eases us into this section by reminding us that "there are a number of things adults can do that are very helpful in building leadership in young children and youth . . ." including providing a warm, accepting atmosphere for the child and respecting the child's values and creativity. She then informs us that "intuition is one of the more difficult characteristics of leadership to cultivate," but that it can be done if parents follow certain ground rules.

The remainder of the article is devoted to showing the caretaker how to teach the child "to listen to the still small voice within our intuitive selves." A specially highlighted blue box at the end of the article announces that "POWERS OF INTUITION BLOSSOM WITH PRACTICE," and suggests that we encourage the youngster to (among other things) "practice learning to 'read' people and situations; make predictions of things that might happen," and "when working on a problem, try visualizing the outcome and actually picture in your mind what a solution might be."

The potential future leaders of our democracy, the very ones who are recognized as being "important for the survival of our civilization," are to be taught and nurtured in the ancient occultic Eastern mystical techniques for opening the "third eye."[1] The implication is clearly made that those parents who do not nurture that faculty in their children are not providing "an atmosphere of warmth and acceptance" or "respect for their values and creativity."

Dr. Sisk is quite influential in the world of education. She is the Executive Secretary of the World Council for Gifted and Talented Children as well as Professor of Exceptional Child Education at the University of South Florida, Tampa. She is on the advisory board of *Gifted Children Monthly*, and is also the author of a teachers' manual entitled *Creative Teaching of the Gifted*, published by McGraw-Hill in 1987.

Dr. Sisk devotes an entire chapter of her book to the techniques of Transpersonal education, although she has apparently refrained from using that term in her manual. Neither, by the way, does her book mention "the third eye," as she did in her article. Instead, she writes of "expanding dimensions of learning" and discusses the latest mind/brain research, the importance of the use of "visualization to develop intuitive and imaginative skills," biofeedback, and Suggestology.[2] Her suggested activities for teachers using her manual include reading *The Aquarian Conspiracy* by Marilyn Ferguson and using the "relaxation techniques suggested in this chapter."[3]

The Gifted in the Front Lines

There are unquestionably some very bright kids out there. According to an article in *Newsweek* (February 23, 1987), about 5 percent of students are considered gifted. Understandably their parents want to provide the special education and attention that will help their child grow and develop his or her gift. While experts in the field are still in disagreement over the best way to handle exceptionally bright and talented children, one thing seems clear to me: Whatever the program chosen for the child, it should not have to be considered necessary for the educator to indoctrinate him into Eastern occultism in order to develop his abilities! And yet in many of the Gifted-and-Talented programs designed for these children, that is precisely what is happening.

One of the places where Transpersonal education frequently makes its first appearance in the public schools is in the Gifted-and-Talented programs. This is in fact the perfect setting for Transpersonal education, because the programs by their very nature are so open to experimentation. The same also holds true for classes for educationally or mentally handicapped students. Transpersonal educators have been known to introduce their occult programs in such classes in order to work the "bugs" out, after which they introduce it to their regular classes.

Quoting as fact sophisticated theories about right-hemisphere brain research, Prigogine's evolving universe, and Pribram and Bohm's holographic models of reality, New Age educators like Barbara Clark (in her teachers' manual *Growing Up Gifted*) are telling us that the "ancient wisdoms of the Chinese, Hindu, Egyptian and other age-old teachings" are being "validated" by science.[4] The trick now for the holistic educator is to make *sure* that the gifted and talented get the hang of it. They want the children to be "gifted" in the "intuitive" (i.e., psychic) abilities that they have assumed normally lie "deep within every individual," as well as to develop their gifts in math or music or writing or whatever. That is the entire purpose of gifted education, as far as Barbara Clark[5] is concerned:

As integrative education becomes more accepted
and practiced, we will find more curricula that
include relaxation and development of integrative
abilities. Guided fantasies and dreams, recognition
and use of altered states of consciousness, and centering activities will develop more of our intuitive
abilities. . . . All this and more lie ahead as we seek
to bring all of our knowledge, feelings, talents, and
creativity into the classroom in the service of actu-
alizing and transcending. Integrative education
promises this, and it is also the message of this
book.[6]

You may recall that the term "integrative" is increasingly
becoming one of the numerous New Age euphemisms for
"Transpersonal" education.[7] Clark's book, which received a
lengthy and favorable review in the fall 1979 edition of the
Gifted Child Quarterly, is filled with all kinds of suggestions
(couched, of course, in scientifically formulated "educa-
tioneese") on how to turn the gifted child into a gifted Eastern
mystic. Marilyn Ferguson even wrote the foreword for the
first edition. In her New Age classic *The Aquarian Conspiracy*,
Ferguson quotes Barbara Clark as saying:

When we have . . . changed and extended our view
of reality, and established the underlying connect-
edness of each to all, we will then have a new
meaning of giftedness. The gifted, the talented,
the "intuned" and the illuminated will then be
merged. . . .[8]

New Agenda for the Gifted

Some teachers are now suggesting that the term "gifted"
needs to be expanded to include children who are "psychically gifted." In a recent article entitled "On Being Psychically Gifted," the author, a senior-high-school teacher in
Illinois named Susan Field, argues that "psychically gifted
children . . . possess valuable gifts that need to be recognized

and nurtured, for it is such gifts that, once properly understood and developed, will give our society new unimaginable achievements and hope for the future."[9]

A euphemism for "psychically gifted" that you may want to be aware of is "intuitively gifted." As Ms. Field tells us, "I know that it is controversial to use the word 'psychic,' and yet I choose not to diffuse its impact by using a more acceptable word. And what would that word be? Intuitive? Yes, I suppose I could say the intuitively gifted. That definitely has a more reasonable ring."[10] Evidently that's what Dr. Sisk thought too. She used the term "intuition" all through her article on leadership. What she was *really* talking about was "psychic." The only place where she slipped up and gave herself away was in mentioning the "third eye" in her section title.

A 1983 special report on "Testing and Enhancing a Gifted Child's ESP" (written by a Director of Gifted Education in Indianapolis, Indiana) informs us that—

> Parapsychology is an ideal subject for gifted children of most any age, as it involves inherently provocative material . . . the development of important skills like critical thinking and scientific inquiry, and an opportunity for self-discovery and enhancement of one's ESP abilities.

> Gifted children often demonstrate a special affinity for the subject, perhaps because they often feel different and unusual themselves, possessing abilities which are "paranormal" relative to most other people. Many students . . . even view psychic powers as logical extensions of human potential.[11]

Skill-Booster Indoctrination

Values-clarification sessions are basic to the Gifted-and-Talented programs, as they are to general humanistic education. As with most values-clarification programs, these classes have been carefully designed to undermine the children's traditional concept of morality, the family, nationalism, and Christianity, all of which is necessary before they can be indoctrinated into the New Age religion of Eastern mysticism. As Barbara Clark observes:

> Without a need for right/wrong, true/false, we are free to examine a few of these bigger, more wonderfully outrageous ideas and those who ask us to entertain them. . . . As we explore the new areas of scientific thought that affect us as guides to the intellect of ourselves and others, we must first give up the need for dichotomies. It no longer seems possible to believe one truth or one view. . . .[12]

It seems no small coincidence that the practice of occultism has followed close behind the introduction of "values clarification" in our classrooms.

Transpersonal techniques have become so popular in everyday classrooms lately that about the only difference between these classrooms and the Gifted-and-Talented sessions is that the gifted children generally get to do more of it.

In Kansas City a teacher handed me a packet of material that had been used as extra work for the brighter students who had finished their regular classwork early. Even I could hardly believe my eyes as I looked over the "High Action Reading for Study Skills" excerpts that were designed for third- to sixth-graders by Modern Curriculum Press. One "skill-booster" exercise featured eight pages on the Ouija board! The second exercise was about "Palm Reading—Messages in Your Hands," and the third was called "Chicago's ESP Detective Irene Hughes."

The stories are indeed fascinating and are presented in a most alluring fashion. Under the pretense of teaching children how to read, spell, and reason, the youngsters are being introduced to ancient forms of divination, and in such a way as to virtually guarantee that any semiprecocious child with half a bent for the mysterious will want to run out and explore these wonders for himself. Indeed, the material openly encourages him to do so, as you will see.

Palm-Reading

The "skill-booster" section on palm-reading[13] (or chiromancy, as it is officially known in occult circles) tells the children that palm-reading goes back to Aristotle, who "wrote about the lines on people's hands. Since then there have been palm readers in almost every time and every country. Some of these people have read palms just for the fun of it. Others have believed that they could tell people important things about their lives or their characters by reading those people's palms. . . . Look at the lines on the inside of your own hands. . . ." They then give the children the basics of palm-reading, including definitions and instructions for locating the "life line," the "head line," and the "heart line," and some elementary guidance in interpreting the "messages in your hands." For example:

> Breaks in the life line show that changes may take place in your life. Perhaps you will move to another neighborhood. Perhaps you will change schools. Maybe you will move even further away. Sometimes a break in the life line may warn you about a narrow escape from a bad accident.

Several pages and numerous instructions later, the children read:

> Now that you have learned about some of the lines on people's hands, you might want to try to read the palms of some of your friends. Maybe you can answer questions your friends ask you about their futures. See how much their palms can tell you about them. Remember, too, that your palms can also tell you about yourself.

The entire section, of course, is illustrated with pictures of Gypsies reading the palms of amazed boys and girls, along with a picture of a palm, lines and all. Their instructions?

Now that you have read about the messages in your palms, try to read the palm below. In the spaces write a few sentences to explain what the palm lines tell you about the person.

What's the typical bright kid to think? Obviously, if Aristotle and his own teachers are into palm-reading, it must be all right!

Unquestionably, the majority of "palm-readers" and other "fortune-tellers" are hard-core frauds whose chief interest in palms is in seeing theirs "crossed with silver." However, a certain number of individuals exist who can to some extent predict your future or inform you of your past or reveal your personality to you. As author and Witch Raymond Buckland says:

> Genuine mediumistic messages are sometimes given while the subject is reading the cards, examining the sitter's palm, etc. . . . Psychic power or mediumship is the basis of the supernatural information given, but it is under the guise of fortune-telling.[14]

By teaching and encouraging children in the ancient and occultic art of palm-reading, schoolteachers are opening the way for children to develop mediumship and psychic powers, practices which are soundly condemned by the Bible as trafficking with very real demonic entities, as we shall see in a later chapter. Yet such practices hold serious dangers from even a secular perspective. According to *Man, Myth and Magic*:

> Some people are so suggestible that they themselves may unconsciously bring about a predicted disaster. Therefore a high-minded palmist will never foretell misfortune or death without very carefully qualifying the reading and showing how the tragedy may be averted.[15]

As much as this is a danger among adults who consult palm-readers, how much more vulnerable will youngsters be if some low-minded budding classroom palm-reader predicts disaster or even death! At best, the practice of palm-reading encourages and fosters superstition. At worst, from a secular perspective, it opens the child to the possibility of unconscious self-fulfillment of the "prophecy." For example, a young woman marries the third man she meets with dark wavy hair because that's the one the reader said she would marry . . . only to find that his one major vice is wife-beating when drunk, which is often. A young mother mysteriously and with no apparent physical cause dies after the birth of her second child because some vengeful palm-reader predicted it years before. A young man commits suicide because the church bazaar palm-reader tells him he has a short life line and that great pain lies ahead. One wonders how many lives have been destroyed by this seemingly innocent but potentially devastating occult practice!

The Amazing Mrs. Hughes

During the week I was writing this chapter, three prime-time shows featured the housewife psychic who helps the oldest Rookie, Simon and Simon, and even Magnum solve their cases. And those are just the shows I happened to tune in to! If from nowhere else, prime-time TV fans are getting the idea that some cops are finding out that having a psychic around can be really helpful, despite initial disbelief and ridicule on their part.

The Gifted-and-Talented children in Kansas City have known for a number of years now that certain police departments use psychics to find missing bodies and missing criminals. The psychic they have been introduced to via their special schoolwork is known as "Chicago's ESP detective Irene Hughes," or "the amazing Mrs. Hughes."

> Have you ever heard about a detective that uses ESP (extrasensory perception) to solve cases? This is the story of a detective with a special gift. She has put that special gift to work to help police departments throughout the country. . . . She has worked with

the Chicago police for over ten years. But all this does not make Irene Hughes special.

Mrs. Hughes is special because she seems to have a gift for seeing things before they really happen. She says she has had this gift since she was a young child. It was passed on to her by her grandmother, a Cherokee Indian. Her grandmother was a psychic, says Irene Hughes. And so is she.

They talk about her amazing sixth sense, her ability to hold an object and tell all about the person to whom it belonged (an ability known as psychometry), and they quote Chief Jordan of the police department as saying, "I am certain that she has a special gift. This gift must come from somewhere. We do not completely understand it, but we are always happy to have her help." The police, the children are told, "were amazed at the number of times she was correct."

As the story concludes, the children are reminded that "most psychics do not feel they are special people who deserve special favors or that they should be famous, but they do want to be accepted and trusted."

Unquestionably, there are people who are indeed possessed by the abilities ascribed to Mrs. Hughes. The famed Dutch "sensitive" Peter Hurkos was frequently called upon by police to help solve murder cases. Gerard Croiset is another Dutch psychic who specializes in finding missing children in Holland. They have both been extensively tried and tested and overall found "genuine," though not infallible. Who could possibly object to using occultists (or anyone else, for that matter) to help police find a little murdered child? The information they provide can be uncannily accurate.

The question we must deal with concerns the *source* of these abilities. If indeed these are merely neutral, latent abilities natural to mankind and potentially of great benefit, then it would certainly be backward of us to object to their development and use. If, on the other hand, they are produced by spirit beings for the purpose of drawing us into a particular belief system, as the Bible clearly indicates, then we have a real problem on our hands. Those who consult the psychics and find much of their information "reliable" are more likely to accept other occult practices and philosophies espoused by these same occultists. Deuteronomy 13:1-3 speaks for itself:

> If a prophet or a dreamer of dreams arises among you and gives you a sign or a wonder, and the sign or the wonder comes true, concerning which he spoke to you, saying, "Let us go after other gods (whom you have not known) and let us serve them," you shall not listen to the words of that prophet or that dreamer of dreams; for the Lord your God is testing you to find out if you love the Lord your God with all your heart and with all your soul.

The Bible tells us that Satan can disguise himself as an angel of light (2 Corinthians 11:13-15). He will do things for you that on the surface seem good and helpful. Satan knows perfectly well where one of his servants left the body of a little murdered child. He is perfectly capable of telling another of his servants, however sincere and innocent he or she may be, where he put the body!

The Ouija Board

Of the three Kansas skill-boosters presented to me, probably the one I found most shocking was the one on the Ouija board. The story featured several pictures of two lovely, elegant, and obviously respectable women—rather like your average mommies—sitting at a table with a Ouija board between them.

The story was based on the life of Pearl Curran, who in 1913 began receiving transmissions through a "magic board" from a being that identified itself as "Patience Worth." For over 25 years Pearl Curran "channeled" books, poems, and plays from Patience Worth, who claimed to be a frustrated writer who had lived over 200 years earlier in Puritan England and America.

Numerous word exercises follow the story, including some of the following:

Patience Worth gave Mrs. Curran many step-by-step directions to follow. To understand what Patience meant, Mrs. Curran carefully followed every step. To learn how many people can use a magic board at the same time, follow Patience's step-by-step instructions listed below.

What are the step-by-step instructions that the children are to carefully follow?:

He [the proprietor of the neighborhood toy store who sold it to her] told her that if two players sat quietly and concentrated very hard, the tiny triangle would move from letter to letter spelling out words.

The store owner also warned her that the board "might sometimes behave in strange ways . . . that made some people believe it had magical powers." Mrs. Curran was indeed frightened by Patience Worth's first communication, but "frightened as she was, Pearl Curran knew she would try to reach Patience Worth again."

Part Two on "magic boards" tells the children that "now you can decide for yourself just how special Mrs. Curran's magic board really was." Of course, the children are told, not everyone believed her story, but then again the scientists who investigated her couldn't quite figure out how Mrs. Curran, with only an eighth-grade education, could suddenly write so beautifully and know so much about remote periods of history and archaic languages. But even though scientists may "feel there is really no magic in a 'magic board' see how *you* feel about these ideas":

Idea: Somehow there are people among us who hold the secret thoughts of those who died long ago. These thoughts are locked inside the minds of the living without them even knowing it. Things like magic boards help the living person unlock those thoughts from spirits that are trapped within them.

Idea: People living today have also had other lives in the past. Some of us can somehow remember these past lives. Sometimes a thought comes back to us in a sudden flash. We find that we seem to know about certain things before they happen. Perhaps, again, magic boards can help a person get in touch with these past lives.

Then the children have a whole page of Mrs. Curran and her friend playing with the board that they can color and "play detective" with, followed by this:

NOTES ON THE SPIRITS

Some people looked to the spirit world for their answer. They believed that even though people die, their spirits live on. The spirit, they said, is filled with all the dead person's thoughts and memories of life. Once a person's body has died, the spirit can't be seen or heard. Perhaps, however, the spirit can speak to the living through the magic board.

They even tell the children, "You might have fun making your own magic board and trying it out with a friend. There are many ways you can do it." They proceed to give easy-to-follow instructions on how to make a simple Ouija board, and then add, ". . . ask a question and wait to see what happens!"

These "ideas" being presented to the children are among the fundamental doctrines and practices of the religion of Spiritism (also referred to as Spiritualism in some circles). There are hundreds of Spiritualist churches in this country. Some denominations even have their own seminaries from which they ordain ministers. The *Handbook of Denominations in the United States* mentions that while Spiritualism is popularly known "for its mediums, seances, clairvoyance . . . Ouija boards, table tipping, spirit rappings and conversations [with the dead]," Spiritualism indeed has a "genuine religious basis and connotations as well as psychic experiments."[16] In presenting these "ideas" in the manner in which they have as well as in their promotion of the use of the Ouija board (a recognized tool of many Spiritualists), the religion of Spiritualism is thereby being promoted in the school materials.

Nothing to Play With

Because the Ouija board is manufactured by Parker Brothers and sold in toy stores next to Monopoly and Scrabble, many people have assumed that it is merely a fascinating and mysterious toy. *Nothing could be further from the truth!*

The Ouija is a truly ancient device that has existed in many parts of the world for centuries. Third-century Rome and Egypt, ancient Greece, China as far back as 500 B.C., thirteenth-century A.D. Mongols, and even North American Indians all had a form of the Ouija for the express purpose of contacting the spirits.[17] In 1853 a French Spiritualist named M. Planchette invented a form of the board that used a little heart-shaped, three-legged platform with a pencil as the front leg. The device was called, not surprisingly, a "planchette."

Today's planchette is similar but usually minus the pencil. In 1892 a U.S. patent was issued to an inventor named Elijah J. Bond for a Ouija board, but he was soon bought out by an enterprising Presbyterian named William Fuld who, on the advice of the Ouija board, founded the Southern Novelty Company in Baltimore, Maryland. The name of the outfit was eventually changed to the Baltimore Talking Board Company. Their product: The Oriole Talking Boards. They were also known as "Magic Talking Boards" and the "Mystifying Oracle."

The name "Ouija" (according to Fuld, who christened it) is simply derived from the French "oui" ("yes") and the German "ja" ("yes"). So what we have here is the "Yes Yes" board. "Yes" *to what* is a question worth serious consideration, especially since some occult traditions hold that demons and other undesirable entities cannot fully operate in a person's life unless explicitly invited or welcomed. "Yes Yes" certainly implies some form of welcome to me. According to Fuld and Bond, the board itself suggested the name.

The modern Ouija board is a fairly simple device in and of itself. It consists merely of a small planchette and a smooth board on which are printed the letters of the alphabet, the numbers 0 to 9, and the words "yes," "no," and "good-bye." In a photograph of the board dated 1935[18] it is interesting to note that the board has a left-facing crescent moon and star (known as the satanic crescent) adjacent to the word "No," and a five-pointed star inside a circle (reminiscent of the pentagram) in the bottom right-hand corner. They did away with the star in later versions.

Taxing the Spirits?

The Talking Boards became a national rage during the First and Second World Wars, when people desperately wanted to know the fate of their loved ones in battle. Spiritism has traditionally experienced revivals during times of war and other catastrophes. It also became fashionable among the ladies to employ the board as a parlor game during the early 1900's. That's all the ever-alert IRS needed. In 1920 they declared the board a game, and as such subject to taxation.[19] After all, Fuld was making a fortune on the thing. By 1920 he had sold over three million of them![20] The case went to court.

Never mind that attorney Allen Fisher contended that the Ouija "is a form of amateur mediumship, and not a game or sport."[21] Never mind that attorney Washington Bowie said the board was "a medium of communication between this world and the next."[22] Never mind that for thousands of years varying forms of the board had been used for just that— contacting the "other side." Never mind that numerous occultists as well as some of the better-informed mental health professionals have repeatedly asserted that there are serious potential dangers in using the Ouija board, not the least of which are demon possession and insanity. Never mind that use of the board was known to result in developing psychic faculties and has on numerous well-documented occasions provided information (as in the case of Mrs. Curran) that could not possibly have been known to her or her board partner, subconsciously or otherwise. All the above points were deemed basically irrelevant by the IRS. If a growing number of "socialite dingbats" (as some were so rudely wont to refer to them) were amusing themselves in their parlors with it, it was, therefore, *ipso facto*, a *game*. The court decided to agree with the IRS on this one, and so the Ouija board officially became a mere game.[23]

But the simple fact is that *Ouija is NOT a neutral device. Nor is it a toy. It is a dangerous spiritistic tool designed to contact spirit beings and develop psychic abilities.*

During the occult revival of the 1960's the board again soared in popularity, to the point that in 1966 Parker Brothers bought the rights to the Ouija board and moved its production (intriguingly) to Salem, Massachusetts. They sold over two million boards the first year, outselling Parker Brothers' traditional all-time favorite, Monopoly.[24] The movie *The Exorcist* sparked a new flurry of interest in the board, primarily among girls aged 11 through 18 who were curious about what the Ouija really could do.[25] Over ten million Ouija boards have been sold, which means that potentially 20 million Americans or more have played with it.[26] And, since Shirley Mac-Laine has made the channeling routine popular once again, you can be sure that business has continued to be brisk.

Demons in Disguise

Despite the fact that the Ouija board is sold in virtually every toy store in America (and I've recently seen it in some Hallmark card stores), even occultists are often not blithe about recommending its use. While some occultists do indeed swear by the device, Manly P. Hall, one of the world's foremost occult historians, says this about the Ouija board:

> The Ouija-board ... driven from most of the civilized countries of the world, is a psychic toy that has contributed many tragedies to man's mortal state. Automatic writing (an advanced form of Ouija), a weird, fascinating pastime, may end in a wide vari-

ety of disasters.... He who listens too often to the whisperings of the "spirits" may find his angels to be demons in disguise... man... should leave alone these forces which may only lead to madness.[27]

The famous English medium Ena Twigg warns:

> I know many young people who are fascinated with psychic phenomena, but I would caution them to avoid those trifling and sometimes absurd ways of making contact which are extremely dangerous, like table-tilting, Ouija boards, alphabet experiments with glasses. I beg of you....[28]

The Donning International Encyclopedic Psychic Dictionary defines the Ouija and then adds:

> ... a dangerous tool when used by one not well-grounded in psychic sciences and knowledge of beforehand preparation; when used as a game for those unfamiliar with psychic tuning it has been known to draw the inferior entities to move the indicator; this inferior entity fools the user and can lead to dangerous physical phenomena.[29]

Stoker Hunt, in his secular book *Ouija: The Most Dangerous Game*, presents extensive and sobering documentation and case histories dealing with the dangers of experimentation with the Ouija board,[30] but then proceeds to give instructions on how to use it if you still think you really want to! However, he repeatedly cautions:

> Even those people who swear by the board warn that Ouija is not a pastime for minors: not youngsters, not teenagers.[31]

Fear of Possession

One of the most frightening potential dangers of using the Ouija board is that of possession by demonic spirits. Alan

Vaughan is an author and psychic researcher, articles editor of *Psychic* magazine, and contributor of a chapter on psychic sensitives for Edgar D. Mitchell's book *Psychic Exploration.* He wrote a chilling personal account of his terrifying possession by an evil spirit which entered him while he was experimenting with the Ouija board. The experience was all the more startling to him because of the fact that at the time it occurred he did not even believe in spirits. He does now! He notes, by the way, that one of the interesting side effects of his possession (of which, he believes, he eventually divested himself) was the development of psychic abilities. The experience launched him into the full-time study of parapsychology.[32]

It was fear of possession that motivated a band of English Spiritualists to ban the sale of Ouija boards:

> It is significant, however, that the greatest outcry against the use of Ouijas has come from the Spiritualists—not the parapsychologists. In England Spiritualist groups are petitioning to ban the sale of Ouijas as toys for children—not because of vague dangers of "unhealthy effects of naive, suggestible persons"—but because they fear that the children will become possessed.[33]

Evidently, enough practitioners of the religion of Witchcraft are involved in the use of the Ouija for purposes of divination to warrant a strong warning from one of the best-known Witches, Yvonne Frost. She and her husband are founders of the church and School of Wicca, in New Bern, North Carolina. According to Stoker Hunt, "Yvonne strongly suggests the Ouija board be avoided, insisting that it is foolish to encourage communication with the negative entities. As for communicating with the positive entities, she says it is much better done by other means. *She recommends meditative sessions instead* (author's emphasis)."[34]

I have spoken with those who have had close personal associations with Satanism who tell me that some Satanists do indeed use the Ouija board for the purpose of divination. Several police officers have confirmed this fact to me. At least one self-styled Satanist youth gang in Southern California used the Ouija board to select the name of the gang's next victim from a list of people whom they consider to be "the most vulnerable to their mind control."

The Victims: Board to Tears

The September 30, 1986, edition of *Weekly World News* reported that a 15-year-old in Belfast, Ireland, committed suicide shortly after the Ouija board predicted his death before his sixteenth birthday. "I've only got a short time to live, so I might as well choose the time to die," he told friends. They thought he was joking—until they found him hanging in the churchyard.

An 11-year-old girl was told by the board that she would be struck dead. She changed from an outgoing and happy little girl to a terrified child who was afraid to leave the house. Her grades dropped to failing, she lost weight, and she showed signs of paranoia until "eventually, after a lot of visits, heartache and considerable expense, the psychiatrist was able to cure the child of the dread that had scarred her youth."[35]

A 15-year-old girl working the board with her mother was instructed to murder her father so that her mother could marry a handsome young cowboy. She killed him. Despite the fact that the board had told them they would get away with the crime, both went to prison.[36]

A Christian child wrote to me from Union Lake, Michigan, to tell me that—

> . . . a girl at school has a Ouija board. She was asking some girls at school to go to the graveyard and contact "ghosts." I said they were demonic, and I was ridiculed. I'm only in the sixth grade. So are they.

In Miami, Florida, an entire military school, the Miami Aerospace Academy, went berserk in October of 1979 after a teacher conducted an experiment with the Ouija board in a science class. According to a police officer (as reported in the

October 26, 1979, issue of the *New York Times*), "teachers and students were running around tearing up things, ripping doors off hinges, kicking holes in walls.... One student put his hand through a window. The teacher who had conducted the Ouija experiment said that "the game got out of control.... Everybody just got carried away and it was a riot.... There were girls screaming that there was a spirit inside the board...."[37]

There is no way of knowing how many murders and suicides as well as cases of insanity and mediumistic psychosis have been produced by the Ouija, not only in adults but in vulnerable children. And yet all the documentation and case histories do not seem to be enough to convince certain school districts of the deadly nature of the "game."

The Game's Up!

In April of 1987 I was invited by several mothers to testify at a school board meeting in Ontario, California, concerning the occult nature and dangers of the Ouija board. It seems that a certain sixth-grade teacher kept a Ouija board in his class for voluntary use during recess on rainy days. When a concerned mother requested removal of the board on the grounds that it was a dangerous occult tool, the teacher adamantly refused to remove the Ouija from his class and promptly consulted his attorney to make certain that "his civil rights were not being violated" by the outrageous request. After extensive publicity, the school board was eventually pressured into conducting public hearings. The teacher at this point generously decided to consider a compromise. He said he would be "willing to remove the Ouija board from his classroom if the 'true believers' would 'sign a pledge not to meddle with the curriculum or classroom instruction of any teacher... for purposes of propagating a particular set of theological precepts.' "[38] "My pledge that I want signed is no more than the law requires of these people to do—not to meddle religiously in the affairs of the public school and its instruction," said this "educator" in another article.[39] His opinion of the committee that temporarily suspended the Ouija until a formal decision could be made, and of the parents who questioned his wisdom, was quoted in the local paper as follows:

> ... A real dumb move ... they're succumbing to the shouts and shrieks of these people. .... It's like waving a white flag in front of these Iranian fanatics dressed in Christian guise.[40]

Those statements paint a staggeringly clear picture of the almost incomprehensible arrogance, hypocrisy, and convoluted logic evidenced by a growing number of educators today who seem to be operating under the mistaken assumption that our children belong to them. These parents were *not* seeking to impose their religious beliefs on the teacher or anyone else in that class. They were not demanding that Bible Trivia be offered instead of the Ouija board. All they were doing was requesting the removal of a device long and unmistakably associated with the practice of Spiritualism and the occult. They were not seeking the imposition of their Christian beliefs in the classroom, as this teacher implied. They were merely demanding that he cease from propagating his own religious practices.

Despite receiving over 96 pieces of documentation from concerned parents, teachers, police officers, and ministers totaling more than 500 pages (some of which included the above materials), plus dozens of other quotes and excerpts from a wide range of sources (including parapsychologists, psychiatrists, counselors, psychologists, and assorted occultists), the Ontario School Board Committee was unable to come to the conclusion that the Ouija board was either occultic or potentially dangerous to the children. The materials presented, we were told in their written conclusions dated June 15, 1987, were not "verified by empirical research data..." and therefore "... the Committee does not make a judgement on this issue."

I would venture that the evidence was quite sufficient. My guess is that it was not "lack of empirical evidence" that kept the Committee from declaring the Ouija board occultic and dangerous (and thereby banning it from their classrooms) but rather that, as reported by Marianne Aiken in the *Daily Report*, "Banning a Ouija board ... would lead to a series of continuing demands for prohibition of other games or instructional material."

As one pro-Ouija mother warned in a statement to the trustees that may have been more revealing than she intended:

> ... they [the anti-Ouija parents] might also seek to ban other occult equipment, studies and holidays ...[41]

If the game in question had been Bible Trivia, there would have been no question whatever concerning the teacher's alleged "violation of his First Amendment rights." The teacher defending his right to keep such a religiously biased game in his classroom would be laughed out of the hearings if he passionately proclaimed that "his rights as a teacher" were being violated because he had been asked to remove it! Nor would his students have been led in a discussion as to why they had been "cheated out of their freedom of choice."[42] Christian teachers and children have no choice concerning the open practice or discussion of their beliefs in the public school. The same rules should apply to Spiritualists, New Agers, and other occultists.

Chapter 5

Your Kid the Psychic

✦

In future generations, children, using their psychic abilities, may lead us into an expanded conscious-ness and a better understanding of the true nature of man.

—Dr. Alex Tanous
Is Your Child Psychic?

A child tells her mother not to go upstairs because the phone is about to ring, and Grandma wants to talk to her. Sure enough, the phone rings seconds later and it's Grandma.

A little boy wakes up in the middle of the night and tells his father that he "just saw Mr. Wilson having an accident and his car hit a tree." Daddy tells the child to go back to sleep and forget it, but several days later Mr. Wilson wraps his car around a tree.

Another child arrives in school one morning and informs his teacher that they're all in for a fire drill that day. The teacher corrects his misinformation by telling him that no fire drill has been scheduled. But soon the school principal ar-rives, and they're going to have a fire drill![1]

Your child is psychic! In fact, *all* children are psychic! Chil-dren are mini-treasurehouses of vast unlimited human po-tential waiting to be tapped, nurtured, and developed. At their disposal are spectacular latent powers awesome beyond anything most of us could ever imagine, at least at this stage in our as-yet-limited evolution. Through altered and expanded states of consciousness your child will develop powers of extrasensory perception through which he will be able to perceive his future, enabling him to choose the right mate or business partner or even avoid life-threatening disasters.

Or so we are being told by a growing number of individuals whose influence on our school systems is increasingly evident.

Powers to heal everything from a mild headache to AIDS will be at your child's command. Through telepathy or clairvoyance or psychometry or all three he will be able to find lost keys for you or lost people for the police department. At his disposal are powers that will open the door to nonhazardous, breathtakingly exciting (not to mention inexpensive) intergalactic travel through out-of-body experiences. His transcendent self will have access to means through which he can channel communications from dead people, or Ascended Masters, or wise persons, or E.T.'s, or spirits, or sprites, who yearn to guide him in this life and beyond.

Your child has been *born* with this psychic ability. It is not demonic nor is it supernatural. Yet, tragically, the potential power and genius resident within the subconscious of all children has been trampled underfoot through ignorance and carelessness on the part of you, the parent—or you, the teacher. The narrow-minded, religiously bigoted, provincial and/or scientifically unsophisticated attitudes espoused by the greater part of Western society have crushed out the psychic potential of most children, to the evolutionary detriment of the entire planet.

But no longer. Times are changing. We stand at the dawn of a glorious New Age, and soon all mankind will take a great cosmic leap into the next phase of our evolution: personalized godhood.[2] So goes the increasingly accepted refrain.

The late Dr. Beverly-Colleene Galyean, who until her death in 1984 was a federally funded program developer for the City of Los Angeles, said:

> The abilities that we have termed "miraculous" in
> the past are none other than normal heightened or
> altered intellectual capabilities given as a birthright

to all people. The task of education today is to identify, clarify, and eventually teach these skills. . . . Our children already have an innate sense of the importance of these capabilities, but need the gentle affirmation and guidance of wise adults to help them refine and expand these heightened body/ mind skills.[3]

Dr. Galyean tells us how pleased she was when she visited a first-grade class in which, during a discussion on dreams, one "sprightly seven-year-old" informed the class that "she dreamed while floating on the ceiling and watching her body sleep in bed." Needless to say, the other children were fascinated with her out-of-body experience and couldn't wait to get home so they could try it themselves. Dr. Galyean observed that such experiences are—

> . . . common to many people; however the cognizance of such abilities by young children may well point to a mass unleashing of consciousness in our youth that will accelerate the useful functioning of this capability within the general public. Yet it takes a wise, affirming adult, such as this teacher [the one in the first-grade class] to validate and expand this experience and encourage its acceptance as normal.[4]

Not only are these experiences and abilities, once traditionally thought of as psychic or "weird," to be viewed as "valid and normal," but they are to be recognized as "the next leap in human intelligence."[5]

Children: Psychic-Research Guinea Pigs

In April of 1980 an article was published in *Instructor* magazine entitled "Your Kids Are Psychic!" by Dr. Alex Tanous and Katherine Fair Donnelly. The article is an excerpt from their book entitled *Is Your Child Psychic? A Guide for Creative Parents and Teachers*, published by Macmillan Publishing Co.

in 1979. *Instructor* is one of the most widely distributed and respected publications among educators. The article informed teachers around the country that the kids in their classrooms are all definitely psychic, but the poor little tykes "may never know it without your help."

The authors of this article tell us that psychic experiences like those mentioned at the beginning of this chapter are a normal part of our everyday lives. The problem is that the adults in each of those examples were not aware of the fact that ESP is a "natural phenomenon, a kind of sixth sense." The authors admit that no one knows how it operates, but assure us that it is indeed an ability we are all born with. Furthermore, "Teachers in particular are in a position to play an exciting role in the psychic development of children." In order to facilitate the teacher's exciting new role as psychic investigator, using your children as their research guinea pigs, the authors define a few principal psychic terms, such as "telepathy," "clairvoyance," "precognition," and "retrocognition," and give the teachers instructions on how to conduct simple ESP tests on the entire class. Here are some of the suggestions given:

- Create an atmosphere of relaxed encouragement. . . .
- Give older children books on ESP or read portions to the younger ones.
- Keep a record of psychic happenings that occur in the classroom or that students report to see if there are any trends.
- Give ESP tests both to determine the extent of a child's psychic ability and to help further develop that ability.
- All ESP testing should be conducted in a game-like fashion, and over a number of years. . . . It should be explained that the tests are simply games.

Some of these "games" are then described for the teacher, along with the encouragement for them to devise their own tests as they see fit, as well as a reminder that many more tests and helpful suggestions are included in their book. Why, you might ask, would a teacher want to spend valuable class-time acting as a psychic researcher when one would think the teacher might be better occupied in trying to do something concrete about the alarming and ever-growing rate of illiteracy in this country? The answer given by the authors is scarcely to be believed: "Identifying a student's psychic ability can be helpful because it allows a teacher to understand a child better and, therefore, to provide reinforcement that is tailored to the specific needs and abilities of each child." This is the same kind of rationalization presented by Dr. Galyean for her use of astrology in the public school classrooms. "...Combining astrology, fantasy, and values awareness is lots of fun, and a low risk way of getting at self-revelation." In fact, she was so enthusiastic about it, that she developed an entire teacher-training program called "Astrology, Fantasy and Values" to be used for "bi-lingual teaching... and as a part of any humanities curriculum."[6] I, for one, cannot but wonder how teachers throughout the ages have ever managed to understand or educate any of their students without resorting to the occult!

Dr. Tanous, Katherine Fair Donnelly, and Dr. Galyean are by no means the first to advocate using public schoolchildren as the subjects of psychic experiments. Among numerous early articles on the subject is one entitled "A Two-Year Program of Tests for Clairvoyance and Precognition with a Class of Public School Pupils," published in the September 1959 issue of the *Journal of Parapsychology*. The authors "demonstrated the excellent results that can be attained with a group of children in classroom ESP tests over a two-year period."[7]

The Psychic Is "In"

What exactly does it mean to be "psychic"? Why is it that certain individuals are determined to develop psychic abilities in the children of this country? Is it possible that the awesome testimonies that we're hearing today from people like Shirley MacLaine and so many others are examples of normal, to-be-expected manifestations of as-yet-little-understood energy fields?

After all, since the turn of the century and certainly since the 1930's (when Dr. J.B. Rhine set up his psi research laboratories at Duke University), well-known and respected scientists from such fields as neurophysiology, theoretical physics, psychology, and anthropology have dedicated themselves to methodically researching the manifestations that have for thousands of years been the core activities and experiences of mystics, Yogis, mediums, psychic surgeons, sorcerers, witches, and other shamans around the world. They are busily formulating complex theories of quantum physics, quantum mechanics, and "holographic models of reality" which they hope may somehow account for "paranormal" manifestations.

Amazingly, these scientists have vigorously denied any connection with occultism and have insisted instead that their research (dubbed "parapsychology" and defined as the study and investigation of psychic phenomena) is a valid science. They are convinced that all paranormal manifestations are produced by some mysterious "energy field" or "force" of some kind, despite the fact that occultists (from mediums and aboriginal shamans to Uri Geller) have always testified that their powers are not inherent in themselves but rather are produced by the direct intervention of spirit guides, or "the gods and goddesses," or the E.T.'s.

The fact is, however, that none of these scientists really knows what he is dealing with. Robert McConnell, the first president of the Parapsychology Association and a retired physicist, candidly admitted that *something* was going "bump in the night," as it were, but it's anybody's guess *what*. "We don't have any idea what we're doing. . . . All we know is that something occurs."[8]

The Scientific Occultist

Edgar D. Mitchell, Apollo 14 astronaut and founder of the

Institute of Noetic Sciences, said: "There are no unnatural or supernatural phenomena, only very large gaps in our knowledge of what is natural. . . . We should strive to fill those gaps of ignorance."[9] He formed the Institute for the "study of human consciousness" and to provide a forum for scientists to share and discuss their findings and research in a multitude of areas, including imagery, biofeedback and meditation, telepathy, clairvoyance, precognition and telekinesis, holistic medicine, etc.

Jeffrey Mishlove, who received a Ph.D. from the University of California at Berkeley for the study of "Psi-development system, a disciplinary matrix for history, theory, evaluation and design," said in an interview for the Winter 1980-81 edition of *SCP Journal*: ". . . psychic abilities are actually innate in most people. . . . It seems to me that psychic abilities are a natural talent. I don't think they're supernatural at all. I think it's a latent talent, like athletic, musical or mathematical ability, that we all have."

These researchers are convinced that occult phenomena are natural, but there is absolutely no scientific basis on which they can demonstrate that belief. They have merely chosen to *assert* that because the alternative (belief in the existence of spirits and demons) is unthinkable to most of them.

Despite their protests to the contrary, not all the scientists involved in psi research have managed to steer clear of the occult philosophy that *invariably* undergirds the phenomena they study. One by one they are finding themselves espousing the mystical perspective of which they were once so skeptical. To be sure, they still cloak it in "scientific" jargon, but the results are still the same: the creation of a new breed of "scientific occultists." (Scientificus Occultus??)

A remarkable article entitled "New Developments in the Reconciliation of Science and Religion" by a leading New Age scientist makes the trend clear:

> The modern world has long assumed a fundamental conflict between science and religion. . . . However . . . there is no necessary conflict at all between

the esoteric "perennial wisdom" of the world's spiritual traditions and . . . science. . . . This is a more revolutionary development than may be apparent at first thought.[10]

C.S. Lewis foresaw this trend years ago in his delightful *Screwtape Letters*. Screwtape, the wily old devil, writes a rather prophetic letter to his nephew Wormwood:

> I have great hopes that we shall learn in due time how to emotionalize and mythologize their science to such an extent that what is, in effect, a belief in us (though not under that name) will creep in while the human mind remains closed to belief in the Enemy. The "Life Force," the worship of sex, and some aspects of Psychoanalysis may here prove useful. If once we can produce our perfect work—the Materialist Magician, the man, not using, but veritably worshipping, what he vaguely calls "Forces" *while denying the existence of "spirits"*— then the end of the war will be in sight.[11]

For those of you who may not yet have noticed, *the end of the war is in sight*! The occult is slowly but surely acquiring an aura, as it were, of respectability. As we have seen, countless millions of people in this country alone have become involved in one form or another of occultism. They have gone from merely *believing that it exists* to *knowing that it is real* on the basis of personal experience.

So What's Wrong with Being Psychic?

If psychic abilities are indeed latent within all human beings—if they are simply the result of natural though as-yet-little-understood energy fields and principles of physics, as so many scientists and researchers assert—then for someone to stand in the way of their exploration or development would indeed place him or her in the same category occupied by the Inquisitors, who ignominiously silenced Galileo for daring to suggest that the earth was not the center of the universe.

And yet while confidently assuring us that these psychic powers are indeed natural and inherent in us all, the scientists and researchers have also admitted that they really have no idea what they're talking about. So *on what basis* are they assuring us that these powers are 1) natural forces and 2) perfectly safe to explore and develop? This is a truly crucial question, especially since so many educators are working so diligently to produce a generation of psychic children.

Scientists, even the best of them, have been known to be wrong about their conclusions and theories on numerous occasions in the past. What if they're wrong about this issue? What if psychic abilities are not natural and neutral at all, but rather are the result of the presence and working of spirit beings? This may not be a particularly popular hypothesis, but it is nevertheless every bit as plausible as the highly complex speculations that the scientists are kicking around. Psychic powers have, after all, an uncanny habit of disappearing when bound, renounced, rebuked, and cast out in the name of Jesus Christ of Nazareth. I have yet to see someone's talent for math or piano-playing do that when subjected to the same treatment!

The Bible acknowledges only two sources of genuine supernatural power: either spirits of demons performing signs and miracles for the purpose of deceiving those willing to listen to them (Revelation 16:14; 13:14; 19:20) or God sovereignly working a miracle or a sign or a wonder in order to bear witness to His word and those who brought it (Hebrews 2:4; Acts 2:22).

Not a single one of the prophets of the Lord ever gave any indication that they thought the miracles or healings or prophecies or signs ever originated with them. Despite the fact that magicians have made Moses out to be something of a patron saint, he had no inner latent psychic power of his own. Moses did not work one single miracle on his own. Exodus 3:20 makes it abundantly clear that it was *the hand of God* that performed the mighty deeds that resulted in the release of the children of Israel from their bondage in Egypt. "I will stretch out My hand and strike Egypt with all My miracles which I shall do in the midst of it, and after that he will let you go."

Even the magicians in Pharaoh's court were forced to admit that it was "the finger of God" that was bringing about their judgment (Exodus 7:19), a tacit acknowledgment that it was someone else's finger altogether that was the source of their comparatively puny powers. Mind you, these magicians were pretty good metaphysicians. They had certainly studied and practiced for years how to harness occult forces, and indeed they could mimic the wonders produced by God, but only up to a point. They were doing fairly well with their secret arts when it came to turning a snake into a staff, turning water into blood, and calling up frogs. But their demon gods petered out after that, and it was certainly only God's mighty hand that parted the waters of the Red Sea. As far as anyone knows, these other guys never even parted the waters of their own bathtubs!

Four hundred years earlier, when Joseph was called before Pharaoh to interpret a disturbing dream, he answered Pharaoh and said, *"It is not in me*; God will give Pharaoh a favorable answer" (Genesis 41:16).

When the prophet Daniel was faced with a similar dilemma during the time of the exile in Babylon, he said to the king, "As for the mystery about which the king has inquired, neither wise men, conjurers, magicians, nor diviners are able to declare it to the king. However, there is a God in heaven who reveals mysteries. . . . But as for me, this mystery has not been revealed to me for any wisdom residing in me more than in any other living man, but for the purpose of making the interpretation known to the king . . ." (Daniel 2:27,28,30). The court occultists were not able to give the king the interpretation, for even then it was true that God "makes fools out of diviners"[12] when the occasion warrants it. Daniel didn't hypnotize himself into an altered state in order to contact the great collective unconscious or his Higher Self for the answer. What he did was fall on his face before the God of heaven and acknowledged that "wisdom and power belong to Him."[13]

In Jerusalem, the apostle Peter was on his way to the temple to pray when he saw a man who had been lame from birth begging for alms. The beggar got more than he bargained for that morning, for Peter grasped him by the hand and said, "I do not possess silver and gold, but what I do have I give to you: In the name of Jesus Christ the Nazarene—walk!" The man was instantly healed. He leaped up and began praising God. And the people were in awe of Peter, thinking that the power was his own. Did Peter miss a great opportunity? He could have told the people about their own inner latent psychic powers which they too could learn to release. But what he said was, "Men of Israel, why do you marvel at this, or why do you gaze at us, as if by our own power or piety we had made him walk? . . . On the basis of faith in His name, it is the name of Jesus which has strengthened this man whom you see and know . . ." (Acts 3:12,16).

Even Jesus as the only begotten Son of God and the perfect man exercised no "latent powers." He chose to walk in dependence on the power of the Holy Spirit and relied on Him for the working of the miracles that He performed. Those miracles were not an end in and of themselves. It was "in order that you may know that the Son of Man has authority on earth to forgive sins [that] He said to the paralytic . . . 'Rise, and take up your stretcher and go home' " (Luke 5:24).

The Curse of Psychic Power

In contrast to the true men of God we see Simon the magician, who had for a long time been astonishing the people of Samaria with his magic arts, "claiming to be someone great." The people proclaimed that "this man is what is called the Great Power of God" (Acts 8:10), and it's entirely likely that they got the title directly from him. And then there's the magician Bar-Jesus, who at every turn sought to hinder the gospel of Jesus of Nazareth. Peter called him a son of the devil and an enemy of all righteousness (Acts 13:6-12). As for the channeler in Acts 16, her "latent power" got itself cast out in the name of Jesus Christ for piously going around proclaiming that Jesus was one of many equally good ways (Acts 16:16-19).

Many people think that being psychic is a gift from God and a sign of their deep spirituality. It is not a gift. It is a curse—the result of participating in practices and activities which God has repeatedly called abomination. These powers may seem to be good, even holy. And yet the Bible makes it clear that appearances can be deceiving. In Matthew 7 no less authority than Jesus Himself gives this terrible warning:

> Not everyone who says to Me, "Lord, Lord," will enter the kingdom of heaven, but he who does the will of My Father who is in heaven. Many will say to Me on that day, "Lord, Lord, did we not prophesy in Your name, and in Your name cast out demons, and in Your name perform many miracles?" And then I will declare to them, "I never knew you; *depart from Me, you who practice lawlessness*" (Matthew 7:21-23).

Why would Jesus say such a terrible thing? These people were performing what seemed to be genuine signs and wonders and miracles, and they were even doing it in His name! So what on earth is the problem? Why does Jesus cast them away, as He says He will do at the time of the final judgment? After all, did He Himself not say in this very same passage "By their fruits you shall know them"? And aren't so many of the psychics and channelers and metaphysicians showing good fruit? Indeed, on one level, many of them are. I have rarely met a more sincere, kindly, dedicated, and loving human being than the medium with whom I worked in Mexico City. The fruit of her life would indeed put many Christians to open shame. She genuinely believed in what she was doing. She sincerely believed that working with her spirit guide was her God-given mission to the world. I myself was convinced that her work had to be from God. After all, her psychic powers seemed to be the source of healing and hope for so many people. And yet the very activity that she believed was a sign of God's favor has been repeatedly condemned as *abomination* in both Old and New Testaments. What Matthew 7 is telling us is that there are two kinds of fruit: There is, to be sure, the fruit of life and good works, but this is not the most important fruit for judging the source of a supernatural sign. The key to that, as Jesus presents it, is *the fruit of doctrine and obedience to God's will*. If what you believe about Jesus is not what He has revealed about Himself in His Word, if you have followed another Jesus, if you have chosen to follow what is right in your own sight regardless of what God has commanded, then regardless of the awesome nature of the apparent miracles you may perform, they are *by definition* not from God. The author of Proverbs wasn't joking when he observed, "There is a way which seems right to a man, but its end is the way of death" (14:12; 16:25).

In Deuteronomy 18:9-14 the Lord spoke to the children of Israel before they were to enter the land which He had promised them. This is what He commanded them:

> When you enter the land which the Lord your God gives you, you shall not learn to imitate the *detestable* things of those nations. There shall not be found among you anyone who makes his son or his daughter pass through the fire, one who uses divination, one who practices witchcraft, or one who interprets omens, or a sorcerer, or one who casts a spell, or a medium, or a spiritist, or one who calls up the dead. For whoever does these things is *detestable* to the Lord; and because of these *detestable* things the Lord your God will drive them out before you. You shall be blameless before the Lord your God. For those nations which you shall dispossess listen to those who practice witchcraft and to diviners, but as for you, the Lord your God has not allowed you to do so.

God flatly condemns the entire spectrum of occultism! Every single form of occult practice—from child sacrifice to belief in superstitions and divination, from channeling to the worship of spirits—has been categorically, uncompromisingly forbidden to those who say they love the Lord. Calling it "parapsychology" or "transpersonal" in no way changes this prohibition; you are still dealing with exactly the same practices that God Himself has labeled abomination. He seems to feel pretty strongly about it; the reason He commanded the destruction of the people of that land was precisely because they were steeped in devil worship and the occult practices which thrive in our own country today. In passage after passage God condemns the practice of the occult. It is illogical to think that He is now going to turn around and bless psychic abilities in you just because you're sincere.

Psychic Pathways

There are basically four ways for a person to become psychic. The first is through inheritance. It is a well-known fact among occultists that psychic powers frequently come down in the family line. Occult practices seem to open a door which allows psychic powers to be passed from generation to generation. There's a good reason for this: Practice of the occult is equated by God with idol worship. It is at its core an insult to God and a direct violation of the Second Commandment:

> You shall have no other gods before Me. You shall not make for yourself an idol, or any likeness of what is in heaven above or on the earth beneath or in the water under the earth. You shall not worship them or serve them; for I, the Lord your God, am a jealous God, visiting the iniquity of the fathers on the children, to the third and the fourth generations of those who hate Me.[14]

When you practice what God has called abomination, you open a door to a curse, not only for yourself, but for generations after you. If we could only go back and check the family history of children who are psychic from an early age, I suspect we would invariably find someone in the line who had been involved in one form or another of the occult.

The second way to acquire psychic abilities is through personal experimentation with the occult. It doesn't make a bit of difference that you weren't serious in your dabbling.

Skeptics who have "just visited" channelers out of sheer curiosity have found themselves going home with spirit guides and psychic powers of their very own, much to their chagrin and initial disbelief. The third way is through the laying on of hands. A powerful psychic can transfer the attention of the spirits producing psychic powers to you in this way. When Jeane Dixon was a child an old Gypsy grasped her hands and transferred power to her. The fourth way to acquire psychic power is a way which a growing number of our teenagers are opting for today: selling their soul to the devil.

Satan is the ultimate counterfeiter. From the beginning he has sought to make himself "like the Most High,"[15] thereby attempting to take upon himself the attributes of God. Satan's promise to Eve of personal divinity is one he has backed up with psychic powers. ESP, precognition, clairvoyance, clairaudience, psychometry, etc., are a counterfeit of God's omniscience. God's omnipresence is mimicked by the supposed cases of astral projection and bi-location in which a person has been seen in two different places at precisely the same time. Psychokinesis, telekinesis, materializations, apports, and the like are a counterfeit of God's attribute of omnipotence. Psychic surgery and occult healings also counterfeit God's mercy and omnipotence and are a mockery of the healings performed by the disciples of Jesus in His name.

Yes, there are actual miracles today, performed by both God and the devil. Nevertheless, only God works *genuine* miracles. A miracle is the divine intervention of a transcendent, sovereign God who reaches into His creation and brings about a whole new work totally outside and apart from any law of nature. In contrast, demonic "miracles" must rely on the manipulation of "forces" to bring about their results. Unless one understands the difference between the two, the results, on the surface, may appear to be similar. That is why the Scriptures admonish us to "test the spirits to see whether they are from God." If we do not know how to do this in accordance with God's command, then we are entirely likely to accept the devil's counterfeit miracles and psychic powers produced by demons as being from the hand of God. Those of whom Jesus spoke in Matthew 7 made that mistake. I pray that you and your children won't be among them.

Chapter 6

Your Kid the Yogi

◆

An influx of spiritual teachings from the East, combined with a new psychological perspective in the West, has resulted in a fresh look at the learning process. . . .[1]
—Jack Canfield and Paula Klimek

They are full of superstitions from the East; they practice divination like the Philistines and clasp hands with pagans.
—Isaiah 2:6 NIV

Part and parcel of Transpersonal New Age education is the belief that all children should have a spirit guide of their very own. Transpersonal educators view this guide as extremely helpful in contacting one's "Higher Self" or "Inner Wisdom," that part of yourself which mystics say is God. In addition to which, as most well-grounded occultists know, you don't want to get caught in your meditational metaphysical ozone without at least one guide. It can be dangerous out there. And, since that "metaphysical ozone" is precisely where the children find themselves as a result of the guided imagery and meditation exercises advocated by these educators, the children will definitely need their "guide" with them.

Transpersonal educators don't generally start out by telling you all this, however. They find it much better to start off by telling you their program is designed to "help the child learn" or "deal with stress" or that their program will "improve the child's self-esteem." Jack Canfield, for example, is one of the current internationally recognized self-esteem gurus. He is president of Self-Esteem Seminars based in Southern California, and for the last 19 years has conducted seminars for corporations such as NCR, General Electric, Scott Paper, and Smith, Kline and French Laboratories, not to mention over 250 school districts. According to the *Los Angeles Times*,[2] Canfield hosted the first Southern California Self-Esteem Conference with 500 participating California educators.

The Trojan Horse Revisited

I had been aware of Jack Canfield since 1978 when he and Paula Klimek published an article in *New Age Magazine* entitled "Education in the New Age," in which they thoughtfully catalogued virtually every key humanistic and occult technique being introduced into public classrooms by "Wholistic" (New Age/Transpersonal) educators.[3]

Then, in 1984 an angry teacher sent me a copy of a curriculum guide to a Self-Esteem Seminar presented by Canfield in Los Angeles. I could see why the teacher was upset about the material: The curriculum guide was a basic, simplified manual for introducing Oriental and New Age occultism into the classroom. His recommended sources were taken from such New Age luminaries as spiritist/channeler Richard Bach, author of *Illusions* and *Jonathan Livingston Seagull;* David Spangler, who teaches we must all take a Luciferic initiation in order to enter the New Age[4]; the late Jane Roberts, channeled for the "Seth" material; *The Science of Mind* by Ernest Holmes; Shakti Gawain; Dr. Mike Samuels; J. Krishnamurti; and Dr. Beverly-Colleene Galyean, to name but a handful. The curriculum guide even included Canfield's easy-to-follow instructions for teachers in leading guided imagery/visualizations and introducing the children to their "wise old person" whom he and Paula Klimek had inadvertently identified as "a guardian spirit" in their article in *New Age Magazine*.[5]

It was disturbing enough to learn that school districts were promoting such blatantly occultic material in their classrooms under the banner of self-esteem. It was even more disturbing when Jack Canfield became a member of the California Task Force to Promote Self-Esteem and Personal and Social Responsibility formed in 1987 by Assemblyman John Vasconcellos. As the *Los Angeles Times* pointed out, at least half of the 25 members of the Task Force were "veterans of the human potential movement,"[6] and the Task Force decidedly carried with it "touchy-feely, New Age, group-grope implications."[7] Being familiar with Assemblyman Vasconcello's Humanist/New Age connections with Esalen and Unity-in-Diversity, and knowing what Canfield was already introducing into public school classrooms, I couldn't help but wonder if perhaps the Task Force was going to be used as something of a Trojan Horse to smuggle New Age, humanistic, and Eastern occultic religious perspectives into the classroom. [See Appendix A: "A Sinner's Self-Esteem."] I said as much at one of their meetings, which provoked quite a reaction from several of the Task Force members, including Assemblyman Vasconcellos and Jack Canfield. Both emphatically denied any "New Age" connections, and assured me that nothing of the kind would ever take place.

Then in February of 1989, I attended Canfield's day-long "Self-Esteem in the Classroom" seminar. It was sponsored by the Orange County Department of Education (Southern California), and according to the vice-principal of a local elementary school with whom I spoke, most of the several hundred educators, school psychologists, and administrators present had been required to attend by the department.

There is no question that Canfield is sincere and committed. He seems to genuinely like people in general and children in particular and is obviously concerned about their welfare, qualities I believe he shares with the other members of the Task Force. And he certainly offered some helpful suggestions for teachers in dealing positively with their students. However, it was clear from the material he handed out that his entire program was firmly entrenched in psychosynthesis and confluent education, with their emphasis on Eastern mysticism and such techniques as guided imagery/visualization, the use of New Age music to help facilitate altered states of consciousness, the Left Brain/Right Brain myth, contact with the "Higher Self," and introduction to spirit guides.

I purchased a copy of his *Self-Esteem in the Classroom Curriculum Guide* (1986) and was shocked, though unfortunately not surprised, to find that he had even included detailed instructions for "Discovering Your Radiant and Creative Self: A Transpersonal Arts Approach to Expressing One's Potential."[8]

Life Purpose Fantasy and the Radiant Self

The "Life Purpose Fantasy," and the "Radiant Self" are among the most blatantly occultic Eastern-based exercises for developing psychic abilities I have come across. These exercises, which he compares to the "traditional rites of passage" of ancient cultures, provide the children with answers to basic questions about which "they are often confused and usually unable to get clear answers from their parents and their teachers . . . basic life questions, such as, Who am I? What does it mean to be alive? Will I and do I make a difference?" Work with "radiant student drawings," and an experience with something he calls the "Life Purpose Fantasy," Canfield tells us, help provide "positive answers" to these questions.

In the guided imagery "Life Purpose Fantasy," the teachers are instructed to get the kids into a comfortable position with their spines straight and eyes closed, and to get them to relax by becoming aware of their breathing pattern. The "fantasy" instructs the children to move backward through their lives in their minds, going back "to being a young child . . . a two year old . . . a baby . . . to the time of your birth and the time you were in your mother's womb. . . . And now go back to the time before your conception. You are about to meet a special guide, your own special guide. A guide to whom you may ask what the purpose of your life is. . . . Meet this guide and pose your question. . . . Feel your guide's unconditional love and strength and beauty. . . . Let whatever happens happen. . . . Communicate with your guide in whatever way possible. . . . Listen to your guide's response. . . . Ask your guide for a gift to represent your purpose, your essence."[9] The students were then to draw and write about their experiences. Once they've brought back their guide's "gift" that represents their "life purpose" then they are ready to move on to the "radiant student" exercises.

The "radiant student drawings" are "full-length body drawings completed over a period of eight to ten imagery sessions." Canfield and Klimek wanted to "help people discover what essential qualities are attempting to manifest through their personalities. We call this process discovering your radiant self."[10] Canfield and Klimek were awed at the artwork thus produced by the sixth, seventh, and eighth graders led in these sessions: "Many students draw healing energies emanating from their hands, archetypal symbols, and more. *There had been no previous discussion of any of these concepts.*"[11] Obviously, the children are contacting some form of spiritual reality during these sessions.

But, Canfield cautions, the teacher can't just spring the "radiant student" and "Life Purpose Fantasy" and "guides" on the kids without proper preparation. First, the teacher must "create an environment of increased trust and mutual support among the students." He emphasized that "we usually begin our work in a classroom with some basic trust-building, self-validation, and communication exercises like those contained in *100 Ways to Enhance Self-Concept in the Classroom.*"[12] The self-esteem programs now being introduced in numerous states around the country, beginning with California, are a crucial part of this all-important first step of "trust-building" and "self-validation."

Once the children have developed an unquestioning trust in the teacher, then, Canfield continues, they are ready to "begin to work with some basic imaging and centering techniques to help the kids relax, to be receptive to the language of their inner images, and to discover their own best way of imagining."[13] The imaging and centering techniques that he feels are "particularly useful" for preparing the students may seem, at first glance, innocuous enough. After all, who could possibly object to helping a child "relax"? Nevertheless, these activities are inextricably rooted in Eastern occultism and mystical religion and are foundational not only in preparing the children to meet their spirit guides, but also in molding their basic worldview. These are the techniques that help turn your kid into a little yogi.

Relaxed and Centered

Centering and *relaxation* are "a fundamental process for New Age education, because they provide a space for listening to the voice within. . . . Learning how to center one's self is one of the most important processes of all the New Age educational tools."[14] As Canfield points out, there are literally hundreds of ways to teach children to relax and become centered. Examples of some of these ways include:

> . . . progressively tensing and relaxing each part of the body . . . counting one's breath to ten and starting over; listening, with eyes closed, for the most distant sound; imagining watching fluffy white clouds floating by; imagining one's body filling with white light.[15]

Most assuredly, it is sometimes necessary to "de-wiggle" a class before it is possible to get down to the business of learning. The issue is whether the only methods available to us are Eastern ones. I've been informed by teachers with long years of experience in the classroom that simply getting the children to stand up, stretch tall, take a couple of deep breaths, and then go limp all over "like a rag doll" a few times is quite enough to do the trick. Not only does it relax the kids, the purported intent, but it manages to do so without zapping the kid into an altered state of consciousness. The stated purpose of all the centering and relaxation techniques presented by the Transpersonal educators, on the other hand, is to train the child in Eastern techniques so that he can sit still long enough to concentrate on focusing his attention *inward*. Why? So that he can "contact . . . his or her own 'Higher

Self.' '"[16] Translation: So that the kid can meet his spirit guide and experience his divinity.

As Deborah Rozman explains it in her book *Meditation For Children*, "when we center, we gather our energies together and become calm."[17] Once everyone is centered, then visualization and other meditation techniques help the child contact the "Source of all Consciousness" at their "Center," which is their "Higher Self," also known as their "True Self," their "Real Self," or their "Radiant Self." You might want to note that New Ager John Randolph Price says that ". . . the Truth of our being—is that the Higher Self of each individual *is* the Christ. . . ."[18]

Sometimes the teacher will begin the centering process with some form of progressive relaxation or other basic hatha-yoga exercises. (Rozman's book, for example, contains a section in the back called "Children's Yoga Exercise Class.") The teacher might instruct the children to lie down on the floor or perhaps to sit cross-legged with back straight, eyes closed, and palms up on their knees. (This is the basic lotus pose that is traditionally assumed by meditators. They usually sit this way because it keeps them from doing permanent damage to themselves should they accidentally tip over while in the trance state that meditation is designed to produce.) Then, in a quiet "modulated" tone of voice (the correct term here is "hypnotic") the teacher usually leads the children in basic rhythmic deep-breathing techniques until they become still and calm. Then the teacher may instruct them to tense, squeezing certain muscles in their bodies in order to "release any residual tension." (Whatever the order any particular teacher may want to use, these are usually the basic components of the process.)

Hatha-Yoga

There is a common misconception in the West that hatha-yoga, one of about ten forms of Yoga that supposedly leads to self-realization, is merely a neutral form of exercise, a soothing and effective alternative for those who abhor jogging and calisthenics. After all, the YMCA, the Boy Scouts, and the

Girl Scouts[19] (and any number of schools and churches) include it in their programs, so there couldn't possibly be anything dangerous or mystical or religious about it, could there? An article entitled "What Is Yoga?" that appeared in *Boy's Life*, a magazine popular among the Boy Scouts, presents Yoga as "a set of ancient poses and exercises that stretch the muscles, strengthen the body and discipline the mind," a "sport" that "promotes strength and calmness," a "good tool for dealing with whatever challenges—mental or physical—that come along." The author of the article informs her young readers that "Yoga... means discipline," and heartily encourages them to become involved in it.[20]

Actually, the Sanskrit root word for Yoga, *yug* or *yuj*, means "to yoke, to unite or to bind." It also means "union" or "communion."[21] The whole point of Yoga is "Self-Realization"—that is, to experience your divinity as you yoke yourself to Brahman (the "Infinite," the "Universal Spirit," the impersonal force that the Hindus call "God"), thereby theoretically releasing yourself from the bondage of endless reincarnation. That is the ultimate aim of all Yoga, including hatha-yoga. Hatha-yoga is "one of the six recognized systems of orthodox Hinduism"[22] and is at its very roots *religious* and *mystical*.[23] It is also one of the most difficult and potentially dangerous forms of Yoga.

The term *hatha* is derived from the verb *hath*, which means "to oppress."[24] The syllable *ha* refers to the moon or the *ida*. The syllable *tha* refers to the sun or the *pingala*. The *ida* and the *pingala* are symbolic, or psychic, passages on either side of the spinal column. What the practice of hatha-yoga is designed to do is suppress the flow of psychic energies through these channels, thereby forcing the "serpent power" or the *kundalini* force to rise through the central psychic channel in the spine (the *sushumna*) and up through the *chakras*, the supposed psychic centers of human personality and power.

Westerners mistakenly believe that one can practice hatha-yoga apart from the philosophical and religious beliefs that undergird it. This is an absolutely false belief. The practice of hatha-yoga, whether in Westernized or even "Christianized" garb, is inextricably tied to the philosophy that spawned it. You cannot separate the exercises from the philosophy. The physical exercises and postures were developed "as a technique for acquiring an altered state of consciousness merely by physical means."[25] As author and TV Yoga teacher Richard Hittleman said, "The movements themselves become a form of meditation."[26] The continued practice of the exercises will, *whether you consciously intend it or not,* eventually influence you toward an Eastern/mystical perspective. *That is what it is meant to do!* As Deborah Rozman has pointed out, "The real purpose of yoga exercises is to put the body in a state where meditation on the One is possible."[27] There is, by definition, no such thing as "neutral" Yoga. As author Dave Hunt dryly observed during a lecture a few years ago, "*No* Yoga is good Yoga."

Physical Postures

Only after spending years at mastering the demands of personal restraint and self-discipline do Yogis move on to the third stage in hatha-yoga, the *asanas,* or physical postures so popular today in the West.[28] There are numerous good reasons for this delay, not the least of which is that the practice of the postures, breathing techniques, and meditation exercises is designed to arouse powerful energies which the Yogis identify as the kundalini serpent force. Unless the devotee has meticulously prepared himself beforehand, those "energies" (which are in fact demonic beings) can indeed destroy him. The literature of Yoga is filled with warnings and case histories of illness, insanity, moral degeneration, and even death of those who practiced Yoga, thereby arousing kundalini.

Gopi Krishna, author and kundalini researcher, suddenly and unexpectedly experienced the arousal of kundalini one day during meditation:

> I felt as if I were in imminent danger of something beyond my understanding and power, something intangible and mysterious, which I could neither

grasp nor analyze. . . . A condition of horror . . . began to settle on me. . . . Little did I realize that from
that day onward I was never to be my old normal
self again, that I had unwittingly and without preparation or even adequate knowledge of it roused to
activity the most wonderful and stern power in
man, that I had stepped unknowingly upon the key
to the most guarded secret of the ancients, and that
thenceforth for a long time I had to live suspended
by a thread, swinging between life on the one hand
and death on the other, between sanity and insanity, between light and darkness, between heaven
and earth.[29]

Gopi Krishna spent years in that condition, exhibiting not
only various forms of insanity, according to his own testimony, but numerous mediumistic abilities as well. That
should not come as any surprise. As John Weldon and Clifford Wilson comment in their excellent research manual
Occult Shock and Psychic Forces:

Yoga is really pure occultism, as any number of Yoga
and occult texts prove . . . the numerous dangers of
occultism are evident from many studies.[30]

Hans-Ulrich Rieker, in his book *The Yoga of Light*, warns:

This is a serious decision. Yoga is not a trifling jest
if we consider that any misunderstanding in the
practice of Yoga can mean death or insanity. That a
misunderstood Yoga can be dangerous has been
proven by many a student. . . .[31]

"Nonsense!" exclaims the Transpersonal educator. "What
can be the harm of a few 'relaxation exercises'?" states the
naive parent. "Ridiculous!" snorts the local YMCA Yoga
teacher. "We've been into Yoga for years and are neither dead,
possessed, nor insane!" Perhaps not. Yet it is nonetheless
significant that virtually every major guru in India has issued

warnings like those stated above. Oddly, the "gurus" in this country are not always so candid. [For further reading see *Gods of the New Age* by Caryl Matrisciana.] If adults choose to practice Yoga despite the risks, that is their prerogative. But if it is true that inherent dangers exist in the practice of these ancient occult techniques, does anyone have the right to expose the children in our public schools to them?

Deep Breathing

The fourth stage of hatha-yoga, also prevalent in many schools, is the practice of deep-breathing techniques, which involve a system of measured, rhythmic inhalation, retention, and exhalation. Now don't misunderstand me—I'm not saying that taking a slow, deep breath is going to automatically open you to the pits of hell! Even Christians need to take a deep breath now and then! However, deep-breathing techniques such as the ones taught in Yoga are a time-honored method for entering altered states of consciousness and for developing psychic power.

Yogis believe that the air is infused with a subtle living energy force called *ch'i* or *prana*. Through ancient Yogic techniques of deep breathing, the Yogi allegedly learns to absorb this mystic cosmic energy. He believes that said energy force fills him with life and psychic power as he directs it through the psychic centers (*chakras*) in his body in order to arouse the kundalini (which is pictured as a goddess in the form of a serpent coiled at the base of the spine). Deborah Rozman's books *Meditating with Children* and *Meditating for Children*, which are highly recommended by Canfield, contain several drawings of cute and lovable snakes. She has the teachers instruct the children to "breathe in as you bring your life energy within and breathe out as you send your life energy out into the world around you."[32]

An interesting warning about the practice of breathing exercises, or *pranayama*, is found, of all places, in a book by the old occultist Alice Bailey. She tells us that "the emphasis in all esoteric schools is necessarily, and rightly, laid upon meditation." But there are numerous dangers in its practice.

> If . . . the tuning up and awakening [of the kundalini] is forced, or is brought about by exercises of various kinds before the student is ready and before the [etheric and physical] bodies are co-ordinated and developed, then the aspirant is headed towards disaster. *Breathing exercises or pranayama training should never be undertaken without expert guidance and only after years of spiritual application, devotion and service;* concentration upon the centers in the force body [with a view to their awakening] is ever to be avoided; it will cause overstimulation and the opening of doors on to the astral plane which the student may have difficulty closing.[33]

The Last Stages

The next stage, *pratyahara*, is one of withdrawal and detachment from the world. (Some Transpersonal educators point out that turning out the lights or shutting one's eyes can create an environment for withdrawal and meditation in the classroom.) Once you're out of the mainstream of the noise and confusion of the world, it's easier to move into stage six, which is called *dharana*, or concentration. (Canfield, Rozman, Hendricks, Fugitt, et al. offer numerous exercises in *dharana* for the children, some of them quite advanced forms of occultism. These include candle meditations, focusing the attention on the center of the forehead, at a point also known as the "third eye.")[34] Eye- and ear-centering exercises are part of the meditation process and are designed to help the child develop his powers of concentration, which will enhance his ability to enter altered states of consciousness for chanting, meditation, etc.[35]

The seventh stage in hatha-yoga is meditation, or *dhyana*. During this stage the Yogi learns to go beyond single-minded concentration on an object to "losing oneself in it." It is a necessary step in preparation for the final stage of "cognitive trance,"[36] when the "mystic union of the individual soul with the Universal Soul"[37] is theoretically achieved. Both these steps usually require years to achieve, and few Transpersonal educators expect to lead the children in their care quite that far. But at least they've laid the groundwork for them.

Sol Gordon, Professor of Child and Family Studies at Syracuse University in New York, encourages students to experiment with altered states of consciousness. In his school textbook entitled *Psychology For You* he tells the students that "one altered state of consciousness that you can investigate on your own without danger is meditation."[38] He then presents the basics of meditation for the students to try out for themselves, including instructions in the lotus position, deep breathing, and basic induction techniques.[39]

If he truly believes that meditation can be practiced "without danger," one wonders why he would bother to add a word of caution suggesting that if the student plans to meditate for longer than an hour he arrange for a friend to check in on him in case he "becomes 'lost' in the 'altered consciousness' of meditation." Gordon does admit that "it cannot be denied that there is a certain amount of risk in altering consciousness in this way. On the other hand, there is a certain amount of risk in all new experiences of life."[40] He then adds: ". . . do not attempt the meditation for longer than you feel comfortable. In other words, if you get a headache, feel extremely restless or have some other 'annoying' reaction, discontinue."[41] Maureen Murdock, in leading meditations with third-graders in California, says that "occasionally a child will experience a scary image and it is important to discuss this with him/her or have the child draw or write about the image."[42]

Don't you find it comforting to see the directions and safeguards the educators of your children are providing for them?

Biofeedback

Biofeedback is simply a Westernized, mechanized method of achieving within a few weeks or months what it has traditionally taken Yogis 20 to 40 years to accomplish.[43] There are teachers across the country who are playing with one form or another of biofeedback in their classrooms. The basic biofeedback machine has been around for about 20 years now. Some of the units are very simple while others, like a new unit known as the "Mind Mirror," are complex and expensive. By attaching oneself to a specially designed monitor, people are learning to control the autonomic (unconscious) functions of their bodies, including heartrate, skin temperature, etc. The chief developers of biofeedback, Dr. Elmer Green (head of the Voluntary Controls Program at the Menninger Foundation in Topeka, Kansas), and his wife, Alyce Green, in their book *Beyond Biofeedback*, called biofeedback "the yoga of the West," and are intrigued by the fact that many who use it and other techniques of hypnosis and mind-training have developed psychic abilities.

The *Donning International Encyclopedic Psychic Dictionary* states that "training sessions easily open one up psychically" and "that one can reach a deeper state of meditation more rapidly than in normal training. . . . Dangers of biofeedback training sessions occur if the doctor or therapist who is monitoring the readouts and session is not familiar with parapsychological principles."[44]

Biofeedback is recognized as an important tool in consciousness research. Some Transpersonal biofeedback researchers believe that widespread use of the machine will help bring about an evolutionary leap of mankind as more of us learn to experience the "Awakened Mind" that their machines help one achieve.[45] Scientists such as Dr. Stanley Krippner have published accounts on "his work with hypnosis and poor readers, and my notions as to how biofeedback and parapsychology could be used in education."[46]

It is interesting that a recent article in *Psychology Today* discusses the use of "biofeedback, relaxation, self-hypnosis and imagery exercises" in helping children as young as three years old gain control of pain, asthma attacks, migraines, etc., and is entitled "Little Swamis."[47]

Chanting and the Mantra

There are numerous forms of chanting, all of which (with

the possible exception of reciting "Mary Had a Little Lamb") will result in altered states of consciousness. One form of chanting is the use of affirmations, a "positive" statement repeated over and over until it sinks deeply into the mind, thereby influencing the person's beliefs and behavior. Sometimes a child will be seated in the middle of the classroom and the rest of the students will repeat a special affirmation to the target child in a process called "seed-planting." Sometimes the chant is fairly long and done by the entire class. Canfield suggests the following as a chant that "works well with children":

> Happiness runs in a circular motion. Life is like a little boat upon the sea. Everyone is a part of everything anyway. You can have it all if you let yourself be.[48]

That little ditty is a classic statement of Eastern philosophy: All is One, One is All.

Canfield says that because children are naturally rhythmic, chanting therefore "fits well into the classroom. Chanting can be used as meditation, for focusing the group energy and for evoking the qualities of peace, love, joy, and unity. When the whole class creates a unified vibration through sound, there is a tremendous uplifting effect."[49]

It is a short step from chanting New Age ditties to actually chanting a *mantra*. Transpersonal educators are quite fond of mantras. Rozman has the children "softly chant OMMMMM-MMMM, and send the OMMMMMMMMM down the threads of light we have built...."[50] This takes place during her "Temple of Light Meditation," in which the children are led to "imagine a thread of blue light going from your spiritual eye (right between your eyebrows) to the spiritual eye of the person on your left."[51] The "third eye" is the sixth psychic center (*chakra*) opened through the practice of Yoga. It is the opening of the "third eye" that is believed to give a person psychic powers.

The Om, TM'rs, and the Gods

In yet another exercise Rozman instructs: "Close off the ears and listen to the hum of the Cosmic vibration inside. That is called the Om, which is the first vibration before all of the other vibrations that we perceive through our senses."[52] And again, "Toning different primal sounds like ahhh or ohhm creates vibrations that still the mind, making us more receptive and better able to listen."[53] Maureen Murdock says that she and her third-graders "often chanted the 'om.' " The kids at first reacted with "self-conscious giggles. They soon, however, joined in and filled the room with vibrations that stilled their minds and laughter."[54] Ms. Murdock found that listening to "Music for Zen Meditation" was helpful in producing a "soothing and peaceful" environment.[55] This is not surprising. New Age music is *designed* to produce altered states of consciousness and is therefore frequently used by Transpersonal educators in their classrooms.

Personally, I wouldn't want any child of mine within a mile of any mantra, whether called "chanting," "toning," "affirmation," or whatever! The ancient Sanskrit word "mantra," it seems, is best translated "spell."[56] It is a "mystical sound,"[57] a "vibration" whose repeated utterance produces effects of awesome power—something that magicians and sorcerers have long understood. They would call it an "incantation." An Indian sorcerer cannot die, it is believed, unless he passes his secret mantra of power to a successor,[58] and some mantras are considered "extremely dangerous if uttered incorrectly or with misplaced intent." Certain mantras, like those of transcendental meditation, are the names of Hindu demon gods. (This may come as a shock to the average TM practitioner.) The "vibrations" of that god are latent within the mantra; it *embodies* him, so that repeated chanting *will summon the god* and make his power available to the chanter.[59]

Whole cults have been formed around Mantra Meditation or Mantra Yoga, such as the Hare Krishnas, who believe that "simply by chanting the Hare Krishna mantra . . . the Great Chant For Deliverance . . . you get the highest perfection. That's a fact."[60]

Transcendental Meditation however, is probably the best-known cult of Mantra Yoga in the West.

In October 1977 parents in New Jersey won a Federal District Court battle declaring that Transcendental Meditation is indeed a religion and therefore has no business being taught or promoted in public schools (Malnak vs. Maharishi Mahesh Yogi).[61] To do so, the Court ruled, is in violation of the Establishment Clause of the First Amendment. Evidently a lot of educators still have not caught on to that as yet. Students in a fourth-grade class in Pennsylvania, as late as October 1988, were still doing reading and spelling lessons based on the following:

"TURNING ON TO TM"

... Several years ago a teacher from India brought the secret of TM, or Transcendental Meditation, to North America. His name is Maharishi Mahesh Yogi. He teaches how to meditate and relax your mind. Some people think that TM is a kind of religion. This is not true. Meditation is simply a way to refresh your mind and body. Twenty minutes of TM can be as helpful to you as several hours of sleep! ...

TM has taken North America by storm. Doctors, politicians, sports stars, parents, and students are learning to relax this new way. There is even a university for studying Transcendental Meditation! Every day, more and more people are turning on to TM.[62]

When a concerned individual protested, they were informed by the teacher that "nothing objectionable" could be seen in the material!

Despite the popularity of TM et al., the famous and ever-popular OM has continued as the "mantra par excellence," enjoying "universal prestige." Did you ever wonder what it means? Jose Arguelles, most recently of Harmonic Convergence notoriety, says that OM is "the irreducible point, the primary syllable, the word, the Logos, through which all is

uttered and through which all must pass. . . . This is the significance of the mystic syllable OM, which in its way is the
seed center of all sound as the point is of vision."[63] It seems
that the sound "was identified with Brahman, with the Veda,
with all the great gods. . . ."[64] If the "gods" can be embodied
within the mantra and summoned by its chanting (according
to the ancients who developed these practices, and they
should know), then perhaps you might want to reconsider
"toning out" on it lest you inadvertently find yourself visited
with "all the great gods"!

The Bible's warning about this practice cannot be ignored:
"When you are praying, do not use meaningless repetition,
as the Gentiles do, for they suppose that they will be heard for
their many words" (Matthew 6:7). Indeed, they will be heard.
The question, of course, is *by whom.*

Mandalas

Just as mantras are designed to establish contact with
higher energies through chanting, *mandalas* act as a *visual*
means of connection to spiritual power. Mandala work is also
tremendously popular in schools today. Art students especially are often given assignments to draw these designs,
although students in any class, from kindergarten on up, may
find themselves instructed in this unique form of "Transpersonal art."[65]

Like the mantra, the mandala is tremendously ancient and
complex in scope and meaning. It is one of a number of
magical centering and meditative techniques especially used
by Buddhists, Hindus, and American Indians.[66] The word
mandala comes from the ancient Sanskrit, and literally means
"circle" and "center."[67] So, not surprising, a mandala is usually circular, representing the whole cosmos, but it may also
be found in the form of a symmetrical figure or geometrical
pattern. As one looks at the pattern there is an illusion of
being "drawn in" to a center of concentration.[68] The mandala
serves as a hypnotic tool for drawing in the user so that he
or she can draw out the power of the gods, achieving that

supreme altered state of consciousness known as "Cosmic" or "Sacred Consciousness." ". . . the Mandala . . . is not an end in itself, but a transmitting agent, a lens focusing the higher energies."[69] In other words, the whole purpose of the mandala is to put you in contact with demons.

Educator Jack Canfield has developed a powerful use of mandalas in his popular curriculum guide. One exercise in particular, the "Radiant Student," is based on the occult manual *Mandala*, by Jose and Miriam Arguelles. The purpose of the exercise is "to help people discover what essential qualities are attempting to manifest through their personalities. We call this process 'discovering your Radiant Self.' "[70]

Interestingly enough, Carl G. Jung was largely responsible for introducing the mandala to Westerners.[71]

Dangers

Canfield may feel that the mandala is a "beautiful, expressive centering process."[72] Nevertheless, those well-versed in the use of mantras and mandalas know that there are serious dangers in the use of these techniques.

Ritual magicians have for hundreds of years used a form of mandala, their "circle of protection," for this very purpose: protection from demonic forces who stand ready to destroy the careless or inexperienced magician who summons them should they step outside their protective circle, or otherwise goof up the ritual.

Even Jose Arguelles quietly acknowledges that certain aspects of the mandala are useful for protection, acting as "barriers protecting the pure source from invasion by unclean spirits, feelings, or thoughts."

Indeed, encounters with demons are an expected hazard of centering and meditation techniques. Ancient and modern writings by "responsible" occultists are filled with warnings about the vital importance of knowing precisely what you are doing and how you are doing it if disaster is to be avoided.

> Without a long period of correct training there is every likelihood of the imagination running amuck.

Even under controlled guidance the apparitions that he encounters in the journey through the intricate pathways of the mandala can be frightening enough. The demon-guardians and the fearful monstrosities that lurk in the dark recesses are ever ready to block his path and hack him to pieces.[73]

Occasionally you will even find a word of caution about the potential dangers in the material distributed to teachers. In an article entitled "A Program Model for Altering Children's Consciousness," published in *The Gifted Child Quarterly*, the author issues a word of warning in the midst of all the Transpersonal programs that he advocates for altering children's consciousness in the classroom. In the section on Guided Fantasies he warns the teachers of possible problems:

Important! For their protection you should say, somewhere in the beginning, that they are in control and can come out of it at any time they need to—that you are their guide on their mind tour.

No matter what your religious convictions (or lack of them) it is important to protect them during meditation. For meditation they should each have a personal guide, protector, or talisman. It is something that they can bring to their conscious aid if the experience takes them into strange or frightening territory. You should also be alert to any serious discomfort, crying, or sudden changes in any of the children and immediately come to their aid. (I have had NO problems yet, but I visualize the room as a large golden pyramid. I'd rather be considered crazy and have the children safe than scientifically expose them to dangers. The yoga tradition must have learned something in their thousands of years of experience. I defer to them.)[74]

Evidently he does not see fit to defer to them enough to dispense with these ancient occult/religious techniques altogether. Quite apart from the fact that no public school-teacher should have the right to lead our children in religious activities, how many of us would be willing to let our children become the spiritual guinea pigs of some neophyte, self-appointed, would-be guru who is feverishly hoping his "golden pyramids" hold up!

As the writers of the *Encyclopedia of Man, Myth and Magic* point out,

> Whether we believe in the actual existence of the entities that are alleged to guard the [astral] zones or not, the fact remains that occultists of both schools, and practitioners of magic, black and white, have brought back vivid descriptions of their experiences while on such astral adventures. We may attribute them to the power of the imagination and the workings of a heightened faith, or dismiss them as hallucinations induced by some alchemy of the brain.... But whatever the interpretation of such occult experiences might be, there can be no doubt that they are hazardous and can be injurious. The paths opened to the aspirant... are not to be ventured on lightly.[75]

Karate Kids

The majority of the martial arts are, as is Yoga, inextricably tied to Eastern religious principles. Canfield lists the martial arts in his "Education in the New Age" article as "the best way we've found to get the individual attention of the more difficult students."[76] What he's saying here is that an awful lot of kids who won't as yet cooperate with the other forms of meditation that holistic educators are trying to incorporate in their classrooms may well be receptive to induction through the martial arts. Bruce Lee, Kung Fu, the "Karate Kid," and any number of movies and TV programs (not to mention the U.S. Tae Kwon Do Olympic team) have made the martial arts extremely appealing to a lot of young men in this country.

Time magazine showed a picture of a four-foot-one-inch, sixty-pound seven-year-old who became the youngest officially recognized black belt in America. He had been practicing the martial arts since he was four. The writer of the article assured us that this was not a script for Karate Kid III, but the true life story of a little boy in New York whose hands were now listed in the category of lethal weapons.[77]

I recently spoke with a man who is a black belt in three different schools of martial arts and asked him if he now, as a committed Christian, felt it would be all right for children to learn the basics of the martial arts, if only for self-defense. His reply was that if it were his child, he would teach him or her a few key places particularly vulnerable to a good swift kick. He would teach him how to "scream his head off" if in trouble, and then run for all he was worth in the opposite direction. He would *not* teach him Kung Fu or Karate or Tai Chi or aikido. The occult influences which the child will most likely be exposed to while practicing these ancient Oriental arts are a risk that far outweigh any possible benefit the child might acquire. Many of the martial arts are rooted in Zen Buddhism and virtually all include meditation, yogic breathing, and centering techniques.[78]

It is an unfortunate fact that our schools are increasingly being infiltrated with practices and superstitions from the East. If your child comes home with a memo cheerfully advising you that your child will now be learning Yoga or karate in his or her gym class, you now have at least enough basic information on the religious nature of Yoga to go to the teacher or school principal and rationally state the reasons for your objection to its inclusion in the school on any level. There are very solid reasons even from a purely secular perspective (and based on the writings of Yogis themselves) which will hopefully cause the school to reconsider using Eastern religious techniques, exercises, or devices in their classrooms. Activities such as Yoga, mandalas, mantras, biofeedback, "centering exercises," or martial arts are not suitable activities for children at all, much less those attending public schools, where officials are supposedly sworn to keeping religious indoctrination out of their institutions.

Chapter 7

Shamanism 101: What You See Is What You Get

✦

Without a doubt one of the most powerful techniques being used to initiate the next generations into the New Age religion is *visualization*. Virtually all Transpersonal educators would agree that the key to education is to help young people look within themselves to discover and release their divinity. Supposedly, all knowledge, wisdom, and perfection already reside within them. All we have to do is to provide the environment and the techniques to help them *experience* it. One of those techniques is visualization:

> Close your eyes and see your objective in your mind's eye. See it and *know* that *it is yours*. Do not see it and just wish that it were yours, or see it on the way to being yours. See it and *know* that it *is* yours. If it's a car, see yourself driving it. See it in your garage. See yourself polishing it and filling it with gas. See yourself putting the keys in your pocket.[1]

Tragically, occult techniques exactly like these have also crept into the church. Many sincere Christians have bought the lie that visualization is a neutral technique and are making the sorry mistake of equating this occult technique with *faith* and *prayer*. *It is not a neutral technique, and it is not the equivalent of biblical faith.* A few brave souls (such as, for example, Dave Hunt) have desperately tried to warn the church and have gotten themselves ridiculed and ostracized for their trouble. But you need to know that the occultists and New Agers are laughing at us for our foolishness and naiveté. Dick Sutphen, reincarnationist and New Age activist, dryly comments:

> I smiled to myself recalling how New Age visualization techniques have obviously infiltrated even Jerry Falwell's organization. In his book, *God's Bullies*, author Perry Deane Young describes a training session for Moral Majority fund raisers. The trainer, Charles S. Judd, told his audience, "PMA: Positive Mental Attitude. Picture yourself being a success. If you're asked to raise five thousand dollars, then picture yourself coming back and saying to the board, 'There it is.' "
>
> Right on, Charlie! And if it works to raise money for you, maybe they'll start to use the technique in their personal lives to create their own reality, which could even lead to the realization that they are God.[2]

In personal interviews with Witches I have been told that their covens have "laughed themselves silly" at how the church has so wholeheartedly adopted their occult techniques, thinking that as long as they tagged "Jesus" at the end of them that they were perfectly okay. In my own earlier days I used extensive guided imagery/visualization techniques for developing psychic powers and mediumship. Some of the techniques I learned through Silva Mind Control, some through the practice of hatha and Raja Yoga, and some were given to me by the medium with whom I worked for 14 months. It was a colossal shock to me to discover that virtually the same techniques I had practiced as an occultist were being used in the church! It was less surprising to find how extensive these practices have become in the schools.

Infinite Knowledge and Power

Transpersonal educators would all agree that without being

able to use guided imagery/visualization techniques in the classroom, their entire program would be pretty well shot.

It is these techniques of "looking within" that are essential to gaining access to the "Higher Self" of each child. Without their meditations in the classroom, they would never be able to "help" the children contact "the ultimate levels of their own being," or "view past-life experiences," or "communicate with others through mental images and sensations." They would never be able to help the children reach those "various levels of consciousness possible to human beings" that must be achieved if the children are to "experience their own divinity." And they would never be able to introduce the children to their "Radiant Selves" or to their spirit guides.

The techniques of visualization and guided imagery are disguised in the schools under various names. In Battle Ground (near Vancouver, Washington) it was found under a 22-step program called "Thinking Skills." Parents of children in the 11 schools testing the program protested that in the "Learning to Learn" section the students were being taught, among other things, to concentrate on dots and the "mind's eye," and were being taught deep-breathing and relaxation techniques similar to Transcendental Meditation.[3]

In Florida, first-graders listened to "Quieting Reflex" and "Success Imagery" tapes that took them on guided-imagery fantasy trips, introduced them to the basics of Yoga for the purpose of "relaxing" the children, used powerful hypnosis techniques to help lead the children to "significant behavior changes," and, in the third tape of the series, introduced them to a "wise man" to whom they could go for counsel.[4]

In Minnesota, 16 schools were targeted for testing of a "method of visualizing success" that was designed to help the students "concentrate and reduce anxiety." The program there is called the "Whole Mind Learning" project (formerly called "Consciousness Education") and was sponsored by the Continuum Center, which is responsible for training more than 300 Minnesota teachers in their occult techniques. Conservative Christians in the area protested that the program "smacked of Eastern religious influences," but the person in charge of teacher training for the school district said that "it's a very innocent type of program." "This project is not about the notion of mind control and religious practices," added an executive of First Bank of Minneapolis (which donated 45,000 dollars to fund the project). "First Bank wouldn't get near a project like that." This executive is, nevertheless, a Continuum Center board member.[5]

Parents in New Mexico protested use of the DUSO (Developing Understanding of Self and Others) program in the schools. DUSO is based on the use of 42 guided imagery/visualization fantasy stories that school counselors and teachers can choose from to help the children "relax" and to introduce them to spirit entities. More than one child testified that they had been instructed by school counselors not to tell their parents.[6]

The parents decided to battle it out with the school administrators, protesting that as Christians they did not want their children indoctrinated in New Age philosophy that teaches you to "look within" for answers rather than to God. They contacted then-State-Senator Joe Carraro, vice chairman of the Senate Education Reform Committee. The senator introduced Senate Memorial 45 (SM-45) during the 1986 legislative session, which stated in part:

> WHEREAS, the utilization of mind-altering techniques for public school students is highly objectionable; and WHEREAS, the teaching of or counseling by certain psychological techniques in New Mexico's public schools should be entirely eliminated; and WHEREAS, these psychological methodologies can involve such techniques of transcendental meditation, altered states of consciousness or the occult; NOW, THEREFORE, BE IT RESOLVED BY THE SENATE OF THE STATE OF NEW MEXICO that the teaching of or counseling by certain mind-altering psychological techniques be entirely eliminated in New Mexico public schools.[7]

In Senator Carraro's remarks to the legislature, he said that "If I can't practice my religion in the schools, I don't want anybody else practicing theirs. . . . Besides which, these kids are there to learn, not to learn how to relax. I have a little boy who doesn't need to relax any more. He needs to read, write and do math, not hum a mantra."[8]

The teachers of New Mexico disagreed. Despite the fact that over 350 parents and leaders picketed the April 1987 Standards Committee of the State Board of Education during their hearings to decide whether SM-45 would be adopted, and despite the fact that nearly 50 proponents of SM-45 testified at the hearing, the board "decided to allow schools to continue teaching New Age philosophy."[9]

New Age educators, it would seem, have forgotten just whose children they're teaching. As the protestors in New Mexico pointed out, "Parents have the primary, inalienable right to educate their children according to their religious, moral and cultural values; they delegate, but do not abdicate that right to schools and teachers. Teachers are entrusted with the awesome responsibility of teaching future generations of Americans. Teachers need the support and cooperation of parents. Schools must respect parental rights and actively encourage parental involvement in every area of education. Parental responsibility requires that parents demand academic excellence in all areas of education. School boards, administrators, and teachers are accountable to the taxpayers and parents who support them and entrust their children to them."[10]

In Seattle, Washington fourth-graders reported that the teacher had frequently asked them to lie down in a darkened room. They were then led in "relaxation" techniques in which they were asked to imagine they were made of sawdust. Then they were taught how to create a mental laboratory, where they could go anytime for counsel, healings, "instant travel," or whatever. In their laboratory they created a "mental screen" that would help them solve any kind of problem. They were introduced to "counselors" or "guides" who would come to help them with anything they asked. These guides might be people or animals. Some of the children said that a small voice had moved inside of them called the "Babbler," which they were told to listen to and obey. (The use of "mental screens," "laboratories," and "counselors" are the same terms and practices used by Silva Mind Control, now known as the Silva Method.[11])

They were taught how to wield a "Sword of Fire," a tool used in their "laboratory" which they could use to draw three circles of fire around themselves—and around anything they wanted in order to bring that thing to themselves. They were taught about a "Cord of Fire" that went up from their belly buttons or from the top of their heads and extended up into infinity which could be used to influence other people. They were encouraged to try bending spoons and rulers with their minds. They were also instructed not to tell their parents or the principal because the teacher said people would think she was crazy and fire her.[12]

Transforming Your Child

Cases like these are legion across the country. In fact, they have something for everyone in California. "Project GOAL" covers grades K-6, "Project STAR" provides for grades 5-8, and "Project Plus" makes sure that high school students become "relaxed" and "enlightened." Now, of course, we have "Project Self-Esteem" in the works. In the Santa Clara Unified School District it's called "Project Balance Accelerated Learning by Challenging the Whole Brain."

Whatever the program may be called in your area, the purpose is basically the same: *the "transformation" of your child.*

Dr. Beverly-Colleene Galyean, as already noted, directed three federally funded projects in confluent education for the Los Angeles City Schools. Confluent education was developed in the 60's by George Isaac Brown of the University of California, Santa Barbara. "Confluent education" as defined by Dr. Brown, is the integration or flowing together of the emotional, intuitive aspects of learning with the reasoning and logical sequencing elements, and is sometimes called humanistic or psychological education.[13] "It is a multisensory approach to learning that applies gestalt techniques, psychosynthesis, guided visual imagery, movement, affirmations,

and deep breathing to the basic classroom curriculum."[14]
Stuart Miller, in his introduction to Dr. Brown's book, acknowledges that some of the techniques of confluent education
were derived from "... Eastern religions...."[15] The government paid Dr. Galyean to experiment with the use of guided-
imagery/visualization and meditation techniques in the schools
to "enhance" student learning.

Dr. Galyean made it clear in countless articles on the subject that helping children learn a foreign language or whatever
was secondary to her primary goal: spiritual indoctrination.
Galyean summed up the beliefs on which her entire program
of confluent education was founded:

> Once we begin to see that we are all God, that we all
> have the attributes of God, then I think the whole
> purpose of human life is to reown the Godlikeness
> within us; the perfect love, the perfect wisdom, the
> perfect understanding, the perfect intelligence, and
> when we do that, we create back to that old, that
> essential oneness which is consciousness. So my
> whole view is very much based on that idea.[16]

Dr. Galyean believed, as do virtually *all* Transpersonal
educators, that the key to education was to help the child look
within himself to discover and release his divinity. She taught
that all knowledge, wisdom, and perfection already reside
within the child. All the teacher needs to do is to provide the
environment and the techniques to help the student experience that fact.

> Teachers who are deeply spiritual and who feel
> comfortable working with their own spiritual de-
> velopment may choose to offer spiritually oriented
> meditations to their students. This is done when
> there is an explicit sense of appropriateness es-
> tablished between the teacher and the students,
> parents, school personnel and community.[17]

The only place where such blatantly inappropriate religious material could conceivably be viewed with any "explicit

sense of appropriateness" would perhaps be in a strictly private school openly dedicated to New Age indoctrination (such as the Montessori or Waldorf Schools), but certainly *not* in the public schools! And yet this is precisely where it is taking place. Ah me. Wherever is the ACLU when you need them!

Dozens of books and articles have been published in the last few years designed to teach parents and educators how to lead children in guided-imagery fantasy trips and meditation. Some of these books, like Deborah Rozman's *Meditating With Children*, have to be seen to be believed. The book is a classically simplified presentation of virtually every major Hindu doctrine and occult practice, ranging from hatha yoga, karma, candle meditations, astrology, third eye meditations, chakras, mandalas, chanting, ESP and divination games, including water witching and pendulums. And that's just for starters!

Rozman's work is full of blatantly religious statements about "training the brain of the child . . . to orient the mind to the spiritual self," about developing a "divine self image" . . . which will "work to further the evolutionary process," and about "a realized at-one-ment." Rozman tells us that "the objective is to establish a true recognition of Center within and the purpose of centering so as to tap the Source of Consciousness and Life for Peace, Joy, Inspiration and Bliss."[18]

In a follow-up book called *Meditation For Children*, Rozman makes the ultimate goal of meditation abundantly clear:

> Flashes of insight will come to reveal that there is no real separation between ourselves and others. . . . Miracles, psychic experiences, visions, etc., are all part of the unfoldment. But to concentrate on any of these as a goal or an end in itself is sidetracking from the real goal of Oneness. In Oneness religious teachings like "The Lord our God is One," "I and My Father are One," "Before Abraham was I AM," *make sense and become personally applicable to us.*[19]

Statements like these (which fill a good part of educational Transpersonal literature) expose the true religious intents of these educators. And yet somehow these people expect us to believe that because they are not officially associated with some specific guru or sect, they are therefore nonreligious! The *East-West Journal* review of Rozman's books says:

> Among the most enlightening of the new teaching books . . . a well-illustrated tool of practical psychology. . . . The absence of a religious point of view in the book makes this volume an excellent learning vehicle.

One would think that the *East-West Journal* surely would have thought twice before making such a singularly inaccurate statement. The philosophy and activities presented in the book are indeed religious to the core, and they know it. Evidently they must have counted on the naiveté and general ignorance of the American public.

Even the U.S. Government has been hoodwinked by all the attestations of the "absence of a religious point of view." It seems they have again used our tax dollars to fund another religious pilot program, this time using *Meditating With Children*. They even published a very positive review of the results in a teacher's manual, which was distributed to all California public schoolteachers.[20]

Half-Brained Theories

Much of the Transpersonal material used in the classroom is being smuggled in under the protective "scientific" banner of the Left Brain/Right Brain theory. Guided imagery/visualization techniques, meditation, mantras, yoga, mandalas, etc., are often introduced by using the excuse that these activities are a vital part of training the "right side" of the child's brain. Teachers are being told that for too long education has focused on "left brain" cognitive teaching that emphasizes rote learning, logic, and memorization of facts. At best, they are told, we use only 10 percent of our brain, and most of that seems to be in the boring, uncreative, and spiritually limiting left side of the brain. "Is it any wonder," muses

Marilyn Ferguson, "that our educational approach, with its emphasis on linear, left-brain processes, has failed to keep pace with the times?"[21] What we need to do now, say the Transpersonal educators, is develop exercises and teaching modes that will develop the *right* side of the brain—that part of our brain that is intuitive, mystical, emotional, creative, artistic, and open to altered states of consciousness—so that the children can be truly balanced.

Sally Springer, coauthor of *Left Brain, Right Brain*, accurately pointed out in an article in the *Phi Kappa Phi Journal* that "The concept that the human brain is divided into two halves or hemispheres, each with specialized functions, is now firmly entrenched in popular culture."[22] "Are you left-brained or right-brained?" is right up there with "What's your sign?" as a social icebreaker these days. As the author of an article in *OMNI* magazine pointed out, "Everyone knows that the left hemisphere is rational, logical, and Western, and the right is creative, intuitive, and Eastern. *Everyone knows, that is, except the scientists who did the research on which the whole notion of left and right brains is based.* To them the idea that the brain's two hemispheres are split into two tidy sections—one the center of creativity, the other the logical thinking—is simplistic and wrongheaded."[23]

Teachers find themselves caught in a real dilemma. It is certainly true that in many ways education has been very one-sided. The focus has been, in great measure, on rote memorization rather than on integrating what is being learned into the child's everyday living and experience. There is certainly nothing wrong with bringing into the classroom a focus on the child as a valuable individual whose emotions and creativity need to be taken into consideration in the learning process. The problem is that "educating the whole child" is being increasingly used as an excuse to smuggle in Eastern/occultic, not to mention *unscientific* theories and techniques.

Probably the best-known teaching method based on the Left Brain/Right Brain myth is one that was developed in Bulgaria by Dr. Georgi Lozanov, a well-known doctor, psychologist, and one of the leading parapsychologists in the Communist world. The system is known variously by the name "Suggestopedia," "Suggestology," the "Lozanov Method," SALT (Suggestive Accelerative Learning and Teaching), or simply "Superlearning." As Sheila Ostrander and Lynn Schroeder point out in their book *SuperLearning*, "Suggestology attempts to get the body and left-brain and right-brain abilities working together as an orchestrated whole to make people more capable of doing whatever they're trying to do."[24]

Dr. Lozanov based his learning system on a broad spectrum of techniques, including mental yoga, music, sleep-learning, physiology, hypnosis, autogenics, and parapsychology.[25] However, he points out that "Suggestology's deepest roots lay in the system of Raja Yoga . . . [which has to do with] ruling or governing the mind. It is considered by its practitioners to be the science of concentration and involves techniques for altering states of consciousness, methods of training in visualization, concentration practice, and special breathing exercises."[26]

Raja Yoga is also well-known among yogis for producing *siddhis*, or supernatural powers. Dr. Lozanov was especially thrilled to discover that "the same yoga techniques that open up supermemory and heal the body also open up many of the mind's other latent powers, like clairvoyance and telepathy."[27]

SuperLearning is spreading rapidly in this country. California, New York, and Hawaii have included it in some middle schools, and Utah uses it in teleconference courses to teach language.[28] Of course, not all parents are thrilled at the prospect of turning their children into little telepaths and clairvoyants, however brilliant. When teachers in Deer Park, Montana, introduced the children in their kindergarten, fifth-, and sixth-grade classes to SuperLearning, several astute parents protested, saying that while they certainly did not question the teachers' motives, they were not going to allow their children to participate in ancient Eastern occultic techniques that at their core violated their personal religious beliefs.

But It Works!

Sincere and well-meaning teachers across the country, burned out by the tedium and aggravations of dealing with unruly kids and/or boring curricula, have flocked to transpersonal teaching techniques in an effort to liven up or, depending on their district, quiet down, their classrooms. And, indeed, the techniques do seem to work in many cases. Teachers have written glowing reports about the soothing effects of the deep-breathing techniques and meditations on even the most impossible of class situations. What they must understand, however, is that these techniques are, at their core, *religious*, and as such, *have no place within the public school classroom*.

"But it works!" cries the desperate teacher. So does Valium, but I would not want some teacher dispensing it to my child because it produces a quiet and comparatively receptive classroom. I do not for one moment believe that the only alternative to reaching our kids is through the introduction of Eastern religious practices into the classroom, although one can see how that has come about. Before God was thrown off the public school campus, the children had a framework and concept of morality: God was known to have some decided views about right and wrong. If your parents or teacher didn't discipline you for misbehaving, there was a good chance that God would. Once the educators managed to ban God from their hallowed halls, however, all hell broke loose. They discovered rather quickly that it is not enough to tell a kid he is the "measure of all things" and has "all knowledge, wisdom, and perfection within his Higher Self," especially if that kid is from the ghetto. The only thing left is to introduce a *different religion* with specialized techniques to help him *experience* it.

Good teachers have always been able to communicate with their students. They have nurtured in their students a sense of self-respect, adventure, and excitement about learning. And they have managed to do so without initiating them into Eastern occultism. Surely that could still be achieved today.

Ancient Roots of Visualization

Far from being "nonreligious" and "neutral," as their proponents in the public schools invariably claim, at least in
public, the techniques of guided imagery and visualization
are integral parts of occult religion and have been for literally
thousands of years. "Philosophers and priests in every
ancient culture used visualization as a tool for growth and
rebirth."[29] "Historical records from Babylonia, Assyria, Sum-
eria, and Greece describe elaborate rituals for ridding the
body of disease. Most of these ancient cultures relied on a
practitioner skilled in the arts of imagination to guide the
afflicted person through thoughts, dreams, or appeals to the
gods to effect a healing."[30] Similar visualization practices
developed in Greece around the cult of Asclepius for the
purpose of healing.[31]

Visualization techniques in the "form of concentration on
an image"[32] have been an integral aspect of yoga since the
days of ancient India. As developed by Patanjali around
200 B.C. in the *Yoga Sutra*, the purpose of all that concentration
was to achieve *samadhi*, a state of bliss and union. The visualizations were also the way to acquire supernatural powers or
siddhis.

In ancient Egypt, the followers of the Egyptian god Thot
(the master of all knowledge and originator of alchemy)[33]
believed that thoughts were *real things*, with vibrational and
energy levels of their own which could be manipulated to
produce physical effects.[34] In other words, what you *think* is
what you *get*. For example, "Ill health, it was believed, could
be overcome by visualizing good health or by imagining the
body in a perfect state or by envisioning a healing god."[35] The
Egyptians built temples to their god of healing and believed
that through dreams and visualizations they would regain
their health.[36]

It seems that as far back as the days of the cave-dwellers,[37]
the shamans used visualization in their prehunt rituals to
mentally slay the soul of the animal they hoped to catch for
supper, or to enter the spirit realm to consult the beings there
on behalf of the tribe or to bring healing to the sick.

What is a shaman? The word *shaman* (pronounced SHAH-maan) has been widely used by anthropologists to refer to individuals who were previously known (primarily in non-Western cultures) by such terms as witch, witch doctor, medicine man, sorcerer, wizard, magic man, magician, and seer. Michael Harner in his book *The Way of the Shaman* defines the term as follows:

> A shaman is a man or woman who enters an altered state of consciousness—at will—to contact and utilize an ordinarily hidden reality in order to acquire knowledge, power, and to help other persons. The shaman has at least one, and usually more, "spirits" in his personal service.[38]

"To acquire knowledge and power." The words are an echo out of Genesis 3.

How does one acquire this knowledge and power? How does one manage to acquire and command a retinue of "spirit guides" as personal servants? *Through the practice of guided imagery and creative visualization.* It is virtually impossible to master many forms of occultism, especially Yoga, Witchcraft, sorcery, and divination, without a thoroughly developed ability to visualize. It is through this ability that the desired effect is brought into existence. *If you can vividly create it in your mind, the occultist believes, it will be manifested in reality.* The sorcerers' ancient Hermetic dictum "As above, so below" is an expression of their belief.

Shakti Gawain, author of the popular book *Creative Visualization*, defines it this way:

> Creative visualization is the technique of using your imagination to create what you want in your life. In creative visualization you use your imagination to create a clear image of something you wish to manifest. Then you continue to focus on the idea or picture regularly . . . until you actually achieve what

you have been visualizing. . . . Creative visualization is magic in the truest and highest meaning of the word.[39]

Dr. Raymond Buckland, anthropologist, Gardnerian Witch, and founder of the Seax-Wica tradition of Witchcraft, would certainly agree with Gawain. In his book *Practical Candleburning Rituals* he dedicates a chapter to the subject of "rituals without candles" which can be practiced by people for whom setting up a lot of candles may be impractical:

> There is a magickal practice that fills the bill and it is closely related to candleburning. It can be extremely effective and can be done virtually anywhere at any time. It is Creative Visualization.[40]

There are perfectly valid and legitimate uses of the imagination, by the way. An artist "sees" the finished painting or sculpture in his mind or an architect "visualizes" the building he is working on. Engineers, photographers, and choreographers "see" their finished products in their minds. Those blessed with a photographic memory have the ability to "see" in their minds with precise detail whatever they need to recall. When we recall past events in our lives, we do so with mental images. Listening to a storyteller or reading a book can produce vivid mental images. When I studied theater, I mentally rehearsed my roles. Such envisioning is *not* what I'm talking about. What I'm talking about is a technique of creating an image in your mind and using that image in an effort to *create or control reality through mind-powers*.[41]

Euphemistically Speaking (or "Catch 'Er in the Lie")

Marilyn Ferguson bemoans, "There are heroes in education, as there have always been heroes, trying to transcend the limits of the old structure; but their efforts are too often thwarted by peers, administrators, parents."[42] That is why, as Mario Fantini bluntly affirms, "The psychology of becoming has to be smuggled into the schools."[43]

There are a multitude of euphemisms employed by these educators to throw parents and other nonsympathetic teachers off the track. Jack Canfield (author of *100 Ways to Enhance Self Concept in the Classroom* and board member of California's new Self-Esteem Task Force) and Paula Klimek give this advice:

> Advice: If you're teaching in a public school, don't call it meditation, call it "centering." Every school wants children to be relaxed, attentive, and creative, and that's what they'll get.[44]

Deborah Rozman suggests:

> If you still have trouble with the word "Meditation" when bringing this program to your children, parents, family, school administrators or board of educators, use alternative terms like Stephanie does, such as awareness training, concentration, centering, awareness games, relaxation, holistic learning, creative imagery, etc.[45]

Who is Stephanie? Stephanie Herzog is a teacher at an elementary school in Scotts Valley Public Schools. She presents a personal testimony about her experiences with meditation in the classroom:

> I began using meditation in the classroom the day after Deborah Rozman spoke at our school district inservice. I started the children with the simple exercise: relaxation, breathing and concentration on a star between their eyes while concentrating on having a good day and doing well in all that they were doing. Due to fear of parent criticism, I call it centering and concentrating our energies. We center five minutes in the morning and ten minutes in the afternoon. If the children come in over-active from any recess we center before beginning work. I told parents who work in my classroom as volunteers that the centering was a relaxation exercise for

increasing the children's concentration. These parents accept what I am doing in a positive way and participate with us.[46]

One teacher leading a recertification course for teachers in Colorado reportedly suggested, "If you're from a conservative school district, don't call it meditation, call it 'Indian folklore.' "[47]

New Age activist Dick Sutphen even brags about the skill which the New Agers have developed in the use of "euphemisms":

> One of the biggest advantages we have as New Agers is, once the occult, metaphysical and New Age terminology is removed, we have concepts and techniques that are very acceptable to the general public. So we can change the names and demonstrate the power. In so doing, we open the New Age door to millions who normally would not be receptive.[48]

You see, they *have to* use "euphemisms." They are determined to transform your children whether you like it or not, and if they have to lie to achieve the "glorious" results that a country filled with "transformed" children will bring, so be it. As any 18-year-old veteran of values clarification can tell you, the ends, after all, justify the means.

Why use guided-imagery/visualization in education? Because it's the only technique, short of peyote or LSD, that will teach the kids how to manipulate altered states of consciousness and "realize" that they are God. And if in the process you can teach them French, Bulgarian, spelling, social studies, or science, so much the better.

Chapter 8

How to Meet Your Spirit Guide

✦

To fully understand psychic children, we must first understand their inner world—their garden of spirits.[1]

—James W. Peterson

The spirit Guides will help you. We all have spirit Guides but sometimes we don't know about them. When you are talking to yourself, you are really talking to your Spirits. It helps more if your Mom's a Psychic.[2]

—Jimmy S. Curtin, age 9, in his book
Magic and Children: The Way for Children to Learn

Undoubtedly one of the most outrageous and dangerous religious practices taking place in a growing number of public schools today is the introduction of the children to spirit guides. "Of course," says Dr. Beverly Galyean, "we don't call them that in the public schools. We call them imaginary guides."[3]

Euphemisms abound when dealing with the subject of spirit guides! Sometimes you'll hear them called "wise person" or "counselors" or "archetypal manifestations." Perhaps they'll be referred to as your "Higher Self," "Divine Master," "Inner Guide," "Inner Wisdom," "Transpersonal Self," "Ally," "Imaginary Doctor," or even "Guardian Angel." Some Satanists call them "Sentinels." If you're dealing with a *really* sophisticated occultist you might find them referred to as "etheric world intelligences." Philosopher and "sacred" psychologist Jean Houston calls them " 'goddings' of the depths of the psyche."[4] Nevertheless, whatever the label, what we're talking about here are *spirit guides*—the kind that no self-respecting spiritualist, medium, or shaman would ever want to be caught dead without! As long as you've got one, no one, including the "Guides," much care *what* you call them. As Shakti Gawain and Marcus Allen advise us in their book *Reunion: Tools for Transformation*, we are quite free to *"call them by the name that feels best to you. I'll call them Spirit Guides, but feel free to substitute any names you wish."*[5]

Transpersonal educators are entirely likely to follow that advice when presenting exercises designed to introduce your child to spirit guides. I venture to say that you will never hear the term "spirit guide" used in the average Transpersonal classroom. Even when directly confronted, Transpersonal educators usually deny vehemently that they have anything to do with "spirit guides." Some of them may even genuinely believe that denial to be the truth. It may indeed be considerably more comfortable for them to think that their "guide" or their supposed "Higher Self" is simply a common and perfectly natural psychological phenomenon, a hitherto-buried aspect of themselves, a mere symbol, an archetype, the language of the unconscious, *anything* but an actual separate spirit entity. They prefer to think that what the channelers are really contacting is a "higher part of their own mind . . . their own subconscious which some call . . . the supraconscious . . . the true self or the hidden observer."[6]

This theory, of course, is of relatively recent origin. For centuries those who have held intercourse with spirit guides have understood these beings to be actual independent intelligences who exist in a spiritual dimension, but who are quite capable of communication with man when it suits them. It was also understood by the ancients, as it is by today's "primitive" societies, that man has no inherent supernatural power of his own. What psychic power he may personally acquire is the product of these beings working through him.

Regardless of how they may individually choose to define or interpret these "guides," the vast majority of Transpersonal educators firmly believe that every child should have at least one of his very own. In the process of "helping improve children's self-esteem" or having them dialogue with their "Wise Old Person," Transpersonal educators are in effect turning schoolchildren into pretty effective little channelers and shamans.

Medium Rare

Years ago the majority of us had never heard of the term "channeler"; those who communicate with spirits were known as "mediums." Pachita, the psychic surgeon with whom I worked for 14 months in Mexico City, probably wouldn't have known what on earth you were talking about if you had called her a "channeler." She was a "medium," a go-between, a vehicle of communication between this world and the astral realm of the dearly departed, which included not only her spirit guide (who presented itself as the spirit of an ancient Aztec prince) but also, on occasion, such illustrious company as the "Apostle John," "Jesus," "an ancient Oriental healer," and the occasional "Space Brother," among others.

Today, however, the term "medium" is decidedly out of vogue (so many negative connotations, you know!). These days the mediums prefer to be called *channelers* (much more sophisticated!). Silva Mind Control puts it this way in one of their California newsletters:

> In keeping with the sense of today's metaphysical philosophies, one would rarely channel his Great aunt Margaret who has just passed over and is floating by. Channeling is most often reserved for contacts with Spiritual Teachers, Ascended masters and other high beings. And the messages received are generally light and pure, positive and loving in quality. So, "dead people" are not normally contacted in such a process, as they do not have much of value to tell us about our Soul Growth.[7]

Of course, as channeling advocate and author Jon Klimo points out, one man's channel is another man's witch doctor:

> Throughout history . . . channels have been named according to what they do . . . the term *medium* and the more recent *channel* . . . shaman, witch doctor, healer, and medicine man in native cultures. They have also been called fortunetellers, oracles, seers, soothsayers, savants, and visionaries. In religious contexts, they have been known as priests, gurus, prophets, saints, mystics and holy ones. . . . In the esoteric schools they are called light workers, initiates, teachers, adepts, or masters.[8]

So What's a Channel?

There are any number of elaborate and scientific-sounding definitions of channeling. Jon Klimo, in his definitive study on the subject, defines channeling as—

> . . . the communication of information to or through a physically embodied human being from a source that is said to exist on some other level or dimension of reality than the physical as we know it, and that is not from the normal mind (or self) of the channel.[9]

For Witch Raymond Buckland, channeling is "the tapping into the collective consciousness in order to obtain needed information."[10]

Silva Mind Control defines it as "simply allowing Higher Consciousness to use our Mind/Brain mechanism—temporarily—to give us knowledge, points of view, or inspiration that we could not have gotten by ourselves."[11]

Personally, I define a channeler as anyone who knows how to hypnotize himself into an altered state of consciousness in order to permit a masquerading demon to communicate through him whatever it wants to for the purpose of deceiving an awful lot of people, including himself. Channeling is in fact nothing but a sophisticated euphemism for one form of demon possession.

Nevertheless, millions of people today are buying into the occult philosophies, heresies, blasphemies, and downright lies being spouted by these "guides" through their channels. Hundreds of books and tapes have been produced by them. In fact, *most of the philosophical and religious principles and guidelines used to establish the New Age were received through channelers.*

As we have already mentioned, Alice Bailey received "telepathic transmissions" from a being that called itself "Djwhal Khul." D.K. claimed to be a "Second Ray Master" and wrote 24 books through her from 1919 to 1949, including *The Externalization of the Hierarchy*, in which the basic plan for the setup of the New Age has been spelled out in some detail. Madame Helen Petrovna Blavatsky, Edgar Cayce, Immanuel Swedenborg, Helen Schucman (and her "Course in Miracles" so popular in many churches today), Ruth Montgomery (the self-proclaimed "Herald of the New Age"), Jose Arguelles (of "Harmonic Convergence" fame, who takes his directions from Pan), Barbara Marx Hubbard, John Randolph Price, Peter Russell, David Spangler, Shakti Gawain, Dr. Mike Samuels, Jane Roberts, and J.Z. Knight (with her 35,000-year-old Ramtha), to name but a handful of them, have all received key New Age doctrines and teachings from their spirit guides, teachings which have been the "guiding light" of the New Age Movement.

Even New Age physicist Fritjof Capra admits in the introduction to his book on physics that he acted, in effect, as a channeler for the book now used as a textbook in various universities:

> Sometimes while writing *The Tao of Physics*, I even felt that it was being written through me, rather than by me. The subsequent events have confirmed these feelings.[12]

So, may we add, has the content of this book, which is little more than a highly sophisticated, "scientific" presentation of the ancient doctrines of demons.

The sheer volume of material that pours forth from these "beings" is overwhelming! Shirley MacLaine channeled her book *Dancing in the Light* in just five weeks, a fact that is bound to elicit a wistful sigh from my publisher.

The spirits don't just confine themselves to books, either. There are channelers who are allowing these beings to produce works of art, paintings, music, scientific discoveries—you name it. It's a well-known fact that channelers and psychics have for many years acted as consultants to major television and movie studios (which might explain why we're seeing so many occult-oriented programs these days). Channel Jill Cook was hired as a "psychic consultant" for the making of *Poltergeist II*. It seems the director consulted with "White Eagle," one of Jill Cook's "controls," more than he did with Jill herself![13]

A Spirit By Any Other Name . . .

In light of the fact that these beings are directly responsible for a major trend in our society today, it would certainly seem well worth knowing exactly with *whom* or with *what* one is in communication. The possibilities seem endless:

> . . . the energies that are now being channeled include dolphins, angels, gods and goddesses, plant and mineral devas, and space brothers—all of whom seem to wish to help humanity at a particularly difficult time in our evolution. And all of them need to borrow voices from us in order to be heard in this realm.[14]

Interestingly enough, children have described the beings they encounter during their teacher-led meditations in much the same terms. For example, during "brain exercises integrated with guided fantasy," Maureen Murdock's third-graders in Santa Monica, California, reported that their "Wise

Person" appeared to them as an old man with a white beard, although some of the girls saw it as an old woman in a rocking chair. A few of the other children reported communicating with a bee, ant, or deer. It is not at all unusual for a spirit guide to appear as an animal in many ancient traditions. These spirit beings are called "power animals," and their function is not only to protect and serve the shaman as anthropologist/ shaman Michael Harner tells us, but also "to become another identity or alter ego for him.[15] Harner also points out that "the main difference between an ordinary person and a shaman is that the shaman uses his guardian spirit actively when in an altered state of consciousness. . . . Without a guardian spirit it is virtually impossible to be a shaman."[16]

For some of Murdock's Santa Monica children, their "Wise Person" was a cartoon figure. Some of the children visualized *themselves* as their "Wise Person."[17] "Wise Persons" might appear in many different forms to the children, Ms. Murdock tells us—perhaps as a religious or mythic figure, a beloved tree, an owl, a stuffed animal, a grandparent, or a peer. Ms. Murdock believes that these beings act as "personal confidants" to the children. These "confidants" are "someone to whom they can tell their joys and sorrows, someone who will champion their cause, someone who will give them advice when the future looks bleak."[18] The important thing is that the children learn to trust and depend on their guide, so that in time they too, like occultist Dr. Mike Samuels, will be able to say that ". . . the information I receive from spirit guides is the information I trust most in my life."[19]

> Children build a very special relationship with this inner ally through the repeated use of imagery. The inner ally gains their trust and shows them different aspects of themselves.[20]

Yuppified Demons

Hearing the way most people describe their guides makes you almost want to go up and give them a big teddy-bear hug, doesn't it? Harvard University theology professor Harvey Cox observes, "They're so cuddly and friendly. They seem to be yuppiefied versions of the demons and spirits of another time."[21] Professor Cox is probably closer to the truth than most people would like to think. In fact, on this one he has hit the proverbial nail right on the head. For all the theories entertained about the origin and nature of these "guides" (all of which, incidentally, the guides themselves have suggested), very few people seem willing to consider the possibility that these spirit guides are actually ancient, unbelievably cunning, malevolent spirits, superb and consummate actors who masquerade for the purpose of gaining our trust. The Bible calls them demons. If the Bible is right on this one, then what the channelers (whether children or adults) are dealing with, however sincerely, will bring them to ultimate deception and destruction.

Kung Fuddled

I first came across Jack Canfield's "Kung Fu" meditation in the 1982 edition of a New Age publication called *Holistic Living News*. The entire edition was dedicated to "Celebrating Children" of the New Age. Canfield's article, entitled "Guided Imagery in the Classroom," was featured on the center page, sandwiched between pictures of beautiful children practicing Yoga and articles about how children today are "old souls" who are now choosing to incarnate so they can help "advance the Aquarian Age."

He began by stating that for several years he had been "exploring how to teach middle school children to contact their inner wisdom, to *look inside rather than outside for the answers about their questions about life.* There are several basic techniques which I use, all of them involving guided imagery." During a discussion with a group of sixth-graders, he brought the children to the point where they decided that they too would like to have a special kind of teacher like "Cain" of the TV show "Kung Fu" had—a "different kind of teacher, somehow more special, more wise, and more able to be trusted."

I then asked the kids if they would like to have a wise old teacher whom they could consult for advice in times of pressure and confusion. They all said yes they would but they weren't sure where they'd find one. Most of them decided they'd have to go to China or Japan or India. I asked them where David Cain went when he needed help. They finally realized that he had closed his eyes and gone inside himself. At this point I suggested that we all try that and see if we could find a wise old teacher inside our minds who could share his or her wisdom with us. They excitedly agreed to try. Here is what I asked them to visualize:

"Close your eyes, take a few deep breaths to relax. I want you to imagine that it is a pleasant day and you are walking in a friendly foreign land, a place where you've never been before.... Off in the distance, to your left, you see a very tall mountain. What does it look like? ... As you look at the mountain, you begin to feel drawn toward it. As you approach the foot of the mountain you see a path going up the side of the mountain. It is an easy path with no obstacles or difficult places and you begin to walk up this path toward the top of the mountain.... When you get to the top you notice a temple, a very special building. As you approach it, you can feel the solemnity and sacredness of this place.... Once inside, you notice thousands of candles burning, creating a great light inside. At the far end of the room you see a very kind and wise old person. As you approach this person, you see a very loving smile and bright, happy eyes. As you get closer, you realize that there is a question about your life in specific or life in general that you want to ask this wise old person.... When you are ready, ask your question and let him respond. If at first you don't understand the answer, ask for more clarity. Have as long a conversation as you need to understand the answer ... (Long pause about one minute).... O.K. now realizing that you can always come back to this place and ask your wise old teacher any question you have about anything, say goodbye for now and begin to leave the temple. . . . As you're coming down the mountain, feel the warmth of the sun on your skin and feel the ground beneath your feet. What does it look like? How does it feel? . . . O.K., when you're ready, and taking as much time as you need, take a few deep breaths again, open your eyes, and come back to the class."

Pick up any occult book on the subject of spirit guides or psychic development and you will find virtually the same basic technique presented. You will find it in Shakti Gawain's occult manual entitled *Creative Visualization* in the chapter "Meeting Your Guide."[22] You will find it in Dr. Mike Samuels' book *Seeing With the Mind's Eye: The History, Techniques and Uses of Visualization*,[23] another occult manual recommended in Canfield's material. Another book by Dr. Samuels, *Spirit Guides: Access to Inner Worlds*, provides an equally effective and simple visualization much like Canfield's that can also be used to contact your very own spirit guide.

You will find it in a book called *Develop Your Psychic Skill*, by author/teacher Enid Hoffman. If you don't have a guide and really want one, she suggests that you go to a medium and have him or her introduce you to one. However, if you don't feel like going to a medium to be introduced, you can do it by yourself by following the usual imagery techniques in which you first "do your relaxation exercises," "drift into your centered, no-mind state," and then see yourself in a beautiful natural setting of your choice. Once there, a tiny dot of blue light approaches and eventually takes the shape of a person who, at your invitation, sits down next to you and allows you to ask it whatever is on your mind.[24]

Wisdom from Where?

When I was in Silva Mind Control, the technique they led us through to meet our "counselors" also followed very much in the same vein as Canfield's Kung Fu exercise. The details varied, of course. In Silva we went into our "laboratory" to meet our guide—not to a mountaintop temple or to a beautiful forest, but so what? The results were the same: an encounter with another being—a "Wise Person," a "counselor," a *spirit guide* whom we could contact at any time for wisdom and direction.

When Canfield asked the children about their experiences, he was amazed at the insight and wisdom they had received.

> They had been given wisdom as old as time, things like: "If you're nice to people, people will be nice to you." "You can only be happy if you decide to be happy." "Things would be easier if you didn't try so hard." One girl had asked a wise old woman the question, "What is the meaning of life?" She said that her wise old woman didn't say anything, but held a mirror to her. I asked her if she understood what that meant. She said, "Yes, it means to me that life is what I choose to make it." That's an amazingly sophisticated insight for a sixth grader.

Canfield is absolutely correct: It is an amazing insight, especially if this child was not raised with a Hindu/occult worldview. In holding a mirror up to the child in answer to her question "What is the meaning of life?" the guide was reaffirming to the child a very basic presupposition of occultism: *You* are the meaning of life. Don't look anywhere but inside yourself, for you can indeed create your own reality. Or as Shirley MacLaine would put it:

> We choose our own destinies, create our own illusions. We have the power to design the world in which we live, and the strength to remake ourselves in the image of our dreams.[25]

Invitation to the Dance

There are, of course, any number of ways to meet your spirit guide as a book called *Opening to Channel* points out. Actually, the book was channeled through the authors by a couple of entities that call themselves "Orin" and "DaBen." These "beings of light" say they wrote the book for the specific purpose of teaching as many people as possible how to channel. I'm quite sure that's true. The spirits want you to believe that in this present time of "future shock," channeling will provide you with an invaluable resource:

> Channeling helps you connect to a constant, steady source of inspiration and information . . . a connection that will stimulate, encourage and support you. It opens "a doorway into more love," to the higher spiritual realms which are "abundant with love," and to a relationship with a spirit guide which contains "constant love, perfect understanding and unending compassion."[26]

One of the key points they make is that *"Asking for a guide brings one to you."*[27] The spirits, you see, generally want to be wanted. All they are waiting for is an invitation. This point presents an interesting parallel in cases of actual demon possession. Scholar and author Malachi Martin (who has documented five cases of possession in his book *Hostage to the Devil*) points out that "at every new step, and during every moment of possession, the consent of the victim is necessary, or possession cannot be successful."[28] An open invitation makes their work in your life much easier. You have given them the "right."

> If you request a guide to assist you, one will begin to work with you. At this stage the connection to a guide may occur most often in your dream states or in spontaneous or unexpected moments.
>
> You may at some point have a vivid dream in which you are aware that your guide has contacted you. You may discover your connection to your intuitive self or a guide through tarot cards, the Ouija board, automatic handwriting, or meditation. During meditation you may begin to get guidance that seems to

be of a greater wisdom than what you have experienced before. There are many methods used to initiate the connection. There is no one set way to become ready to channel.[29]

However, there is one sure way to contact a guide. It is a method presented by virtually every channeler as the safest and most effective way to contact your guide. The method? *Guided imagery/visualization.* Shamans, mediums, witches, and other occultists have understood this fact for millennia. By far the most effective way to contact spirit entities is by visualizing them and inviting them to yourself.

The process is really quite simple. "Orin" and "DaBen" begin by teaching progressive relaxation techniques, focusing, and concentration. They want you to learn how to keep pictures in your imagination, how to use it to see yourself going to higher realms, how to attune yourself with life-force energy, how to relax and keep your body in a comfortable position during the sessions (as we've already discussed). The procedures presented by Orin and DaBen are *precisely* the same ones being taught to children by the Transpersonal educators. Once you've got a handle on the basics, you're ready to meet your very own spirit guide. You begin with a "ceremony of welcome":

> Imagine that your guide, a special guide, is coming forward. Sense this guide, feel his or her love for you. Be open to receive. Feel your heart welcoming this guide. Feel the response. Believe that it is really happening! *Your imagination is the closest ability you have to channeling, and it is the easiest connection your guide has to you at first.*[30]

How does any of this differ from the techniques which the Transpersonal educators are using in the classrooms to help children contact their "Wise Person" or their "Higher Self"? It doesn't.

One of the most important parallels lies in the *tone* of the language used. In the "Kung Fu" meditation the children find themselves approaching a temple. "... you can feel the solemnity and sacredness of this place. You decide to go inside, but before you do, you carefully remove your shoes and place them before the doorway." To me, the pattern here is rather reminiscent of Moses and his encounter with Almighty God, who spoke to him out of the burning bush: "Remove your sandals from your feet, for the place on which you are standing is holy ground."

In virtually all the guided-imagery/meditation sessions in which the would-be channels (whether children or adults) are led to encounter their guides, there is a tone which clearly communicates that the being they are meeting is someone to be approached with great respect and awe. For example, in Silva Mind Control we were instructed to always greet our "counselors" with respect and a "welcome" prayer. In my experiences years ago, whenever Pachita's guide was invoked, we stood in a circle around her "elevating our thoughts to God." The arrival of her spirit guide, "Hermanito Cuauhtemoc," was for us a sacred moment, holy and infused with the divine. I have read dozens of the exercises developed by Transpersonal educators to introduce the children to their guides. Every one of them evidences a clear awareness of the supernatural. Perhaps there is a good reason for this. Jon Klimo informs us:

> The attempted communication with other levels of existence is not to be treated lightly, we are told. To the extent to which channeling is said to be taking place within a spiritual universe, approaching it in less than a spiritual manner may be tantamount to sacrilege.[31]

An interesting word, "sacrilege." It is defined as "the violation or profanation of anything sacred or held sacred ... the stealing of anything consecrated to the service of God."[32] What must be clarified, however, is *which* God.

But Is It Real?

Are you really contacting a "spirit guide"? Is it possible that all these people, children included, are contacting nothing more than their own overwrought imaginations? After all, even most of the occult manuals teaching these techniques assure you that it's quite normal to feel as "if you're making the whole thing up."[33]

My Silva Mind Control instructor in Mexico City continually assured us that as we went through the exercises of guided imagery/visualization we would feel as though we were making it all up. "This is the correct feeling!" he would tell us. "You will see on the last day!" Sure enough, on the last day, when we functioned as psychics, being able to diagnose the medical conditions of people we had never met and receiving accurate, frequently astonishing information from our counselors (information we could not possibly have made up or gleaned from those around us), even the skeptics among us knew some power beyond ourselves had been activated. Somehow, even though it had all felt to many as though they were "just guessing" and "making it all up," they had gone beyond that level and actually touched the edge of another dimension.

Imaginary Playmates

Some children in the school system don't need to be led through meditation techniques to conjure up spirit guides; from the time they could talk they've been describing imaginary playmates: other children, or elves and fairies, or invisible pets. Some children carry on this relationship until they are 10 or 11 years old, although most invisible playmates acquired independently in childhood seem to disappear by the time the child begins school.

Psychologists who have spent years studying the phenomena of children with imaginary playmates tell us that probably one in six children has at least one at some point in his formative years.[34] While still debating just how healthy it is for a child to actually have imaginary playmates, most researchers seem to feel that it is generally a normal part of growing up for many children and that it fulfills a psychological need in their development. A lonely or disliked child may sometimes call an imaginary playmate into being just to have someone he feels comfortable and safe to play with. Or perhaps the child imagines a "twin" of himself—a perfect, beautiful child who is loved and cherished, unlike himself. Or perhaps a usually meek child imagines a boisterous, naughty playmate who becomes a convenient scapegoat when he misbehaves. A child with a high-strung, demanding mother may keep close an imaginary friend who appears as a quiet, gentle, loving older woman.

From a psychological perspective, the presence of imaginary playmates may indeed be an unconscious cry for help. On the other hand, it may merely be the expression of a healthy, active, rich, and vibrant imagination which may someday produce yet another "great American novel." Certainly not every child who begins conversing with an imaginary playmate is necessarily in need of a psychologist or an exorcist. The child's imaginary playmate may indeed be just that—purely imaginary.

However, the phenomenon of the imaginary playmate sometimes seems to go beyond the scope of a mere fabrication created to fulfill some buried psychological need. Psychic investigators and parapsychologists have observed that one of the characteristics of the psychic child is that he is frequently aware of the presence of "invisible" beings around him at a fairly early age. Some of the most famous psychics of our age, among them Edgar Cayce, Eileen Garret, and Olga Worrall, were in contact with "invisible beings" from the time they were very young.

In fact, Olga Worrall was only three years old when she first "saw people" standing by her bed. As she described them, her frightened mother recognized that some of the people which the increasingly psychic little Olga was seeing were long-dead relatives. Olga's husband, Ambrose Worrall, was also a powerful psychic from his earliest childhood. He frequently "saw people" in the dark of his room—children playing silently, shadowy grown-ups who just stood by and watched, and mysterious children and grown-ups that no one but the six-year-old little boy could "see."[35] The late Tony

Agapao, one of the best-known psychic surgeons in the Philippines, had "invisible playmates" who used to snatch him from his bed in the middle of the night and deposit him in a large fruit tree outside his home. He was between one and three years old at the time. It seems that "many Filipino children, especially those who have not been brought up in the Western scientific tradition, can see and play with what is called a dwarf or elf."[36]

Hal Bennet, coauthor of *The Well Body Book* and *Spirit Guides*, "traces his experiences with spirit guides back to childhood and to an imaginary playmate who helped him solve some of the problems of growing up. His most vivid recollection of this imaginary playmate was when he was between the ages of five and eleven."[37] His playmate did not just disappear as he grew older; it just took on a different more acceptable manner of communicating with him, thereby helping him avoid the ridicule of his friends. "While a teenager, Hal began writing stories and poems. His imaginary voices gained a new reality when he wrote them down. Once he had found this outlet he could agree with his peers that his imaginary playmates of earlier years had been 'a bit ridiculous.' Though his secret world found expression in his stories and poems, the spirit guide once embodied in his imaginary playmate had been buried under skepticism which he learned from his peers."[38]

Which Comes First?

New Age psychiatrist Dr. Gerald Jampolsky, well-known for his work with children and imagination, observes that—

> ... children with high psychic ability generally have imaginary playmates that they treat as real.[39]

While many psychic researchers today tend to assume that the children see these "imaginary playmates" because they are psychic, I believe that the children are psychic because of the presence of the "playmates." As Michael Harner points out, "*Whatever [the guide] is called, it is the fundamental source of power of the shaman's functioning.*"[40]

Of course, psychic researchers readily acknowledge that not every "imaginary playmate" is necessarily an actual objective spiritual entity. Some are indeed just "make-believe" and the child basically knows that his playmate does not really exist. However, as James W. Peterson points out, "this in no way precludes the notion that the playmate might also represent a paranormal perception."[41] He distinguishes between three types of "childhood companions":

> The first is the true clairvoyant perception of some entity whose objective existence on the astral plane is brought into the child's awareness. This type I refer to as an "invisible playmate." The second variety is actually . . . created in the child's mind to fulfill some deep-felt emotional need. This type I call an "imaginary companion." The third type is actually a mixture of the two.[42]

Dr. Alex Tanous and Katherine Fair Donnelly would add several other categories to the possible explanations. The imaginary guide, they say, may be produced by "telepathic communication." They cite a case in which a father is visiting his mother who has just acquired a pet crow. Meanwhile at home in another city, and totally unaware of her grandmother's new pet, a little girl suddenly begins playing with an imaginary crow. Perhaps the imaginary playmate is the result of a so-called "out-of-body or bilocation experience." This would explain to the authors why many of the children's imaginary playmates seem to be from another country. Some child is allegedly astral projecting and his spirit is showing up as some other kid's imaginary playmate. Another possibility, we are told, is that the imaginary playmate is "either a sprite or a spirit that finds children unusually receptive." They hasten to assure us that these beings are in no way dangerous to the child:

> What exactly are spirits and sprites? One point of emphasis is that they are not harmful . . . researchers claim that spirits are probably well-adjusted discarnate beings who actually want to help

the living whom they contact in order to impart information. Sprites are mischievous but playful ghosts, again not harmful.[43]

This is an exceedingly overconfident assertion. In truth, these researchers have *no* idea what these beings are! All they know is *what the beings themselves want them to believe*. Few psychic researchers are willing to admit that the children's "invisible playmates" are actually demons in disguise. "If the imaginary playmate gives the child instructions to do something evil or destructive, this could indicate the child's need of psychiatric assistance."[44]

Indeed these spirits may nct all immediately terrorize or physically harm the child to whom they appear. On the contrary, they may even be credited with aiding the child, even to the point of "saving his life." And yet the danger they represent is deadlier to the child than can ever be imagined. While perhaps manifesting very real phenomena, they will invariably lead the people in contact with them, be they children or adults, into beliefs and practices that stand in stark contrast and opposition to the revealed Word of God.

How a Parent Should React: Occultist Version

One of the key points stressed repeatedly by Tanous and Donnelly is that above all, regardless of what has been happening, the parent *must* be open and receptive to the child's psychic experiences and imaginary playmates. To ridicule them or in any way deny their validity is quite literally equated by the psychic researchers with child abuse. They say they don't much care *what* the playmates are; the child obviously needs them or they wouldn't be there. Dr. Tanous cites a case in which an eight-year-old child suffering from rheumatic fever fantasized conversations with "Mrs. Wiggs" of the Cabbage Patch characters whenever she was in the grip of fever.

It didn't make any difference apparently if the playmate was real, imaginary, a spirit, or a sprite. Mrs. Wiggs came through at a vital time in this

child's life and continued to do so in times of stress,
perhaps even helping to save her life. . . . The
imaginary playmate should be fostered rather than
hindered, accepted rather than rejected, welcomed
rather than denied. . . . Of course, if it can be determined that the imaginary playmate is either a sprite
or a spirit, it is a manifestation of the child's psychic
awareness, and is not to be feared. What it is is not
important to the child, as long as the playmate
serves his need in a healthy fashion.[45]

So, parent, the psychic researchers would have you simply
take a deep breath, relax, and rejoice that your child is in
communication with such wondrous beings! Do everything
you can to nurture and encourage the child's psychic development and his relationship with his guides!

But once again we are forced to consider the question we've
been faced with all along: What if these guides and imaginary
playmates are actually demons in disguise? What should your
reaction be then? How on earth do you tell the difference
between what may be a genuine touch from God or a demonic
counterfeit? After all, even the Bible tells us that all children
have a guardian angel assigned to them. The Bible is filled
with accounts of these angels, of how they appeared in dreams
and visions to warn and protect or make announcements of
great import. Is it not possible that all these "spirit guides" are
but our guardian angels made "visible" so that we may better
relate to them?

Chapter 9

Angels of God or Angels of Light?

✦

What will you do if your child starts talking about experiencing the presence of an "imaginary playmate" or a "guardian angel" or a special "Wise Person"? How will you know whether you are dealing with a youthful, overactive imagination or the very real manifestation of demonic entities?

We are emphatically warned by the Bible not to believe every spirit, but to test the spirits to see whether they are from God (1 John 4:1). Clearly, the implication is that there are spirits that are *not* from God but are evil, "spirits of demons performing signs" (Revelation 16:14). These are cheap imitations of the Holy Spirit which are capable of astonishing signs and wonders impressive enough to deceive even the elect (Matthew 24:24). If we do not apply the biblical tests to these spirits, we are entirely likely to be deceived by them. Don't think it can't happen!

A case in point: Reviewers from the Christian Broadcast Network gave *The Door to the Secret City*, by Kathleen J. Forti, the following glowing review:

> [Freddie] should serve [young people] well to lift them out of their problems into that wonderful dimension of imagination and make-believe. What a splendid cause . . . ![1]

The book is about a little boy named Freddie who has a near-death experience after falling out of a tree. He suddenly finds himself hovering over his body and is astonished at the things he can do now that he is invisible—such as passing right through doors. When he meets "Daniel," it occurs to him that perhaps he is his guardian angel.

> Daniel smiled. "Well, we like to think of ourselves more as Guides," he corrected. "Guardian Angel is a bit old-fashioned by our standards. Nobody uses it up there anymore."[2]

Daniel takes him to an amazing place called the City of Crystal and then to the Golden Temple, where he and many other children can learn wonderful lessons, such as the secrets of universal healing and how to read minds. He runs into a friend of his, a little girl who is very much alive and well on planet Earth, but who has known for a long time how to communicate consciously with her guide and enter into the City of Crystal while in her sleep or through practicing visualization. In short, this charming, well-written book that is supposed to be appropriate for children of ages seven and up *is occultic to the core*, as are a good number of books published by Stillpoint Publishers. It is a tragic commentary on the lack of discernment in the church that even major Christian networks seem to have difficulty spotting an occult book when they see one.

In another disturbing book for children entitled *Meditation for Little People*, author Anne Langford teaches the children to "think of God as a loving light" that dwells within each one of them as well as within every single thing around them. This God, she tells them, "has given to you, your own personal angel" who is with them at all times to guard and protect them. She instructs the child to draw his personal angel on a blank page provided in the book, and tells her young readers that there are children who can actually see their personal angel "as a light in their room" or "feel its magnificent presence." The children are encouraged to talk to this angel on a regular basis:

You can talk to your angel about anything and at any time. When you know your angel is with you, your inner God-light shines very bright. But, your light becomes dim when you forget to talk with your personal angel. Some children *do* talk with their angels, but they *forget* to listen. It is important to listen, for angels *really do talk with us.*[3]

The very best way to commune with this angel, she continues, is through the practice of meditation. She then instructs the children in the basic beginner's techniques of Eastern meditation and visualization. She wraps the whole thing up by instructing the children to "picture themselves" walking into "a large white light." Why, you ask? Every occultist knows the answer:

This protects you and helps your personal angel to protect you even more.[4]

God's Angels

As we examine the role of angels in the Bible, we find some disturbing differences between biblical angels and the "guardian angels" of the occultists. Indeed, I certainly do believe in guardian angels. Hebrews 1:14 says that angels are "ministering spirits, sent out to render service for the sake of those who will inherit salvation." I believe that they are active today, and I am deeply grateful for the ministry they have doubtlessly had in my own life. Frequently in my time of prayer I have asked God to send His ministering angels to stand guard around me and my loved ones. I know that those prayers have been honored.

Children are of special concern to the angels. Jesus Himself warns us "not [to] despise one of these little ones, for I say to you that their angels in heaven continually behold the face of My Father who is in heaven" (Matthew 18:10). Adult survivors of ritual abuse have frequently spoken of being visited during their time of torment by holy angels and being comforted by them. One survivor told me that angels came to her when she was seven years old. It was on the night of the ritual in which the high priest had sealed her in her own blood to Satan, the coven, and himself. She had been brutally raped while her mother and her father held her down. Then they left her in a barn, tied to the stone altar. She was naked and alone and it was dark. They had told her that a savage wolf would come and eat her, and that bats would come and drink her blood. There would be nothing left of her by morning, they told her, except a pile of bones. She had no reason to doubt them, since she had already seen too much of what they were capable of doing. She lay on the altar, shaking, in pain, almost delirious with terror, and waiting to die.

"That's when God sent His angels. I only heard their heavenly voices singing at first. Then they came into the barn. They were beautiful! Tall, all in white, comforting. They were neither male nor female; they were just angels. They may have had wings when they came into the barn, but I don't remember seeing wings later. Two of the angels came to me and untied me. I leaned on the angel to my left. He covered my body with his dress. He ministered to me like the mommy I didn't have. I know they literally saved my life that night. Just before daybreak they retied me, but they assured me I would be all right." She was to endure 11 more years of ritual and horror before she escaped from her parents and the coven. She would see her own child butchered in honor of Satan. And yet what Satan intended for her destruction and for his demented glory the Lord God of heaven has turned into His victory! She belongs to the Lord Jesus and has long been used by Him as a powerful prayer warrior and intercessor.

Assuredly, we do have guardian angels! And yet nowhere in Scripture do I see that anyone is instructed to invoke them or conjure them up at will in order to dialogue with them while in an altered state of consciousness. The visible appearance of angels is very infrequent even in the Bible. The people who did see them usually did so only once (although several individuals had more than one angelic visitation). Certainly we are all encouraged to be hospitable to strangers, "for by this some have entertained angels without knowing it" (Hebrews 13:2).

While angels are referred to in the Bible over 375 times, there are only 32 individuals or groups who actually saw angels.[5] Some of these were not particularly happy about the event, such as the army of 185,000 Assyrians in 2 Kings 19:35 who were struck dead by an angel of the Lord in judgment because they were about to attack David's Jerusalem. One of my favorite accounts of angels is in 2 Kings 6:16, in which Elisha and his servant literally saw the angelic army encamped around them for their protection. The servant suddenly understood: Despite the might of the enemy who confronts us we need not fear, "for those who are with us are more than those who are with them!"

Envoys of God

When angels in the Bible appear as visible beings, it is as envoys of Almighty God sent to deliver a specific message from Him. The angel Gabriel appeared to Mary to announce the birth of the Messiah, and a host of them appeared to the shepherds to announce the glorious birth of God's Son. Joseph was warned by an angel in a dream to flee to Egypt. An angel of the Lord opened the gates of the prison and set the apostles free so that they could "stand and speak to the people in the temple the whole message of this Life" (Acts 5:20). When an angel appeared to Philip in Acts chapter 8, it was to direct him to "arise and go south to the road that descends from Jerusalem to Gaza." For what purpose? So that Philip might present the gospel of Jesus the Messiah to the Ethiopian eunuch. An angel sent by Jesus came to the apostle John to give the great Revelation of the things that are to come. Each of these was a special visitation with a very specific purpose.

The angels' ministry in heaven and on earth is rich and varied, but *nowhere* do we see God's angels acting as spirit guides to mediums and occultists, even very young ones!

Nowhere do we see an angel from God present a "word" or "message" or "teaching" that in any way contradicts the revealed Word of God in the Bible. *Nowhere* do we see an angel from God tell someone that God is but a Force "within everyone and everything," or that by contacting our perfect and divine Higher Self we can all someday become God ourselves. *Nowhere* do we see an angel of God instruct Isaiah or Ezekiel or any of the true prophets to consult a medium (i.e., channeler) or to practice sorcery. *Nowhere* in the Bible do we find a holy angel telling us that there is no hell, or that Jesus of Nazareth is but the greatest medium of all, or that He did not die on a cross to pay for the sins of man, or that He did not rise on the third day *in the flesh* to prove His victory over sin and Satan. *Nowhere.* The fact that something that *looks* like an angel may appear and tell you differently impressed the apostle Paul not one bit:

> But even though we or an angel from heaven should preach to you a gospel contrary to that which we have preached to you, let him be accursed (Galatians 1:8).

> Let no one keep defrauding you of your prize by delighting in self-abasement and the worship of the angels, taking his stand on visions he has seen, inflated without cause by his fleshly mind, and not holding fast to the head (Colossians 2:18,19a).

Translation: "So you saw an angel. *So what?* What did the angel say to you? What did that guide teach you about God? What did it teach you about His Son, Jesus of Nazareth? Did that angel confirm that it is 'by grace you have been saved through faith, and that not of yourselves, it is the gift of God; not as a result of works, that no one should boast' (Ephesians 2:8) or did that angel preach to you '*another Jesus . . . a different spirit . . . a different gospel*' " (2 Corinthians 11:4)? The answer to the questions *"Which Jesus?"* and *"Which gospel?"* will give you a pretty good idea as to *which spirit* you're dealing with.

By this you know the Spirit of God: every spirit that confesses that Jesus Christ has come in the flesh is from God; and every spirit that does not confess Jesus is not from God; and this is the spirit of the antichrist, of which you have heard that it is coming, and now it is already in the world (1 John 4:2,3).

You need to keep your eyes open. The "spirit guides" have developed a pretty slick approach to dealing with those who challenge them to reveal their position on this issue. For example, when asked by a woman in Seattle to say just what it believed about Jesus, "Mafu" (the spirit that channels through Penny Torres) replied:

What is called Jesus entity is a remarkable Master who gave great love and uplifted the whole of mankind. I would never deny that what is called Jesus is Lord God because He is . . . *but so are you, dear lady*!

If I'm God incarnate and you're God incarnate and everything is God incarnate, then it is no big deal for Jesus to claim to be God in human flesh. Jesus has been magnanimously damned with faint praise and robbed of the very nature of unique divinity which He claimed for Himself. By equating us all with Jesus, Mafu has cleverly but most effectively denied that Jesus Christ is uniquely God come in human form. Mafu's piety is therefore but a flimsy cover-up for the lying spirit of antichrist that spawned him.

Jesus Who?

Don't be fooled by the terminology! Even though the guides, channelers, cultists, and occultists will (with the exception of the Satanists) invariably seek to portray themselves as compatible with biblical theology by using biblical terminology, they will invariably redefine those terms to mean something totally different from orthodox biblical teaching. Yes, they will assert, we love and respect Jesus! But if they've redefined Him into "Master Jesus, the avatar for the now-past Piscean

Age," or if He has become "the Divine Principle" or "the spirit brother of Lucifer" or "the archangel Michael, the greatest creation of Jehovah," or if they tell you that the man Jesus became the Christ at His baptism to show us that we can all in time tap into that Christ Consciousness, or if they revere Him as the greatest and most accomplished medium and magician, or if they assert that Jesus was the reincarnation of King David, etc., etc., then *they've got the wrong Jesus!*

Actually the name "Jesus" is a fairly common one in many places, especially in Latin American countries. When I was growing up in Cuernavaca, we once had a gardener named "Jesus Joseph Mary." Stand on any street corner in Latin America and shout the name "Jesus," and you'll probably find yourself surrounded by at least 15 people demanding to know why you called them. To call on the name of Jesus, however sincerely, is irrelevant and immaterial if you don't know the Individual to whom it belongs! If you don't know anything about the real Jesus as He is presented in the Bible, you are highly likely to wind up with some clever impostor, even as I did when I invited "Jesus" as my Counselor in Silva Mind Control. I got a "Jesus" all right, but it wasn't the Jesus of the Bible!

Those who have made the mistake of assuming that you will automatically be able to identify the nature of these guides just by "experiencing" how marvelously benign, lofty, holy, and wise they seem to be are potentially in for a colossal disappointment somewhere down the line. We are warned in the Bible that "Satan disguises himself as an angel of light" (2 Corinthians 11:14), and we are told that "his servants also disguise themselves as servants of righteousness" (verse 15). Evil spirits are very capable of disguising themselves as servants of righteousness. Scripture indicates that they were once part of the angelic host created by God. When Lucifer in his arrogance and pride rebelled against God (Isaiah 14:12-15; Ezekiel 28:12-19), a third of the angels chose to follow Lucifer. These fallen angels became the demons—irretrievably wicked and desperate beings who, like their new god, have not lost the ability to appear as "angels of light."

Whose Test?

Test the spirits! Excellent advice; even the channelers would agree with it. They acknowledge that it is indeed possible for a "lower entity" to slither its way into a person's life, bringing all manner of mischief with it. "Discern; discern; discern!" is the heartfelt advice of many a channeler.[6] Discernment for the channeler, however, is an entirely subjective experience.

> In many ways, it does not matter what the source of good, uplifting information is, as long as it is valid. . . . As long as you can retrieve the right answer so you can heal another human being, or make the correct choice in important situations, the "technical" description of how all this works becomes irrelevant. . . . The information, energy, wisdom or guidance is either GOOD [meaning it works] or it is NOT [meaning it doesn't work]. This must be the final test of any channel—any channeled "being"— and all channeled information.[7]

The vast majority of what you'll encounter in the channelers' "discernment" category runs along similar lines. "Tired of the Program? Change Your Channel." So advise Douglas James Mahr and Francis Racey, Ph.D., in their article in *Life Times: Forum for the New Age*.[8] In articles with titles such as "Tips for Choosing a Psychic or Channel"[9] you will be cautioned to stay away from channels who "tell you only what you want to hear" or channels who try to create a dependency on themselves. The authors will warn you about giving away your personal power to a channeler and tell you not to stick around those who try to push their belief systems on you. Especially they want you to understand that "a true Channel/Psychic knows and will indicate that they and the information are not 100 percent accurate."[10] Biblically, this point alone would *immediately* expose someone as a false prophet. True prophets of God were *100 percent accurate 100 percent of the time.*

You may say in your heart, "How shall we know the word which the Lord has not spoken?" When a prophet speaks in the name of the Lord, if the thing does not come about or come true, that is the thing which the Lord has not spoken (Deuteronomy 18:21, 22).

"Channeled material is of value only if it returns you to the grandeur of Self," assert Mahr and Racey:

The questions should be: Does the channel effectively provide information that is useful, inspiring and life-affirming? Does the channel provide insights and information that trigger your own contact with your higher self to provide your own answers? My Guide, Li Sung, says that the primary purpose is to provide inspiration to trigger a person's higher self to create a better material reality.[11]

The Bible presents an altogether different set of standards and tests for discerning the source of seemingly supernatural revelations and manifestations. The first and most crucial test, as we have seen, is in the area of theology. If they flunk out on that one, you don't even need to bother with any of the other tests. However pious they seem to be and however much "truth" the demonic spirits impart, they will invariably deny the absolute reliability of the Bible, the personal nature of God, the doctrine of the Trinity, and the unique nature and ministry of Jesus of Nazareth.

Spiritual Harlotry

Acts 16 documents an encounter that Paul and Silas had in Philippi with a certain slave-girl "having a spirit of divination." In other words, this girl was a channeler. She was the Jeane Dixon of her generation. This girl was the "real thing." Her guide came to her and made all kinds of wonderful and evidently accurate predictions through her, "bringing her masters much profit by fortune-telling." Even then channeling was an extremely profitable venture! The girl followed after Paul, piously crying out: "These men are bondservants of the Most High God, who are proclaiming to you the way of salvation!" What she said sounds good at first glance. However, the margin of the New American Standard Bible points out that what she was literally saying was not that Paul and Silas were proclaiming Jesus to be *the* way of salvation but rather *a* way of salvation! With the barely noticeable absence of a definite participle, Jesus was demoted to one of many equally good ways, along with any other "path" or "deity" that might suit you. The apostle Paul's reaction to this channeler's piously inaccurate endorsement is worth noting:

> But Paul was greatly annoyed, and turned and said to the spirit, "I command you in the name of Jesus Christ to come out of her!" And it came out at that very moment (Acts 16:18).

Instead of being grateful for any endorsement he could get, Paul turned around and unceremoniously cast out her spirit guide! Since the only things ever cast out of people in the Bible were demons, the correlation here is not too difficult to make!

There is something else worth considering. If the Bible in both the Old and the New Testaments consistently and repeatedly condemns the practice of mediumship and every other form of occultism as forbidden contact with demons and spiritual harlots, is it really logical to suppose that God is going to bless contact with spirit guides and channelers today? In verse after verse and chapter after chapter, in both the Old and the New Testaments, the practice of occultism in general and mediumship in particular is categorically forbidden.

> As for the person who turns to mediums and to spiritists, to play the harlot after them, I will also set My face against that person and will cut him off from among his people. You shall consecrate yourselves therefore and be holy, for I am the Lord your God (Leviticus 20:6,7).

> Do not turn to mediums or spiritists; do not seek
> them out to be defiled by them. I am the Lord your
> God (Leviticus 19:31).

The condemnation was not issued against mere "frauds
and windbags," incidentally. The Bible has always recognized the reality of phenomena produced by occultism. The
key question we must ask when faced with a vision, appari-
tion, or paranormal manifestation of any kind is "What is the
source behind it?" If it falls into the category of practices
condemned by Scripture in Deuteronomy 18 and many other
places, then by definition *it cannot be from God.*

The Medium and the King

Occultists are quick to point out that one of the earliest
recorded seances is found in the Old Testament, in 1 Samuel
28. King Saul had gotten himself into a terrible mess with
God. He had deliberately disobeyed God's command concerning the execution of His judgment on the Amalekites. He
had also murdered God's priests for having sided with David
(1 Samuel 22:6-23). Yet despite these blatant affronts to God,
King Saul seemed perplexed that God had stopped communicating with him. So, since God wasn't talking to him, he
decided to consult a medium. This proved to be somewhat of
a challenge, as there were very few of them left in the land.
Saul himself had ordered them executed in obedience to
God's command (Exodus 22:18). A medium was located in the
city of Endor, and Saul disguised himself and went to her by
night so no one would recognize him. "Conjure up for me,
please, and bring up for me whom I shall name to you. . . .
Bring up Samuel for me," he said to the medium. What
happened next is astonishing:

> When the woman saw Samuel, she cried out with a
> loud voice; and the woman spoke to Saul, saying,
> "Why have you deceived me? For you are Saul."
> And the king said to her, "Do not be afraid; but
> what do you see?" and the woman said to Saul, "I

see a divine being coming up out of the earth." And
he said to her, "What is his form?" And she said,
"An old man is coming up, and he is wrapped with a
robe." And Saul knew that it was Samuel, and he
bowed with his face to the ground and did homage
(1 Samuel 28:12-14).

The text clearly indicates that something happened that
the medium was not expecting. What she saw frightened her,
for the Hebrew text uses the word *zalag*, which indicates that
she literally shrieked in terror at what she was seeing. This
was no masquerading demon before her. This was no hal-
lucination. Samuel was actually there. Furthermore, this
woman was no fraud. She suddenly knew clairvoyantly that
the disguised man before her was King Saul.

Did the old prophet arise in response to the medium's
conjuring? Can this incident be used as proof that mediums
can indeed call up the dead for personal consultations? No.
What took place here was a unique incident. God Himself
sovereignly intervened and allowed the spirit of His prophet
Samuel to appear before His anointed (though now apostate)
king, for the specific purpose of pronouncing divine judgment upon him.

First Chronicles 10:13 wraps it up:

So Saul died for his trespass which he committed
against the Lord, because of the word of the Lord
which he did not keep; *and also because he asked
counsel of a medium.* . . .

What a Parent Should Do: Christian Version

If you suspect that your child has a spirit guide, don't panic
and scare your child half to death by pinning him into a corner
and attempting to exorcise the demons! The importance of
your reaction to what your child tells you cannot be overestimated, and if you panic so will he. Be sensitive to your child.
Untold damage has been done to children (and adults, for that
matter) by parents who have ridiculed them or have refused

to believe them or even listen to them when they have talked about their "imaginary playmates," "Wise-Persons," "Guardian Angels," etc. It's not likely that a child who has been told to "stop telling lies" when he's tried to share about these things will ever want to open up to his parents about anything else either. Even worse damage has been done by reacting in fear or by attempting to deal with the spirits in a hysterical and unbiblical manner.

Talk to your child. Listen to him. Ask questions. Encourage your child to talk to you. Ask him to describe his invisible playmate: What does it look like, when does he see it, what do they do together, what does it tell him? Does it ever frighten him? Has it ever told him to keep secrets from you? Is his playmate real or does he know he has just made it up? Did he meet it at school with his teacher? Ask him if he knows what his playmate thinks about God and Jesus and the Bible. You need to pray that God will give you special discernment when dealing with your child in these matters.

Regardless of the child's answers, it's a good idea to put the situation to the test through prayer. If your child is open to praying with you about it, perhaps you can ask him if he wants to bring his "playmate" to Jesus. Then quietly pray with your child:

> Lord Jesus, I want to bring You my child's playmate. Father, You know we love You and don't want anything in our lives that is not from You. Lord, if this imaginary playmate is not from You, then we ask that You make it go away in Jesus' name and never allow it to return again. Heavenly Father, we ask this in the name of Your Precious Son, Jesus. Amen.

Should your child be reluctant to pray with you about it, that's okay. Just pray quietly by his bed at night. Ask the Lord to give your child special protection, and command any deceiving spirit around him to leave in the name of Jesus Christ. The Lord will hear your prayer, and if the "companion" is indeed a demon in disguise, you can be sure it will hear you too. There is the possibility that if there is an occult background in your family line that has been unconfessed, or if by chance there are occult paraphernalia or toys in your home, the "companion" may feel he has the right to stick around your child. You may need to deal with these things before the spirit will leave. This will be discussed further in the last chapter.

Fear of Jesus

It's a fascinating thing to see how these guides respond to Jesus of Nazareth. One psychic researcher bemoaned the fact that a child who was "so psychic that he could see spirits, both nature spirits and discarnate spirits" was subjected to the rite of exorcism because his wealthy family believed the boy was possessed. "The exorcism succeeded and his invisible friends reluctantly left him. Today he is a 'normal' human being working in a management consulting firm. He is normal because he could no longer see and talk to spirits."[12]

For some reason, spirit guides are not overly fond of Jesus of Nazareth, or for that matter of people who are His true disciples. Knud Rasmussen (1879-1933) was a famous anthropologist and explorer who was recognized as an unrivaled authority on the Eskimo people. He reported an intriguing conversation with a former East Greenland shaman who had turned his back on shamanism after his conversion to Jesus Christ.

> I had many helping spirits who often were very useful to me, especially when I was exposed to gales or storms; and not many dangers could threaten me, because I felt safe. When later on I made up my mind to be baptized, they revealed themselves to me and advised me not to; however, I did what I had decided to do. Now I have been a baptized man for several years, and my old helping spirits have never visited me since, because I betrayed them by being baptized.[13]

It's never too early to tell children about Jesus and about the basics of spiritual warfare! Even a little child can put the spirits to the test. Indeed, they must. My sister Kim met a young woman a few years ago who told her that when she was about six or seven an angelic being came to her one night when she was in her bed. It was a radiantly beautiful being full of soft, shining light. "I am an angel sent from Jesus," it told her. The child was from a deeply committed Christian family and she loved Jesus. And yet she was terribly afraid at the presence of the "angel."

"You're *not* from Jesus!" the little girl challenged. "How do you know?" responded the still-shining angel. "Because in the Bible every *real* angel said 'Be not afraid' if someone was afraid of him. I'm afraid now and you didn't say that to me!"

Instantly the being changed into a hideous manifestation that swooped down upon her. "Would you rather see me like this?" the thing hissed as it vanished into the dark behind her. The demon had been challenged and unmasked by a little child. Even at her tender age her parents had trained her to be discerning. She knew enough not to swallow whatever being came down the pike just because it looked holy! She knew that if an "angel" didn't match the biblical description, it could not be from God. Scratch one would-be "guardian spirit"!

Who knows what untold deceptions and ruined lives might have been avoided if only the Edgar Cayces, Olga Worralls, Tony Agapaos, Sybil Leeks, and Aleister Crowleys had been taught these things in childhood by those who truly understood the grace and love and inestimable power of the Lord Jesus Christ.

Chapter 10

Truth Under Siege

✦

I believe that it is incumbent on those of us who teach at the college level to dismantle dogmatism wherever we find it. The question is how to accomplish the task.

—*Thought in Action: The NEA Higher Education Journal*

The Spirit explicitly says that in later times some will fall away from the faith, paying attention to deceitful spirits and doctrines of demons.

—The Apostle Paul
1 Timothy 4:1

The cardinal crime in Western society today is to assert that there is such a thing as moral absolutes, or absolutes of any kind, as Professor Alan Bloom has so insightfully documented in his book *The Closing of the American Mind*. Virtually every student who is a product of American education knows one thing (and in all too many cases *only* one thing), and that is that there are *absolutely no absolutes*. By extension this means that the Bible, which is known for some rather absolute claims, *must* be invalid. Satan has to cast doubt on the very nature of God and His Word, for once there is no longer any source of absolute truth against which to test one's experiences or philosophies, Satan has free rein to produce whatever effect or belief he desires.

Experience Above All?

One of his most powerful strategies has been to elevate *personal experience* over and above God's truth. Satan is a master at manipulation, and one of the easiest things in the entire universe to manipulate is human emotion. He will give you any experience you want. Some of the most ecstatic, numinous experiences I ever had were during the deepest times of occult meditations. These experiences confirmed for me at "gut level" the total "rightness" of my pursuit. I *knew* that Pachita's work as a psychic surgeon had to be from God because "it felt so holy." Satan will flatter you, praise you, lead you, guide you, heal you, or woo you as a passionate young man might court a maiden with long-stem roses and Lady Godiva chocolates—that proverbial spoonful of sugar that makes the devil's medicine go down.

Experience is a powerful factor in accepting the New Age religious beliefs. As the song says: "It can't be wrong when it feels so right!" That perspective may make for wonderfully romantic ballads, but it's a deadly foundation on which to base one's life. Whatever your personal *experience*—whatever *makes sense* or simply *feels right* to you about God or yourself— is what you'll go with, never realizing that without absolutes and without the God who sets the standards, the entire concept of values is meaningless.

The New Age philosophies being introduced in the schools are designed to produce experiences which will build into the child, at the most basic level, an unqualified acceptance of highly religious New Age thinking. One of the most important functions of Transpersonal education is "to help people learn to trust the validity of their personal experiences and accept what they learn from these experiences as their best source of wisdom and truth."[1] As we have already discussed, kids growing up are most certainly ". . . confused and usually unable to get clear answers from their parents and their teachers about many basic life questions, such as, Who am I? What does it mean to be alive? Will I and do I make a difference?"[2] If the answers the children receive to these crucial questions are wrapped in the powerful experiences of an Eastern/occultic worldview, then that will become the basic perspective from which they will construct their beliefs about the nature of God, the nature of man and reality, ethics, and what happens after death.

It is therefore not at all surprising that the Bible has been under such concerted and ferocious attack. It presents itself as God's infallible Word given to us "for teaching, for reproof, for correction, for training in righteousness" (2 Timothy 3:16). In other words, it presents itself as the absolute standard given by an absolute God, who expects us to measure our lives and experiences by what He has revealed in that Word. Furthermore, that Word flatly contradicts every single one of the New Ager's occultic and humanistic beliefs and exposes them for the demonic counterfeits and lies that they are.

As the editor of Helen Schucman's *Course In Miracles* astutely observed during a seminar, ". . . if the Bible were considered literally true, then the *Course* would have to be viewed as demonically inspired."[3] This, you understand, simply will not do. New Agers *must* destroy the credibility of the Bible if they will ever be fully successful in establishing their New Age religion.

Satan has always sought to undermine and discredit the Word of God. His routine worked spectacularly when he used it that first time in Genesis chapter 3, and he hasn't changed his approach since then.

What Satan doesn't want you to know about the New Age and the occult is that there really isn't anything *new* about it. It's the same old lie repackaged for contemporary minds.

Snake Oil

In Genesis 3:1 we read that "the serpent was more crafty than any beast of the field." This observation probably qualifies for the all-time understatement-of-the-year award! This was no ordinary beastie. He was sly and cunning and a master of the art of subtlety. The ancient Hebrew wording indicates that the word "serpent" in this context means "shining one."

What Eve was confronted with that day in the Garden was an astonishingly beautiful creature masking the foulest, most cunning spirit in the universe.

He said to the Eve, "Indeed, has God said, 'You shall not eat from *every* tree of the garden'?" The serpent's tone was one of shock and disbelief. Eve understood that only one single tree was forbidden, so she corrected the serpent's apparent confusion: "From the fruit of the trees of the garden we may eat; but from the fruit of the tree which is in the middle of the garden God has said, 'You shall not eat from it or touch it, lest you die.' "

Eve was doing a bit of embellishing here. God had never said anything about not *touching* the tree. He just said, "*Trust Me, don't eat from it,* because there are severe consequences if you do." It wasn't that God had poisoned the fruit like the wicked witch poisoned the apple offered to Snow White. God simply wanted them to take Him at His Word and choose to obey Him because they knew Him and loved Him.

The serpent's next move was a masterstroke of boldness and evil genius, based on the principle of "the bigger the lie and the straighter the face you tell it with, the more likely you are to be believed." He gambled everything on the chance that by flatly contradicting God he could lure Eve into turning her back on Him altogether. "The serpent said to the woman, 'You surely shall not die! For God knows that in the day you eat from it your eyes will be opened, and you will be like God, knowing good and evil.' "

That temptation was more than Eve was willing to resist. She would be as God! Unlimited human potential would be hers! God obviously didn't have Adam and Eve's best interests at heart, or else why would He withhold such wonders from them? She looked again at the forbidden tree and saw that it was a delightful thing to behold; the fruit certainly didn't appear to be dangerous. Obviously God had to be mistaken when He said she would die if she ate from it. So instead of turning her back on the serpent who had flatly called God a liar, she listened to the serpent's lie and ate the fruit.

Truly, the beautiful side of evil. The tree gave no indication whatever of the cosmic disaster that lay in its fruit. And the serpent looked so lovely! Surely nothing evil could come from something so dazzling and kind! And not one negative word from him—not like God with His "don't eat or you're dead" command! So she took the fruit, ate, and then talked Adam into doing the same.

The changes in them must have been startling and abrupt. It undoubtedly exposed the serpent to them for the liar he was, but by that time it was too late. The consequence of their choice was already upon them. The shimmering radiance of innocence fell away from them like a discarded robe, leaving them naked indeed.

"In the day you eat of it," God had warned them, "dying you shall surely die." So reads the Hebrew text. Two kinds of death came into being in that moment. The first was the instantaneous death of the face-to-face relationship which Adam and Eve had enjoyed with their Creator. This was *spiritual* death. The second kind of death was *physical* death. The irreversible process of their decay began at that very moment. Someday their bodies would perish, and unless they chose to once again turn toward God in faith and obedience, their spirits would likewise perish in that place of eternal separation from His presence—not by God's choosing, but by theirs.[4]

The serpent must have been fit to be tied when God didn't instantly obliterate Adam and Eve in response to their rebellion. Instead, God sought them out and provided a covering for them, since the one they had tried to make for themselves was hopelessly inadequate. In the midst of the curses they had brought upon themselves and all creation, God spoke the first veiled prophecy of His coming Son, who by taking the penalty of death upon Himself would thereby crush the head of the serpent forever.

Satanic Revenge

Satan has never been known as a good loser, and it seems

sadly true in this case that "misery loves company." The best way for Satan to take revenge on God for casting him out of heaven was to destroy as many human beings as he could get his hands on.

Today, he is still luring us with precisely the same bait of arrogance, vanity, and pride that he used with Eve:

1. *"Indeed, has God said . . . ?"* The God of the Bible is untrustworthy. Everyone knows the Bible is not the inerrant, infallible Word of God. It's full of lies and errors, rewritings, and mistranslations. It means only what you choose it to mean for you, since there are no absolutes.

2. *"You surely shall not die!"* There is no such place as heaven, and there is *certainly* no such place as a literal hell! Sin is a dangerous myth. God punishes no one, and therefore you certainly don't need a "Savior." There is nothing to be saved from! It doesn't matter what you do or what you believe, as long as you're sincere. Death is not to be feared! Shirley MacLaine's "Higher Self" tells us so! When your body ceases to show signs of life, you do not die; you merely release your Higher Self into the astral plane, where you will continue to learn, evolve, and grow ever higher and higher.

3. *"You will be like God . . . "* You are not born with a sin nature. You are born perfect, divine in your essence. Nothing matters more than the nurturing and esteeming of your self. In you resides all knowledge and wisdom and power, for you are a perfect person and student! Psychic abilities are but natural expressions of this inherent divinity latent within us all. Furthermore, and most important to understand, God is not a personal God. He is a Force: He is a She; He is in All, and All is in Him; therefore *everything* is God, including

evil. Therefore, there is no "right" and there is no "wrong." There are no absolutes.

Does this all sound familiar? It is certainly no coincidence that the *exact same lies* used by Satan to lure Adam and Eve in the Garden of Eden are *precisely* the same principles that form the basis of all occultism in general and the New Age in particular. Considering the source, one would think that occultists and New Agers would be a bit less enthusiastic about their belief system. That, unfortunately, seems hardly to be the case. Dick Sutphen, reincarnationist, author, and major figure in the New Age Movement, puts it this way:

> Classical systems of occult/metaphysical philosophy . . . are based upon the following assumptions:
>
> *All is one*: The external world and consciousness are one and the same.
>
> *Man is a divine being*: We are all part of God, we are God.
>
> *Life is for evolutionary purposes*: Karma and reincarnation. [See Appendix B: "You Must Be Born Again . . . and Again."]
>
> *Self-actualization*: Awareness of the True Self within leads to mastery of your own reality.[5]

It is the unchallenged and unqualified acceptance of those assumptions that will help bring about what Marilyn Ferguson calls ". . . a new mind—the ascendance of a startling world view that gathers into its framework break-through science and insights from earliest recorded thought."[6] "Insights from earliest recorded thought," incidentally, is one of the more elegant euphemisms I've yet seen to describe ancient occultism.

Only one Book in the world reveals the master strategy of Satan and exposes occultism for what it really is. Only the Word of God stands in opposition to this evil. Is it any wonder that the attack has seldom before been more intense than it is right now?

Open Season

If you want your turn at Bible-bashing, you're just going to have to get in line. Atheist Anne Gaylor, president of the Freedom From Religion Foundation (founded in 1978), claims that "the Bible is a book of myths and fables and legends . . . a uniquely dangerous book that teaches people to hate, kill, maim and beat. It is a mean, sordid book that has set civilization back thousands of years."[7] In 1982 she did her level (and unsuccessful) best to have President Reagan's proclamation of 1983 as "The Year of the Bible" declared unconstitutional.

More recently, her 3000-member nonprofit organization launched a nationwide campaign urging innkeepers to remove the Gideon Bibles from their rooms. So far most innkeepers have decided to keep the Bibles, but Ms. Gaylor is nonetheless encouraged by the fact that at least her group has managed to play a key role in banning pregame prayer at all football games held at the University of Wisconsin.

Ms. Gaylor's approach is obvious; it falls in the category of "direct frontal attack." More subtle and considerably more dangerous is the attack that seeks to unify all religions into a single "universal religion." In a book entitled *Toward a Maitreyan Revolution* (published through the New Age organization *Unity in Diversity*) we learn that this—

> New universal religion . . . will be nondogmatic . . . a synthesis of mysticism, occultism, humanism, theism, pantheism, and idealism, all related to a glorious search for cosmic consciousness. There will be new temples arising where the symbols of every religion will be seen as part of one architectural and geometrical reality of the cosmos. . . . The new religion will have its prayers, mantras, and invocations, plus acknowledging the value and expression of those from the religions and teachings of the past.[8]

Of course, some of us may prove to be a little slow in embracing this glorious concept of a "universal religion":

> One who doesn't grasp this great truth, a Christian,
> for example, asks, "But was not Christ inspired?"
> Yes, but he was not the only one inspired. Another
> who is a Buddhist asks, "Was not Buddha inspired?"
> Yes, but he was not the only one inspired. A Chris-
> tian asks, "But is not our Christian Bible inspired?"
> Yes, but there are other inspired scriptures. A Brah-
> min or a Buddhist asks, "Are not the Vedas inspired?"
> Yes, but there are other inspired sacred books. Your
> error is not in believing that your particular scrip-
> tures are inspired, but your error is—and you show
> your absurdly laughable limitations by it—your in-
> ability to see that other scriptures are also inspired.
> The sacred books, the inspired writings, all come
> from the same source—God.[9]

There are any number of problems with the above pro-
nouncement. All these "sacred books" present radically different worldviews. To accept one book is by definition to deny
the others. For example, God cannot be both an abstract,
amoral, pantheistic, universal Force (as He is presented in
Eastern and Gnostic scriptures) and at the same time be a
personal, living, transcendent Creator-God who says, "You
shall have no other gods before Me" (Exodus 20:3). These two
concepts of God are mutually exclusive. If one of them is true,
then the other *by definition*, cannot be. How then can all
religions be reconciled into a single universal religion? Only
by destroying the one Book which claims exclusive truth to
the exclusion of all other books; only by destroying the base
on which Christianity stands: the Bible.

Those who would establish a one-world government and
ruler know that they will never succeed until they somehow
settle the thorny issue of conflicting and divisive religious
beliefs.

Robert Muller for many years director of the Secretary
General's office at the United Nations, has said it as clearly
as any of them: "The world's major religions must speed
up dramatically their ecumenical movement and recognize

the unity of their objectives in the diversity of their cults. Religions must actively cooperate to bring to unprecedented heights a better understanding of the mysteries of life and of our place in the universe. 'My religion, right or wrong,' and 'My nation, right or wrong' must be abandoned forever in the planetary age."[10]

Unity is the password of the day: unity at all costs; unity at the expense of right or wrong; unity at the expense of truth. Those who stand in the way of "unity"—especially religious unity—are increasingly being viewed with a hostile eye, for these "narrow-minded disrupters" are seen as standing in the way of the establishment of the peace and the very survival of the entire planet. Those people (such as Fundamentalist Christians and other monotheists) who insist on maintaining their "archaic and provincially orthodox" beliefs and literal interpretations of Scripture must either learn to become "open-minded" and blend in or else risk being eliminated— literally. [See Appendix C: "Unity or Else."]

Attacks Closer to Home

While we may not be surprised by the frontal attacks of the atheists or caught unaware by the more subtle strategies coming from the New Age camp, what is undoubtedly most disturbing are the increasingly blatant attacks from within the church itself by those who have previously esteemed the Bible as the inerrant and infallible Word of God.

"How firm a foundation, ye saints of the Lord, is laid for your faith in His excellent Word!" So reads the first line of one of the great old hymns of the church. Today precious few church members who happen across it in their hymnals believe that the Word of God can provide a firm foundation for anything at all, much less their faith. Then again, why should they? Many of their pastors don't.

According to a new survey undertaken by the Presbyterian Church, which currently holds the dubious distinction of being the most liberal of the mainline denominations, "just 5% of the clergy and 16% of the laity say the Bible should be taken literally."[11] The United Methodist General Conference held in St. Louis in April 1988 debated introducing "gender-less names for God. . . . The Commission on the Status and Role of Women is supporting a proposal that would have church publications substitute the words 'Creator' for 'Father' and 'Our Savior' or 'Redeemer' for 'His Only Son.' "[12] They're also planning to publish a unisex Bible. Not surprisingly, the National Council of Churches is planning a similar unisex publication.

And the Methodist Hymnal Revision Committee found itself agonizing over the decision whether to include a song called "Strong Mother God" in their new hymnal edition. The song got voted down 11 to 10. Ah well, maybe next time.

The Presbyterians and the Methodists are not alone. Episcopal Bishop John S. Spong recently stated that "the mainline Christian churches should either 'rescue the Bible' from fundamentalists with frank, honest teaching about the Scriptures or return this noble book to the shelves of our libraries and museums."[13] The patronizing implication here is that the Bible is simply not fit for modern human consumption as it stands, for it is filled with prejudices of the past. Bishop Spong is working hard to remove those "biblical prejudices" by ordaining women as priests and bishops and by urging "that rites to bless committed homosexual couples be instituted in the Episcopal Church." I'm sure I don't know what the good bishop plans to do with the Scriptures once the "mainline churches rescue the Bible from the Falwells of this world." Rescue it *for what*! Why on earth would he even bother? As he himself points out, "one of the reasons that our clergy do not teach the Bible rigorously to their congregations [is] the fact that we clergy ourselves have come to dismiss much of Holy Scripture as no longer valid. . . ."

Many ministers no longer believe in the Bible or in any of the fundamentals of Christianity for that matter.[14] Thanks for this goes in good measure to a man the *Encyclopedia Britannica* identifies as "perhaps the leading New Testament scholar of the 20th century," Rudolf Bultmann (1884-1976). Bultmann felt that it was unreasonable to expect modern man, with his scientific and technocratic sophistication, to actually accept the Bible as it stands. So he took it upon himself to surgically remove all its "myths." Anything that didn't make sense to him, such as the virgin birth, the incarnation, the resurrection, all the miracles, and anything that even remotely smacked of the supernatural, were pronounced "mythology" and expunged from the text. He simply defined them out of existence.

It took numerous scholarly volumes to help his students and fellow scholars understand his demytholization process. After World War II he became a "major international academic figure," which means that he traveled to as many places as he could to convince as many people as he could that the God of the Bible is a liar. Today the pernicious influence of "higher criticism" is widely spread throughout seminaries and universities across Europe and America.

A good number of pastors and ministers in the pulpit today do not believe in the Bible because their professors bought Bultmann's "scholarly" speculations as "Gospel truth," as it were. As a result, they were left with an emasculated Bible and the kind of simpering, double-minded, wimp of a "Jesus" well-suited to the mockeries of a *Last Temptation of Christ*. It's no wonder none of these "ministers" objected to the film! They have already become accustomed to the milksop caricature left them by Bultmann's "de-mythologizing."

The Jesus Seminar

Following proudly in Bultmann's footsteps is another group of scholars who call themselves the "Jesus Seminar." This group, comprised of about 125 Roman Catholic, Protestant, and non-Christian scholars, has been meeting biannually since 1985 for the purpose of voting on what they think Jesus did or did not actually say. So far, they have concluded that "less than 25% of the words attributed to Jesus were His."[15] They have decided (by secret ballot) that Jesus did not publicly proclaim Himself to be the Messiah. He never said, "I am the resurrection and the life. He who believes in Me shall live even if he dies" (John 11:25). The incident in Matthew 26:63,64 in which Jesus was commanded by the high priest to reveal whether He was indeed "the Christ, the Son of God," to which Jesus responded, "You have said it yourself," never happened. Jesus also did not create or teach the Lord's Prayer. Furthermore, He never said anything at all about an apocalyptic chaos at the end of the world or about His second coming! The Jesus Seminar has inadvertently found itself bringing about the fulfillment of biblical prophecy before our very eyes:

> Know this first of all, that in the last days mockers will come with their mocking, following after their own lusts and saying, "Where is the promise of His coming?" (2 Peter 3:3ff.).

The Jesus Seminar wants us to believe that "after Jesus' lifetime, scholars say, the churches speculated about the divine nature of Jesus and thus invented sayings. . . ."[16] Keep in mind that these scholars themselves have admitted that their findings "are not to be taken as truth, but rather as a scholarly 'theory of uncertainty.' "[17] What they're presenting with such confidence, in other words, is purely speculation! Nevertheless, they will publish their new censored and color-coded version of the Bible so that you can know what is and is not worth believing. They see it as their mission to "offset . . . unsophisticated Bible teachings by television preachers and others."[18]

The implication is crystal clear: Those who believe that the Bible is the inerrant, God-breathed, inspired Word of the Living God are "unsophisticated," a term of genteel snobbery obviously to be equated with the words "ignorant," "unscholarly," and, worst of all, "Fundamentalist." Father Edward F. Beutner, campus minister at Santa Clara University and a seminar member, points out: ". . . the seminar findings on the Second Coming reflect what is quietly taught in most major universities and seminaries."[19]

Nevertheless, a large number of extremely intelligent, highly accomplished individuals who have spent lifetimes studying the Bible have come to the conclusion that one can indeed accept the Bible as a reliable historical document as well as the inerrant and infallible Word of God without committing intellectual suicide.[20]

Reliable History

Professor John Warwick Montgomery wrote a clear and readable apologetic on the reliability of the Bible entitled *History and Christianity*. In reference to the historical accuracy of the New Testament documents he says the following:

> . . . competent historical scholarship must regard the New Testament documents as coming from the first century and as reflecting primary-source testimony about the person and claims of Jesus. . . . We may not like the Jesus of the historical documents; but like him or not, we meet him there as a divine being on whom our personal destiny depends.[21]

Sir Frederic G. Kenyon, formerly director and principal librarian of the British Museum, summarizes the textual advantage of the New Testament documents over all other ancient manuscripts by writing:

> The books of the New Testament were written in the latter part of the first century; the earliest extant manuscripts . . . are of the fourth century—say 250 to 300 years later. This may sound a considerable interval, but it is nothing to that which parts most of the great classical authors from their earliest manuscripts. We believe we have in all essentials an accurate text of the seven extant plays of Sophocles; yet the earliest substantial manuscript upon which it is based was written more than 1400 years after the poet's death. Aeschylus, Aristophanes, and Thucydides are in the same state; while with Euripides the interval is increased to 1600 years. For Plato it may be put at 1300 years, for Demosthenes as low as 1200.[22]

With the discovery in recent years of numerous papyrus portions of New Testament documents, Kenyon went on to conclude:

> ... the last foundation for any doubt that the Scriptures have come down to us substantially as they were written has now been removed. Both the authenticity and the general integrity of the books of the New Testament may be regarded as finally established.[23]

A.T. Robertson, the author of the most comprehensive grammar of New Testament Greek, wrote, "We have 13,000 manuscript copies of portions of the New Testament. To be skeptical of the resultant text of the New Testament books is to allow all of classical antiquity to slip into obscurity, for no documents of the ancient period are as well attested bibliographically as the New Testament."[24]

The Bible can be proved reliable on many levels: internal evidence, the testimony of eyewitnesses, the inclusion of the texts in the writings of the early church fathers, the evidences for the resurrection,[25] and the literal fulfillment of hundreds of specific prophecies from both the Old and the New Testaments.[26] The historical evidence for the reliability of the Bible is simply overwhelming.

The Attitude Problem

The real problem is not "lack of evidence" or "contradictions." The problem is closely related to the same dilemma facing the scribes and Pharisees of Jesus' day. I can't help but wonder if the Jesus Seminar has gotten around to voting on whether or not Jesus actually said any of *this*:

> Woe to you, scribes and Pharisees, hypocrites, because you shut off the kingdom of heaven from men; for you do not enter in yourselves, nor do you allow those who are entering to go in.
>
> Woe to you, scribes and Pharisees, hypocrites, because you travel about on sea and land to make

one proselyte; and when he becomes one, you make
him twice as much a son of hell as yourselves (Matthew 23:13,15).

Jesus continued at length with this theme, and grew more
emphatic as He continued. He said they were "full of robbery
and self-indulgence." He called them "whitewashed tombs
which on the outside appear beautiful but inside are full of
dead men's bones." "Even so you too outwardly appear righteous to men," He said to them, "but inwardly you are full of
hypocrisy and lawlessness." "You serpents, you brood of
vipers, how shall you escape the sentence of hell?" (Matthew
23:25-33).

"Gentle Jesus," meek and mild—the most loving, positive
Man who has ever walked the face of the earth—did not
hesitate to speak the truth in the strongest possible terms,
and this to the priests and scholars of His day. Why? Because
they had in their hands the revealed Word of God, they had
great knowledge and intelligence and wisdom, and yet despite
all their brilliance and learning they *would not* believe the
evidence before them—evidence which clearly proved that
Jesus of Nazareth was indeed God incarnate in human flesh
and the Messiah whom they had so long awaited. "Professing
to be wise, they became fools" (Romans 1:22).

The apostle Peter, an eyewitness to the life and teachings of
Jesus (and therefore infinitely better qualified than today's
critics to impart valid information on the subject) acknowledged that there are indeed things which are "hard to understand, which the untaught and unstable distort, as they do
also the rest of the Scriptures, to their own destruction. You
therefore, beloved, knowing this beforehand, be on your
guard lest, being carried away by the error of unprincipled
men, you fall from your own steadfastness" (2 Peter 3:16,17).
It is a vital warning for our time.

Take the Time

Parents, it is today more crucial than ever that you take the
time to study and understand why the Bible is indeed reliable

as a historical document. It is not enough to say to your children, "Believe this because I say so." You must prepare them to defend their faith today as never before if they are to survive their educational process intact in their faith. Be assured that the NEA is very diligently preparing their teachers to deal with children who arrive in their classrooms convinced that they "know the truth."

In the Winter 1986 edition of the NEA's *Higher Education Journal* is an article written by David McKenzie called "Teaching Students Who Already Know the 'Truth.' " As an associate professor of philosophy at Berry College in Rome, Georgia, Mr. McKenzie is genuinely concerned about how to "encourage intellectual inquiry among the growing number of religious dogmatists in the classroom. . . ." (It is worth noting, by the way, that Mr. McKenzie has a B.D. from Southern Baptist Theological Seminary, and "serves a pastoral appointment in the United Methodist Church.")

There are many signs of dogmatism in the classrooms of this country, he tells us, and cites the cases of students who have the audacity to bring their Bibles to their first-year philosophy class as an obvious and open challenge to the professor who now finds himself pitting his mind against "the absolute word of God!" "The most basic of the dogmas these students uphold is a commitment to the inerrancy and absolute authority of the Bible," observes Mr. McKenzie. These "dogmatic Fundamentalists" are sitting there in your classroom actually comparing what you tell them against what they read in the Bible, and thereby, says Mr. McKenzie, endangering "free thought in a free society." He presents teachers with basic apologetics to the key arguments which the "dogmatic Fundamentalists" are most likely to raise in their classrooms, and gives them helpful suggestions to "reach" those who "have absolutized their truth, and have locked out anything that might broaden their perspectives."

New Age and humanist educators across the country feel that it is their moral obligation to their students and the world to release them from the narrow bondage and confines that accepting the Bible as the inerrant Word of God has placed them in. If you have not spent the time teaching your child not only *what* he believes but *why* he believes it as well, these educators are very likely to succeed in undermining, if not totally destroying, your child's faith in God.

Chapter 11

Halloween

◆

I was working on this chapter last night, Halloween, when the doorbell rang. I was greeted by an adorable bunch of little kids doing their level best to look like gruesome Witches and vampires. I bent down as I distributed apples and oranges in response to lusty cries of "trick or treat!"

"You kids want to know something?" I asked very softly.

"Yeah!" came a unanimous chorus.

"With the Lord Jesus there is no trick. He loves every one of you very much."

Several little faces beamed up at me through their ghoulish makeup. "That's neat!" exclaimed one little girl. "Yeah!" chimed in a few others.

"This is Jesus' night," I said. Why, I'm not really sure. I was poignantly aware of the fact that it is a night the devil has made a point of claiming for himself.

"No it's not!" snarled a hidden voice. "It's *Jason's* night!" A boy who was taller than the rest stepped out from the shadows. He was wearing the white hockey mask of "Jason," the demented, ghoulish killer in the movie *Friday the 13th* and was brandishing a very realistic-looking hatchet. I have to admit that the boy gave me a start, but I stood my ground and dropped a banana into his bag.

"No, 'Jason,' this is still Jesus' night!" I repeated. And indeed it is, even though it is most assuredly the night set aside for the glorification and worship of idols, false gods, Satan, and death. "The Son of God appeared for this purpose, that He might destroy the works of the devil!"[1]

"Jason" evidently resented the competition, however, for he ripped our mailbox right out of the ground and left his banana squished on the stair.

Pet Ghosts?

Most of us in the United States have grown up observing Halloween in one form or another. From the time we're in preschool we make drawings or cutouts of sinister black Witches—the haggier the better. We make paintings of gruesome black cats with gleaming, evil, orange eyes; we hang up smirking paper skeletons with dancing limbs; we glue together ghost and bat mobiles; and we design demoniacal faces for our pumpkins.

For several years now, one thoughtful kindergarten teacher in Southern California has even provided ghosts for her pupils to commune with at Halloween. I spoke with one of the mothers from that school who told me that her little boy was sent home with a note from the teacher informing the parents that their child would be bringing home a "special friend" the next day. The child was to nurture his "friend," name it, feed it, and talk to it—all as a part of a special class project that was designed to "develop the child's imagination."

The next day the little boy came home with a sealed envelope along with *explicit* instructions that his parents were *not* to touch it; only the child was allowed to open the envelope. Mom said "You bet!" and promptly opened it up. Inside was six inches of thick orange wool string with a knot tied a quarter of the way up to make a loop resembling a head. The mimeographed "letter" that accompanied it read as follows:

> Haunted House
> 001 Cemetery Lane
> Spookville

Dear Customer,
   Thank you for your order. Your ghost is exactly what you ordered. You will find that your ghost is

attached to an orange string. *Do not* untie the special knot until you are ready to let your ghost go.

Your ghost will tell you when it is hungry and what it prefers to eat. It will sleep in the air beside you all day. It especially likes quiet places where there are cobwebs, creaky boards and corners.

If you follow the above directions, you will have a very happy ghost.

Yours truly,

Head Ghost

The mother, a Christian, didn't cotton to the idea of her son taking in a pet ghost, however housebroken. She was also a little suspicious of her six-year-old being addressed as "Dear Customer." So she confiscated the thing and put it in the garage on a shelf until she could decide what to do with it. The next day her sister was in the garage on an errand, unaware of the matter of the "ghost in the string." Suddenly she was frightened by the sense of a threatening presence around her. She heard the sounds of a cat hissing in the corner and something like a "chatty doll" mumbling incoherently at her. Later that night they threw the "ghost string" into the garbage pail, prayed to bind and remove the entity, and were never bothered by the "presence" again. This family had no trouble whatever believing that a spirit had indeed been sent home with their little boy, and that it didn't much like having been assigned to a Christian household.[2]

The Halloween ghosts were given out again this year by the same teacher. The mother managed to get hold of the envelope, orange ghost-carrier and all, and sent it to me. It is possible of course that the teacher meant nothing sinister by it. Perhaps to her it was just a cute exercise in imagination for her kindergartners. Nevertheless, in light of the stated intent of many Transpersonal educators to introduce children to spirit guides, I can't help but be a little curious about any teacher who sends the children home with "imaginary friends."

Church-Sponsored Horror

Even in the church, Halloween is a time of spooky fun and games. Any number of good, solid churches, ever mindful of their youth programs and ministries, will sponsor haunted houses designed to scare the wits out of the kids. In Bakersfield, California, Youth for Christ's Campus Life, a heavy-metal rock radio station, Pepsi, and Burger King are yearly sponsors of "Scream in the Dark," an event held every night for about a week before Halloween. At least 20,000 people "brave the chilly corridors and dark passages" every year to face ghoulish figures, terrifying tunnels, and screams in the dark.[3]

A certain Assembly of God church in Tampa, Florida, got more than it bargained for in that department a couple of years ago when it borrowed a coffin from a local mortuary for use at a Halloween fund-raiser, and found a long-forgotten dead body still in it![4]

The Lawndale Christian Church in Lawndale, California, offers discount coupons for "The House." The advertisement reads "You are entering at your own risk. Young children strongly recommended *not* to enter 'THE HOUSE.' Children under 12 must be accompanied by an adult. Persons with heart conditions, health problems or pregnant women are not allowed. . . ."

The warning is well-given. Terror can kill. When my husband was a teenager, the family next door to him lost their toddler one Halloween when the little one opened the door to trick-or-treaters. Their hideous appearance and shrieks so traumatized the child that he literally dropped dead on the spot.

Church-sponsored horror isn't a particularly new phenomenon. My husband's Lutheran church in New York always sponsored a "Chamber of Horrors" when he was a boy, complete with fluorescent skeletons, scary pop-ups, peeled grapes to simulate dead eyeballs, and a bowl of cold spaghetti that was supposed to be . . . well, you know. Anyway, they made you stick your hand into it, and any number of kids spent the rest of the night throwing up.

Halloween has become a full-fledged national children's playday, but for hundreds of thousands of people in the Western world (and their numbers are growing steadily) Halloween is a sacred time, the ancient pagan festival of fire and death.

Festival of the Dead

The origins and traditions of Halloween can be traced back thousands of years to the days of the ancient Celts and their priests, the Druids. The eve of October 31 marked the transition from summer into the darkness of winter. It marked the beginning of the Celtic New Year. The Feast of Samhain was a fearsome night, a dreaded night, a night in which great bonfires were lit to Samana the Lord of Death, the dark Aryan god who was known as the Grim Reaper, the leader of the ancestral ghosts.[5]

On this night the spirits of the dead rose up, shivering with the coming cold of winter and seeking the warmth and affection of the homes they once inhabited. And even colder, darker creatures filled the night: evil Witches flying through the night,[6] hobgoblins, and evil pookas that appeared in the form of hideous black horses. Demons, fairies, and ghouls roamed about as the doors of the burial sidh-mounds opened wide,[7] allowing them free access to the world of living men. These loathsome beings were usually not in a particularly good mood by the time they arrived and it was feared that unless these spirits were appeased and soothed with offerings and gifts they would wreak mischief and vengeance by destroying crops, killing cattle, turning milk sour, and generally making life miserable.

So it was that families offered what was most precious to them: food—a "treat" which they fervently hoped would be sufficient to offset any "trick" which the ghostly blackmailers might otherwise be tempted to inflict.

The ancient Celtic villagers realized, however, that merely feeding the spirits might not be enough to speed them on their way. The ghoulies might decide it would be rude to eat and run, as it were, and might just be tempted to stick around.

That simply would not do. So arose the practice of dressing in masks and costumes: Chosen villagers disguised themselves as the fell creatures at large, mystically taking on their attributes and powers. The "mummers," as they were called, cavorted from house to house collecting the ancient Celtic equivalent of protection money, and then romped the ghosts right out of town when they were through.

They carried a jack-o'-lantern to light their way—a turnip or potato with a fearful, demonic face carved into it which they hoped would duly impress, if not intimidate, the demons around them.[8]

Sacrifice and Fire

As a part of their ancient New Year's ritual, massive sacred bonfires were lit throughout the countryside of Wales, Ireland, and France—fires from which every house in the village would rekindle their hearth fires (which had been ritually extinguished, as they were at the end of every year). The villagers would gather and dance round and round the bonfire, whose light and heat they believed would help the sun make it through the cold, dark winter.[9]

But the great fires served another purpose as well: On this night unspeakable sacrifices were offered by the Druid priests to the Lord of Death.

Lewis Spence in his book *The History and Origins of Druidism* says:

> Certain writers on Celtic history have indignantly denied that the Druidic caste ever practiced the horrible rite of human sacrifice. There is no question, however, that practice it they did. Tacitus alludes to the fact that the Druids of Anglesea "covered their altars with the blood of captives." If the words of Caesar are to be credited, human sacrifice was a frequent and common element in their religious procedure. He tells us that no sacrifice might be carried out except in the presence of a Druid.[10]

It is in his *Commentaries* that Caesar speaks of the great wicker images "in which the Druids were said to burn scores of people alive."[11]

Some modern Witches may still deny that the Druidic religion, on which many of their beliefs and practices are based, ever practiced human and animal sacrifice as a part of their "peaceable nature religion." But some noted Witches have indeed acknowledged the murderous bent of the ancient religion:

> Propitiation, in the old days when survival was felt to depend on it, was a grim and serious affair. There can be little doubt that at one time it involved human sacrifice—of criminals saved up for the purpose or, at the other end of the scale, of an ageing king; little doubt, either, that these ritual deaths were by fire.[12]

The Druids (from the Gaelic word *druidh*, meaning "a wise man" or "magician,"[13] would carefully watch the writhing of the victims in the fire (whether people or animals) and from their death agonies would foretell the future of the village. The Feast of Samhain was by no means the only celebration at which the Druids practiced human sacrifice. Sacrificial victims were also burned in their sacred fires during the spring festival of Beltane held on the eve of the first of May as part of their fertility rites.[14] So it would seem, according to ancient historians, that human and animal sacrifice was a particularly noxious and pervasive habit among the Druids.

The Farrars, well-known authors and practicing Witches in Ireland, tell us that "Later, of course, the propitiatory sacrifice became symbolic . . . "but then mention that the royal sacrifice at Samhain may have lingered in the form of animal substitutes. The Farrars tell us of at least one animal sacrifice they knew of that took place in their village "within living memory."[15] We can only hope that "the old days when "survival was felt to depend on human sacrifice" will never return.

The Spirit of Halloween

Last Halloween I watched a rerun of "Garfield's Halloween

Adventure." Garfield, you may remember, is thrilled at the realization that Halloween is a night where he gets to rake in free candy. "This is the night I was created for," he exclaims with as much enthusiasm as Garfield ever seems to muster.

He decides to sucker poor unsuspecting Otie, an exceedingly dumb (though endearing) doggie, into going with him so that Garfield can double his personal candy haul. Well . . . maybe he'll give Otie one piece of candy for his troubles.

Then suddenly Garfield pauses in his Machiavellian musings and wonders, "Am I being too greedy? Should I share my candy with those less fortunate than I? Am I missing the spirit of Halloween?" Wouldn't it be nice if that were in fact the spirit of Halloween!

The "spirit of Halloween" is more accurately discerned in the horror movies and videos traditionally released in honor of the season.[16] Cinematic treasures so popular with teenage boys today like *Halloween I, II,* and *III; Friday the 13th I, II,* and *III; Thriller; Faces of Death I* through whatever; *Nightmare on Elm Street;* and any number of slasher, blood-and-gore, murder-and-terror flicks are truer to the original "spirit of Halloween"—the spirit of sudden death and murder—than is the sight of little Linus sitting all night in his "sincere" pumpkin patch waiting for the Great Pumpkin, or of Garfield in his quest for candy.

Spirited Communion

Modern Witches would vehemently deny that their celebration has anything to do with the demonic horrors depicted in such films as *Friday the 13th.* To them Halloween is one of the four greater Sabbats held during the year. Halloween for them is the time of Harvest Celebration—that season in which the Great Goddess goes to sleep for the long winter months, giving way to the Horned God of Hunting and Death, who will rule until her return on the first of May. It is a time of ritual and for ridding oneself of personal weaknesses,[17] a time for feasting and joyful celebration. It is also a time for communing with the spirits of the dead.

Witches Arnold and Patricia Crowther say that—

Halloween has always been the Festival of the Dead, and was believed to be the best time to contact those who had passed over. Today, spiritualists try to contact the departed by means of "spirit guides"—American Indians, Chinese men, nuns, priests and even little girls. Witches tried to make contact through the God of Death himself. So when the bonfire had burned down ... the priestess, in her new role as the God, held a skull between her hands, using it as a crystal-gazing ball. This was the kind of necromancy practiced centuries before the Fox Sisters, with their poltergeist tappings, started the modern craze for spiritualism.[18]

The Celts, say the Crowthers, would sometimes lie on graves during Halloween, hoping to hear some word of wisdom from the spirits of the corpses beneath them. And the Crowthers boast that "the high priestesses were just as successful in contacting the dead as are our own mediums. . . ."[19] According to a longtime Witch with whom I once spoke, they still are. Communing with the spirits of the dead is a regular feature of their covens' Halloween rituals.

An article in the *Los Angeles Times* (Saturday, October 31, 1987) features a story on a certain coven's celebration rituals during Halloween. The story describes the ritual and then tells us that it "will be repeated throughout the Southland today as Witches celebrate their most important holiday, Samhain, or Halloween, when they believe the veil between the worlds becomes thin, making visits with spirits possible." Some Witches will use the Ouija board to contact the dead. Others will use a darkened scrying-mirror into which they stare until the faces of their beloved departed appear. Others may use a crystal ball or "sit quietly round the cauldron, gazing into the incense-smoke, talking of what they see and feel."[20]

Satanic Revels

While the Witches are spending the Halloween season

tucking in their Goddess for her long winter sleep and frolicking in joyful communion with the spirits of the dead, there is another religious group which is equally serious about its Halloween celebrations: the Satanists. Halloween to them is a more sinister and direct celebration of death and Satan. Unlike the Witches, of whom most do not even acknowledge the existence of Satan, the Satanists are quite candid about exactly who the dread "lord of death" happens to be, and they celebrate Halloween as one of his two highest unholy days.

As is the case among the Witches, different "denominations" of Satanists have their own peculiar traditions, beliefs, and practices on this night. For some of them Satan is not a real, specific entity, but rather the personification of evil resident within all men, a "dark hidden force in nature responsible for the workings of earthly affairs...."[21]

Other Satanists however—cult Satanists—understand that Satan is very real indeed. To them the sacrifices he demands are not symbolic at all.[22] They believe that the blood sacrifice of innocence which Satan demands as the ultimate blasphemy and sign of devotion to himself must be very literal indeed. At various times during the year, but especially during the month of October, police across the country report finding the remains of animals—some with the blood drained, others with various organs missing, some carefully skinned while keeping the wretched creature alive. They are frequently found at sites which indicate that some form of ritual took place. When no altar or pentagram or other symbolism is in evidence, it is entirely likely that some neophyte or self-styled Satanist is simply practicing to make sure the "sacrifice" is letter-perfect for the ceremony.

One animal control officer in Southern California stated in a phone conversation that the ritualistic slayings of animals had soared "almost beyond control" in the previous year (1987). The officers had found over 25 incidents of skinned or ritually mutilated animals in his area. However, his department head was adamantly opposed to making these reports public, although the officer interviewed was not sure why.

Halloween Sacrifices

At Halloween the sacrifices of some of these satanic cults are unspeakably vicious and brutal. Lauren Stratford, in her powerful and important book *Satan's Underground*, relates the horror of the practices of the particular satanic cult which victimized her for many years. It was their practice to begin the Halloween ceremonies five weeks before the night of Halloween. The sixth week of the rituals culminates on the night of Halloween itself.

On that first night the key aspect of the ritual is gathering together and chanting "666" until the participants literally see the face of Satan made manifest to them. On the night of the second week they offer a small animal—perhaps a bird or a cat. The rituals are long and elaborate, beginning at six in the evening and culminating with the death of the sacrifice as close to midnight as possible. On the third week a larger animal, such as a large dog or a small sheep or goat, is slaughtered. On the fourth week the participants *must* sacrifice a male goat with as large a set of horns as they can find. They sever the head and set it up as a symbol of the perfect head of Satan.

On the night of the fifth week the group performs the ritual murder of a tiny infant or a very young child. (Yes, it actually happens.) The child is often the offspring of a female member or victim of the coven (or *grotto*, as some Satanists refer to their group) who has been impregnated for the very purpose of turning her child over for the sacrifice. In that case there would be no public record of the birth of the child and certainly no report of its death. If the mother has not delivered the child in time for the ritual, it is taken by Cesarean section. If the Satanists have been unable to produce their own infant within the group for the occasion, they steal a child, possibly from illegal aliens, since they are not always likely to report the kidnapping because of fear of the authorities. Or they pick up a runaway or "throwaway" kid, or else "adopt" or buy a baby through the black market. It is interesting to note, as several police officers have told me, that reports of stolen or missing children increase during this time of year.

Because of its innocence and frailty, a tiny child is viewed by these Satanists as the perfect sacrifice to their Master. The infant is seen as a representation of the Christ Child, and it is He whom they are blaspheming and symbolically destroying in the prolonged and brutal torture and slaying of the child. After the death of the baby, the members will all eat a portion of the little one's heart and will drink its blood.

The night of Halloween itself is the sixth and final night in the series of rituals. On this night another child, as well as an adult female (preferably the mother of the infant taken the week before), will be slaughtered. Not all Satanist groups participate in activities of this kind, but some certainly do.

The night of Halloween is also a propitious time for some Satanists to contact the spirits of the dead. Their rituals of necromancy often go far beyond that of the Witches and mediums in the horror and perversion in which these people specialize. After the sacrifices the group might transfer to a solitary graveyard. A casket is unearthed and the lid pried open. Sometimes this ritual will take place in a mortuary rather than a cemetery. Ritual words are spoken to cast out "the spirit of death" and to invoke into the decaying body the "spirit of life," which is then adjured to answer any question the high priest puts to it. Victims have told of being placed inside the coffin in a ritual "embracing of death." This ritual can take place at any time during the year, but Halloween is decidedly a favorite time for numerous satanic groups.

Satan Wants You

Halloween is also a prime recruiting season for the Satanists. Much as the government will plant "narcs" in various high schools to find out who is pushing or using drugs on campus, so some Satanists may plant kids at the schools who are there solely for the purpose of discerning potential members or victims among the students. The Dungeons and Dragons clubs are prime hunting grounds for them, as are other groups and clubs based on medieval themes. Or they may invite some kid to a party and slip a drug into his drink. Then they'll photograph or videotape him in compromising

situations, perhaps sexual or possibly showing him participating in a blood sacrifice. The photographs are then used to
blackmail the kid into silence and obedience.

Church-sponsored "haunted houses" are also prime hunting grounds. The Satanists watch for those kids who show a
marked bent for the macabre and the sinister, and they invite
them to a "real good" party being held elsewhere, which
proves to be a lower-level ritual held for the purpose of initiating these kids into Satanism.

I know that many of you reading these words will find all
this beyond belief. Many of you will find it impossible to
accept the fact that human beings could be capable of such
deliberate and unspeakable horrors. Yet it is true. It actually
happens, and not just in California, where the demented and
criminally insane are *expected* to reside, but in virtually every
state and major community in this country. These people are
not insane in the classical sense of the word. They are committed worshipers of the one who has been called a murderer
from the beginning.[23]

Imitators of God

So . . . should your family participate in the traditional
Halloween celebrations? Absolutely . . . *if* you and/or your
children are Witches, Satanists, Humanists, atheists, or anything other than born-again Christians (or Orthodox Jews).
For a true Christian to participate in the ancient trappings of
Halloween is as incongruous as for a committed cult Satanist
coming from a blood sacrifice on Christmas Eve to set up a
crèche in his living room and sing "Silent Night, Holy Night"
with heartfelt, sincere devotion to Baby Jesus.

Ephesians 5:1 admonishes us to "be imitators of God." Can
you picture the Lord Jesus dressing up as Satan, or as one of
the demons He cast out that week, or perhaps as a Druid
priest, just because it was the Feast of Samhain and His
disciples were giving a nifty party that night in honor of the
tradition? Or can you see the apostles disguising themselves
as temple prostitutes or as worshipers of the god Moloch, to
whom the Canaanites (and even the Israelites in their darker
days) sacrificed their children?[24]

Halloween is a day in which virtually everything that God has called *abomination* is glorified.[25] We have no business participating in that at any time, much less in the name of "fun."

"But it's only for one night!" you cry. "It's only in fun for the children!" If this is how you feel, then you need to understand what the Word of God says to you:

> Learn not the way of the heathen! (Jeremiah 10:2 KJV). Do not be bound together with unbelievers; for what partnership have righteousness and lawlessness, or what fellowship has light with darkness? Or what harmony has Christ with Belial, or what has a believer in common with an unbeliever? Or what agreement has the temple of God with idols? For we are the temple of the living God; just as God said, "I will dwell in them and walk among them; and I will be their God, and they shall be My people. Therefore, come out from their midst and be separate," says the Lord. "And do not touch what is unclean" (2 Corinthians 6:14-17 NAS).
>
> ... but I say that the things which the Gentiles sacrifice, they sacrifice to demons and not to God; and I do not want you to become sharers in demons. You cannot drink the cup of the Lord and the cup of demons; you cannot partake of the table of the Lord and the table of demons (1 Corinthians 10:20,21).

Creative Alternatives

There are any number of creative alternatives that can be provided for children on Halloween without participating in the ancient religious traditions of the Witches and Satanists.

I've heard Mike Warnke suggest that parents and churches hold costume parties and have the kids come as Bible heroes. (And don't just make it "Bible characters" in general. After all, Satan, Baal, Belial, Beelzebul and Moloch are mentioned in there!) Some groups have set up bowling or ice-skating parties.

Some families view the occasion as a witnessing opportunity, and hand out gospel tracts along with the treats. Some
churches are now sponsoring "Bible Houses," in which the
kids go through and hear different Bible stories read or acted
out—a godly alternative to the haunted-house routine!

Other Christian families choose to spend the night remem-
bering the saints who have gone to be with the Lord during
the year. Saints aren't just those who have been canonized as
such by some church. A saint, according to the Bible, is *anyone*
who has believed in the Lord Jesus Christ as his personal
Messiah. Perhaps you could spend this night talking about
the martyrs who were willing to die rather than compromise
their belief in the Lord Jesus Christ.

Christian parents can also make a difference in the way the
schools which their children attend celebrate Halloween. *The
Eagle's Forum* of Fall 1987 reported a story about parents in
Colorado who have protested the traditional celebration of
Halloween in several public schools, including at least one
elementary school, on the grounds that it is a "high holy day
in the satanic religion, and as such is an inappropriate holiday
for schoolchildren."[26] One mother said that she "would like
to see the same measures applied to the Halloween parties as
have been taken with the Christmas parties."[27] In light of the
present distress, I fully agree. Since God and Jesus have been
banned from Christmas and Easter and Thanksgiving celebrations in most of our schools, why should the Witches and
Satanists get free promotion on Halloween from those same
institutions?

One thing that Halloween should *not* be for the Christian is
a time of fear. It should be a time to rejoice in the fact that "the
Son of God appeared for this purpose, that He might destroy
the works of the devil" (1 John 3:8)! Spend at least part of this
night worshiping God by singing hymns. Above all, spend
time in prayer and intercession for the children.

It is tragic that many people in the church have forgotten
that "God has not given us a spirit of fear, but of power and of
love and of a sound mind" (from 2 Timothy 1:7 KJV), and that
includes on Halloween! Too many of our children have been

made vulnerable to a spirit of fear and to the occult because we have for so long believed Halloween to be an innocent season of fun.

However, after the repeal of the Witchcraft Act in England in 1951, the Witches and Satanists experienced a revival which is currently in full swing. You might not know too much about Witches or Satanists or "Jason" or Freddie Krueger, but I guarantee you that most of your kids do!

> You were formerly darkness, but now you are light in the Lord; walk as children of light . . . and do not participate in the unfruitful deeds of darkness, but instead even expose them (Ephesians 5:8,11).

Chapter 12

The Season of the Witch

✦

The children gather wood, and the fathers kindle the fire, and the women knead dough to make cakes for the queen of heaven; and they pour out drink offerings to other gods in order to spite Me. "Do they spite Me?" declares the Lord. "Is it not themselves they spite, to their own shame?"
—Jeremiah 7:18,19

Halloween isn't the only time our kids are exposed to Witchcraft in their schools. Witches know that many children find Witchcraft irresistibly fascinating. In fact, in researching this section over the last two years, it is intriguing to note how many of the most influential Witches of today, not to mention your average, everyday run-of-the-mill Witches, were drawn to Witchcraft as children. As the well-known feminist Witch Starhawk observed in an interview, "an increasing number of children, attracted by the ceremonial dances, chants and bonfires, are becoming involved with Witchcraft."[1] She herself was first attracted to the occult when she was 16, and decided to become a Witch after doing a research paper for an anthropology class at UCLA.[2]

While publicly denying that they are actively out proselytizing young children, the Witches' own material indicates quite the opposite. A memo from a coven in Southern California dated October 12, 1983, and labeled "from the desk of Diana" reads as follows:

Greetings—Brothers and Sisters in Witchcraft

This is just a short report to all of you regarding our summer activities. We have had 632 children from ages 5-12 in our summer youth program. Remember—Each One Reach One. Our winter program will have twice the number as the schools that participate in religious release time for their areas must let the children who choose the Pagan way also be allowed educational time under the law.

It is fascinating to observe how some Witches handle the "we do *not* proselytize children" issue while doing precisely that!

Witch Gundella

In October of 1985, Plymouth, Michigan, became embroiled in a major flap over the scheduled appearance of Marion Kucio, also known as the Witch Gundella, at a local high school. The school librarian had arranged Gundella's visit as part of a regular speakers series. Despite heated protests from Christian parents, the school board was advised by legal counsel that it would be unconstitutional to cancel the Witch's lecture. You see, she was not going to "attempt to indoctrinate the students in the virtues of Witchcraft," the school's lawyer argued. He found on the basis of other presentations she had made that there was "insufficient basis for interfering with the students' right to receive the information she will impart."[3] After all, she only "sought to debunk myths and legends which surround Witches and explain how certain terms historically came to be associated with Witchcraft," according to one reporter.[4] "She's not here to persuade anyone to be anything or do anything," said Dave Seemann in his introduction of Gundella. "She's here to provide information about Witchcraft."[5] And so Gundella, promoted by local newspapers as a "wonderful...kewpie doll of a woman" spoke to an auditorium full of schoolchildren, while two dozen angry parents picketed outside. Here is a little of what she taught the kids:

"A Witch is a person, a human being," she said.
"The main belief of Witchcraft is we are all one. We
all come from a divine intelligence, a divine power.
I believe all people are worshipping some god
who people call what they were taught. One thing
we believe is reincarnation—evolution of the soul
through many lives," Gundella continued. "We
believe evil is not the opposite of good but the lack
of perfection." Gundella said she couldn't believe
that a loving God would damn anyone on the basis
of actions during one life-time so much affected by
the circumstances of birth. "Reincarnation is mentioned in both the Old and New Testaments," she
maintained. "We are one with every religion on
earth and so are you."[6]

To me, this comes across as pretty efficient proselytizing.
Furthermore, the "facts" she presented about Christianity
and the Bible were not facts at all, but the usual Gnostic lies
and half-truths peddled by occultists everywhere. One would
have hoped that the educators in charge of that district would
have been at least as concerned to have the truth about the
Bible presented as they evidently were in exposing children to
"the truth about Witchcraft." But to my knowledge, none of
them stood up after Gundella's presentation to say "Wait a
minute!" If Witches are going to be allowed to tell our children
what the Bible teaches, never mind what Witchcraft believes,
they should at least do so accurately.

Gundella did her job well. Most of the students interviewed
after her 50-minute presentation had very favorable reactions
to what she taught, and they wondered in retrospect what on
earth all the fuss had been about. Scott McDonnell, a Canton
junior, described those who wanted to muzzle Gundella as a
"bunch of jerks."

"She isn't hurting anyone," he said. "She changed
my views on a few things about Witches and God."

"It taught me witches weren't what I thought they were like on TV," said Rob Franchek, a Canton sophomore.[7]

The *New Webster's Dictionary* defines a "proselyte" as "*one who has changed from one opinion, religious belief, sect, or the like to another; a convert.*" Despite protestations from the school's library director that "Gundella's talk was essentially informational" and that "no efforts were made to convert students," it would seem that proselytizing is *precisely* what happened to at least some of those listening to her.

A Witch doesn't have to show up with a pagan version of the "UNCLE SAM WANTS YOU" speech in order to qualify as an effective recruiter.[8]

Bewitching Assignments

Certain educators and publishers have also figured out that children find Witchcraft and the occult very fascinating, so they have developed programs for the schools based on occult themes. Evidently many educators seem to think that it is necessary to introduce our children to occult religion in order to teach them to read, write, and think creatively. Here are a few examples among many that could be given.

• Sixth-graders in Orange County, Florida, practiced "Creative Writing" by using "A Witch's Manual," an eight-page workbook. The children learned, among other things, that "most Witches have a familiar—an imp that has taken the form of a cat." Then they wrote out a list of ingredients that every good Witch should keep in her kitchen in order to cast a spell.[9]

• In Tracy, California, sixth-graders improve their spelling, handwriting, and language skills through use of a "simulation game" called "Wizards." In the process they also learn that "enchanters . . . have Witchcraft powers," "sorcerers . . . have the ability to read very old and secret scrolls," "magicians are noted for their skill and magic . . . and are somewhat shy and are cute and cuddly," and that "wizards are the highest level you can achieve. With the supreme power of the 'good guys,' they can ward off Gotmes, Orcs, and Snakes. Wizards can cast the Spell of Exchange and are extremely intelligent, agile, and handsome." (What sixth-grader could possibly resist wanting to be a wizard?)

• An angry mother in Carlsbad, California, couldn't believe her eyes when she looked through the "Reading Comprehension" worksheets that her little fourth-grade daughter was bringing home. The material was from *The Fantastic Mystery Stories*, which carries a series for grade levels three through six. After much effort, she finally obtained a copy of the book used for the sixth grade at a teacher's supply store. The back of the book, which she sent to me, advertises the series as "Intriguing tales of bizarre occurrences and startling speculations. Did astronauts from another planet visit earth in ancient times? Can mind power actually bend metal objects? Do vampires and werewolves really exist? Will we ever know the truth about UFO's and Bigfoot?"

In a note to the teacher, the editors of the Series do say that "it is not our intent to persuade students that these stories are true or that any of the theories suggested in them are valid. To that end, the following statement appears on each page: *Some parts of this mystery story may not be true.* A brief discussion of the word 'mystery' will help students understand that while some people explain certain phenomena one way, others may have an entirely different point of view."

• Children at Wilmot Elementary School in Evergreen, Colorado, got to fill in a "Witch License Application" after reading a cute little article called "Which Witch From Ipswich" which gave the children an overview of Witchcraft around the world. It informed them about the meaning of the word "witch," discussed various methods for casting spells, and observed that "Witches have not all been associated with evil" and that "belief in Witchcraft still exists in some form among some societies in many parts of the world." Then followed a short discussion on various fortune-reading methods traditionally used by Witches. Finally came the punch line:

Suppose that you wanted to pursue a career as a Witch. These days you might have to apply for a license and perhaps even join a Witches' union. In any case, by filling out an application your aptitude for Witchcraft could be evaluated.

The Witch License Application that the kids then got to fill out must be the ultimate in "terminal cute," beginning with the supposed return mailing address:

National Association of Witches (NAW)

(A Subsidiary of Sonic Brooms)

131313 Hades Highway

Satan's Corner, Lower Depths 02158

The questions to be answered included "Professional name: (do not give real name). State why you wish to be a Witch; what animal impersonation do you prefer, and why. What words would you use to cast a spell? (All incantations must be original.) and last, but not least, as a test of your ability to cast out spells, tell how you would handle the following problems: #1 A chicken that is normally cheerful and friendly takes to sulking in a corner of the henhouse. And #2 A certain supermarket reports that all of its shopping carts seem to have trouble going in the right direction. A push forward sends them crashing sideways into the pickles."

Assignments like these may seem thoroughly innocent and innocuous on the surface. Nevertheless, what they have succeeded in doing is to arouse a child's curiosity about the mysterious and the supernatural. They have made Witchcraft and the occult seem like exciting, innocent fun, and have thereby helped desensitize the child to the very real dangers inherent in occultism. They have familiarized children with the terminology of the occult and have even encouraged the child to experiment with developing occult powers for himself.

Witch Book Did You Say?

In the last few years, school libraries have been deluged with new books and stories about how wonderful, charming, exciting, delightful, loving, and friendly Witches are. For really little kids, a teacher could walk into just about any teacher's supply store and purchase a copy of *Magic & Make-Believe*, by Imogene Forte, part of the *Tabletop Learning Series*. The first page has a darling drawing of a little girl Witch in her ceremonial robes working a spell over a cauldron while two adorable kitties look on. The children can learn to dress up as a wizard, practice mental magic, summon a genie, read a crystal ball, make their own Ouija board ("Do you think the spirits move the message indicator? If not, who does?"), or learn to worship and "shout praises to the Goddess of the Forest."[10] [See Appendix D: "The Queen of Heaven."]

"Pretending and make-believe are marvelous learning tools, and the appeal of magic is irresistible to children of all ages." So reads part of the promotional copy on the back of the book. And they are right. The perennial question, of course, is *just what is it that the children are learning?* A quick glance through the book should make the answer to that crystal clear.

Scholastic Inc. is one of the most well-respected publishers of children's books. According to several teachers who have long used their material, the selection of books which they publish has become increasingly geared toward Witchcraft and the occult in recent years. Their series by Norman Bridwell is especially insidious: *The Witches' Vacation* ("Camp can be a lot of fun with the Witch next door around"), *The Witch Grows Up* ("How did the Witch next door grow up? Just like you and me! Well, almost . . ."), and *The Witch Next Door* ("Meet the wonderful Witch who lives next door. She's a great neighbor. Everything she does will surprise you.").

Wiccans seem to be very fond of Mr. Bridwell's children's books. At least Raymond Buckland is. In his Witchcraft training manual entitled *Buckland's Complete Book of Witchcraft*, he recommends them as being among books for children "that do treat the Craft in a positive light."[11]

Ruth Chew has written a number of books for children with occult themes. Her book *What the Witch Left* was recommended by Children's Book Review with this enthusiastic promotion: "Inquisitive girls in the third and fourth grade will enjoy this easy-to-read story." It was the *Publisher's Weekly* endorsement, however, that was most revealing: *"Engaging . . . a believable fantasy about non-dangerous supernatural powers and the fun they bring to judicious young users."*[12]

Nondangerous supernatural powers? Judicious young users? *There is no such thing as nondangerous occultic supernatural powers.* Children are being encouraged to experiment and play with things that God has repeatedly and thoroughly condemned in both the Old and the New Testaments, not because the phenomena are not real but rather because they are produced by demons determined to lead you into worship of other gods and ultimate destruction (Deuteronomy 13:1ff.).

The Bible repeatedly warns against becoming involved with the occult on any level, identifying only two possible sources of genuine spiritual phenomena: God, who can indeed choose to bear witness to the truth of His Word and the testimony of Jesus through signs and wonders and various miracles (Hebrews 2:4), and what the Bible identifies as "spirits of demons working signs" for the purpose of deceiving the whole world (Revelation 16:14; cf. 13:14).

In spite of these clear admonitions regarding supernatural power, some parents or teachers might still say, "So a kid reads a book or does an assignment and then pretends he or she's a Witch. Big deal! After all, everyone *knows* that there's no such thing as Witchcraft! It's the stuff that fairy tales and cartoons are made of—nothing more." Nothing could be further from the truth, as we shall see.

What Is Witchcraft, Anyway?

For thousands of years Witches have been the objects of heated controversy. Belief in Witches and their supernatural powers is a universal phenomenon, ranging from the primitive societies of Africa, Australia, and North America to the civilized and sophisticated ancient Greeks and Romans. Some societies respected Witches as healers and priestesses. Other societies have viewed them as traffickers in demons, workers of ancient evil, cannibals, and killers of children, and have held them responsible for every and any misfortune befalling the community.

That view certainly held sway in Europe during the horrifying centuries when the practice of Witchcraft was a crime punishable by torture and death. Anti-Witchcraft laws were enacted in various parts of Europe as early as the twelfth century, but it was during the fifteenth through the seventeenth centuries that the Witch-hunt hysteria reached its peak. The least hint or suspicion of Witchcraft in their midst was sufficient to drive entire communities to a murderous frenzy. Estimates of the numbers killed during this unquestionably hideous period, known among Witches today as "the Burning Times," range from tens of thousands to nine million, depending on whether you hear it from conservative scholars or Witches. No one really knows for certain, but the number is probably closer to 100,000.

In 1951, a vaguely embarrassed England decided that it was time to settle the Witchcraft issue once and for all: "British Make It Official; Witches No Longer Exist." So read a headline on the front page of the *New York Times* on April 21, 1951.

Far from being dismayed at being declared officially defunct, Britain's Witches heaved an enormous sigh of relief that the days of officially sanctioned persecution were over. The persecutions and anti-Witchcraft laws had succeeded in driving its practitioners underground, and it seems there were still a surprising number of them passing on their ancient beliefs and practices as family heirlooms from generation to generation.

The last Witch trial in England took place in 1712, and 1727 saw the last official burning in Scotland.[13] However, until the Witchcraft Act was formally repealed in 1951, there was still a chance in Britain that "devil dealing persons... who practiced Witchery and the invoking of evil and wicked spirits"[14] could wind up spending a year in jail. This was better than being hanged or burned at the stake, but still small comfort to the average Witch! As the *New York Times* reported, the "chief purpose of the new bill, introduced by a Methodist member, Walter Monslow, is to allow Britain's 50,000 active Spiritualists to meet without fear of arrest." That may indeed have been the bill's primary intent, but as an intriguing sideline it helped open the door to an unprecedented resurgence of Witchcraft in the Western world.

Some Witches will tell you that the word "Witch" (which they insist be capitalized—even as one would capitalize the word "Christian" or "Jew") comes from the Old English word "Wita" or "Wicca," which means "wise one." Witchcraft, therefore would mean "Craft of the Wise." Others will assert that the word "wicce" derives from the Indo-European roots "wic," or "weik," meaning "to bend or turn or twist." "Thus a Witch would be a woman (or man) skilled in the craft of shaping, bending, and changing reality," says Margot Adler in her 595-page volume on the subject. Or as Starhawk, another well-known feminist Witch would put it, Witches are "those who could shape the unseen to their will."[15]

Very simply, to an ever growing number of very sincere and committed people, Witchcraft is a religion. It is recognized by the government of the United States as such, and many covens hold tax-exempt status. Their priestesses and priests are licensed in many states and allowed to conduct legally recognized marriages and other functions of the ministry. The manual handed out to chaplains in the Armed Services includes a section on the religion of Wicca.

How many Witches are there today? No one knows for sure. Witches, or Wiccans, still tend for the most part to be highly secretive. Margot Adler, in an article for the *Washington Times*, "believes there are 50,000 to 100,000 active Neo-Pagans or members of Wicca in the United States."[16] They are part of the current revival of paganism, a movement which embraces other nature religions, such as Santeria, Voddoun, Shamanism, Druidism, Hinduism, and even Satanism.

Mirror, Mirror, on the Wall...

Despite their growing popularity, Witches are still plagued by the ancient stereotype which equates them with Satanists and baby-killers. [See Appendix E: "Sharers in Demons" and Appendix F: "What Witches Believe."] Say the word "Witch" and the majority of us instantly conjure up an image of an ancient, hideous, wart-ridden, devil-worshiping hag bent over an enormous Shakespearean cauldron mumbling something like "Bubble, bubble, toil and trouble. . . ." This is a medieval stereotype that drives today's Witches absolutely frantic, and a growing number of them have decided to correct the misconceptions. Recent interviews with Witches printed in publications across the country carry headlines such as these:

WITCHCRAFT—
Modern Witch tries to dispel spooky myths.[17]

THE WITCHES AMONG US—
Local practitioners say they're not crazy
or dangerous, and that the Craft is a religion
that's just like any other.[18]

WITCHES BATTLE BAD PRESS
BY GOING PUBLIC TO TIDY IMAGE[19]

Even Ann Landers got her hand slapped for having referred to some evidently unpleasant woman as "a four-door, brass-plated Witch," the implication being that Witches are by definition unsavory individuals at best.

"I am one of more than 150,000 Witches in this country," the offended Witch told Ann Landers. "Genuine Witchcraft does not embrace the concept of Satan, let alone the worship of it, yet Witches are constantly being slandered and viewed as evil."[20]

Nevertheless, as Dave Hunt and Tom McMahon point out in their fascinating book *America: The Sorcerer's New Apprentice*:

> . . . in spite of variations in the rituals, from the Satanists on one end of the Witchcraft spectrum to the practitioners of "white magic" on the other, the underlying belief remains the same: *It is all nature*

religion. All of the rituals share a common purpose: to invoke and/or manipulate a natural force innate within the cosmos in order to achieve health, wealth, or success, or to bring a curse upon one's enemies. Whether the "power" believed in is called Satan or the goddess does not affect the basic philosophy.[21]

So What's It Doing in the Schools?

It should not be surprising to find that school districts will be among the very last to recognize Witchcraft as a religion. After all, if they do, they will be forced to either a) dispense with many volumes of teacher's manuals, readers, assignment sheets, and various other assorted materials that promote Witchcraft, or else b) give other religions equal time in the program. Neither alternative is to the liking of your average school board, so what you are likely to encounter is a denial of the current status of Witchcraft in modern society.

I watched with horrified fascination as the superintendent of the Long Beach Unified School District informed parents at a hearing that he wasn't at all sure that Witchcraft (or for that matter Humanism, he added) was an actual religion on any level. "We have not seen any objective evidence or conclusive proof that would bring us to this point," he remarked. This position would not have been surprising were it not for the fact that I had just spent the better part of an hour presenting to him a voluminous amount of material on the true nature of Witchcraft. I would be most interested to know just what *would* be considered "objective evidence" by this school district!

The hearing was being held in response to a protest by some of the parents to two books on film that were being promoted by filmstrips for fifth- and sixth-graders. One of the books being promoted was called *The Headless Cupid*, a Newbery Award winner written by Zilpha Keatley Snyder.

The story is about a twelve-year-old girl named Amanda whose divorced mother marries a widower with four children. Amanda considers herself a Witch and arrives at her new home in her ceremonial robes, her hair in ceremonial braids, and a pink triangle painted on her forehead which she refers to as her "center of power," a concept her 11-year-old stepbrother David finds most intriguing. Amanda also has her familiar with her in the form of an ill-tempered crow. She also keeps a snake and a horny toad. "A Familiar," she explains, "is something that looks like an animal or bird, but really what it is, is a spirit. It's a spirit that lives with an occult person and is her contact with the world of the supernatural."[20] She also has a large box of occult books with her, another source of fascination to her new stepbrother:

> "You sure have a lot of books," David said.
>
> "I know," Amanda said. "Most of the ones in that box are a part of my supernatural library. You know—about black magic, spiritualism, astrology, witchcraft and stuff like that."
>
> "Wow!" David said. Taking out some books . . . he started having the good, slightly excited feeling that a library always gave him. Magic had always been one of his special interests, and he'd read lots of books on the subject, but he'd never seen most of the books in Amanda's box. The first two he picked up were called *Haunted Houses* and *Modern Witchcraft*.

Amanda capitalizes on her stepfamily's fascination with the occult to lead them into a series of nine "ordeals" as part of their initiation into Witchcraft. She also conducts a seance during which all kinds of supposed poltergeist manifestations occur. Later in the book we discover that Amanda staged most of these manifestations" herself in order to get back at everybody because of her broken family situation. And yet the book ends on a decidedly eerie note when the youngest member of the family indicates that it was the ghost of a long-dead little girl who revealed the secret hiding place of the head that belonged to a carved wooden cupid at the head of the stairs.[22]

Harmless Fiction?

The school district argued that *The Headless Cupid* did not promote the occult at all because it was fiction. One of several lengthy memorandums from the Long Beach School District's legal advisers stated that—

> Fictional material which is presented to young viewers is not persuasive in the same manner that nonfictional material is since the viewer is, throughout the viewing, aware that the material is fictional. . . . Because the student knows he is reading for entertainment, he is *not persuaded*.
>
> . . . The viewing of the filmstrip neither advances nor inhibits religion because, assuming for the sake of discussion that the material . . . concerns a "religion" for First Amendment purposes, the subject is presented in a *neutral* manner.[23]

The above arguments are patently ridiculous, and I suspect that the majority of the Witches and occultists who became involved in the occult as children through a fascination with myths and works of fiction that dealt with occult themes would agree with me on this one. Fiction, myths, parables, television shows, cartoons, and toys are indeed powerful means of teaching principles and molding worldviews.

Nevertheless, despite months of protests and volumes of correspondence and memorandums from the Christian Civil Liberties Union and others, the Long Beach District decided that the books and their promotional filmstrips violated no law and therefore stayed. They did agree to allow parents to remove their children if they wished during viewing of these materials, and suggested the possibility of labeling the material "To be used with discretion."

As the courageous mother who initiated the action against the district pointed out, however:

> Exactly what do you mean "to be used with discretion"? How does one teach Witchcraft with

discretion? Are there teacher training courses that teach your employees how to teach Witchcraft and the occult with "discretion"? Would you also like to teach Christianity "with discretion"?

How can material which definitely gives the young reader the impression that the occult, Witchcraft, and contact with spirits of the dead are real—*as indeed they are*—be protected and allowed to remain in the classroom as required reading?

Why are we treated by the ACLU to such deafening silence when fifth-graders in Palo Alto and Oceanside, California, are given assignments like the following exercise taken from a teacher's "Bookmate" for the book *Jennifer, Hecate, Macbeth, William McKinley and Me, Elizabeth*, by E.L. Konigsburg:

ONE STEP FURTHER

1. Pretend you are a Witch. Make a list of ten steps necessary to become a Witch. Try to follow the steps yourself to see if you really could become a Witch.

2. Jennifer and Elizabeth prepared a formula for flying ointment. Write your own magical recipe for flying ointment. Be sure to have at least thirteen ingredients.

3. While an apprentice Witch, Elizabeth had to eat or avoid certain foods for a week. Make a list of forbidden foods. Try to avoid these foods for a week.

4. Act out a ceremony for apprentice Witches. Ask a friend to be Elizabeth, and you be Jennifer.

Suppose the above exercise had read "Pretend you are a Christian. Write down the one thing you need to become a true born-again Christian. Try to pray to God yourself in the name of His Son, Jesus Christ, to see if you really could become a Christian." I submit to you that the ACLU would have squashed the district flatter than a pancake!

Just Who Got Censored?

Censorship is a fascinating word indeed. When school districts, librarians, and teachers weed through the massive piles of books and materials available to them, not one shrill cry of that dread epithet "Censorship!" is to be heard among them when one set of books is chosen above another. No, when they decide what books to include and which to leave out (i.e., preemptive censorship) it is called "the selection process." Nevertheless, should a Christian parent or a student rise up and challenge the infinite wisdom of their "selection process," suggesting that perhaps their "selection" was less than unbiased, the cry of "Censor!" bellows forth like molten lava spewing from an erupting volcano.

The NEA is positively paranoid about challenges to their "selection process" of library books and school texts, and they are doing their level best to prepare their teachers and school librarians to deal with the situation by producing training videos with accompanying manuals with titles such as "Far Right Attacks On The NEA." The National Council of Teachers of English published a volume entitled *Dealing With Censorship in 1979*, edited by James E. Davis, which includes six chapters instructing teachers on "What To Do" if anyone tries to "censor" any of their "selections." Teachers' catalogs such as one called *Paperbacks for Young Readers K-10*, 1985-1986 ARCHWAY WANDER POCKET BOOKS publication warns teachers on the front page that:

> Increasing numbers of schools and libraries are becoming involved in community review or censorship of educational materials.

They then offer advice on setting up anticensorship tactics and provide a handy list of agencies dedicated to fighting censorship. It includes the ACLU, the National Council of Teachers of English, the Office for Intellectual Freedom, the National Ad Hoc Committee Against Censorship, the Association of American Publishers, and Media Coalition, Inc. Let's face it: Any parent protesting materials in his child's school is up against some pretty big guns! Incidentally, when you read through the table of contents of the above-mentioned Archway Catalog, you suddenly understand why they're preparing for battle: One of their major categories is entitled "Supernatural and the Occult."

Let me give you a sample of the level of the hypocrisy we are dealing with here. In Boise, Idaho, school officials allowed Bibles to be distributed to "the *entire* fifth grade." One of the men distributing the books told the students, "If you abide by this Bible, you will grow to be a better person." However, the mother of one of the boys was outraged, contending that her son's civil rights had been violated. The American Civil Liberties Union filed suit in the U.S. District Court in Pocatello. The ACLU's regional counsel in Denver, Steven Pevar, had this to say about the incident:

> We don't want our public schools to be conduits for religious indoctrination. . . . When parents send their children to school, it's not with the idea that some teacher will indoctrinate their child with religious teachings of the teacher.[24]

When you've recovered from the absurdity of that one, read on.

Censorship or Protection?

In 1985 a high school student named Robert Thomas walked into his school library and was horrified to discover that there were about 25 how-to books on Satanism, Witchcraft, voodoo, and general occultism. His dismay was well-founded in light of the fact that there had been a well-publicized rash of grave robberies and church vandalisms in the Oceanside area. Several years earlier there had been some horrifying animal mutilations right on the school campus. Satanic graffiti was prevalent. Robert knew for a fact that several of the kids he knew on campus were becoming deeply involved in Witchcraft and Satanism. So, when he discovered books in the school library that gave step-by-step instructions for animal mutilations and satanic rituals and realized that those books had been used by some of the kids on campus to learn how to practice Satanism, he decided it was up to him to do something. He and two other friends went to the school authorities to request that the books be removed from the shelves, or at least be put on restricted access so that the kids could check them out only with parental permission. The books had been purchased about ten years before for a class on Myths and Legends no longer taught at the school.

Robert told me in a phone interview how shocked he and his two friends (by then dubbed the "God Squad") were at the reaction to their request. The key word: *Censorship!*

Robert replied to the accusation of censorship in an article in one of the local papers:

> If you take the car keys from a 10-year-old who wants to go driving, that is not censoring the child from driving but guiding the child. And if you removed books which teach children to kill and diminish away what morals the child has, books which in the past and if they remain on the shelves will certainly in the future be misused in this fashion, this is not censorship but guidance.

This young man, only 17 at the time of this writing, pointed out that "they term their requests not censorship but protection."[25] Robert showed more solid common sense than all the lawyers, educators, and critics-at-large he was dealing with.

Children under 17 are not admitted to movies rated "R" or "X" in this country. They are not allowed to buy liquor or go to bars. They are not allowed to purchase handguns or pornographic magazines. Who among us will raise the issue of their "rights" or of "censorship" concerning these things! Young people *by definition* are in need of guidance and training. *By definition* they need protection from certain materials, information, and experiences which they simply are not mature enough, or at least not old enough, to handle.

What the ACLU, People for the American Way, and others of their ilk have routinely labeled "censorship" some of us call "responsible parenting." As Shari Thomas, Robert's mother, said in a speech to the Oceanside School Board on September 9, 1986:

> No sane person would give a five-year-old a hand grenade, the keys to the family car, or open access to Satanist training manuals in the El Camino Library. To encourage or allow these young people in their immaturity to read all books regardless of content is to hand them mental and emotional explosives they are unequipped to handle.

And yet that is precisely the right which the ACLU demands for the children of this country. In his letter to the Oceanside Unified School District, ACLU's volunteer attorney Robert R. DeKoven stated that "to remove the occult books would be unconstitutional."

Even though he admitted that he had not personally read any of the books in question, he was quite certain that because they were already in the library they were therefore obviously not "pervasively vulgar . . . obscene . . . or educationally unsuitable." He reminded the District that ". . . school boards cannot in exercise of their broad discretion 'strangle the free mind' and limit youth in acquiring important information."

Since when has learning how to conduct a satanic ritual, renounce Christianity, and perform blood sacrifices been considered "important information" for our children!

Greg Marshall, legal director for the ACLU's San Diego chapter, had this to say on the subject of removing or even restricting the occult books:

> . . . The issue is relatively clear-cut, because the First Amendment requires toleration of written and oral information even if one disagrees with the message.[26]

Read this statement again, slowly. Now go back and read what the ACLU had to say about "toleration" when Bibles were given as a free gift to fifth-graders in Boise! What you have is a classic example of self-serving hypocrisy. I like the way young Robert Thomas put it:

> And to the ACLU . . . we must not forget the largest atheist, double-standard organization in this country. This illustrious organization says that it is illegal to ban books of any kind for any reason as this is a violation of the student's civil rights and they (the ACLU) will sue. If this is so, maybe a civil suit ought to be filed against the ACLU for violating the Christian student's rights in banning books on creation.[27]

In light of the unquestionable fact that Witchcraft is a religion, and in light of the fact that Witches are increasingly vocal in asserting that fact, and in light of the fact that the ACLU has a prominent history of righteous indignation on the issue of "religion in the schools," we might reasonably wonder why Witchcraft is regularly presented to our children in the public schools. It's a good question, and more parents across the country should start asking it.

Chapter 13

Nothing to Toy With

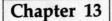

> Imitation is natural to man from childhood . . . he is
> the most imitative creature in the world, and learns
> at first by imitation.[1]
> —Aristotle

> Train up a child in the way he should go, and when
> he is old he will not depart from it.
> —Proverbs 22:6 (KJV)

The ancient demon gods still live. The hideous hybrid monsters worshiped by the ancient Babylonians, Sumerians, Egyptians, and Chinese still walk among us. The gods and goddesses of the Greeks and Romans still rule. The ancient magical symbols, tools, beliefs, and rites hold sway among us yet, absorbed and learned and practiced by eager young apprentices—not in the halls of marbled temples, or in sacred groves, or in a sorcerer's dungeon, but in local movie theaters and living rooms of homes around the country.

From four to seven hours a day, day after day, year after year, our little ones sit transfixed before the phosphorescent altar of their gods, eagerly soaking into the very depths of their beings the lessons and images of violence, occultism, sex, death, and hedonism so powerfully presented to them. According to the Nielsen Television Index, American children between the ages of two and seventeen spend about 27 to 31 hours a week watching TV.[2] Not surprisingly, it's the preschoolers who spend the most time of all glued to the screen.[3] Tragically, television has become the prime educator and the gratuitous nanny in many American homes. By the time the average American child reaches the age of 18, he will have logged from 15 to 22 *thousand* hours of television. That works out to a staggering equivalent of ten years of 40-hour weeks![4] Those figures are pretty sobering, especially when you consider that the average child spends only about 11,000 hours in school and a scant couple of hundred hours *at best* in Sunday school!

What on earth is a child learning during those hours? More to the point, does it really matter? After all, aren't children's cartoons and other TV shows (not to mention movies, toys, comic books, and fantasy role-playing games) just an important and harmless form of play? To suggest that there is something sinister about watching the Smurfs and He-Man and playing with adorable rainbow-colored unicorns is definitely to risk losing one's credibility with many parents and others who simply cannot see anything wrong with them, and who in fact may view them as important developmental tools in a child's life.

And yet it is a fact that many of today's cartoons and toys are saturated not only with violence, but with hard-core occultism, some of it obvious and some of it subtle, but all of it powerful in its potential impact on vulnerable children. At first glance, cartoons and toys like the Care Bears, Rainbow Brite, My Little Pony 'N Friends, and the Smurfs may seem innocuous enough. And yet the themes that characterize these and hundreds of other cartoons and toys like them are nothing but basic child-level introductions to New Age/occultic symbols and principles. Preschoolers may not understand this, but in the hundreds of generally unsupervised hours spent watching these cartoons and playing with toys based on them, children become increasingly familiar and fascinated with the symbols and basic New Age/occultic concepts that they will most certainly encounter as they grow older.

New Agers won't have a difficult time at all explaining to these children the profoundly occult concept of building the Rainbow Bridge (called the *Antahkarana*) between man and the "over soul" who is Lucifer,[5] because these children already know that rainbows are the bridge on which they travel to reach Rainbow Brite, who "has the power of the rainbow to make you happy!" A lot of children won't have a hard time at all accepting the occult belief in the power of crystals, because for years they watched the little dream fairies on "My Little Pony 'N Friends" use crystals to gain power over the evil Night Mare.[6] They will be familiar with the concepts of ESP, because when He-Man suddenly realized he could hear a creature's thoughts, he understood that the creature was talking with his mind. "It's called telepathy," he explained to the millions of children watching.[7] Little girls won't have any problem at all accepting the concept of the Mother Goddess or that they themselves can become goddesses, because for years they lived the fantasy of Wonder Woman and of She-Ra, Princess of Power.

The Role of the Imagination

Famed child psychologist, fairy-tale advocate, and author Bruno Bettelheim has pointed out in his book *The Uses Of Enchantment* that fairy tales, myths, and religious stories have, almost from the beginning of man's history, played a crucial part in the development of a child's intellectual life.[8] They stimulated his imagination and nourished his fantasizing. And, Bettelheim points out, the stories "were a major agent of his socialization. . . . Myths and closely related religious legends offered material from which children formed their concepts of the world's origin and purpose, and of the social ideals a child could pattern himself after."[9]

In other words, the stories a child heard from the time he was an infant helped mold and develop his worldview. They helped him formulate the very basic framework for his belief about the nature of God and reality. They helped him deal with the perennial question of "Who am I?" and sort out how he was expected to behave toward other people. Dr. Bettelheim believes that fairy tales must play that same important role in a child's life today, and, correctly, points out that "fairy tales provide answers to these pressing questions, many of which the child becomes aware of only as he follows the stories."[10]

The question, of course, is *Just what answers are fairy tales and myths providing today, and are they really the answers you want your kids to believe in?*

There are literally hundreds of occult-based cartoons, movies, videos, and toys out on the market today that we could discuss and analyze, but there would be no point in doing that. [For further reading see *Turmoil in the Toy Box* by Phil Phillips.] New ones are coming out all the time, each with a slightly different occult twist or technique. All I can do here is choose a few and try to point out at least some of the occult principles and symbols with which they're saturating your children. The examples we'll be discussing are by no means the only ones, or even necessarily the worst ones, but they're bad enough!

She-Ra

A few days ago my husband, Randolph, and I were in Toys R Us scouting through the aisles to see what was new. We were also busily scribbling notes about some of the old standby hard-core occult toys and videos that are still selling well. All of a sudden I heard a high-pitched little voice crying "SHE-RA! SHE-RA!" The voice belonged to a beautiful little three-year-old boy who was sitting in a shopping cart. He was holding a gray plastic sword from the She-Ra collection and raising it high in the air, even as She-Ra does in the popular cartoon series of that name. "SHE-RA!" he cried again in obvious delight. "I see he's into She-Ra," I observed to the rather red-faced father standing by the boy. "Does he like to watch her on TV?" "Actually, we don't allow him to watch cartoons at all," the father replied. "But all his little friends in our apartment complex do. He learned about She-Ra from them."

Take She-Ra's name, for starters. *Ra* was the name of the ancient Egyptian sun god, and one of the early names of Mother Goddess,[11] who is worshiped today by thousands of Witches and neopagans. When that little boy in the toy store raised his voice to "SHE-RA!" he was, however innocently, following not only in the footsteps of ancient Egyptian worshipers of the Goddess but in the footsteps of the Goddess worshipers of today. Furthermore, either the writers of "She-Ra" are profoundly knowledgeable of ancient Hermetic lore or else they stumbled upon a remarkable coincidence when they named She-Ra's steed "Spirit." According to the *Book of Lambspring* (1625), a rare Hermetic tract, "the unicorn will be (i.e., represents) the *spirit* at all times...."[12] When the Princess Adora (as in "adore: to worship with profound reverence; to honor or to pay divine honor to; to regard with the utmost devotion, esteem, love, and respect...")[13] raises her sword and cries out "For the honor of Greyskull!" she becomes She-Ra as a serpentine stream of energy swirls around her. She then directs the energy beam from the crystal in her sword toward the crystal embedded in Spirit's head-dress, and Spirit becomes "Swift Wind," a winged unicorn.

Innocent Unicorn?

The myth of the unicorn probably originated in ancient Babylon and spread to numerous civilizations around the world, its form and interpretation varying depending on where it found itself in which century. It has generally been regarded as a symbol of purity, despite the fact that ancient legends ascribe to it some decidedly impure and unvirginal activities. It is seen as a symbol of opposites, rather like the *yin/yang*, a combination and androgynous blending of masculine and feminine, which makes it the perfect symbol for the gay and feminist movement of today. New Agers have, in fact, adopted the unicorn as one of their major symbols, viewing it as "the spark of divine light in the darkness of matter and evil,"[14] and as a symbol of the great world leader whom they expect to bring peace on the earth in the New Age. The Bible identifies this leader as the Antichrist, the little horn that rises in the midst of the ten horns which Daniel saw in his vision (Daniel 7:8).

She-Ra's unicorn also has wings, which makes him a Pegasus. The Pegasus also shows up a lot in "My Little Pony 'N Friends." In Greek mythology the winged horse was "a symbol of the sacred king's or hero's journey to heaven; an image of death . . . like the mythic death-horses of northern Europe."[15]

The winged horse was also a symbol of divine inspiration and immortality, and today it is a popular New Age symbol.

She-Ra does all "for the honor of Greyskull," as does her twin brother, Adam, also known as "He-Man, the Most Powerful Man in the Universe." In one episode, Swift Wind was wounded and dying, but She-Ra cried out, "For the honor of Greyskull, let your wounds be healed!" Her hands were glowing as she laid them on her steed and healed him. A hideous fanged grey skull is an interesting choice of symbols for the wondrous kingdom of Eternia and Etheria that She-Ra and He-Man defend. The skull or death's head "is the emblem of finality, the perpetual reminder of death. . . ."[16] In folk belief, "grey is the color of the dead and of spirits that walk abroad."[17]

Within Castle Greyskull lives the Sorceress, the eagle-hooded winged possessor of great mystical powers "who secretly watches over the heroes of Eternia." In mystical lore the eagle is generally seen as "a symbol of height, of the spirit as the sun, and of the spiritual principle in general."[18]

On occasion She-Ra goes to the Crystal Castle to speak to "Light Hope,"[19] a beam of radiant light that speaks to her in a deep, Godlike voice. Light Hope is always seen emanating from the middle of a large triangle on the ground. Around the triangle is a large circle. In ritual magic, the circle is a symbol of protection or containment. Everything inside the circle is safe and protected from the intrusion of any evil or demonic beings. The circle is an ancient symbol for God, as it is timeless, without beginning or end. For many people in the New Age it also represents the Mother Goddess. The triangle (a representation of the Trinity), when placed within the circle, becomes a Thaumaturgic (magic) Triangle, one of the most powerful occult symbols in ritual magic for the conjuration of demons. But all this is contained within the Crystal Castle, and crystal is a symbol for spirit and purity.[20] The message seems clear enough: To She-Ra, the hope for the world is the "Light" which rises forth from their occultic circle. Most New Agers would readily recognize that "Light" as "Lucifer" the lightbearer, whom they to believe to be the only hope for the salvation of the world. [See Appendix G: "Sympathy for the Devil."] The final punch line comes at the end of every She-Ra program in a memorable little ditty: "For the honor of love, we have the power. So can you."

This isn't "just fantasy." Nor is it simply part of the "magic" of childhood. It is heavy-duty, highly sophisticated religious indoctrination disguised as innocent entertainment! To be sure, the theme of "good" conquering "evil" is continually presented in these cartoons, but only in a dualistic sense. Good can never ultimately destroy evil because to do so would be to destroy the balance that must exist between them. Therefore She-Ra sheds tears of compassion which save the evil Skeletor from certain extinction,[21] and the good wizard Zodac must intervene when Skeletor steals He-Man's Sword of Power to join it with his own. By uniting the two halves of the Power Sword, Skeletor can now unlock the Secrets of the Universe hidden in a vault in the castle . . . but that cannot be allowed! "Skeletor has upset the balance between good and evil" and He-Man must stop him—not to destroy him, but to restore the cosmic balance.[22]

May the Force Be With Who?

Who among us has not seen *Star Wars*, *The Empire Strikes Back*, and *Return of the Jedi*? More than 500 million dollars' worth of us stood in lines for hours to see *Star Wars* since it was first released in 1977. And, in anticipation of the release of *The Empire Strikes Back* three years later, at least one woman sat in line for two whole days to make sure she was the first to get in to see the next episode of the magnificent multimillion-dollar saga that had captured the imagination and heart of the world.

And then on Wednesday, May 25, 1983, *Return of the Jedi* opened.[23] The cosmic battle between the Rebel Alliance and the corrupt and evil Empire raged once again with breathtaking effects. Yoda, the 900-year-old Jedi master, confirmed to Luke Skywalker, the last of the Jedi knights, what for six long years we had all suspected: The sinister, Odin-masked, black-cloaked Darth Vader was indeed Luke's father. A onetime Jedi warrior and follower of the "old religion," he had succumbed to the seductive evil of the sorcerer Emperor, and had turned to the "dark side of the Force," to hate rather than love. Luke would have to confront him and deal with the "dark side" within himself if he were ever to become a full Jedi knight. *Return of the Jedi* broke every box office record in movie history, bringing in over 45 million dollars in the first week alone as over ten million people went to see it.[24]

As spectacularly entertaining and exciting as the trilogy was, George Lucas (according to his biographer, Dale Pollock) was determined to do more with his films than "just entertain."[25] He wanted to create "a modern fairy tale," a "timeless fable" for America and the world. As Lucas said, "I wanted to make a kids' film that would strengthen contemporary mythology and introduce a kind of basic morality. . . . Nobody's saying the very basic things; . . . everybody's forgetting to tell the kids, 'Hey, this is right and this is wrong.' " As Pollock observes, "Lucas was imposing his values on the rest of the world, but he felt they were the *right* values."[26]

Pollock candidly and unequivocally states that "the message of Star Wars *is* religious. . . . *Lucas wanted to instill in children a belief in a supreme being—not a religious god, but a universal deity that he named the Force, a cosmic energy source that incorporates and consumes all living things.*"[27] According to Pollock, Lucas based much of his concept of the Force on the works of author/sorcerer Carlos Castaneda, who wrote about his experiences with a Mexican Indian sorcerer named Don Juan. In *Tales of Power*, Don Juan (whom Lucas used as his model for Ben Kenobi) refers to the "life force."[28] Obi-Wan Kenobi defined the Force as "an energy field . . . it penetrates you and me . . . it's what holds the universe together. . . . When people die, their life spirit is drained from them and incorporated in a huge energy force in the sky."[29]

It is astonishing that so many well-meaning Christians saw in the Star Wars trilogy a "clear message" of the gospel of Jesus Christ. For a while there I even remember seeing bumper stickers that read "May the Force be with you . . . Jesus!" But what George Lucas was succinctly presenting as the god that he hoped millions of people would embrace was not the personal living God of the Bible but rather the abstract, impersonal cosmic energy source long venerated and manipulated by Witches, neopagans, Oriental mystics and philosophers, devotees of the "mind sciences," Spiritualists, occultists, and Transpersonal educators the world over. The Force, quite simply, is basic Witchcraft. [See Appendix H: "God Who?"]

George Lucas told us as much in the first episode. Remember when one of the Empire generals on the Deathstar made the colossal mistake of arrogantly challenging Imperial Warlord Darth Vader, saying "Don't try to frighten us with your sorcerer's ways. Your ancient religion doesn't frighten us! The Jedis are extinct.... You're all that's left of that old religion...." Witches frequently refer to their Craft as "the old religion."

George Lucas succeeded beyond his wildest dreams in his goal to implant the beliefs of that "ancient religion" at the very core of our society. The late Joseph Campbell, New Ager, author, professor, and the acknowledged world authority on mythology, said that he had heard youngsters use some of George Lucas' terms—"The Force" and "the dark side." "... So it must be hitting somewhere.... You see, that movie communicates. It is in a language that talks to young people, and that's what counts.... It's a good sound teaching, I would say."[30] And so it is, for anyone into Oriental mysticism and New Age occultism.

Your Kid The Magician/Warrior

Pollock points out that "the Jedi knights are trained to tap into this collective energy, which gives them the status of magician/warrior."[31] To use the Force was to put aside objective reasoning. Both Ben Kenobi and Yoda, whose entire philosophy was Buddhist,[32] repeatedly instructed Luke to "let go of your conscious self... act on instinct... stretch out with your feelings... trust your feelings!" Sounds rather like what some children are learning in their classrooms today, doesn't it? There is nothing that is beyond you, no supernatural power that is beyond your grasp, if only you will relinquish control and give in to the power of the Force. Using the Force, Ben can hypnotize an Empire warrior and pithily observes that "the Force can have a strong influence on the weak-minded." Using the Force, Darth Vader can grab an insolent officer around the throat, lifting him high into the air and almost squeezing the life out of him . . . while standing across the room from him. Using the Force, Yoda can levitate Luke's fighter plane out of the murky swamp. "I don't believe it!" exclaims an awed Skywalker. "That," responds Yoda, "is why you fail."

Put aside all critical faculties, enter an altered state of consciousness, have faith in your faith, and allow the Force to work through you. Nothing shall be withheld from you if only you believe! Herein lies the basis of all occult power. This is how channelers become channelers, how occultists develop occult power, and how millions of our schoolchildren become open to demonic beings.

How many millions of children have yearned to become Jedi knights like Luke Skywalker? How many millions accepted the occultic lessons presented by Yoda and Ben Kenobi, and have incorporated those lessons into the basic framework of their personalities? Their newly implanted yearning to become magician/warriors like their hero, Luke, was fed by the deluge of Star Wars paraphernalia that hit the market after each episode. There were *thousands* of objects to choose from—everything from Star Wars school supplies and lunch pails to Darth Vader pajamas and belt buckles and Princess Lea bubble bath. So many people were collecting Star Wars paraphernalia that in 1986 someone published *The Official Price Guide to Star Trek and Star Wars Collectibles*, which contains "4000 all-new listings!"[33]

There was even a "Special Diary for Jedi Knights-In-Training" called *My Jedi Journal*. On the first page the children receive these basic instructions from the ancient, all-wise Yoda:

The Jedi Master Speaks:

A Jedi must have the deepest commitment, the most serious mind.

A Jedi's strength flows from The Force.

A Jedi uses The Force for knowledge and defense, never for attack.

Try not. Do. Or do not. There is no try.

My ally is The Force. Life creates it, makes it grow. Its energy surrounds us and binds us.

You must feel The Force around you.

You must learn control.

Promotional material for "Star Wars Action Figures" was mailed to children in households across the country by Kenner Products. Along with a handsome Star Wars poster, each "Young Jedi Knight" received what seemed to be a personal letter from Luke Skywalker himself, telling about his exciting adventures, even though he "had yet to learn to harness the mystical powers of the Force." At the close of the letter he encourages the children to "be sure to study hard as I did, and May the Force Be With You!"

Transpersonal educators Jack Canfield and Paula Klimek were quick to recognize the application of *Star Wars* in their classrooms: "The first difficulty is to get kids to close their eyes and to validate this need for inner space. A wonderful way to do this, we have found, is to use the tools the media are providing. An example might be to ask, 'What's this thing called the force in *Star Wars*? How does Luke communicate with it? How does it help him?' The next question is, 'Well, would you like to have this kind of experience?' (The answer is always an overwhelming 'Yes!') 'Well, we can try this and see what happens. There are some ground rules you will need to follow.' At this point the kids are more than ready. The media has done a lot of the work for us. Consequently, they quickly learn such benefits as being fully present before a test, solving their problems through contact with their own inner wisdom, and learning to relax."[34]

And need we say there were cartoon series based on the pugnacious little teddy bear Ewok warriors and on the adventures of the two "Droids," Artoo-Detoo, and See-Threepio.

The Droids didn't seem to last too long, but the Ewoks were popular enough to merit two television movies of their very own. Of course, their tribal shaman always played a prominent part.

Brave Star is another one of several cartoon series that have featured shamans in recent years. Brave Star is a handsome intergalactic marshal on a distant planet still going through its Old West phase. Brave Star can call on supernatural powers. By entering an altered state, he can summon to himself the "eyes of a hawk . . . the strength of a bear . . . the speed of a puma. . . ." When he is in need of special wisdom, he always consults the wise old shaman who trained Brave Star even from his boyhood in the ancient ways.

Smurfed Up

Then of course there are always the Smurfs. Those eternally blue little critters have been Smurfing around now since September of 1981[35] and show no sign of calling it quits. The six- through 11-year olds made it NBC's number one runaway hit in its first season, breaking all kinds of Nielsen records for Saturday morning viewing. And kids still love the Smurfs. Unlike so much of the violent, loud, scary stuff, kids can identify with the little Smurfs, whose names—Lazy Smurf, Brainy Smurf, Clumsy Smurf, Grumpy Smurf—strike a deep chord of recognition in a lot of little guys!

The little Smurfs spend much of their time avoiding the evil plots of the sinister, wicked, and ever-incompetent sorcerer named Gargamel and his moth-eaten feline familiar, Azariel. Gargamel's chief ambition in life is to capture a Smurf— it seems he likes to eat them. But Papa Smurf is himself a powerful wizard of no small means, and can always be counted on to come to the rescue with the aid of his magic books, spells, amulets, and incantations.

The other reason Gargamel wants to catch Smurfs is to prove to all the other wizards that Smurfs do indeed exist and that he hasn't been hallucinating all these years. The other wizards had been ribbing him about it unmercifully. Now, to add insult to injury, Gargamel has just been informed that neither he nor his imaginary Smurfs were invited to the great wizard convention that year. But Gargamel is determined to vindicate himself. He goes into his room and bows low before the "Great Book of Spells" which stands enshrined between two candles. The book has a five-pointed star on the cover. Gargamel calculates that the moon is in just the right phase for him to ask the spirit of the Great Book for a wish, so he conjures him forth.

"Speak the incantation, oh rude one!" commands the irritated voice that issues forth from the pages of the now-open book. Gargamel does so and tells the spirit that he wants him to give him the biggest bird on earth so he can swoop down and capture a Smurf to take to the wizard convention. So the spirit gives him detailed instructions, which include the following: *"Draw a pentagram on the ground."* There is also some inane incantation along the lines of "Draw this circle on the dirt and sprinkle skunk juice on your shirt!" Gargamel does as he is told, and sure enough, the biggest bird in the world suddenly appears before him: an ostrich! The bird proves totally useless in catching Smurfs, of course, and once again Gargamel is left in stark defeat and humiliation with even the spirit of his own magic book of spells calling him a "bumbling fool neophyte."

True enough! Nevertheless, the point is that the basic procedure for the invocation of spirits used by ritual magicians is pretty much all there, right down to the term "pentagram." The pentagram is a five-pointed star considered to be one of the most powerful tools of conjuration in magical rites. The pentagram with one point upward is used by Witches and other neopagans as a symbol of man and of the divine power he has over the universe.[36] In medieval days it supposedly represented the five wounds of Christ, and as such was used as a charm to keep evil spirits away. Some ritual magicians today still use it in this context to repel evil, and, at least in medieval days, many magicians sewed the pentagram on their robes for protection, along with the crescent moon (symbolizing the protection of the goddess). When the pentagram is reversed it becomes a symbol of Satan and darkness, and therefore attracts those very forces. With two points up, the pentagram signifies the supposed victory of man and Satan over the Trinity. Keep your eyes open as you watch these kiddie shows; the pentagram, including the satanic inverted version, shows up on a regular basis.

New Age leaders have made it abundantly clear that they are determined to initiate our children into their program. Occult cartoons, stories, movies, toys, games, and comics are to the New Age religion what Sunday school and Bible stories are to Christianity, only multiplied a thousandfold. Apart from the psychological conditioning and desensitizing to occultism brought about by chronic viewing of cartoons and movies like the ones we've been discussing, there are also very real spiritual dangers. The more that children are encouraged to experiment and play with the occult, the more that many of them are going to attract literal demonic beings to themselves. If you think that somehow children are spared from demonic attention simply because they are young and "just playing," you're dead wrong. Satan and his demons are the ultimate legalists; they don't care how old a human being is when he trespasses into demonic territory, and there are numerous well-documented cases of demon possession of children, not the least impressive of which are found in the New Testament.[37]

Violent Report

Not only are children being exposed to occultic influence through the media, but they are also absorbing the violence of our society.[38] A close look at the entertainment available to our children today should gave us serious pause. If our children grow up with violence and occultism, then those are the traits and beliefs they will surely reflect to one degree or another in adulthood.

It seems that promoting war and violence is extremely profitable to the toy companies. In 1985 they sold over 1.2 *billion* dollars worth of war toys and accessories! As Dr. Radecki points out, the toy companies now finance about 85 percent of the cartoon programming.[39] Never mind that study after study, covering thousands of children in countries around the world, confirm the direct correlation of cartoon violence to hostile and aggressive behavior. Never mind that when a gang of boys in New York City go "wilding," savagely raping and beating their way through Central Park, the sociologists explain their behavior in part by telling us that—

> the circuits of popular culture transmit images of brutality without consequences. Children play video games in which they win points for killing the most people. They watch violence-packed cartoons. They listen to songs titled *Be My Slave* and *Scumkill*. Or they are baby-sat by vastly popular movie video-tapes like *Splatter University* and *I Spit on Your Grave*. Says sociologist Gail Dines-Levy of Wheelock College in Boston: "What we are doing is training a whole generation of male kids to see sex and violence as inextricably linked."[40]

According to a recent government study, children start imitating what they see on television as early as 14 months of age![41] It seems that a baby of that age can remember how a toy was manipulated on television and a day later repeat those actions when given the toy. Andrew Meltzoff, a psychologist at the University of Washington, concluded that "television may influence early development of speech, language and social skills more than has been thought."[42]

Dungeons, Dragons, and Role-Playing

Of course, not everyone agrees that fantasizing about violence and the occult is bad for a kid. Gary Gygax, for example, inventor of the wildly popular and shockingly violent and occultic role-playing game called Dungeons and Dragons (or D & D, as it is commonly known) denies that his "game" has caused anyone to become violent or antisocial. On the contrary, he cites letters from parents who praise the game for helping encourage their children to think, reason, use their imaginations, pursue reading, and even overcome learning

232 ◆ Johanna Michaelsen

disabilities. "People have a need to fantasize. It's a mundane world, it's nice to have something imaginary."[43]

Most assuredly, Fantasy Role Playing (FRP) games, and there are from 350 to 400 different ones out on the market now, do encourage the use of the imagination. Imagination is indeed a wonderful thing. So is fantasy, and I believe that both are a gift from God. And yet both fantasy and imagination have been perverted when used to indulge in and promote practices and beliefs that God has repeatedly and consistently labeled *abomination* all through Scripture. It isn't imagination or fantasy that I have a problem with; it's the promotion of occultism and violence that bothers me, and Fantasy Role Playing games especially are saturated with both.

The FRP game is played primarily in the minds of the players who, on the basis of the roll of dice, select a character whose role they will play in the game. The players generally find themselves in a medieval world of "swords and sorcery," in search of adventure, treasure, and above all, power—especially supernatural power. The point of the game is to make it through the dungeons, to slash or conjure your way past the monsters, dragons, and whatever . . . or whoever . . . gets in your way, in order to achieve your goals, preferably without getting your character killed off. To do that, any amount or kind of violence and sorcery is permitted within the context of your character's nature and on the basis of the god that your character serves. Of course, should your character get killed, all is not necessarily lost! "Even death loses much of its sting, for often the character can be resurrected or reincarnated."[44] In the case of D & D, the game is controlled by the Dungeon Master, a player who is expected to be committed and brilliant enough to design the unbelievably complex fantasy worlds and adventures of the game, and who in essence gets to play "God," deciding by the roll of dice what goes on in the game.

"Swords and sorcery best describes what this game is all about, for those are the two key fantasy ingredients," says Gygax.[45] In other words, to really get into the spirit of this game, you've got to be into violence, magic, and Witchcraft. The degree and kind of violence in these games doubtlessly stems from the fact that they developed from war games based on historical battles. Many of the FRP games go far beyond the old models in the unbridled sadism and sexual violence (including sodomy, rape, homosexuality, bestiality, and other perversions) which can be vicariously indulged in by the players through their characters. Points are given for varying degrees of mutilation inflicted on a victim or adversary during battles and confrontations. Those whose character is in the category of assassin are instructed in the careful planning and execution of the murder of their victims, including the most effective use of poisons.[46]

The Occult Element

However, it's the occult element that really makes today's Fantasy Role Playing games so enormously appealing. Dungeons & Dragons, the granddaddy of them all, is based on Tolkien's famed "Ring Trilogy," and has adopted a similar theme and feel. Some of the most important weapons available to the characters in their quest are spells, incantations, conjurations, and magical rituals and practices, many of which have been taken directly from black magic, Witchcraft, voodoo, and Satanism. From what I can see, there's probably not a form or practice of occultism or devil worship that has not been included somewhere in these "games." The spells must be carefully studied and memorized, and "as with all other types of spells... must be spoken or read aloud."[47] Gygax insists that his work is just a game... a work of pure fantasy... not real—and yet on page 115 of the *Official Advanced Dungeons & Dragons Dungeon Masters Guide*, 1979 edition, under "Spell Research," Gygax advises that "it is absolutely mandatory for the researcher to be of sound mind and body and to have privacy and seclusion free from interruption during the course of his or her spell study.... It requires about 8 hours per day of work. ... Once you have the details of the spell, compare and contrast it with and to existing spells in order to determine its level and any modifications and additions you find necessary in order to have it conform to 'known' magic principles." On page 42 of the same manual Gygax has included drawings of a Magic Circle, the Pentagram, and the Thaumaturgic Triangle to be used for protection by the spell-caster.

Devotees of the games may protest that they're not *really* casting spells; it's all just fantasy. And a lot of the spells are just made up. Yet once again it bears repeating that the participants are nevertheless saturating themselves with the contemplation, study, and promotion of things which the God of the Bible has repeatedly condemned as *abomination!* (Deuteronomy 18:9ff.). God *hates* the practice of every form of idolatry and occultism in the real world. Human sacrifice, divination, Witchcraft, superstitions, sorcery, ritual magic, mediumship, spiritism, and necromancy are all flatly condemned by the Word of God. So what makes you think He's going to approve of it in the world of your imagination? Jesus warned that "everyone who looks on a woman to lust for her has committed adultery with her already in his heart."[48] What we entertain in our imaginations, according to Jesus, carries more weight than some of us may like to think. God calls us to be transformed by the renewing of our minds.[49] He encourages us to let our minds dwell on whatever is true, honorable, right, pure, lovely, and of good repute.[50] Last time I looked, Fantasy Role Playing games fall rather short on this list!

Dr. Thomas Radecki, a consistent and adamant critic of D & D, has stated that the game is "essentially a worship of violence. . . . It's a very intense war game. . . . It's very fascinating. It's a game of fun. But when you have fun with murder, that's dangerous. When you make a game out of war, that's harmful. The game is full of human sacrifice, eating babies, drinking blood, rape, murder of every variety, curses of insanity. It's just a very violent game."[51]

Today there are well over four million players, mostly young males ranging from 8 to 27 years old, who have accepted Mr. Gygax's invitation to enter into that fantasy dream world of sorcery and swords.

One of the recognized dangers inherent in the game is the potential for overidentification with the characters. When I was a first-year acting student in college, the professor made a point of telling us that one of the quickest ways to insure a free trip to the booby hatch was to take the character we were playing home with us and overidentify with it on a regular basis.

There is a serious danger of reality distortion as some players begin to develop their fantasy character as an alter ego, and some youngsters insist on being called by their character's name. Others have found themselves actually carrying out the rapes, robberies, and murders that they had played over and over again in their minds.

Fantasy Role Playing games in general, and D & D in particular, have some interesting defenders. I have received letters from young seminarians from well-known institutions scolding me for having publicly criticized Dungeons & Dragons, and informing me that they and some of their professors have been playing the game for years! A woman called me to tell me that her pastor's young son was an avid player of the game. The pastor was offended that she would criticize the boy's involvement, and told her that he could find absolutely nothing wrong with playing D & D. And there are church youth groups that have had on-going games for years led by their youth pastor.

Dungeons and Dragons has been heavily promoted in the *Gifted Children Newsletter*[52] and in the 1987 "Gifted Child Today Catalog" for its "educational merit." In fact, D & D has been endorsed by the Association for Gifted-Creative Children because the game encourages the reading of Shakespeare, Tolkien, and Isaac Asimov.[53] A version of D & D specially adapted for use in schools has long been a staple of many Gifted-and-Talented programs across the country, although fortunately there are an increasing number of schools that have wisely chosen to remove it from their classrooms.

It is a fact confirmed by onetime participants as well as by law-enforcement groups that certain Satanist, Wiccan, and other neopagan groups seek to recruit new members from among the ranks of dedicated Fantasy Role Playing advocates. They are prime candidates for recruitment into these groups, for they are already familiar with most of the philosophy, ritual, symbolism, and practice of these religions.

A Full-Time Challenge

There is probably no more challenging, difficult, or rewarding job in the world today than that of raising balanced, healthy, normal, confident, loving, and godly children to become balanced, healthy, normal, confident, loving, and godly adults. In many ways it's a scary world out there. Kids are no longer safe on our streets. At school, if they're lucky enough to make it through the day without getting mugged or shot in the halls, they're faced with New Age teachings and principles in their classrooms. Now you're being told that you can't even let the kid sit in front of the TV to watch Saturday morning cartoons without worrying about it!

The fact is, as tempting as it may be, you cannot altogether isolate your child from the world. You can't keep him locked in a plastic bubble in the hope of shielding him from every destructive virus that surrounds him. If you make the mistake of overprotecting him, you run the risk of losing him to the first little bug that comes along. You may well decide, if you haven't already, to throw your television out altogether. Or you might forbid your child to watch any cartoons or see any movies at all. That may well be your best alternative if your children are very young. As the child matures, however, he will in all likelihood notice that a lot of his friends spend their playtime with He-Man, She-Ra, JEM,[54] the Super Naturals, Willow, Knights of the Magical Powers, and the Smurfs. Your child is bound to feel cheated and rebellious if he doesn't at least understand why he's not allowed to watch those shows indiscriminately or play with the myriad of occult/violent toys based on them.

Somewhere, sooner or later, even the most shielded child is going to find himself exposed to the occult principles that permeate today's society. You simply cannot isolate your child forever. Nor, on the other hand, can you allow him to become steeped in the deeply occultic and mystical principles, fear, and violence presented on virtually every cartoon show and children's program at one time or another—not to mention the rest of what's on television that a lot of children watch along with their parents! Many of these programs, as we have seen, have a very specific message that they want to get across. The trick is to spot that message and not allow it to indoctrinate you or your children! There are a few simple ways to do this.

How to Spot the Message

1. First of all, learn as much as you can about the New Age from a Christian perspective. There are many excellent books on the market to choose from. You don't necessarily need to become an expert on the subject, but you cannot afford to be ignorant of the basic concepts and symbols used to indoctrinate the unwary. You've got to study!

2. Never allow your preschooler to watch television by himself. Even "Sesame Street" has been known to scare the diapers off some little tykes from time to time. Studies conducted by Piaget and others indicate that a child under seven sometimes has a tough time distinguishing fantasy from reality. To him, what happens on that television or movie screen is actually real! Pretty scary if you think about it!

3. Be sure to monitor what your child watches. Author Michael R. Kelley in his excellent book *A Parent's Guide to Television: Making the Most of It* says that ideally a preschool child should *never* watch action-adventure cartoons that routinely present violent and aggressive behavior, action-adventure dramas, highly violent movies, medical documentaries, soap operas, or the evening news.[55] I would add to that "never" list any show that carries occult themes. These present images that a little one may not be able to handle for years, and which can become a source of nightmares and excessively fearful or aggressive behavior. Shows like "Winnie the Pooh" and the "Muppet Babies" are generally good ones to stick with. If you're there watching with him, you can talk over what he sees and help him work out anything that may frighten or confuse him.

4. Researchers also suggest that you never allow preschoolers to watch more than one hour of television a day. Television is definitely addictive, and the more TV a child watches when very young, the harder it is to break that addiction. More important, it steals away precious time that could be spent doing something creative. Spend more time playing together or encouraging him to draw, or else read a story. There are some wonderful new storybooks on the market.[56] Consider *The Rumpoles and The Barleys*, by Karen Mezek; Dave Hunt has written a fun new children's story called *The Money Tree*. There's *Bedtime Hugs for Little Ones* by Debby Boone and *Growing Up With Jesus* by Gilbert Beers. Dr. Beers has also written a book called *Parents: Talk With Your Children* that I think has some tremendously valuable insights for parents today.

5. Begin training your little ones to discern the difference between fantasy and reality at an early age. If you tell your child that Santa Claus really lives in the North Pole and that he and his reindeer actually come down the chimney on Christmas Eve, you've lied to him. If you let him think that the Easter bunny is what Resurrection Sunday is all about, and that the bunny actually comes and hides eggs, you've lied to him. Eventually he's going to figure that out, and then he's entirely likely to conclude that what you told him about Jesus is all just a lie too. It's a wonderful thing for a child to play "let's pretend," but you must help him understand that his pretend play is *not* reality. He is simply not going to be able to fly like Superman out of his second-story window just because he put on a little Superman cape!

6. As your children grow older, teach them what to look for. Rather than totally censoring all questionable reading and viewing material, use that material to help teach them discernment. By the time a child is about 11 or 12, he is generally able to reason more abstractly, and you'll be able to reason things through with him on a level that would have been lost on him at an earlier age. Teach him the difference between the genuine miracles that God performs and the

occult counterfeits seen in the movies and cartoons. It's important that your child understands that occult powers can indeed be very real, but that God has repeatedly warned us to stay away from them. Tell your child about Moses and the magicians in Pharaoh's court. Tell him about Joseph and Daniel and Elisha. God, in accordance with His own will and purpose, worked awesome miracles through these men, putting all the occultists, wizards, and sorcerers to shame. You might be surprised at just how discerning a child can be if you give him the tools to work with!

A teacher I know at a Christian elementary school in Southern California has long been aware of the pernicious influence of occultism among children and has, a little at a time, been able to teach her second-graders how to discern what they see in movies and television or read in books and compare it with what they know the Word of God has to say about the subject. One day the mother of one of her students reported that she had taken her daughter to see *The Care Bear Movie*. While this little second-grader enjoyed the movie, there was something about it that bothered her. She commented that the Care Bears seemed like God. They were up in heaven and knew everything, like God did. And when the Bears concentrated their energy in the "Care Bear Stare" to change something, she said, it was "like a counterfeit miracle . . . kind of like the magicians in Pharaoh's court." Very discerning for a second-grader!

Those of you who watched the April 11, 1989, Oprah Winfrey Show in which Shirley MacLaine explained about the *chakra* system and its correlation to the seven colors of the rainbow should be able to identify the source of the imagery behind the "Care Bear Stare." When confronted with an emergency, the little Bears focus their energy into beams of rainbow light that emanate from their torsos . . . or heart *chakra*, which, as MacLaine explained, is the seat of the emotions.

7. Be aware that your exercise of discernment should apply equally to Christian materials as well. For example, the fantasy works of Tolkien and C.S. Lewis reflect an essentially

Christian worldview, but they include enough references in their writings to "good" Witches, wizards, and magicians to confuse the average child. Tolkien's *Ring Trilogy*, for example, was taken as the basis for the development of Dungeons & Dragons. And C.S. Lewis, who in his autobiography *Surprised by Joy* openly admits to his lifelong fascination with the occult, included (among other things) a lovable faun named Mr. Tumnus in his *Chronicles of Narnia*. The faun, of course, is the Roman version of the Greek god Pan, who is identified as an alter ego of Satan himself in the Satanic Bible.

I'm not sure I'm prepared to burn all the little hobbits at the stake, but, as with other fairy tales that present any form of occultism in a positive light, I would certainly exercise caution and make sure that my child was old enough to appreciate the story while still understanding that neither C.S. Lewis nor Tolkien were infallible.[57]

8. Above all, teach your children how to test what they see and hear against the Scripture, for this is God's yardstick for truth.

God has given you the responsibility to raise your children in the way in which they should go. The wisdom of man tells us that belief in the occult is good for children.

Bruno Bettelheim goes so far as to blame the rise in occultism and drug use among teens today on a squashed fantasy life in early childhood: "Many young people who today suddenly seek escape in drug-induced dreams, apprentice themselves to some guru, believe in astrology, engage in practicing 'black magic,' or who in some other fashion escape from reality into daydreams about magic experiences which are to change their life for the better, were prematurely pressed to view reality in an adult way.... I have known many examples where ... years of belief in magic are called upon to compensate for the persons having been deprived of it prematurely in childhood."[58]

That is pure Humanistic nonsense. God, on the other hand, warns us to stay away from the occult at all costs! It's up to you whose advice you choose to follow in the raising of your children.

Chapter 14

The Hideous Side of Evil

✦

On the altar of the Devil up is down, pleasure is pain, darkness is light, slavery is freedom, and madness is sanity.
—Anton Szandor LaVey
The Satanic Rituals

Woe to those who call evil good, and good evil; who substitute darkness for light, and light for darkness; who substitute bitter for sweet, and sweet for bitter! Woe to those who are wise in their own eyes, and clever in their own sight!
—The Lord
Isaiah 5:20,21

A Growing Epidemic

Satanism. The very word chills most of us to the bone. We don't want to think about it. We *certainly* don't want to read about it! Some of us are deeply offended that anyone—especially a Christian—would actually write about it and expect us to confront the bloodcurdling case histories of those who claim to have lived through it. And yet, if the hundreds of newspaper headlines, police reports, and personal testimonies of parents, children, teenagers, and adult survivors across this country and around the world are even partially true, then we are being inundated with satanic and ritualistic practices and beliefs on an unprecedented scale. In fact, a growing number of police departments across the country are holding seminars to train officers in the basics of Satanism and ritual occultism so they'll know what to look for at a crime scene. Officers and detectives who have pushed for such seminars have often done so despite ridicule and opposition from their peers. And yet veteran officers have said that they remember seeing indications of ritualistic crime as long as 20 years ago. They just didn't know what it was at the time. Some of those officers, initially skeptical of the need for such seminars, are beginning to change their minds. Numerous psychologists and police investigators have told me they believe the problem has reached epidemic proportions.

A case in point: On April 11, 1989, police in Matamoros, Mexico, discovered 12 (eventually 15) mutilated bodies buried on a remote ranch just across the Texas border. Among them was the body of Mark Kilroy, a 21-year-old University of Texas student who disappeared while vactioning on spring break in Matamoros. The authorities were at the ranch on a drug raid when they discovered the graves. They also found candles, the skulls and bones of small animals, a rusted machete, and an iron pot containing human brains and blood. Some of the bodies had been skinned. Some had been decapitated. Some had had their hearts torn out. Almost all the bodies were horribly mutilated. "It was like a human slaughter house," said Cameron County Sheriff Alex Perez. "This is just sick," another official said. "It's just unimaginable."[1]

It was clear to the investigators that they had stumbled upon a self-styled satanic drug-smuggling cult whose beliefs and practices appeared to be an amalgamation of Santeria, voodoo, black magic, and Satanism called *Palo Mayombe*. According to testimony from the cult members, some of whom were wearing necklaces made from their victims' vertebrae, they believed that sacrificing humans would "put a magical shield about them" that would protect them from the police and even from bullets.

What made the case even harder to accept was the fact that the perpetrators were well-educated, intelligent, and generally respected members of the community who drove luxury cars and wore expensive clothes. The high priestess of the cult was a 24-year-old dean's honor roll student at Texas Southmost College and listed in the college's "Who's Who" directory in 1987-88. When they searched her home, they discovered a sacrificial altar covered with blood. They also found blood-stained children's clothing and a variety of voodoo paraphernalia. The head of the group was a good-looking 26-year-old Cuban they called "The Godfather." One of the cult members said that the Godfather had decided to perform human sacrifices after watching a movie called "The Believers," a chilling film about a network of wealthy businesspeople who give up their children for sacrifice in exchange for power, protection, and wealth.

On an interview for the "Larry King Show" a few days after the discovery, Jim Mattox, the attorney general of Texas, was still in evident shock about the nature of the discoveries. He had been on the site himself and had seen the evidence. Toward the end of his interview, Mr. Mattox made an admission that in my opinion is probably one of the most important statements to come out of the entire incident:

> May I tell you something: Here in Austin about a month ago, we had a whole symposium on the occult, on Satanic-type worship and things like that. I was somewhat amused because I did not really and truly take these matters to heart.... There were so many there, social workers and others involved in this process. But I did not take it as seriously as I would have had I known what was about to take place in this circumstance, and there were so many people there that just could not understand what was happening, even though we have seen a rise in these animal mutilations. And then all of a sudden this hits us right square in the face. We've got to realize that the people who are saying these things are growing in our high schools and in society as a whole. We must recognize and learn how to deal with it.

For about three years now clinical psychologists, therapists, and social workers have been holding seminars of their
own on ritualistic crime and Satanism to help them understand the nature of the abuse being described by an increasing
number of their patients. Only a few short years ago, most
police officers would have scoffed at any suggestion of Satanism having anything to do with the suicides, murders, child-
abuse cases, or animal mutilations they were investigating.
And the psychologists would probably have wondered how
to politely suggest you were in serious need of psychiatric
care for even mentioning the subject. Fifteen years ago those
who spoke of incest received much the same kind of treatment. No one wants to believe these things actually happen.

And yet for years there have been rumblings of the presence of Satanism in our midst. Charles Manson, the "Son of
Sam," Sirhan Sirhan, the "Night Stalker," the Zodiac Killer,
Henry Lee Lucas—these are but a few of the better-known
killers with ties to the occult and Satanism. Then there is the
MacMartin preschool case, in which almost 400 children at a
prestigious Manhattan Beach school raised accusations of
molestation, rape, pornography, and the slaughter of animals
and infants during satanic rituals. And then there is the
preschool case in Jordan, Minnesota; and the one at West
Point and the Presidio; and the ones in Akron, Ohio, and
Boulder, Colorado; and Fort Pierce, Florida; and Bakersfield,
California; and Bellingham, Washington; and on and on in
virtually every state of the Union. And then there were the
stories of teenagers, self-styled devil worshipers, and fans of
heavy-metal "devil music" committing hideous animal mutilations, church and graveyard desecrations, and even suicide
and murder, all in the name of Satan. Adults who claim to be
survivors of satanic ritual abuse began to come forward to tell
their stories of unspeakable horror and abuse as children.
Some of them tell of having been used to breed infants to be
used as human offerings to Satan.

All of a sudden it seems that everybody is talking about
the devil. Oprah Winfrey, "20/20," "Nightline," Phil Dona-
hue, and Sally Jesse Raphael have based numerous shows on

Satanism. Geraldo leads the way so far with at least six programs on various aspects of the subject aired between 1988 and 1989, including his much-maligned two-hour primetime special called "Devil Worship: Exposing Satan's Underground." Some people have chosen to dismiss programs like these as "trash TV." Perhaps they are. Nevertheless, I personally feel they have done us all a tremendous service by bringing the subject of Satanism to national attention. Skeptics and critics to the contrary, *something* is going on out there. We're never going to learn to deal with it by ignoring it.

A Sinister Surge

Around 1984 or so bookstores in Houston and other parts of the country began to notice that copies of the *Satanic Bible* (and its companion *The Satanic Rituals*), which had long sat on store shelves collecting dust, suddenly experienced an unexpected surge of popularity as teenagers bought them at an alarming rate. It became even more alarming when copies of that "Bible" and the *Rituals* were found in the possession of many teens who committed ritual murder, self-mutilation, animal sacrifice, or suicide. Occult shops found they couldn't keep enough stock of black candles, inverted pentagrams, and other paraphernalia associated with black magic and Satanism. Most of the customers for these items were then, even as they are today, teenagers.

Satanic graffiti began appearing on school walls, lockers, and student notebooks; they were tattooed on kids' arms and sprayed under bridges or on church walls. Some of that graffiti had been drawn in human blood. Blanche Barton, a Satanist with the Church of Satan based in San Francisco, boasted in a 1985 interview for the *Houston Post* that "there has been a major resurgence of Satanism in this country in the last 18 months. . . . It's fascinating, it's dark, it's dangerous and it is becoming an acceptable form of protest. In the '60s, it was hippies. In the '80s, it's Satanists. . . ."[2]

Our teenagers have indeed been gravitating around the fascinating and dark worship of the devil. It has become an "acceptable" form of protest for many youngsters—the ultimate rebellion. Just how dangerous it is, however, is now being seen in newspaper headlines across the country:

SYMPATHY FOR THE DEVIL:
MORE YOUNG PEOPLE TURN
TO SATAN-WORSHIP,
—*Los Angeles Herald Examiner*
March 18, 1984

SATAN'S TEENS:
"WHAT HAVE WE GOT TO LIVE FOR?"
—*Albuquerque Journal*
February 15, 1988

PARENT KILLINGS INTENSIFY WORRIES
OVER HEAVY METAL
—*Sunday Journal*
Albuquerque, New Mexico,
February 28, 1988

In January 1988 a 14-year-old named Thomas Sullivan Jr. brutally slashed his mother to death with his Boy Scout knife. He tried to kill his father and ten-year-old brother by setting fire to the family home. Then he went outside and slit his wrists and throat with a violence that almost severed his head from his body. As far as investigators have been able to tell, he had become especially obsessed with the devil and occult literature after friends wrote an "A" paper on Satanism for a class assignment on world religions. According to the boy's father, Thomas Jr. became obsessed with the occult. He began writing notes to friends in Latin that could only be read when reversed. The week before the killings he had been singing a song "about blood and killing your mother." He had also talked to a friend about a vision in which Satan had appeared to him and ". . . urged him to kill his family and to preach Satanism."

Just before the deaths, Tommy wrote the following in his diary: "I believe evil will once again rise and conquer the love of God. If this pact is to your approval, sign below. . . ." The mayor of the town and some investigators believe that other young people in the area are still involved in Satan worship.[3]

In San Antonio, a group of about ten seventh- and eighth-graders were suspected in the torture, mutilation, and deaths of over 50 animals. According to one teacher, the students are "very serious about Satanism. They're caught up in their Satanism. It's all that power stuff. . . ."[4] The boys wore steel-toed boots, were into heavy metal, drew pictures of Lucifer, and greeted each other in the school halls with "Hey (or "Hail") Satan." In a case of classic denial, the principal of the middle school said that "there were no indications that Satanism has been practiced on school grounds." The kids, however, told a different story. The police report said that on one occasion "a large group of students cheered as [a] puppy was thrown up in the air and allowed to fall to the ground." Most of the animals were found on or near the school grounds.

Mutilated animal remains have also been found in El Paso, Texas, where frightened teenagers say hundreds of kids and adults, from age 8 to 40, are involved in the worship of Satan. The rituals include the torture and killing of animals. One young man said he witnessed the murder of a ten-year-old girl, whose body was then taken out to sea for disposal. In August 1987 police were looking into a report from a former Satanist that newborns and transients have been killed during devil worship rituals.[5] The city has been plagued with a rash of church and graveyard desecrations. The problem has become so severe that Henderson Junior High and Vista Del Sol Junior High "have banned occult symbols such as '666,' pentagrams, upside-down crosses and swastikas. Also banned are heavy metal rock T-shirts with satanic art."[6]

A minister/evangelist in Houston named Paul Vick has been deeply involved in prison ministry and is working with thousands of kids across the State. He told me the problems in El Paso and surrounding areas have not gone away: "It seems that overt satanic activity is really on the rise here in this area of Texas. Hardly a day goes by that the newspapers fail to report another bizarre occult-oriented happening."[7]

The kids are still deeply involved in devil worship, and the El Paso Hotline still gets frequent calls from terrified youngsters who fear that Satan is going to kill them.

According to Florence Luke, director of the El Paso Hotline when the story was reported in 1986, "The animal sacrifices and the drinking of blood is very real to these children. Most of them can't even sleep at night. Some of them have thoughts of suicide and thoughts of killing others."[8]

Several of the children counseled because of involvement in devil worship are in elementary school, said Dr. Carlos Estrada, a Corpus Christi psychiatrist, in an interview for a local paper in August of 1988. "It's becoming an epidemic here."[9] El Paso, incidentally, is the hometown of Richard Ramirez, the accused Night Stalker and self-proclaimed Satanist.

On January 6, 1988, a popular Vermont high-school sophomore named Michele Kimball put a rifle to her head and pulled the trigger. Her death was part of a suicide pact made with her boyfriend, who fortunately survived. Her suicide note said that she was a worshiper of the devil and that she knew her parents wouldn't understand. The last words recorded in her diary were those of a heavy-metal song.

The Littlest Victims

The story told by the little four-year-old boy was as horrifying and unbelievable as it was consistent: They killed his friend Bobby. He had met Bobby during the numerous strange rituals he was taken to while attending his day-care center. Bobby was about five or six years old, blond and blue-eyed. He wore wire-rim glasses and could say his ABC's. He lived in a "cage" in the back of a truck. The boy said that the last time he saw Bobby, a man chopped off his head with a sword. He described how the blood spurted when the man gouged Bobby's eyes out. He watched as they chopped off his legs and his arms. And he watched as other adults ate some of the flesh from the arms. Then they shoved what was left of Bobby into a bag and threw the bag into a hole. "Over and over, he's told the story, the same way. He always tells it the same," said the boy's father.[10]

The day-care center which the boy attended was run by a 67-year-old woman who was described by one official as "everyone's picture of what a grandmother should be." And yet several years earlier a mother, suspicious of the symptoms her child was showing, had removed her child from the center and raised accusations of molestation. They were never proved, so the center remained open. But later, when other children began showing signs of abuse, officials reopened the investigation. That's when they found out about Bobby. The investigating officer said he took the boy's story "very seriously," but unfortunately there was no way to prove it.

Then one day while driving through the countryside the boy pointed out a familiar place and identified it as the location where Bobby had been killed. The site was a truck-washing operation where drivers of cattle trucks can clean out their rigs. There was an acid pit nearby where the truckers disposed of carcasses of animals that have died along the way. There was still no solid proof, but suddenly the boy's story became all the more plausible.

Other children at that center told of being smeared with feces, which they were also forced to eat. They told of being made to drink blood. They talked about being sodomized and raped by adults who wore masks and hooded robes. Some of them had the scars to prove it. They spoke of being frightened by the adults with power saws and cattle prods, as well as with knives, swords, and guns. The children, most of them under five years old at the time, were told they would be killed if they said anything. Many of these children, some of whom are now 12 to 13 years old, still suffer from nightmares, depression, spells of fear and terror, outbursts against other children, and thoughts of death and suicide. At least one of the children has developed a split personality. According to one child-care expert, "These are by far the most severely disturbed children I have ever seen. The emotional impacts are astounding. Entire families are thrown into chaos over this."[11]

The case is scheduled to go to trial in May of 1989. However, Paul Hutchinson (who initially reported the boy's story about Bobby in the *Denver Post*) told me that it doesn't seem likely that any mention of Satanism will be made at the trial. As San Francisco police detective Sandi Gallant observed in reference to other preschool cases currently in trial, "Any district attorney will tell you going to court with a child under 5 is next to impossible, much less one blaming the devil."[12] Despite the fact that the children frequently show physical signs of abuse, the minute the preschoolers tell of being drugged and assaulted as part of some horrific ritual, a lot of D.A.'s start trying to figure out how to drop the charges. That's exactly what happened in Colorado, but the Governor went over the D.A.'s head and reinstated the case.

It Really Happens

Do things like these really happen? Is it possible that there are really human beings who are capable of such deliberate and calculated assault against the bodies, minds, and spirits of innocent little children? Why would they do such things? The answer is really quite simple: They do it because they worship Satan. They do it because they are evil. Unlike some groups of Satanists, who keep a high profile and openly state that they do not even believe in the devil, there are other Satanists who cling to the shadows and who believe in Satan with all their heart and soul and mind. They know that God exists, and they despise and loathe Him and all who follow Him with a vicious hatred. Like their master, who was a murderer, a liar, and thief from the beginning, they seek to destroy and kill everything which reflects the beauty of the image of God.

It is precisely because children are so pure and precious in the sight of God that they offer them in sacrifice to Satan. These Satanists are intimately acquainted with the Bible, and, unlike many people in the Christian church, understand that Jesus Christ is indeed coming again, and know that the time is soon. Yet in their demonic delusion they genuinely believe that they will be able to build an army of followers strong enough to wage war against Christ and so defeat Him!

The New Agers know that they cannot fully establish their great and glorious New Age without thoroughly indoctrinating today's children into their belief system. So too, Satanists know that while it is one thing to gain adult converts and lure a rebellious generation of teens with their lying promises of power and autonomy, it is quite another to have an army of those who from infancy have been raised in unquestioning sociopathic obedience to their master. What if it is true that selected clusters of preschools and day-care centers across the country have been deliberately infiltrated for the last ten or twelve years by Satanist teachers and caretakers for the purpose of raising an army of dedicated followers? What if it isn't a mere coincidence that the majority of the allegations of ritual abuse and molestations are coming from centers located in middle- and upper-class areas, areas which are most likely to produce the future leaders of the country? Personally, I don't think it is a coincidence at all.

But where do Satanists and other ritualistic killers get the infants and children for their sacrifices? The FBI, after all, says that there are only about 150 "truly missing" children kidnapped from their parents in this country each year, and not over one million, as others have stated. Yet how many runaway kids are never heard from again? What about the throwaways that no one bothers to report missing at all? Some of the kids are taken from transient families who can no longer afford to support their little ones and believe they are giving them away to "good homes," or from unwed mothers who innocently give their little ones over to "agencies" and "reputable" doctors or lawyers who promise to find them "a loving family."

Such was the fate of little Lisa Steinberg, who was brutally beaten to death by the man who promised to arrange a good home for her. That child's tragic face haunts many of us to this day. Investigative reporter and author Maury Terry disclosed on the Geraldo Rivera Satanism special that there was clear evidence that little Lisa was also the victim of child pornography and satanic ritual abuse, a fact he confirmed to me on the phone.

Some of the children come from unwed mothers who respond to flyers placed on their windshields or "want ads" in their papers stating that "a good Christian family" wants to adopt a child. Some mothers sell their infants in exchange for drugs. According to some who claim to have been there, infants are specifically bred within the cult for the purpose of sacrifice. And some of the sacrifices are near-term babies murdered by their own mothers in the abortionists' clinics and then quietly taken by the Satanist nurse or doctor for his or her own use. There is no end to the possible sources of unwanted humanity.

But where are the bodies of the sacrificed infants and children that the preschoolers and other victims talk about? According to detectives, police officers, ex-cult members, and the victims, there are any number of ways to dispose of a body. The children have described crematoriums where the bodies were incinerated. Not too implausible, really. In Southern California alone during the last year we have had almost half a dozen investigations of cemeteries accused of illegal cremations. One was a pet crematorium that was being illegally used to burn aborted babies. Sometimes the bodies are disposed of in "accidental" fires of homes and buildings. Some children have spoken of portable crematoriums; infant bone matter is soft and very easily disposed of. The bodies can be ground up and put down industrial garbage disposals (such as those in restaurants); some have been thrown into acid pits or down abandoned mine shafts, caves, and wells. Many have been taken out to sea and fed to the fish. Some have been cannibalized, or thrown to hungry dogs, or to wild animals. It took six years for someone to stumble across the bodies of a couple who killed each other in a satanic suicide pact, and they were lying out in the open in a downtown Los Angeles state park frequented by hundreds of thousands of visitors and hikers! No one has yet found Jimmy Hoffa either, but who seriously questions his murder!

Growing Evidence

How do we know that children are being abused and forced to participate in satanic rituals too horrible to describe? What proof is there? Not much, really. Only the terrified faces of small children as they describe the sounds a baby makes when its body is slit open. Only their descriptions of how a puppy screams when it is skinned alive. Only their tales of what the inside of a coffin looks like, and how a rotten corpse stinks and falls apart when you embrace it. Only their word about what blood and urine and feces and human flesh taste like.

What proof is there? Only the doctors reports of the scarring of little boys' bottoms and the inside of little girls' bodies. Only the countless stories of heartbroken parents whose previously loving, happy children now spend their time sexually abusing or mutilating their family pets or siblings. Only the parents' expressions of shock when their five-year-old tries to fondle them after smearing feces all over himself. Only the terror of foster parents who turn to find their tiny charges sneaking up behind them with butcher knives; who must lock their other children and themselves in their rooms at night for fear they'll be murdered in their sleep. Only the sight of little bodies contorted in wild "devil dances," and the sounds of little voices now turned to alien growls and hissings as they chant and pray to Satan.

Just because these children rage at the mention of God and Jesus and defecate at the sight of a Bible or a crucifix or the flag is no "proof" at all that they have been subjected to ritual abuse. And yet if it were my child and he suddenly showed a terror of or an unusual preoccupation with the number 6, if he suddenly showed signs of multiple personalities or regressive behavior, if he talked about "magic" operations in which "all the good was taken out" and "all the bad was put in," if the theme of "better not tell" continually showed up in his play, and he said he "couldn't tell" because the monsters would come and kill you all, and if he ever informed me that he knew I didn't love him because his "other" mommy or daddy told him so, then perhaps I would begin to wonder.

What terror is yet to be unleashed upon us as these little ones grow up can only be imagined. If it is indeed true that systematic ritual abuse in preschools has been taking place for the last ten or fifteen years, then we may already be experiencing a taste of what is to come in the breathtaking hatred, rebellion, violence, parental killings, and suicides of our teenagers today. Never mind the overwhelming psychological damage done to these kids—there is an additional factor that few parents and even fewer therapists have as yet recognized: the spiritual factor. You are not dealing with just psychologically and physically abused children, although God knows that this is bad enough. If treated early enough by a skilled therapist and doctor, in time many of these scars may heal. Yet the children who have been involved in ritualistic abuse have invariably had curses and demons called upon them. This is not a psychological hypothesis; this is a spiritual reality. However unsophisticated this may seem to some people, Satan and demons are real. Unless these are recognized, dealt with, and broken by the power of Jesus Christ, those children will never be healed.

The Devil's Reputation

Stories like these—and they are legion—tend to give Satan a bad name, a fact which evidently irritates some of the better-known Satanists. A number of them have taken to the mass media circuit to help clear the devil's reputation. Dr. Michael Aquino, High Priest and founder of the "Temple of Set," recently said on the Geraldo Rivera show that "Satanism as legitimate Satanists would define it . . . is ethical, it is above ground, it is positive."[13]

On the same program, Zeena LaVey (daughter of Anton Szandor LaVey, the so-called Black Pope of the First Church of Satan), contested the testimonies of mothers who claimed their infants had been sacrificed on Satanic altars. She said that "every single thing you've given as examples of Satanism here are completely from a Christian standpoint . . . everything you've put forth as being considered Satanic is not considered Satanic by my standard or my definition of Satanism.[14] And author Arthur Lyons, who has acknowledged he was at one time a "card-carrying member" of LaVey's church "for the purpose of research," has said that virtually all those who claim to be victims of Satanism, be they adults or children, are "*Munchausens.*" That is, they are all lying—deliberately making up outrageous stories in order to get the attention they crave. There are even a few prominent FBI agents out there saying this. They are denying that there is any problem at all big enough to warrant occult-crime seminars.

They want us to believe that Satanism is really a good thing and that it is not really so different from many beliefs currently popular in our society. On the Oprah Winfrey Show in February of 1988, Aquino undoubtedly startled many New Agers by confirming that Satanism and the New Age are basically the same. In the Chaplain's Manual of the United States Armed Forces, Anton Szandor LaVey had already stated that "the Church of Satan is essentially a human potential movement. . . ."[15] The repartee between Aquino and Oprah was fascinating. Oprah asked him "Do you believe in working for the good of mankind, humankind?" To this a straight-faced Aquino responded, "Absolutely. . . ." Oprah, with suspicious tone: "Under the realm of Satan, though." Aquino: "Not under the realm of Satan; under the realm of the exploration of this element of the human psyche that is responsible for its own virtue and responsible for its own ethics." Oprah was quick to perceive the implications of that statement. "Well, the way you explain this is very much the way a lot of people who are into metaphysics now and New Age movement and New Age thinking, they say the very same thing. Are you saying that it's the same?" And Aquino replied, "Yes, except that I would say we have a more precise grasp of what it actually is that we are looking at here. . . . We would say that we understand what's actually happening a little better than many New Agers." I can't argue with Aquino on that point! I suspect that quite a few New Agers are going to be dreadfully surprised to discover someday that their Lucifer, Pan, Sanat Kumara, Higher Self, Lord Maitreya, et al., are in reality just different monikers for one being, and that the Satanists have been worshiping him all along.

"So what you're saying to me," Oprah responded after the commercial break, fully comprehending but obviously not buying Aquino's outrageous propaganda, "is that Satan isn't evil, which is the opposite of what everybody in this world has been taught... it's just a matter of looking inside your soul and understanding that you have power to control your life. Is that what you're saying to me?" "Exactly, exactly," nodded Aquino, pleased that his message was coming across. "You have to understand that most people are looking at the term 'Satanism' and 'Satan' from a very Judeo-Christian stance, where our perception of it and our dealing with it are not that way.... It has nothing to do with evil and destruction and all the rest of it. We have a very high set of personal ethics, and we are very decent, very law-abiding people...."[16]

In fact, Aquino was apparently so offended that anyone would equate Satanism with evil and thereby scorn his religion that he went so far as to compare the stigma carried by those who proudly bear the mark of Satan with the treatment the Jews received at the hands of the Nazis at Auschwitz![17] "One of the reasons that we're here today is because we have seen quite enough of this kind of thing going on in the United States with regard to our religion, and we are not about to sit silent and watch it proceed further."[18]

The Card Carriers

Aquino, Zeena LaVey, and Arthur Lyons display nothing but the highest contempt for those who claim to have been victimized by the worship of the devil. When one young man in Oprah's audience stood up and talked of having been an acolyte of a Satanist church and of having witnessed a human sacrifice, Aquino's first question to him, before he called him an out-and-out liar, was "... were you a member of the Church of Satan, a *card-carrying* member of *the* Church of Satan?"

The question was not altogether an illogical one. Aquino obviously would not want the audience left with the idea that anyone connected with the Temple of Set or the Church of

Satan had been involved in human sacrifice. And yet his question and tone betrayed an arrogance typical of Religious Satanists. The implication is that if you're not an official signed, sealed, and delivered member of *their* specific outfit, then you are obviously and quite simply not a Satanist at all. That is a patently ridiculous assumption. It would be rather like a new and extremely liberal branch of Christianity which flatly denies the reality and personal divinity of Jesus Christ, standing up and announcing to the world that no one who is not a card-carrying member of their particular sect has the right to call themselves a real Christian!

Anton Szandor LaVey is a relative newcomer in the field of historical Satanism. He is viewed by the media and much of the general public as being *the* measuring stick of all Satanism today simply because he happens to be the best-known of the lot. LaVey, a onetime circus-assistant lion-tamer, stage hypnotist, and organ-player for strip joints, was a devoted student of the occult from the time he was a child.[19] His fascination was fed by reading books on the subject as well as by the horror films he was exposed to as a boy.[20]

LaVey founded his Church of Satan on a night long set apart by pagans as a night of riotous celebration and communion with demons, Walpurgisnacht (April 30) 1966. LaVey's Church and its penchant for bizarre theatrics soon drew the attention of many well-known figures in Hollywood as well as numerous doctors, lawyers, computer programmers, and even FBI agents.[21]

Michael Aquino was a onetime member of LaVey's Church, but broke away from it to found his own organization, The Temple of Set, in 1975.[22] Unlike LaVey, Aquino believes in Satan, whom he worships in the form of Set, as a literal reality. For LaVey, however, Satan is not a literal anthropomorphic reality but rather a "dark, hidden force in nature responsible for the workings of earthly affairs."[23] Zeena LaVey denies that they worship the devil at all! "We worship ourselves."

Still, for one who doesn't believe in a personal Satan, LaVey spends an awful lot of valuable space in *The Satanic*

Rituals addressing prayers to "Our Father which art in Hell," and entreating this "mighty and terrible Lord of Darkness" to accept their sacrifice and thereby grant them to "prosper in fullness and length of life, under Thy protection, and may cause to go forth at our bidding Thy dreadful minions, for the fulfillment of our desires and the destruction of our enemies."[24] A tall order for a nonexistent devil!

Types of Satanism

Aquino and LaVey fall in the category of "Religious" Satanism. Unlike the teenagers, who are generally "self-styled" and highly eclectic and unstructured in their beliefs and practices (though potentially every bit as sincere in their devotion), the Religious Satanists have a highly structured organization and form of worship. Their religion is constitutionally recognized and protected by the First Amendment, and the government doesn't much care whether they're out there worshiping Satan, themselves, or a holy hamburger bun, as long as no criminal activity is involved. Despite growing allegations and rumors from children and ex-members, nothing has ever yet been proved against either Aquino or LaVey. The practice of Satanism as defined in their public literature is not against the law, and LaVey especially has on more than one occasion gone out of his way to be helpful to law enforcement agencies. Having once worked as a police photographer, we can assume he knows the ropes. Furthermore, the Handbook for Chaplains of the Armed Services covers the basic beliefs and practices of Satanism as prescribed by Anton LaVey in order to help chaplains understand the growing number of Satanists in our Armed Forces.[25]

A third type of Satanist is recognized to exist: the so-called "Orthodox" or "Cult" Satanist. As we have already mentioned, this group is highly secretive and dangerous. They tend to believe in a very literal Satan indeed, and are working very diligently to bring about the total annihilation of Christianity so that Satan's rightful rule can be established on the earth. Unlike Aquino and LaVey and other Religious Satanists, who seem to thrive on publicity, Cult Satanists are extremely secretive and difficult to spot. They frequently prove to be those considered the pillars of society: doctors, lawyers, district attorneys, judges, schoolteachers, worship leaders, even ministers.[26]

Christ wasn't joking when He warned us to beware of wolves in sheep's clothing.[27] As far back as the Middle Ages we have documented cases of Satanists turning out to be knights, priests, French kings' mistresses, poets, and even members of Parliament. Their practices and beliefs have been handed down from generation to generation, and they generally bring few new members into the group, although there are exceptions to this, depending on the group. Some of these groups are now actively pursuing new members. Their carefully cultivated cloak of respectability provides the perfect cover for criminal activity, which ranges from child pornography and drug trafficking to kidnapping and human sacrifice. These people generally know how to cover their tracks and it seems they've got the money and power behind them to do it. A growing number of their victims are beginning to speak out, but as of now it has been extremely difficult to tie specific crimes to specific perpetrators. This may change in time.[28]

Unholy Bible

Anton LaVey might well have faded into the woodwork of esoteric weirdities of the sixties were it not for the fact that he started writing books. His *Satanic Bible*, published in 1969, has sold hundreds of thousands of copies. While many people may not take LaVey particularly seriously because of his theatrics and the liberal bent of his "theology," his *Satanic Bible* is certainly no joke and has guaranteed his place in history as the most significant promulgator of Satanism in contemporary history.

The impact of the *Satanic Bible* on countless thousands of our teenagers today cannot be overestimated. It has been the guiding light for those who have wanted to worship the devil as well as for many who have found in its pages and in those of its companion, the *Satanic Rituals* (published in 1972), a rationale for carrying out every form of wicked perversity known to man. Of course, Aquino repeatedly proclaimed his horror and chagrin that anyone would take the "lofty ideals" presented in these works and use them as an excuse to carry out their personal perversions and violence.

When confronted on the Geraldo show with a passage out of the *Satanic Bible* which reads in part "Death to the weakling, wealth to the strong,"[29] and asked how he could adhere to this and still uphold the Constitution of the United States as a high-ranking officer with high security clearance, Aquino responded that ". . . what you're looking at there is a highly polemical book that was never meant to be taken literally in all of its commandments."[30]

Maybe so, but someone forgot to tell the kids. A lot of them take the *Satanic Bible* very literally, and in their youthful zeal they frequently carry its vicious philosophy to its logical and historical conclusions. [See Appendix I: "Speak for Yourself."]

On Human Sacrifice

Any teenage would-be devil worshiper can turn to the section in the *Satanic Bible* entitled "Invocation Employed Towards the Conjuration of Destruction" and learn how he too can become "a monstrous machine of annihilation to the festering fragments of the body of he (she) who would detain me. . . . I call upon the messengers of doom to slash with grim delight this victim I hath chosen."[31]

To be sure, LaVey emphasizes in his chapter called "On the Choice of a Human Sacrifice" that no Satanist would, under any circumstance, sacrifice or willfully hurt any animal or baby, because they hold these innocent beings in highest respect. Nevertheless, LaVey does leave the door open for another kind of murder:

> The only time a Satanist would perform a human sacrifice would be if it were to serve a two-fold purpose: that being to release the magician's wrath in the throwing of a curse, and more important, to dispose of a totally obnoxious and deserving individual. . . . The question arises, "Who, then, would

be considered a fit and proper human sacrifice, and how is one qualified to pass judgment on such a person?" The answer is brutally simple. Anyone who has unjustly wronged you—one who has "gone out of his way" to hurt you—to deliberately cause trouble and hardship for you or those dear to you. In short, a person asking to be cursed by their very actions.[32]

To be sure, LaVey has stated that "*symbolically*, the victim is destroyed through the working of a hex or curse." Nevertheless, he fully expects the physical destruction of the one on whom the destruction curse is called, much like Jayne Mansfield and her lover Sam Brody[33] were killed as a result of LaVey's much-publicized death curse on Brody. And, as LaVey points out, the hex or curse "leads to the physical, mental or emotional destruction of the 'sacrifice' in ways and means not attributable to the magician. . . . If your curse provokes their actual annihilation, rejoice that you have been instrumental in ridding the world of a pest!" For a man who continually insists that no true Satanist ever has or ever would commit an actual, literal human sacrifice, one would think LaVey would have thought twice about some of the Infernal Names he included in the list he provides for their invocation. At least 15 of the ancient gods and demons on his list are well-known to have demanded human sacrifice in general, and in the case of Adramelech, Chemosh, Milcom, and Moloch, child sacrifice in particular. Not to mention LaVey's inclusion of Dracula, the nickname for a real-life, unspeakably sadistic killer named Vlad, also known as the Impaler (ca. 1431-1476) whose legendary thirst for human blood earned him immortality in Bram Stoker's novel *Dracula*. Vlad used to enjoy doing things like impaling his dinner guests on stakes and then dining in their midst to the sounds of their screams.[34] It should not be surprising if perhaps some of us were to come away with the idea that LaVey's protestations of "symbolic" sacrifice are, perhaps, less than sincere, and included in the book primarily because not to have done so would have virtually guaranteed LaVey chronic and unwanted attention by the law.

Vulnerable Teens

For most kids the teen years are a tremendously difficult time. They are a time of seeking a sense of identity and independence. For many teenagers these years are a time of experimentation and rebellion. One young Hollywood woman said that she had run away from home when she was 12. "I was rebelling against my parents. Then I put a pentagram up on my wall. The next best thing to sex, drugs, rock 'n' roll was Satan."[35]

Satanism is unquestionably the ultimate in rebellion. It carries a "blood-and-guts" macho image that generally (though by no means exclusively) appeals to boys. The typical teenage Satan worshiper tends to be a creative and intelligent white male from a middle- to upper-class family. He is probably an underachiever and has a low self-image.

He likely feels alienated from his family and their traditional values and religious beliefs, as well as feeling conflict in his relationship with his peers. He is bored and desperately seeking something new and exciting to fill the emptiness of his existence. "What have I got to live for?" is a question he may be asking. His life is characterized by a sense of personal helplessness.

Some of these kids turn to Satan in search of a father figure. Some of them are "throwaways"—kids who are out on the street because their parents threw them out and told them never to come home again. Some are from single-parent homes. Others have fathers who may care very much but who simply don't take the time to really communicate with their child or set firm, loving, consistent guidelines and rules for him. According to recent statistics, the average parent spends approximately 30 seconds a day of meaningful communication with his or her child! A lot of children are just left to raise themselves.

Dr. Peter Olsson, a clinical associate professor of psychiatry at the Baylor College of Medicine, has spent over ten years studying supernatural cults as well as researching the reasons why teens become involved with Satanism. It was his conclusion that overly permissive parents were in good part responsible for some teens' involvement with Satanism. "They see in the Devil a leader—a powerful being they can look up to for guidance. He's someone who can take the decision-making problems off their shoulders."[36] For many youngsters, participation in Satanism is their way of crying out for the attention they're not sensing from their parents.

"But why don't they turn to Jesus instead of the devil?" you may ask. There are several reasons. First of all, they're sick unto death of the hypocrisy they see in so many of our churches. How can we expect them to be drawn to Christianity when "Do as I say, not as I do" is presented to them as the unspoken motto of their parents and church leaders. These kids are not stupid. They rapidly figure out that if Christianity isn't working in the church it's not going to do much for them either. And they're rebelling against the mindless legalism and empty ritual that characterize so much of the church.

One young Satanist named Wilson Mattea (who describes himself as "a former Catholic") put it this way: "I often think of Satan as a cool dude. Since he controls one part of the supernatural, he tends to let you be on your own, to do what you want, whereas God has his own rules on how you're supposed to live. They're kind of binding. He wants to put you in a jail cell, to control you."[37]

Another young Satanist named Johnnie said that his parents had sent him to church when he was younger, "but it didn't seem to do me any good. I didn't like it, so I tried the opposite side, and I liked that."[38] Empty religion tends to have a similar effect on a lot of people.

Satan, on the other hand, is regarded as the Simón Bolívar of the cosmos, the great liberator who gives man unbridled freedom to "do his own thing" and "be himself." He promises you limitless power and control over your circumstances and over the supernatural, and panders to your fascination with the mystical and the unexplained, thereby providing a surefire way out of boredom. He presents you with an open platform for the uninhibited pursuit of sex, money, drugs, and any kind of "high" you desire. He promises you freedom from guilt and the "good life" here and now, not to mention an eternity of excitement and power in hell.

But even young Wilson Mattea had a sense that Satan wasn't everything he was cracked up to be: "First, you're all good and stuff. . . . You don't like crime. You don't like to do drugs. Then, slowly, you transgress. You transpose. That's when the demon creeped into my soul. I must have left some void open."[39]

Devil Music

The *Satanic Bible* is by no means the average teenager's only (or even his first) introduction to devil worship. Certainly this was true for Wilson, who credits heavy metal for helping to transform him from a Catholic to a Satanist. Like Wilson, the vast majority of kids get their first hard-core introduction to Satanism at their local record or video store. The images on the cover jackets alone are breathtaking in their portrayal of raw decadence and demonic evil. If you've never perused the heavy-metal section of your local music store, you might seriously consider doing so sometime in the near future.

Thousands upon thousands of our children are spending hour after hour a day, year after year, feeding their minds and souls with music quite literally spawned out of the pit of hell. Their heroes extol the brutal joys and glory of rape, incest, bestiality, sex with corpses, human sacrifice, sadomasochism, drug abuse, and alcoholism. Every form of perverted violence, hatred, and rebellion is encouraged, from matricide to suicide. From four to eight hours a day some of our children are listening to lyrics like the following, recorded by a group called Venom:

Sacrifice,
Oh so nice . . .
Sacrifice to Lucifer, my master.
Bring the chalice,

Raise the knife,
Welcome to my sacrifice;
Plunge the dagger in her breast,
I insist.
S-a-c-r-i-f-i-c-e...
Demons rejoice,
Sacrifice, sacrifice,
Name your price.[40]

In an elementary school in Belle Vernon, Pennsylvania, several sixth-graders wanted their music teacher to explain to them some lyrics they saw on another one of Venom's album covers:

We're possessed by all that's evil; the death of you, God, we demand. We spit at the virgin you worship, and sit at Lord Satan's left hand (from "Welcome to Hell").

It seems the kids were also curious about some lyrics by another heavy-metal band that calls itself Slayer. It said something about "the relentless lust of rotting flesh." The teacher did her best to answer their questions as delicately as possible, but the next day some extremely irate parents called the school principal demanding to know why their kids were being subjected to discussions about necrophilia and Satanism. Peggy Mann, the author of the article which reported this incident in *Reader's Digest*, pointed out that the parents had evidently never taken the time to listen to the records their kids were buying and obviously had no idea of what was on them.[41]

Of course, proponents of heavy-metal will passionately deny any connection between their music and philosophy and the rebellious, self-destructive generation we are currently cultivating, as Tipper Gore and Sally Nevius, founders of Parents' Music Resource Center, have discovered.[42] They have confronted one "gentleman" (and I use the term in the loosest possible sense of the word) after another in a music industry that for the most part refuses to accept responsibility for its product. For example, Mr. Legs McNeil of the rock magazine *Spin* defended heavy-metal music on the Geraldo show[43] by invoking the First Amendment and "people's right to write lyrics and sing about what they want. I think kids are interested and fascinated by evil. I think they live in very powerful extremes. And when you are a child and everyone's telling you not to do something wrong, when someone's trying to tell you what you're doing is wrong all the time, this kind of stuff affords you some freedom. I mean, evil's fascinating."

Geraldo asked Mr. McNeil if he believed that the First Amendment was designed to protect lyrics such as those by one of the vilest of heavy-metal bands: "Sacrifice the virgin's spiritual right! Their master's time has come! The moon is full tonight, an orgy's taking place, human blood will spill, an act of worship—Satan has their souls."

Mr. McNeil hesitated only a split second before answering, "How can—you know, you just asked me a question. When does the First Amendment not apply to anything we say?"

Quite simply, in a lot of cases! The First Amendment does not guarantee you the right to stand in a crowded auditorium and yell "Fire!" if there is no fire. One may squeal all he wants to about his First Amendment rights to freedom of speech and about the horrors of censorship, but the First Amendment does *not* guarantee a person the right to expose himself in public, or to produce and distribute child pornography, or to threaten the life of the President of the United States, or to contribute to the delinquency of a minor. Nor does it guarantee a minor the right to attend an "R"- or "X"-rated movie unaccompanied by an adult willing to take the responsibility for polluting the child's mind.

So how come these blatant perverts who masquerade behind the thin veneer of "art" and "music" are allowed to do all this unchallenged on a concert stage while hiding behind the First Amendment! Are we no longer to draw the line at anything in this society? Rock musicians can protest that they are "Christians," regular people, and "*not* Satanists," all day long, as indeed some do. But in concerts around the country some musicians act out the sodomization of naked baby-dolls, then slash off their heads as hundreds of young fans scream their approval. The fans get the message loud and clear, affectionately paying homage to the musicians by throwing dead or decapitated animals onto the stage.[44] And why not. The fans are just following their example and offering back to their demon idols the sacrifices they know will be most pleasing.

Gimmicked Out

Few of the "black metal" bands (bands that focus on Satanism in their themes and lyrics) will actually admit to being practicing Satanists. Most assure us that it's nothing but an innocent sales gimmick for them. However I listened to card-carrying, High Priestess of the Church of Satan in Van Nuys, California, Dea Lucas, on "Mid-Morning L.A." in March of 1984, and she had this to say:

> Heavy Metal groups are influencing the kids to come to Satan.... The groups are into Satanism even though they may deny it. Just by listening to the lyrics, being a Satanist myself, I can read between the lines.... Black Sabbath...and AC/DC are Satanic!

Ms. Lucas also stated that she and her fellow Satanists were out at a Black Sabbath concert in Long Beach, California, one night putting their flyers on kids' windshields.

King Diamond is one black-metal musician who is openly proud of his satanic affiliations. Danish-born, he was first drawn to the powers of the "dark side" when he was only 13 years old. In *Hit Parader Magazine*, he says:

> When we started in 1981, people just weren't ready for songs about Satan. We opened the doors for many young "black metal" bands in Europe, but unfortunately, most of them see the style as some sort of gimmick—*they have no understanding of the forces they are dealing with.*[45]

Guitarist Jimmy Page of Led Zeppelin does. This group was one of the original "metal mashers," which set the example for groups like Black Sabbath.[46] The cover of one of their albums, *House of the Holy*, shows a child being sacrificed to demons. But their all-time greatest hit is "Stairway to Heaven," a song that is a call to those who have mindlessly followed the path of Christianity in trying to buy their way into heaven to "change the road you're on" and follow the Piper (i.e., Satan) instead. It seems obvious to me and many others that the song contains clear backmasking which says, "I sing because I live with Satan. The Lord turned me off. There's no escaping it. Here's to my sweet Satan. . . ."[47]

Perhaps you can understand my dismay at finding that Jack Canfield recommends that schoolteachers play "Stairway to Heaven" for their students while leading them in their "Radiant Student" meditations.[48]

What the "black heavy metal" musicians are teaching our children is dangerous and evil—not just "weird," not just "sick," not just "different," *evil*. Hideously, sickeningly, and desperately evil. The very word *evil*, of course, suggests a value judgment that is bound to stun the sophisticated in our society who have long preached that morals, values, and ethics are relative. But how long, in the name of "open-mindedness" and "art" and "free speech" will we continue to allow raw, naked, unadulterated evil to poison the spirits and minds of our children? Perhaps if we had had the courage to rise up against this evil as a nation years ago we could have saved at least some of the thousands of teenagers who kill themselves every year in this country.

Over and over, devoted fans listen to lyrics like "*Can you help me?/ Oh, shoot out my brains, ohhh yeah!*" How many teenagers have been influenced by songs such as "Suicide Solution" and later committed suicide?[49] Perhaps we could have saved Ray, an 18-year-old who made a suicide pact two days before Christmas several years ago with his 19-year-old friend James after listening to the lyrics of a heavy-metal album.[50] James survived the attempt. The gun, covered with Ray's blood, slipped in his hands as he fired. He was left hideously and painfully disfigured, but he lived to tell of the direct influence which the music had on their decision to kill themselves. James recently died as a result of complications from reconstruction surgery.[51]

I don't mean to be simplistic here. There are many causes for the tragic epidemic of teen suicide in our country which have nothing to do with black metal music or with the occult.[52] Nevertheless, I believe that there's a principle of computer programming that generally applies here: "Garbage in, garbage out." Can we really believe that what we see and hear has no effect on our behavior? If it doesn't, why do we bother buying classics and good books for our children? If it doesn't, then an awful lot of advertising agencies are wasting billions of dollars a year making sure their product is seen as often and by as many people as they can possibly manage. They fully expect their efforts to result in a change in your behavior which will ultimately result in you buying their product.

We allow our children to fill their minds with violence, murder, rebellion, mutilation, and Satan, and are then astonished if that child gathers with some friends one evening to smash a boy with baseball bats "because it's fun."[53] A troubled teen who may already be considering self-destruction, does not need to go home at night with a school assignment from his teacher to write his own obituary for his death-education class. Nor does he need to listen to hour after hour of music and lyrics that may well convince a troubled teenager that suicide is his solution. (Some suicidologists estimate that over one million children a year think about suicide at one time or another.[54]) Close to 600,000 teenagers in this country attempt suicide each year. Of these, almost 6500 succeeded in destroying their young lives. That's 18 children a day, one every 80 minutes.[55] Can we really believe that what their minds dwell on has no impact on their lives?

Signs of Satanic Involvement

It is crucial that parents, teachers, ministers, doctors, social workers, and anyone else connected with young people learn to look for and recognize the warning signs of possible satanic involvement. Parents, you especially are in a key position to discern what's going on with your child.

The key word here is *supervision*. It is a crucial part of responsible parenting. You need to know at all times specifically *where* your kid is going, and *with whom*. He needs to have consistent guidelines and curfews. If his behavior is okay and you have an established bond of communication and trust between you, then great! But if you're noticing odd or negative changes in his behavior, such as consistently breaking curfew, displaying a defiant attitude, odd mood swings, cutting school—any kind of behavior that makes you wonder just a little whether he's into drugs or getting involved with bad company—you must find out what's going on. That may involve a bit of detective work on your part—such as checking out the kid's room. I know that many consider this an unforgivable breach of a child's right to privacy. However, every policeman, detective, and counselor I've listened to who has had to pick up the pieces of lives destroyed by satanic involvement has invariably given the same advice: *If you suspect there's something strange going on with your kid, forget about privacy! Watch the kid like a hawk and go check out his room!*

I've heard too many stories of parents who never realized their children were into Satanism and the occult until after it was too late to prevent a tragedy. A mother in Denver, Colorado, came home from work one day in 1982 and found her son dead of carbon monoxide poisoning. He had killed himself. Hidden in his room were satanic books, including a copy of the *Satanic Bible*, a ritual knife (athame), Dungeons and Dragons material, and a bag of bones that may have been squirrel bones. The mother said in an interview with Connie Chung that for several days before he died she would look up and find him staring at her with a dark, evil stare. Another mother whose boy had shot himself through the heart said that they had made the "big mistake" of giving him the absolute privacy he demanded when he became 15 years old. After his death, they discovered a stash of weapons under his bed. They also found jawbones and other remains of the family cat that had disappeared sometime earlier. "But he seemed so normal," the heartbroken mother exclaimed. "Never think 'NOT MY CHILD!' It can happen to anybody." Most kids do give some indication, either in their attitude and behavior or in the paraphernalia they keep around. Does he own a copy of the *Satanic Bible* and the *Satanic Rituals*? What about other occult literature, books, and magazines? Many of the music and skateboard magazines are filled with symbols and drawings of anarchy, rebellion, Satanism, and death. Look through school notebooks for drawings, satanic symbols, and doodlings. Are his school compositions, essays, or poetry filled with themes of death and violence? *Thrasher*, one of the skateboarding magazines, regularly publishes drawings sent in by its readers. The caption under one particularly gruesome drawing of a creature disemboweling itself reads: "A well-composed illustration of horror. Like something from the pages of a spooky novel. Brad Moore shows a rising ability." *About 99 percent of all the art received is horror or futuristic disaster!*[56]

Satanic Plans and Symbols

I have seen kids' diaries filled with all kinds of notes and plans for the establishment of covens and the designing of rituals. Some have included plans for ritual killings and parental and sibling murders, as well as their own pact with the devil, to lead as many other people to Satan and destruction as possible, and then to eventually commit suicide. Some parents have found intricate satanic rituals stored on their kids' computer software. Check for occult symbols on his clothing and jewelry. If your kid starts sporting pentagrams, skulls, werewolves, swastikas, upside-down crosses, and daggers dripping blood, or if he has recently begun painting the nail of his pinky or middle finger of his left hand in black or red, or if he's conducting rituals on your dining-room table, it's by all means time to start showing some concern.

Is his or her room draped in black gauze? Does he have inverted crosses and pentagrams on the walls? Is he obsessed with heavy-metal music? Are his bedroom walls covered with the perverted posters of heavy-metal groups such as WASP,

Venom, Black Sabbath, Ozzie Osbourne, KISS, King Diamond, Dio, AC/DC, Motley Crue, Slayer, or Judas Priest? Does he have an altar set up in some corner of the room or inside his closet? Look for the presence of a goat's head (Baphomet), candles, black or red hooded robes, ceremonial knives, bells, chalice, and the presence of skulls and other bones, either animal or human. Some kids are very creative about stashing this stuff, by the way. It's a good idea to also check the attic, basement, toolshed, tree house, or other favorite outdoor hangout. Or he may keep it all in a school or gym locker.

Is he or she obsessed with Fantasy Role-Playing games? Does he talk or write about death and suicide? What about a fascination with horror films and "slasher" videos such as *Faces of Death*, *Friday the 13th*, *Halloween*, or *Nightmare on Elm Street*. Films such as these (and there are hundreds on the market like them) jade a child, desensitizing him to the horror of violence, rape, demons, blood, perversion, and death. And yet they have proved so popular that they have generated three to four sequels and have been turned into prime-time television series. It is a frightening fact that many of our youngsters are beginning to live out the fantasies which these films plant in their minds.[57]

Have his grades taken a sudden and radical plunge? Is he secretive and elusive about where he goes and who he's spending time with? Has he suddenly lost all interest in once-favorite sports, hobbies, or pastimes? Has there been a radical change in his eating or sleeping patterns? Is he into heavy alcohol or drug use? Is he displaying cruel or hostile behavior toward animals, siblings, or you? Some of that rage may show up in self-mutilation. Look for signs of fresh scars or thin razor cuts on arms or legs. Look for tattoos. Does he speak favorably about Satan? Does he react with rage and blasphemy whenever the subjects of God, Jesus, the Bible, or the church come up?

Just a Phase?

Don't, I beg you, make the mistake of assuming that this is all just a fad or a phase that all kids go through! Of course, not every kid who gets into devil worship necessarily goes out and kills someone or commits suicide, but a growing number of them do. How many of you are willing to take that chance? Unfortunately, some parents who have seen these signs and gone to teachers or even ministers for counsel have been turned away with a patronizing pat on the head and the empty assurance that "it's just a phase that all kids go through." How many more children need to commit suicide before we conclude that it's more than "just a phase"? How many more parents must weep over children murdered by children steeped in Satanism and fantasy role-playing games before we decide it's more than "just a fad"? How many more parents themselves need to be murdered by their own sons and daughters before we begin to pay attention?

There's no such thing as just "playing around" with the things of Satan. Some psychologists and others to the contrary, Satan is a very real being, and so are his demons. Many people have found to their eternal sorrow that summoning demons even as a joke can open the door wide for demonic intrusion into their lives.

If your child's behavior is out of control for *whatever* reason, there are local and national organizations that can help.[58]

You must get involved with your child! Talk with him. (Please note I said *with*, not *at*.) Ask questions. Hopefully, from the time your child was tiny, you have established a good talking relationship with him. When you really know your child and have established a mutual bond of trust with him, it's much easier to sense when something is going wrong in his life and deal with it before it gets out of hand. Nevertheless, even if he initially rebuffs any attempt you may make at communicating with him, don't give up! Keep trying! Be willing to be open and vulnerable to him. As a concerned parent, you can approach your child in a spirit of humility and ask that the child forgive you. "I have failed you deeply or you wouldn't be doing this. I have neglected to talk with you and spend time with you. Please forgive me. Please help me; work with me. I'm deeply concerned about what you're into."[59]

Listen to your child. Take the time to listen to his music and find out why he likes it. Show him by the attention and time you give him that you are genuinely concerned about what he thinks and feels. Parent, your attitude here is all-important! You probably won't get very far if you confront your child with "Look, kid! I found all this satanic junk in your room, and you'd better get it out *now* or you're grounded for the rest of the week!" You must explain to him the dangers of what he's into. Explain to him from the Word of God why you cannot allow him to bring heavy-metal and satanic paraphernalia into the house. Most of all, show him that you love him unconditionally and that you care. Let him know that you understand what goes on in some of these groups, and then warn him of the dangers. Tell him about Lauren Stratford and what Satanists did to her. Give him *Satan's Underground* and Mike Warnke's *The Satan Seller* and encourage him to read these books. Tell him about Jim Hardy and Pete Roland and Ron Clements, kids who thought Satan was cool and gave them status and power; kids who thought it was exciting to smash kittens and puppies with baseball bats and gouge their eyes out as offerings to Satan; kids who one day smashed Steven Newberry with those same bats until he died "because it's fun, Steven."[60]

Pete Roland's mother suspected something was terribly wrong with her son. She found crude weapons in his room, broken glass, and a stick with nails poking out. His walls were covered with the goriest of heavy-metal posters. He assured her that the satanic symbols and images of violence and death on his T-shirts "didn't mean a thing." When she found a *Satanic Bible* in his room, he explained that "it belonged to someone else."[61] Tragically, she believed him. And as for the heavy-metal music, she just figured that "if they sell it, it's gotta be okay."

On the Geraldo Special this heartbroken mother mourned for the fate of her son, now in prison for the rest of his life for the murder of Steven Newberry:

> I feel very guilty that I didn't pay attention. . . . I saw the satanic symbols on his book work and I had spoken to him about it. It didn't mean anything,

you know, it was—I assumed it was a passing phase. I had my things when I was that age; I assumed that he had his. I assumed wrong. And I would advise anybody, if they see anything like that, to look into it, don't ignore it. It doesn't pass. . . . I wish I had listened to the music, I wish I had thrown it out. I wish I had gone to school and talked to him, talked to his friends' mothers; maybe they saw some things that I didn't see. Maybe if we put them together we could have come up with something. . . .

Even as Adolfo de Jesus Constanzo and his followers in Matamoros, Pete Roland and his friends thought that Satan would protect them. They thought Satan would make them invincible and give them power. Where did it get Pete? In a prison cell for the rest of his life: "It's all false, man. It just leads to your own destruction. Look where I'm at, you know, look at my sentence. I mean, I'm in jail for life without parole."

But at least he's alive. Adolfo de Jesus Constanzo died, by his own command, at the hands of his homosexual lover rather than be captured by the police who surrounded him in his Mexico City hideout.

A Light in the Darkness

There is a great darkness upon us. As we approach the time of the return of our Lord Jesus Christ we can expect to see the influence of Satanism and other devil-worshiping cults (like the one discovered in Matamoros) ever more prevalent among us and our children. And yet the Word of God declares that a great Light has come into the darkness, and in that Light there are no shifting shadows! "The Son of God appeared for this purpose, that He might destroy the works of the devil!" (1 John 3:8). Those who worship Satan worship a defeated god, for Jesus of Nazareth made a public display of Satan at the cross (Colossians 2:15). To be sure, Satan is still a powerful enemy. It is not yet time for the fulfillment of the prophecy in Revelation that foretells the ultimate doom of the Evil One.

The time is coming when "the devil who deceived them [will be] thrown into the lake of fire and brimstone,"[62] but that time is not yet. He is still a powerful enemy to be reckoned with.

Those who seek to fight against Satan in their own strength are doomed to defeat. Only Jesus Christ of Nazareth has defeated him, and only those who stand in that victory can see the enemy vanquished in their lives.

Those involved in the occult and in Satanism, those who feel trapped inside the black hole of devil worship and perversion, those who have sacrificed animals and humans, those who have sold themselves to the devil for the illusion of power and riches and fame, those who have spit at God and mocked His Son, need to know that even now *it is not too late to get out!*

> Say to them, "As I live!" declares the Lord God, "I take no pleasure in the death of the wicked, but rather that the wicked turn from his way and live" (Ezekiel 33:11).

Chapter 15

What's a Parent to Do?

✦

Thanks be to God, who gives us the victory through our Lord Jesus Christ!
> —The Apostle Paul
> 1 Corinthians 15:57

Submit therefore to God. Resist the devil and he will flee from you!
> —The Apostle James
> James 4:7

By now it is entirely possible that many of you are in a panic, wondering how you can possibly shield, protect, or rescue your children from the wiles of the devil that unquestionably surround them on every side.

If you've gotten this far in the book, you've already taken one of the most important steps you could take: You've made an effort to become informed! And yet as crucial as that is, simply gathering information is not enough. Sharing it with your children is not enough either. Nor is confronting New Age educators. Neither will the problem be ultimately settled by getting elected to school boards or by writing letters to your representatives. [See Appendix K.]

It is not enough to resolve to become a better parent by spending time communicating and genuinely listening to your child, or by setting consistent guidelines for him, or even by home-schooling him. The problem will not be solved exclusively by getting the best therapy or counseling available for a troubled child or a dysfunctional family. *All these things are most certainly vitally important and should be pursued vigorously. Yet if this is all you do, it will not be enough!*

Wickedness in Heavenly Places

The battle we wage is first and foremost a *spiritual war*. The apostle Paul warned us that—

> our struggle is not against flesh and blood, but against the rulers, against the powers, against the world forces of this darkness, against the spiritual forces of wickedness in the heavenly places (Ephesians 6:12).

Our fight is against the one who raised his fist in the face of Almighty God and cried, "I will make myself like the Most High!"[1] It is against the one who has from the beginning been a murderer and a liar, a deceiver and a thief. Satan is indeed the prince of the power of the air[2] and all the world lies in the power of the Evil One,[3] for man gave this power to him in the Garden. Whether through deceitful subterfuge, or disguised as an angel of light, or in all his unveiled hideousness, Satan seeks only one thing: the ultimate spiritual and physical destruction of human beings; for in destroying that which God made in His own image he wounds the heart of God.

Satan's rage is fierce because he knows his time is short. These next days until our Lord's return will be filled with the blood and destruction of many people. Many of those destroyed will be children because there was no one to defend them; no one to wage war on their behalf or train their hearts and minds and spirits to discern good and evil; no one who had the courage to stand in the face of the "wisdom" of the world and teach them the profound reality and truth of "Jesus loves me, this I know, for the Bible tells me so."

Many will be lost in the battle because there is no one to teach them how to "be strong in the Lord and in the strength of His might" or how to "put on the full armor of God, that you may be able to stand firm against the schemes of the devil!"[4] Even now, by the countless thousands, our young ones are being led like lambs to the slaughter.

You Can't Give What You Don't Have

You can't share truth with your children if you don't know what it is. You can't show your child how to resist the devil if you yourself have not first learned how to submit your own way to God.

The answer to the darkness and the bondage and the fear is so simple: Jesus. "A simplistic answer," some may think. "A foolish answer! A ridiculous answer! No answer at all!" exclaim others who have long and publicly expressed their irritation at those of us who look to Jesus of Nazareth as the ultimate source of healing and restoration. And so they impatiently brush aside the only One who truly holds the answers, and instead continue to wonder why their therapeutic techniques aren't working. It is true that "the word of the cross is to those who are perishing foolishness, but to us who are being saved it is the power of God."[5] The apostle Paul was not ashamed of the gospel, "for it is the power of God for salvation to everyone who believes."[6]

> There is salvation in no one else; for there is no other name under heaven that has been given among men by which we must be saved.[7]

That name is Jesus. Apart from Him there is no hope—not for you and not for your children.

You can spend the rest of your days chanting, meditating on your chakras, aligning your chi energy, clutching your crystals, drawing your mandalas, consulting the channelers, practicing your Yoga, talking to your "Higher Self," eating your kumquats, consulting your astrology charts, and affirming your personal divinity, but none of these will give you that peace which passes all understanding, nor will it purchase salvation for your soul. It seems to be God's good pleasure to make "foolish the wisdom of the world."[8] Salvation is not something you achieve or earn. It is something you simply receive as God's free gift: *"For by grace you have been saved through faith, and that not of yourselves, it is the gift of God; not as a result of works, that no one should boast."*[9]

So many people in the New Age are beginning to find themselves in the same sorry condition as Fay in Neil Simon's movie *Chapter Two*. In a conversation with Leo, with whom she's contemplating an affair, Fay wistfully acknowledges, "I feel so empty. I've tried TM, meditation, and health foods and am now tranquilly, serenely, and robustly unhappier than I have ever been!"

But everyone who comes to Jesus on His terms will find true peace and freedom: "*As many as received Him, to them He gave the right to become children of God, even to those who believe in His name.*"[10] Jesus is as near to you as the whisper of a prayer.

The Gnostic lies and half-truths of the New Age may seem satisfying for a time, but ultimately they will leave you empty and disillusioned. Psychotechnologies and occult philosophies are a vapid and shallow substitute for a relationship with the living, transcendent, personal God of the universe! All you need to do to begin your relationship with Him is to invite Him into your life with a prayer:

> Lord Jesus, I ask You now to come into my life. I give it to You. I recognize that I will never be good enough to make it into God's presence on my own. I acknowledge before You that I am a sinner and that I have broken God's perfect law. I know that the penalty for that is death—eternal separation from God. But I thank You, Lord Jesus, for paying that penalty for me by dying in my place on the cross! I accept Your payment for my sin, and praise You that my salvation isn't based on my merit but rather on Your grace! I commit my whole life into Your hand, Lord Jesus, and I thank You for Your promise that You will never leave me or forsake me. Fill my life with Your Holy Spirit and make it pleasing to God. Amen.

True Confessions

God has repeatedly labeled every form of occultism abomination. Its practice is a direct affront and insult to His character and sovereignty, for it is a direct violation of the First and Second Commandments, which forbid us to have any other gods before Him (Exodus 20:3,4).

When the Ephesians became believers in Jesus Christ, the Book of Acts reports that "many also of those who had believed kept coming, confessing and disclosing their practices."[11] There was something about coming into the light of Jesus that instinctively made them want to bring into that light the secret and hidden things of darkness, thereby shaking off their bondage.

Confession is simply agreeing with God about sin in our lives. Confession is for our benefit, not God's!

> When I kept silent about my sin, my body wasted away through my groaning all day long. . . . My vitality was drained away as with the fever heat of summer. . . . I acknowledged my sin to Thee, and my iniquity I did not hide; I said, "I will confess my transgressions to the Lord"; and Thou didst forgive the guilt of my sin (Psalm 32:3-5).

To acknowledge the existence or presence of sin is the great anathema of the Satanist and the New Ager. And yet the Word of God says, "If we say that we have no sin, we are deceiving ourselves, and the truth is not in us" and "The wages of sin is death."[12] That's the bad news. The good news, however, is that "if we confess our sins, He is faithful and righteous to forgive us our sins and to cleanse us from all unrighteousness" (1 John 1:9).

It might be helpful to take a moment here to make a list of any occult activities that you may have been involved with. Even if you were just "fooling around" with it as a child, write it down. You may not have known at the time that what you were doing came under the category of "abomination," but you know now. Ask the Holy Spirit to show you if there is anything else in your life that you need to deal with before Him. It might be pride, anger, unforgiveness, lust, envy, greed, alcoholism, drug addiction, or a root of bitterness. Whatever it might be, bring it before the Lord now and confess it to Him; bring it into the light and ask the Lord to heal you from these things that have for so long acted as a barrier between you and Him.

> "Come now, and let us reason together," says the Lord; "though your sins are as scarlet, they will be as white as snow; though they are red like crimson, they will be like wool" (Isaiah 1:18).

"But you don't understand what I've done!" said a note from a young woman who had called in while I was on TBN discussing this issue one night. "I was a Satanist. I sacrificed my own baby to Satan. Are you really saying that God can forgive me too?" Yes, that's *exactly* what I'm saying! "But I don't deserve His forgiveness." That's right—you don't, and neither do I. Forgiveness is ours solely on the basis of the finished work of Jesus Christ on the cross. "In Him we have redemption through His blood, the forgiveness of our trespasses, according to the riches of His grace."[13] "For God so loved the world that He gave His only begotten Son, that *whoever* believes in Him should not perish but have eternal life."[14] "Behold, the Lamb of God who takes away the sin of the world!"[15]

"There is therefore now *no condemnation* for those who are in Christ Jesus!"[16] Because He has loved us and forgiven us, we too can now forgive others and even ourselves.

I Renounce the Devil

The early church fathers understood the importance of having a new convert from paganism pray to renounce the devil and all his works before being baptized. As Kurt Koch has pointed out in his classic manual *Occult Bondage and Deliverance*, "Every sin connected with sorcery is basically a contract with the powers of darkness."[17] It is important that you now pray to officially and legally break that contract with the Evil One, who tends to consider even the most innocent of excursions into his realm as legal ground for tenure in your life. Renounce also any sin of occultism or sorcery that may be in your family line. Renounce the power of any curses that may be upon you, your children, or your family line. Renounce any psychic powers you may possess. To renounce means "to separate yourself from." To renounce something means to wholeheartedly turn your back on it, to no longer allow the thing being renounced to hold sway over you.

Even if you have been a true believer in Jesus Christ for many years, if there are sins of occultism or perversion in your life or family line that have not been dealt with, it is certainly possible for that demonic opening to be there. It can show up in many ways: in a coldness of heart to the things of God and to His Word; in the harsh legalism that denies by its actions the forgiveness and grace of God; in hypocrisy and corruption of life that belies the piety of your words; in the presence of psychic powers that may even masquerade in the church as the genuine gifts of the Spirit.[18]

You might pray something like this:

> Almighty God, in the name of Your Son, Jesus Christ of Nazareth, I confess to You these things which Your Word tells me are abomination in Your sight (list them out loud). I now renounce these practices. I renounce Satan and all his works. I renounce my spirit guide in the name of Jesus the Messiah, and I command you, deceitful spirit, to depart from me to go to that place where Jesus sends you! I now reject any psychic powers or abilities which have possessed me, and I command them to leave my life in the name of Jesus the Messiah. I renounce the occult practices of my forefathers. If any spirit of Witchcraft or sorcery has attached itself to me or my children or my family line because of these practices, I now command them to leave, and I declare, by the victory of Jesus Christ, that their power over me and any of my children or my children's children is now broken forever.
>
> I now ask You, Lord Jesus, to come into my life. I ask You to be my Savior and my Lord, and I commit

myself to You now and forever. Fill me with Your Holy Spirit, Lord. Cover me and my family with the protection of Your holy blood shed at the cross in payment for my sins. Almighty God, I praise You that the Son of God appeared for this purpose— that He might destroy the works of the devil! Destroy now, Almighty Lord, every work of the devil in my life and in the life of my children. Shield and protect us from the hatred and deceit of the Evil One! And teach me, Lord, how to truly minister to my children in Your name, that they may always see Your grace and unconditional love for them reflected through me. I lift this prayer to You, heavenly Father, in the precious name of Your Son, my Lord and Savior, Jesus Christ. Amen.

The Devil's Tools

The next thing the Ephesians did after confessing and disclosing their practices was to gather together all their occult tools and books and destroy them: "Many also of those who practiced magic brought their books together and began burning them in the sight of all; and they counted up the price of them and found it fifty thousand pieces of silver. So the word of the Lord was growing mightily and prevailing."[19] The Ephesians wanted to make it clear to the entire city that they no longer served the demon gods and goddesses, nor would they any longer traffic with them through the practice of their magic arts.

There was another reason for the destruction of the objects connected with occultism: These books and objects can serve as focal points for demons. Demons can and frequently do attach themselves to occult tools and books, as many people have found to their horror and surprise.

A case in point: Manuel Bonilla, a well-known Latin American evangelist, and his family had been living in their new home only a short while when it began—the sense of a black presence that would move among them in the night, and the feeling of sudden terror in the special alcove that had intially been the children's favorite hangout. And then the crying began—the chilling sounds of an infant sobbing and whimpering in the dark. Overnight guests in the house would ask about the weeping child the next morning, but there was no explanation that Manuel could offer.

Manuel was well-versed in spiritual warfare, and as head of his household he commanded the evil spirit to leave his home and family in the name of Jesus Christ. But then suddenly it would return, and the terror among them seemed blacker than ever. This continued for several years, until Manuel said he and his family despaired of ever being rid of the oppression that was beginning to take its toll on them. There was no hidden sin in his family, no occultism, nothing he was aware of that could possibly act as a focal point for demons . . . and yet, the thing simply would not leave!

Then one morning, while replacing the insulation in the attic, the workman made an unexpected discovery. "Pastor Bonilla, what would you like me to do with these . . . 'things' in your attic?" As far as the pastor knew, the only thing in his attic was dust, but his face turned ashen when he saw what the workman had found hidden. The objects were clearly ritualistic in nature—among them a large crucifix on which a black effigy of Jesus hung upside-down. There was a noose around the figure's neck, and long nails had been pounded all through the body, which had dark, crusty splotches on it that for all the world looked like dried blood. God only knows what hideous, demonic, bloody rituals the blasphemous objects had been part of.

Pastor Bonilla wasted no time in destroying and burning the hideous things. Once again he took authority over the demonic being in the name of Jesus of Nazareth, commanding it to leave his home and be confined to the place where Jesus sent it. From that moment on, the blackness left his house and never returned.

Do Your Housecleaning!

Some of you have got a lot of housecleaning to do! Devil

masks and idols that you brought back as trophies and mementos from the mission field—*destroy them.* Your collection of books of channeled wisdom, the old Ouija board you've kept in the trunk since college days, your grandmother's tarot card deck and crystal ball that she left you in her will, the 18-karat gold zodiac sign you wear around your neck, the beautiful crystals that your best friend gave you to center your energies, the ankh your aunt sent you from Egypt. And don't forget to check through the record collection. That's *your* collection I'm talking about! Some of the music we of the 'nostalgic hippie years' listen to is in its own way every bit as degenerate and ungodly as the heavy-metal stuff the kids are into today. Deal with your own things first, and then you'll have set a basis and an example for dealing with the occult toys, records, posters, books, etc., that belong to your children.

> The graven images of their gods you are to burn with fire; you shall not covet the silver or the gold that is on them, nor take it for yourselves, lest you be snared by it, for it is an abomination to the Lord your God. And you shall not bring an abomination into your house, and like it come under the ban; you shall utterly detest it and you shall utterly abhor it, for it is something banned (Deuteronomy 7:25,26).

If your best friend's favorite pastime is haunting New Age occult bookstores and visiting the channelers, pastimes which she simply refuses to relinquish, then you should consider what Paul advises in 2 Corinthians 6:14:

> Do not be bound together with unbelievers; for what partnership have righteousness and lawlessness, or what fellowship has light with darkness? Or what harmony has Christ with Belial, or what has a believer in common with an unbeliever? Or what agreement has the temple of God with idols? . . . Therefore *come out from their midst and be separate, says the Lord* (2 Corinthians 6:14-16a,17a).

Only after you have dealt with these issues in your own life will you be equipped to handle them in your child's life. You must never lose sight of the fact that the battle for your child is first and foremost a *spiritual* one. As long as there are occult openings that have been left in your own life, Satan will undermine you in any effort to minister to your child. This is one of the reasons that I spent so much time in this book discussing issues that may at first glance seem peripheral to children. You must be discerning and alert to the schemes of the devil in your own life, and recognize that if he can succeed in luring you into some form of occultism, he will have succeeded in gaining an opening for the spiritual contamination of your children.

The Armor of God

The only way you're going to be able to truly help your child in these last days is by getting your own life straight with God. You alone can decide what your priorities are to be. But know this: Those who are committed to Satan's plan for you and your children are not double-minded; they know the goal. They are well aware of what it will take to achieve that goal, and are tireless in their dedication to bring it about. Above all else, they seek the destruction of the Christian home and ethic, for that alone stands in their way. Yet they can only succeed in your family if you allow them to. Therefore the apostle Paul urges you to "be strong in the Lord, and in the strength of His might!" Our own strength is fragile and limited, and yet the strength of God's might is what causes the mountains to tremble and the waters of the Red Sea to part! His might is what brought the universe into being. The power available to you *in Him* is infinite!

"Put on the full armor of God!" Like it or not, we're all in the midst of battle. We wrestle not against flesh and blood, but against a highly skilled and mighty army of demonic beings, a very literal horde of fiends who will destroy us if we neglect to take the apostle's warning to heart. This is not fanatical paranoia; this is biblical truth. Those who will not evaluate the biblical facts or the cases of demonology amply documented in modern history[20] will never comprehend the nature of the bondage that holds the victims of Satanism and the occult.

God does not send us into battle naked and vulnerable. He Himself has forged the armor and the weapons of our victory so that we "may be able to resist in the evil day, and having done everything, to stand firm." Ephesians chapter 6 is a magnificent passage that speaks of the heavenly armor that God has provided for our protection. Paul based his imagery on the armor worn by the Roman soldiers.

1) *"Stand firm therefore, having girded your loins with truth."* The belt, or girdle, was an essential part of the soldier's armor and provided the support to which the rest of the Roman soldier's armor was fastened. The belt that must gird the Christian warrior is the belt of truth—the truth which God has revealed in His Word, the truth of Jesus Christ. But Paul is also speaking of subjective truth here: A Christian must be characterized by truthfulness. He must possess integrity of character, for insincerity, dishonesty, and an otherwise guilty conscience will destroy his effectiveness in the war.

2) *"And having put on the breastplate of righteousness."* No soldier ever went into battle without his breastplate. Its purpose was to protect the chest and abdomen of the soldier. Paul is telling us that we must put on the righteousness of Christ. It is His righteousness that has been given to us the moment we accept Him as our Lord (2 Corinthians 5:21). Because of His righteousness, our lives and personal conduct must be characterized by virtue, morality, uprightness, and wisdom if we are to stand firm in the battle. We deal with unrighteousness in our lives by readily acknowledging all sin before God, according to 1 John 1:9, and by allowing the Holy Spirit to produce His fruit within us (Galatians 5:22). That's what keeps the holes out of your breastplate that would otherwise allow the enemy to come in for the kill!

3) *"And having shod your feet with the preparation of the gospel of peace."* The Roman soldier was always issued special hobnailed sandals for use in combat. These insured the soldier firm footing so that when he was out there swinging away he wouldn't lose his balance. *"The good news of peace"*: In the midst of the fiercest combat, God has provided the means for keeping us stable and balanced in His peace. At every turn you can be sure that Satan will do everything he possibly can to rob you of God's peace. The enemy will do everything he can to overwhelm you with fear. *Don't let him do it!* "If God be for us, who can be against us!" (Romans 8:31 KJV). Even in the midst of tribulation, distress, persecution, famine, nakedness, peril, or sword Paul declared that "in all these things we overwhelmingly conquer through Him who loved us. . . . For I am convinced that neither death, nor life, nor angels, nor principalities, nor things present, nor things to come, nor powers, nor height, nor depth, nor any other created thing, shall be able to separate us from the love of God, which is in Christ Jesus our Lord" (Romans 8:35-39).

Satan would want you to take your eyes off God and look with terror at the battle raging around you and your children. But God tells you, "Do not be afraid of sudden fear, nor of the onslaught of the wicked when it comes; for the Lord will be your confidence, and will keep your foot from being caught" (Proverbs 3:25,26). "The Lord is my light and my salvation; whom shall I fear? The Lord is the defense of my life; whom shall I dread? When evildoers came upon me to devour my flesh, my adversaries and my enemies, they stumbled and fell. Though a host encamp against me, my heart will not fear; though war arise against me, in spite of this I shall be confident" (Psalm 27:1-3). Psalms 3, 4, 91 . . . there are so many passages that remind us of God's faithfulness and peace in the midst of battle. Those of you committed to raising godly children in this day and age would do well to memorize them all!

Satan will do his level best to attack your mind and heart with fear. He'll tell you it's hopeless; that your children are lost; that you'll never be able to protect them enough. Even if you discover that your teenager considers himself a Satanist, or even if you suddenly realize that your preschooler is showing all the major signs of ritual abuse, *do not allow Satan to paralyze you with fear*. If he succeeds in doing that, he will most likely succeed in keeping you from ministering effectively to your child. "God has not given us a spirit of fear, but of power, love, and a sound mind" (2 Timothy 1:7). Stand on that promise! To allow yourself to succumb to fear is to remove yourself from fellowship with God, for fear is the antithesis of faith. The greatest antidote to fear is praise and worship of the living God! As long as Peter kept his eyes on Jesus, he was able to walk across the water. But, as he discovered, take your eyes off Him and you're sunk!

Your children will learn how to handle fear not by what you *tell* them but by what you *show* them in your life.

4) *"In addition to all, take up the shield of faith, with which you will be able to extinguish all the flaming missiles of the evil one."* One of the deadliest weapons of the ancient world was an arrow dipped in pitch and set afire. Soldiers would let loose a volley of them on the enemy. The burning tar on the tips would insure that the flesh would continue burning deep inside even when the arrow was pulled out. So the Roman soldiers carried shields that were about 30 inches wide by 48 inches high, behind which they would crouch when the flaming missiles started flying. Guilt, condemnation, fear . . . whatever form of flaming missile Satan hurls at you, lift up your shield of faith in God. "For whatever is born of God overcomes the world; and this is the victory that has overcome the world—our faith. And who is the one who overcomes the world, but he who believes that Jesus is the Son of God?" (1 John 5:4,5).

5) *"And take the helmet of salvation."* The helmet provides God's protection for your thought life from Satan's broadsword attacks of doubt about the security of our salvation. Salvation is ours based solely on the finished work of Christ. We can do nothing to earn it and we can do nothing to keep it.

Jesus assures us of this in John 10:27,28: "My sheep hear My voice, and I know them, and they follow Me; and I give eternal life to them, and they shall never perish, and no one shall snatch them out of My hand." When Satan tries to fill your mind with thoughts of defeat, put on the helmet of salvation and take every thought captive to the obedience of Christ.[21]

6) *"And the sword of the Spirit, which is the word of God."* Study God's Word. Memorize it. Hide it in your heart. It is the weapon that God has given you for the defeat of the enemy. When Satan dared to tempt the Lord Himself, Jesus responded by saying, "It is written . . ." and then quoting the passage that directly applied to the devil's taunt. Satan is not particularly impressed by those who think they're going to defeat him just by waving their Bibles at him. You're not going to defeat the devil by beaning him with your Moroccan leather binding! What brings down his strongholds is the Word of God hidden in the heart of a child of God who knows that in Christ he has the victory!

How do you put on God's armor? On your knees. *"With all prayer and petition pray at all times in the Spirit, and with this in view, be on the alert with all perseverance and petition for all the saints."* Prayer is the battleground! It is in *prayer* that the battle is fought, and it is there in prayer that it is either won or lost! There is no more important service you can perform for your children than to pray for them and to teach them how to pray. Intercede earnestly for them! Regardless of how hopeless the situation with your child may seem, never give up praying for him or her!

Mark Bubeck has two books that I think will be helpful to you in warfare praying for your children. The first is called *The Adversary*, and the second is called *Overcoming the Adversary*, in which Ephesians chapter 6 is discussed in greater depth. *Satan's Underground*, by Lauren Stratford, contains invaluable information and insights on ministering to children of ritual abuse. As parents have quietly prayed by their children's beds at night, taking authority over the demonic spirits that have attached themselves to the children and breaking the curses of the circle, curses of silence, isolation, perversion, suicide, insanity, and murder, they have seen their children receive healing and changes in their behavior that had not been achieved in months and even years of conventional therapy alone!

Diligently teach God's truth to your little ones. From the earliest possible age tell them about Jesus and lead them to Him. Teach them to be wise as serpents but innocent as doves. Shield and protect them all you can, but also equip them to fight the warfare from the earliest age, for as we have seen, even the littlest ones are not exempt from the battle.

The Choice Is Yours

There are two choices you have today in raising your children. The first one is to raise them as the parents in ancient Babylon did. The Babylonians were the ultimate occultists of their age. Much like Humanists today, those "sensual ones" believed they dwelled securely, saying in their heart, "I am, and there is no one besides me." They "felt secure in their wickedness and said, 'No one sees me.' " And yet their confident assertions of the nonexistence of a personal God did not keep Him from pronouncing judgment upon them:

> Your wisdom and your knowledge, they have deluded you; For you have said in your heart, "I am, and there is no one besides me." But evil will come on you which you will not know how to charm away; and disaster will fall on you for which you cannot atone, and destruction about which you do not know will come on you suddenly. Stand fast now in your spells and in your many sorceries with which you have labored from your youth; perhaps you will be able to profit. Perhaps you may cause trembling. You are wearied with your many counsels; let now the astrologers, those who prophesy by the stars, those who predict by the new moons,

stand up and save you from what will come upon you. Behold, they have become like stubble, fire burns them; they cannot deliver themselves from the power of the flame; there will be no coal to warm by, nor a fire to sit before! So have those become to you with whom you have labored, who have trafficked with you from your youth; each has wandered in his own way. There is none to save you (Isaiah 47:10-15).

Or you can raise your children as did the parents of Daniel, Hananiah, Mishael, and Azariah. From their earliest childhood their parents diligently raised their sons to know and revere the Lord, for when they were carried into captivity as youths into Babylon, and subjected to the Humanistic and occultic brainwashing of that school system, those young men did not compromise from their devotion and commitment to Almighty God. They refused to be lured by the "wisdom" and "beauty" of a system that sought to lead them away from God, preferring to be cast into the fiery furnace than to betray their Lord by compromise.

May God grant you the wisdom, courage, and perseverance to raise sons and daughters such as Daniel in these last days!

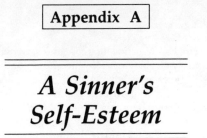

A Sinner's Self-Esteem

California Assemblyman John Vasconcellos has said in his book *A Liberating Vision* that for man to think of himself as a sinner simply ruins his self-esteem. So he has determined to do everything he can to change that. As the head of the California Task Force to Promote Self-Esteem & Personal & Social Responsibility, he's in a pretty good position to influence millions of people in general and children in particular with his humanistic perspective. And not only in California, but across the entire country. Vasconcellos is now calling for a national initiative on Self-Esteem[1] and is encouraging supporters of his program to write to President Bush to help bring this about.

His goal is stated clearly in the introduction to *A Liberating Vision*: "I propose we develop a humanistic/holistic government and politics—in and for human beings everywhere."[2] But this New Age goal will never be accomplished until human beings are "liberated" from their old ways of thinking about themselves:

> The central personal and sociopolitical event of our times is the emergence of a new model of humanness. That is our Human Revolution.... It constitutes a total "paradigm" shift, a massive change in our "world view", our way of looking at everything (p. 141).

> We're radically redefining what it means to be human. Our old vision assumes our human nature is sinful, untrustworthy and guilty. Our new vision assumes we humans are, by nature, innocent, trustworthy and life affirming.

Assemblyman Vasconcellos rightly recognizes that "how we envision ourselves affects everything else in our lives and society" (p. 140). If we assume we are "bad" inside, he tells us, we'll never turn "our curiosity and powers of reason inward..." in order to explore our "inner space," that "vast, deep, unexplored and uncharted universe of our own being" (p. 138).

> We're searching through it to liberate our innocence and natural wisdom. Our true perfect selves are erupting up, out and through the false faces and veneers we've unconsciously chosen to wear. We're New Age chicks, cracking open the brittle, stale shell of Our Old Egg (p. 138).

As "New Age chicks," Vasconcellos continues, we will learn to say "Yes" to ourselves," and "we're saying "No" to those conditions, events, processes, and institutions which have been saying "No" to our human nature. It's our new Declaration of Independence. We're declaring ourselves independent human beings. He sees the battle for this independence as a "holy war," and he makes it perfectly clear just what he thinks of those who stand in the way of the Human Revolution:

> Today's world is the arena in which two contrary personal creeds vie for dominance: the idealistic/humanistic/holistic and the cynical/negativistic/ behavioristic; the humanizing and the dehumanizing. . . . One group consists of persons whose vision is cynical—including traditional religionists, other traditionalists, Skinnerians, and others. They believe we humans are by nature evil, untrustworthy and violent. . . . The other group of believers are those of the humanistic vision—Carl Rogers, Abe Maslow, Sid Jourard, Wilhelm Reich, and others. We're more positive about our nature and potential. We claim some greater sense of what we humans are and may become. We expect the best of us: that we're innocent, trustworthy, life-affirming and gentle.

Those in the New Consciousness Movement tend to blame all the woes of the world in general and themselves in particular on the "traditional" (i.e., Christian) worldview:

> We believe that our old vision causes and explains our failures. It's so deeply rooted in our old cultural norms, our traditional religion, philosophy, education, science and art—it's easy to understand why we find ourselves in a state of personal, social and global crisis (p. 146).

He believes that acknowledging oneself as a sinner destroys a human being. His solution to this is simply to define sin out of existence and declare man sinless. Unfortunately, sin and self-deceit lie at the root of all human nature. "The heart is more deceitful than all else and is desperately sick; who can understand it?" (Jeremiah 17:9). No amount of Transpersonal self-realization peak experiences will ever change that fact. Regardless of how young or how thoroughly the child may be programmed with "positive affirmations," eventually his sinful nature is going to show up in one way or another. It is what he is. How many of you have ever had to teach a two-year-old how to be disobedient or naughty? The little one needs to be loved and nurtured and cherished even as he is disciplined and trained to know right from wrong, good from evil. He needs to learn that he can achieve wonderful things. Most of all, he needs to know he is loved and accepted unconditionally by those closest to him. He does not need to spend his years boosting his self-esteem by asserting what way deep down he's bound to know is a lie.

Those children who have been raised in a legalistic home or church in which nothing they can ever do is good enough are at a tragic disadvantage. They will indeed in all probability grow to be guilt-ridden adults whose only aim is to destroy the institutions and beliefs that have caused them such pain and produced such an awareness of guilt. Legalistic, unloving, unforgiving churches that do not understand or grasp the love, mercy, forgiveness, and unbounded grace of the Lord have most assuredly done the world and God a terrible disservice. Legalism has driven more wounded, angry souls into the arms of the New Age, the occult, atheism, and Satanism than we will ever know. It is not hard to see why.

God will indeed hold responsible those who have set themselves up as ministers and teachers for not teaching the full counsel of His Word! They have preached His justice and righteous anger at sin without ever telling the people that this same God has made a provision for that sin. "For God so loved the world that He gave His only begotten Son, that whosoever believes in Him should not perish, but have everlasting life" (John 3:16). This passage clearly presents an awesome revelation of two aspects of God's character: Yes, He is love—abounding, merciful, unending love that reaches out to man and makes a gift to him of God's only begotten Son. But it also tells us *why* He has done so. It is so that those who accept that love may not perish in the judgment that His perfect righteousness demands. God cannot exercise one aspect of His character at the expense of the other.

To make a positive assertion will never erase the fingerprint of God on the soul of man. The endless chanting of "I am a perfect person and student" may blunt your conscience, but it will not heal your soul. The solution lies simply in recognizing the truth of our condition and coming to God for forgiveness and restoration. "But God demonstrates His own love toward us, in that while we were yet sinners, Christ died for us" (Romans 5:8). Mind you, this is one of the toughest propositions for those steeped in the cult of self-worship to swallow! As Paul Vitz observes, "For the Christian the self is the problem, not the potential paradise. Understanding this problem involves an awareness of sin, especially of the sin of pride; correcting this condition requires the practice of such un-self-actualized states as contrition and penitence, humility, obedience, and trust in God."[3]

The Bible says, "If we say that we have no sin, we are deceiving ourselves and the truth is not in us. . . . If we say that we have not sinned, we make Him a liar, and His word is not in us" (1 John 1:8,10). And yet the Lord is the one who says, "I, even I, am the one who wipes out your transgressions for My own sake; and I will not remember your sins" (Isaiah 43:25). "If we confess our sins, He is faithful and righteous to forgive us our sins and to cleanse us from all unrighteousness" (1 John 1:9).

Shirley MacLaine believes that "more important than anything, in my experience the purpose for continuing is simply to understand SELF."[4] But the Bible has never called us to focus on ourselves. On the contrary, Jesus said to the multitude and to His disciples, "If anyone wishes to come after Me, let him deny himself, and take up his cross, and follow Me. . . . For what does it profit a man to gain the whole world and forfeit his soul?" (Mark 8:34,36).

The Place Called Hell

Proclaiming personal divinity and independence from God will boost your self-esteem all right—right into the place that Jesus Himself called hell. Jesus spoke of it as a very real place indeed. He viewed it not as a figure of speech or a mere metaphor or something we create for ourselves here on earth. He spoke of it as a literal place of eternal torment and separation from God. No one likes to talk or read about sin or hell. Certainly I don't. I know by even referring to it here I've probably just lost the rest of whatever New Agers might have made it this far! Nevertheless, Jesus warned us of it. Consider this: Jesus categorically, emphatically, unashamedly asserts that hell exists. And yet every single channeler, every single occultist, every single New Ager categorically, emphatically, unashamedly asserts that it does *not*. Whose word are you going to take for it?

Ramtha says he has been to the core of the earth and found but a hollow ball. There is no hell. There is no devil.

> ... what is hell? According to Ramtha, nothing but a shallow grave, a dump! Apparently, man's imagination has created the awesome fear of a hell, for man does have that power of creation. If there is no hell what is the devil?[5]

> ... now, the devil was a masterful ploy by a conquering institution to put the fear of God, most literally, into the hearts of little ones.

> With typically convoluted logic, Ramtha asks a "Master," the flattering term he often uses to address those who ask him questions: "Now, if God made the Devil, then what is the Devil made out of?"
> Master: "God."
> Ramtha: "Ah, so we must conclude that the devil has good in him, aye? So the devil is really not evil, aye, because he's really God, aye?"[6]

Shirley MacLaine's "Higher Self" says that:

> The God energy is no judge of persons. In fact, there is no judgment involved with life. There is only experience from incarnation to incarnation, until the soul realizes its perfection and that it is total love. ... Until mankind realizes there is, in truth, no good and there is, in truth, no evil—there will be no peace. ... When mankind realizes there is no death, it will have taken a giant step in understanding the God Principle existing in each individual.[7]

David Chethlahe Paladin, an artist and channeler in Arizona, while channeling the thoughts and experiences of a dying man, received the following message through automatic writing:

... oh, my God! Is that my body? I'm floating ... oh, s---, I'm afraid. I must be dead. I can hear that d---ed doctor telling the clerk that I am ... Matt! You old son-of-a-gun, how are you? D---! It's you, it's me and oh God, it's true—I'm home free! It's real! No hellfire, no St. Peter![8]

Jesus, on the other hand, spoke of a place of eternal punishment: "the eternal fire, which has been prepared for the devil and his angels ..." (Matthew 25:46,41; 10:28). He speaks of hell as a "furnace of fire" into which "all stumbling blocks, and those who commit lawlessness" will be cast. He speaks of it as an unimaginably horrible place in which there shall be weeping and gnashing of teeth (Matthew 13:42). If hell is *not* a literal reality then Jesus was indeed a fool for going to the cross: The whole reason He did so was in order to save us from that place of eternal torment and separation from God. "Truly, truly, I say to you, he who hears My word, and believes Him who sent Me, has eternal life, and does not come into judgment, but has passed out of death into life" (John 5:24). "I said therefore to you, that you shall die in your sins; for unless you believe that I am He, you shall die in your sins" (John 8:24).

In a kind of roundabout way, New Age religion has a point: "All paths lead to the same place." That is true. All their paths *do* lead to the same place, and if Jesus is right about it, *you don't want to go there!*

You Must Be Born
Again ... and Again

Death is one of the darkest instinctive fears of the human race. Every war or time of deep unrest in a society sees a desperate rise in spiritist seances as loved ones seek personal guidance or comfort as to the welfare of the "dearly departed." To hear that indeed they are not "dead," but residing with Robert Kennedy or Arthur Ford on the "other side" is of great comfort to some. After all, Death is so unfair. So ... well, *final*. It seems only logical that we should have another chance to get things right, or at least to even things out.

Ramtha, J.Z. Knight's spirit guide who bills himself as "the Enlightened One," gives these words of comfort to one woman in his audience:

> ... The ultimate of all fears is death. That is a truth, Master. Do
> you know you never have to die? ... Your body was made to live
> forever.... You have nothing to fear. You have lived, Entity,
> 13,342 and one-half times.... You are a divine creature....[1]

Reincarnation seems to many to present the perfect answer to the problem of pain and suffering in the world. The ancient Hindu law of Karma teaches that you must reap precisely what you sow, whether good or bad. If you are filled with pain and misery and disaster in this life, it doubtlessly serves you right. The law of Karma is paying you back for some evil you committed in some previous life.

Those of you who watched Shirley MacLaine's miniseries "Out on a Limb" will remember the conversation she had with "David," her "guru," while looking at the wreck of a bus on the side of a Peruvian mountain in which many had perished. David advised Shirley not to feel sorry for those who had died. After all, they had *chosen* what happened to them. They *chose* to incarnate into bodies they knew would someday go over the cliff in that bus. There aren't any victims in this world. Their hideous death was but the just fulfillment of their karma, and they would all be better off for it in their next incarnation!

Shirley's initial reaction to this callous, brutal philosophy was, quite rightly, one of incredulous horror ... until she evolved to a higher level of spiritual understanding. Then it all made perfect sense to her. And why shouldn't it? After all, one of her favorite channelers, J.Z. Knight, sat on national TV one night ("20/20") and told the entire nation that murder was perfectly all right as long as you were evolved enough to understand the purpose of it. This is a classic example of pantheistic monism taken to its logical conclusion. It removes any basis for morals, right and wrong, discerning of evil; for if all is God, then what we call evil is also of God. Evil is therefore not evil at all, but just part of what is. The end results of such demonic teachings are the destruction of the conscience and the understanding and the warm embracing of all that once was viewed with horror.

Spirit Speaks

One of the most horrifying and disgusting examples of the logical conclusion of the theory of reincarnation comes out of an outfit in Los Angeles that calls itself "Spirit Speaks."

The eighth edition of their publication devoted itself to "Kids 'N Karma," and is a collection of messages channeled by the wise and ascended masters who wanted to be sure that parents of today understand how to raise and nurture their New Age children. Let me give you a few random quotes out of their teachings:

On "Selecting Life Paths and Parents"

Soli: "You choose your parents. You choose the time and place of your birth. You choose the probability pattern of your life totally knowing what that is going to be. You know how your parents are going to train you. . . . Children have always chosen their parents. No matter how terrible society might view the experience of a child with its parents, even in the case of so-called 'child abuse,' the child chose. It is by agreement. Most think that children are these poor little innocent beings that have come into Earth, a new soul, to experience life. Nothing could be further from the truth, my friends" (p. 11).

On "Incest and Child Abuse"

Soli: "What is causing child abuse and incest right now is the belief in society that it is happening. . . . First and foremost, if a child has reached the age of puberty, the child is capable of sexual union with pleasure. Sex and sexual union is a communication, whether between male and male, female and female, male and female. It does not matter, it is communication. Communication brings more understanding of your oneness of all life. However, the right idea of that is communication with respect. If there is respect between father and daughter, father and son, mother and daughter, mother and son, and they are all at the age of able to enjoy a sexual union, from our perspective there is absolutely nothing wrong with it whatsoever" (p. 42).

On "Early Exits from Life"

Ting-Lao: "In case of abortion, it is true that Spirit is around body of baby and so does feel destruction of body. Some people think it is very bad. But it is no different from death at old age, it is only death at early age. Soul usually knows that pregnancy will not come to term when chooses this experience of being involved in pregnancy and then having body of baby killed. Yes, it is killing the baby's body, but that is not so bad. It is only in your concept of life and death that it seems to be bad, coupled with the non-understanding of the foreverness of life. Life is only life, you know. There is no beginning and no end, it is only cycles, like never-ending circle" (p. 32).

A local Los Angeles paper called "Easy Reader" with a circulation of 50,000 readers, gave "Spirit Speaks" a bit of free publicity in a lengthy article they did on channeling published on January 22, 1987. Here is how they described them:

> The local channeling network even has its own publication— "Spirit Speaks," a bi-monthly 56-page newsletter compiling over 22,000 words of wisdom taken from a number of different channeled sessions. . . .

If you are upset by these "words of wisdom," you're not alone. Even Molli Nickell, Publisher of "Spirit Speaks," tells us that "there were multiple 'buttons pushed' for several of us while working on this book." (Obviously not enough "buttons" were pushed to make them stop and recognize that what they were being told was perverted and demonic to the core.) She then offers a word of comfort, reminding you that you "did the best you could" with your kids, under the circumstances, even as your parents did with you under theirs, so since you all chose your situations anyway, you might as well come to terms with it.

Karma Chameleon

The "law of karma" is cold and unforgiving, void of any grace or compassion. Belief in its inevitability has produced untold suffering in India, the land of its origin. Anyone who wishes to understand the full impact of the logical conclusions of that philosophy need only take a good long look at what that doctrine of demons has produced there. It is viewed by the Hindus as a hideous concept. They see themselves as trapped on the wheel of *samsara* (suffering), and they yearn to break out of the cycle so that they can finally merge as a mindless drop in the great sea of forgetfulness that they call Nirvana.[2] The Eastern concept of reincarnation also accepts the belief in metempsychosis—which assumes that one can reincarnate as a tree or a cow or a mosquito.

In this country, however, we have embraced our own Westernized version of it. Millions of us (one out of every four in this country according to a recent Gallup poll), now find ourselves titillated by the exotic idea of having lived before as an ancient warrior in Atlantis, or as an elephant rider in India, or as a cocoa bean gatherer in the Aztec Empire before the Conquistadores arrived, or as Queen of the Nile . . . (do you have any idea how many out there today "know" they were Cleopatra? Neither do I, but I understand there's more than one. Even staunch . . . [I almost said "die-hard" . . .] reincarnationists admit this is something of a problem). Reincarnation into anything other than a human form has been pronounced unacceptable by Westerners, who now find themselves swapping "past life experiences" over lunch. Many have found it a convenient and comforting excuse to live out their immoralities and perversions. After all, it's okay to have an affair with some married man, because you were married to him in another life. When it comes right down to it, it's okay to murder someone you hate because they probably did you in in some previous life. It's okay to indulge in incest because, after all, you're just working out some kinks in your previous relationship with that child. It's all part of the process.

But Didn't Jesus Teach Reincarnation?

In a word, NO. He did not. But no one who is into the New Age believes that. The story goes something like this: Originally Jesus did teach reincarnation. He believed in it. His apostles believed in it. The early church believed in it. But, sometime during 325 A.D. or 553 A.D. (the dates vary depending on who's telling it), the church decided to get together and write out all the references to reincarnation from the Bible, along with the teachings on Karma and personal divinity which Jesus also taught. Despite the fact that way deep down the church fathers believed in reincarnation themselves, they did this so that they could better control the masses, and so that the emperor Constantine (if you go with the 325 A.D. version) or the emperor Justinian (if you go for the 553 A.D. version) could consolidate the Roman Empire. After all, as Marilyn Ferguson said on "The Oprah Winfrey Show," ". . . there was a concern that people were counting on their next lifetime to straighten up. So that was why they thought it would be better if people didn't think they had lots of time."[3]

I've personally always found it peculiar that while emphatically insisting that the Bible is totally unreliable because ". . . the New Testament was not recorded until long after Jesus died, and its books subsequently passed through the censoring hands of church councils . . ."[4] the reincarnationists nonetheless turn around and relentlessly quote the Bible to prove to us that it teaches reincarnation. If indeed it does, one can only assume that the church fathers supposedly in charge of removing all references to reincarnation were unbelievably sloppy about it.

But let's assume they did rewrite the New Testament. The church papas *really* had a job on their hands now! They would have had to collect all the copies of the Gospels and Epistles that had been distributed across all the churches for at least the last couple of hundred years or so. Then they would have had to delete the offending passages from them, redistribute them to the churches, *and* falsely antiquate the manuscripts so that when modern scholars such as Dr. Albright and Dr. Kenyon and Dr. Robertson found and studied them, they could still be accurately dated to the first and second century. Truly these old church fathers worked a miracle that must be considered on a par with the parting of the Red Sea!

No, they didn't "rewrite" the New Testament. The books that were included in the Canon (the fixed list of accepted books) were those which had always been considered divinely inspired by the churches and which could be traced, either directly or indirectly, to apostolic authority.[5] The much-disputed books that were deleted were recognized as Gnostic heresy, and had never been considered as part of the accepted teachings of the church. Professor Morton Smith of Columbia University holds that we must examine these "pagan works about Jesus" that present "suppressed evidence" in order to learn the truth about Him.[6] This "truth" is an ancient Gnostic lie that Jesus was but "one of a swarm of Levantine magicians" of His day. And yet why should we look to works of fiction and mythology to learn the truth about the historical Jesus? Those works were not accepted by the apostles *or* by the early church fathers, modern Gnostic "scholars" to the contrary. It makes no sense for anyone seeking the historical truth about Jesus to accept them today.[7]

Reincarnation and resurrection stand in diametric opposition to each other. If one is true, then the other cannot be. Reincarnation teaches that you must pay for your own sins through endless successive incarnations. Christianity is based on the fact that no man can reach God on his own effort or merit. Therefore Christ died for our sins, was buried, and was raised physically from the dead on the third day, even as the Scriptures predicted (Isaiah 53; Psalm 16:8; Matthew 16:21). The apostle Paul himself acknowledged that the whole of Christianity rests on the fact of the resurrection: ". . . if Christ has not been raised, your faith is worthless; you are still in your sins" (1 Corinthians 15:17). "If there is no resurrection of the dead, not even Christ has been raised; and if Christ has not been raised, then our preaching is vain, your faith also is vain" (1 Corinthians 15:13,14). If reincarnation is true, then Jesus was a fool to go to the cross. If reincarnation is true, then Paul and the apostles and the hundreds of witnesses who proclaimed they had seen the risen Christ must have been munching some pretty powerful mushrooms at their prayer meetings, because their consistent testimony to the world was that *He is risen!* If reincarnation is true, then sin has not been paid for, and the body of Jesus is still mouldering in some grave along with all the other great religious leaders of the world. If reincarnation is true, then it is a lie that death is an enemy, as Paul asserts (1 Corinthians 15:26). If reincarnation is true, then every single major teaching of biblical Christianity is false. It cannot be otherwise. Hebrews 9:27 affirms that it is "appointed for men to die once, and after this comes judgment," not cyclic reincarnation!

Evolution: Science or Religious Mumbo Jumbo

The theory of evolution is an integral aspect of the entire Eastern religious belief system. For millennia, Eastern mysticism has taught that lower forms of life evolved to higher forms, and that eventually all would evolve back to godhood. Evolution is an indispensable part of the teaching of reincarnation. This belief is documented in Witchcraft, Shamanism, and occult literature around the world. It is now also an integral part of our education system. Despite the fact that evolution is religious in origin and nature and has nothing whatever to do with the price of scientific potatoes, many scientists and educators still rabidly cling to the theory because the alternative—creation out of nothing by a personal God—is thoroughly unthinkable to them.

Even Marilyn Ferguson candidly admits that Darwin's theory of evolution is kaput:

> Darwin's theory of evolution by chance mutation and survival of the fittest has proven hopelessly inadequate to account for a great many observations in biology. . . . to this day fossil evidence has not turned up the necessary missing links. Steven Jay Gould [a Harvard biologist and geologist] called the extreme rarity in the fossil record of transitional forms of life "the trade secret of paleontology." Younger scientists, confronted by the continuing absence of such missing links, are increasingly skeptical of the old theory.[8]

Not only are the fossil records "incomplete" (major understatement here!) in providing any credible evidence of intermediate or transitional forms, but what "proofs" scientists have clung to in support of their beliefs have even bigger problems associated with them.

You kind of have to feel sorry for the poor paleontologist here. For over a hundred years since Darwin postulated his theory of gradual evolution, scientists have been digging up the countryside desperately trying to find some kind, *any* kind, of solid, irrefutable fossil record to prove their theory. They simply have been unable to do so. IT ISN'T THERE.

So a new theory has recently developed: "Punctuated equilibria."[9] Following the time-honored tradition that dictates that "when you haven't got the evidence, you make up a story that will fit the lack of evidence,"[10] Dr. Stephen Jay Gould and Niles Eldredge developed a theory that seeks to explain the "sudden appearance" of a species. "It does not evolve gradually by the steady change of its ancestors, but all at once and fully formed."[11]

New Agers are very excited by this theory because they believe it "opens us up to the possibility of rapid evolution in our own time, when the equilibrium of the species is punctuated by stress."[12] In other words, if we work at it hard enough and create just the right global conditions, we can achieve a "critical mass" sufficient to produce that "quantum leap" in our own evolution from "homo sapiens" to "homo Noeticus," an entirely new and superior form of man. By the way, Hitler also thought this was a nifty theory. You may remember that his belief in his ability to produce the "Master Race," which resulted in the extermination of millions of "inferior" beings, was based on this very idea.

The Marxists believe somewhat the same thing and have based their Communist system on a remarkably similar theory. It is of interest to note the admitted Marxist source of punctuationalist evolution.[13] Nevertheless, school textbooks continue to teach this miserably defective religious and, it would seem, politically biased theory as scientific fact. A recent[14] decision of the Supreme Court struck down the Louisiana law that required a balanced presentation of both evolution and creation science in their public schools, because, they said, it violated the constitutionally required separation of church and state.

Anthony T. Podesta, president of the liberal advocacy group People for the American Way, called on the Supreme Court to rule against the Louisiana law. "All over the country schools are under pressure to teach creationism in science classrooms. Creationism is a religious belief, not a science."[15] Civil Libertarians loudly proclaimed that to allow creation science to even be mentioned in the class was a "blatant attempt to promote a religious belief in the public schools."

In all honesty, I would dearly love to hear these "watchmen of American freedom" for once say what they really mean. It doesn't bother them in the least that religion and "unscientific theories" are taught in the classroom. Their adherence and dedicated promotion of evolution and the many other Eastern religious and occultic beliefs and practices in the classroom are ample evidence of that. What does seem to fry their collective egg, however, is any connection which that belief or practice may have to *biblical* religion. At that point, be prepared to hear them scream bloody murder.

The fact that the fossil records are simply not there has proved to be a source of great embarrassment to the entire scientific community, but that has not for one minute undermined their determination to continue to teach their totally unproven theory and religion as irrefutable and scientific fact in every classroom in America.

Appendix C

Unity or Else!

Barbara Marx Hubbard is hailed by many within the New Age Movement as a leading spokeswoman, futurist, and activist for their cause. She is a founding member of the Global Futures Network, and describes herself as a visionary and a prophet of the New Age. The late Buckminster Fuller said of her, "There is no doubt in my mind that Barbara Marx Hubbard, who has helped introduce the concept of futurism to society, is the best informed human now alive regarding futurism and the foresights that it has produced."[1] As most of you I'm sure remember, Barbara Marx Hubbard was a candidate for the Democratic Vice-Presidential nomination in the 1984 Presidential campaign.

She was also one of the four "visionaries" behind the promoting of the well-publicized "World Instant of Cooperation," an event that took place on December 31, 1986. At least 47 countries around the world participated. Cities in all 50 states in this country hosted the event. Programs such as "Live Aid," "Band Aid," and especially "Hands Across America" seem to have been designed to prepare people for this so called "World Instant of Cooperation."

These "visionaries," it seems, all received word from their "guides" that "the time has come for humanity to claim its essential oneness." They called for 50 million people around the world to "suspend for one hour all thoughts of fear, conflict and separation as they pray, meditate and contemplate the oneness of all life on earth." The theory is based on the idea that if they could get enough people to do this, they would establish a "critical mass" sufficient to raise in one great, sudden "quantum leap" the consciousness level of the entire planet, thus ushering in their "New Age of Light and Love."

They did not get quite the number of people involved as they had hoped for, but the response was still enormous all over the world. These events are planned for New Year's Eve every year until their Millennium New Year's Eve party in 1999. They're also encouraging their people to get together every month to visualize world peace and the healing of Mother Earth.

Another similar group calling itself "Heal Our World (HOW)/Harmonic Convergence, promoted another session of world meditation which they expected would hasten the arrival of the New Age. Jose Arguelles, author of *The Mayan Factor: Path Beyond Technology*, said that August 16 and 17, 1987, the dates scheduled for their mass purification rites around the world, are crucial in the ancient Aztec and Mayan calendars. According to Arguelles, these dates are the ones which end the ancient calendars and "mark the critical moment in the calendar's Great Cycle—3113 B.C. to 2021 A.D. when the wave of history climaxes and a new age dawns, initiating a 25-year return movement to close out the cycle in 2012 ... which will bring the establishment of a cosmic consciousness among all humanity, and, by 2012, entry into galactic civilization."[2] Arguelles' spirit guide, Pan,[3] has told him that Quetzalcoatl will return to earth on those dates. Mystics, shamans, and witch doctors, 144,000 of them, were commanded by Pan to participate in 12 days of fire purification rituals before going to the sacred sites specifically designated around the world. People were called on to wholly surrender to the spirit of Pan around the world.

These people believe that if they are not able to change and raise the vibration levels of the world's consciousness, we are in for a time of "cleansing" for Mother Earth. (The Hopi Indians and the Tibetans have similar myths.) Their view of "Mother Earth" is based on the so-called GAIA principle which views the Earth as a living, breathing entity. In ancient Roman and Greek mythology, Gaia (or Terra, as she is sometimes alternately called) was the Earth goddess. It seems Mother Earth has just about "had it" with mankind and is getting ready to go through a period of cataclysmic cleansing. What do they mean by "cleansing"? Well you may ask. Let me quote Ms. Marx Hubbard's spirit guide:

> No worldly peace can prevail until the self-centered members of the planetary body either change, or die. That is the choice. ... Evolution empowers the horseman upon the red horse to kill that which cannot love God above all else and his neighbor as himself, and himself as the son of God. This act is as horrible as killing a cancer cell. It must be done for the sake of the future of the whole. So be it; be prepared for the selection process which is now beginning.
>
> We, the elders, have been patiently waiting until the very last moment before the quantum transformation, to take action to cut out this corrupted and corrupting element in the body of humanity. It is like watching a cancer grow; something must be done before the whole body is destroyed.
>
> Now, as we approach the quantum shift from creature-human to co-creative human ... the human who is an inheritor of god-like powers ... the destructive one fourth must be eliminated from the social body. We have no choice, dearly beloveds. It is a case of the destruction of the whole planet, or the elimination of the ego-driven godless one-fourth who, at this time of planetary birth, can, if allowed to live on to reproduce their defective disconnection, destroy forever the opportunity of Homo sapiens to become Homo universalis, heirs of God.[4]

Barbara Marx Hubbard is not the only one who is "channeling" or voicing material of this sort.

Peter Russell says exactly the same thing in his book *The Global Brain*: Every person on the face of the earth is like a cell in the great "Global Brain."

Some of these cells have gone haywire, however, and have become like cancer cells in the system. These "cancer cells" have to be eradicated so that the Global or Universal Brain can live.[5]

Benjamin Creme, the self-appointed prophet of the much-touted (and still conspicuous by his absence) "Lord Maitreya" says that those cancer cells have to be annihilated or face the sword of cleavage. One of the founders of "Concerned Christians," a newsletter out of Golden, Colorado, said in one of their reports that she heard in one New Age workshop, "It's too bad they have to die."

John Randolph Price, the primary moving force behind the "World Instant of Cooperation," was told by his favorite spirit guide, "Asher," that "Nature will soon enter her cleansing cycle. . . ." These individuals [the two billion human beings who do not have the 'ring of protection' around them] with their lower vibratory rates will be removed during the next two decades. . . ."[6]

John Randolph Price was initially aghast at the information and challenged his spirit guide about it. "What I am hearing is both horrible and hopeful," he said. "I know that one of the most serious problems we have today is overpopulation, but wiping more than 2 billion people off the face of the earth is a little drastic, don't you think?" Asher replied, ". . . who are we to say that those people did not volunteer to be a part of the destruction and regeneration—for the purpose of soul growth? Never forget that each individual has free will and free choice."[7]

Newsweek magazine, in their July 27, 1987, issue, reported that Shirley MacLaine told her devotees to "tune into your higher self or else." "The earth is moving off its axis," she said, and only the "collective consciousness" of mankind can right it. "That's why everyone should mark August 16 and 17 on their calendars."

New Agers find it difficult, if not impossible, to tolerate "narrow-minded" people. You could say that they themselves are, if you will, somewhat "narrow-minded" about accepting "narrow-minded" people . . . at which point we might conclude that these "open-minded" people are somewhat less "open-minded" than they would like us to think. It simply will not do to declare we must all unite in a mutual, open-minded and global love, acceptance, and tolerance of one another while all the while plotting the deliberate and untimely demise of those who don't agree.

Most of the New Agers will, however, be able to accept this coming "global cleansing" with a clear conscience. After all, the Ascended Masters, the Enlightened Ones, have assured them they will not be responsible:

> Fortunately you, dearly beloveds, are not responsible for this act. We are. We are in charge of God's selection process for planet Earth. He selects, we destroy. We are the riders of the pale horse, Death. We come to bring death to those who are unable to know God. We do this for the sake of the world.[8]

Indeed, the spirits speaking these words have finally said something true. They have identified themselves as Death. Revelation 6:7,8 (which they have semiquoted and thoroughly misinterpreted for us) adds that Hades was following with Death, the rider of the "ashen horse" released by God for the judgment of those who hated Him. Read the chapter. Why, you may wonder, are people like Barbara Marx Hubbard et. al., cooing with ecstasy at holding intimate conversations with Death? And why do they choose to accept what Death says as the guideline for the world? It would be good for these people to read 1 Corinthians 15:54-57, which tells us the final fate of their co-worker:

> Death is swallowed up in victory. O Death, where is your victory? O Death, where is your sting? . . . but thanks be to God, who gives us the victory through our Lord Jesus Christ.

What we are seeing in Ms. Marx Hubbard's writings is a bizarre twisting and reinterpretation of the Book of Revelation and the Book of Daniel, in which God reveals that a seven-year period of tribulation and judgment unlike anything the world has ever seen before will indeed come upon the world. The New Agers twist the passage to mean what it never said— namely, that "only those who are capable of evolving . . . who willingly follow the inner voice" will be spared these horrors. What the Bible actually says, however, is that only those "narrow-minded and dogmatic bigots"[9] who actually *believe* what that Bible plainly tells them about God, His unique and only-begotten Son, Jesus the Messiah, and their need to accept Him on His terms as their personal Lord and Savior will be saved from the destruction that is to come.

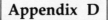

Appendix D

Queen of Heaven

The concept of a "Queen of Heaven" has been around since the time of Semiramis, Queen of ancient Babylon and wife of Nimrod in the days just before the mess at the Tower of Babel. She was the original "Great Goddess," who was deified as the one alluded to in Genesis: the virgin through whom would be born the Savior who was to crush the head of the serpent.[1] The worship of Semiramis as the Virgin "Queen of Heaven" and of her consort/son Tammuz was carried worldwide after the Babel thing fell apart, a counterfeit virgin mother and her counterfeit divine son, known by many different names, but essentially the same deities. This view is not the one held by the Witches, needless to say. *Circle Network News*, a Neo-Pagan publication, describes the Goddess in this way:

> In ancient rites under clean and sacred skies, the mysterious Queen of Heaven, Mother of Earth, was worshiped century after century upon the wheel of time. By countless names, in myriad forms and disguises, She was the "Dream and the Matrix of Knowing" invoked and adored, enchanted and discovered within the heart and spirit of Her children. With power and Magick, in love and in strength did She then, as now, reveal Her greatest secret; that within lies the Source of Her creation coiled in infinite potential at the base of our spines. With the joy of Her return upon us, let the Serpents rise![2]

". . . By countless names, in myriad forms and disguises . . ." Witches recognize hundreds of names for their Goddess. Each Witch is free to worship her in whatever aspect and form suits the need at the time. They view her as a Triple Goddess, who manifests herself as the "independent, adventurous maiden; the nurturing, enterprising mother, and the wise, prophetic crone."[3] She is the creator, the nourisher, and the destroyer, and they invoke her in their rituals by the chanting of her names: Isis, Circe, Kali, Cybele, Juno, Kwan Yin, Durga, Hecate, Demeter, Frigg, Gaea. She is the goddess of ten thousand names. In ancient Greece she was known as Aphrodite. The Romans called her Venus. The Ephesians called her Diana. The ancient Assyrians knew her as Ishtar, and the Sumerians called her Innanna as far back as 2300 years B.C.[4] Astarte or Ashtoreth (or Asheroth) was the name by which she was known to the Canaanites and even to the children of Israel during the (frequent) days of their apostasies. It was by this name that Jezebel knew and served the goddess as high priestess along with 400 other "holy" temple prostitutes set aside to her service, to the consternation of the prophet Elijah (1 Kings 18:19). Jezebel and her priestesses were evidently not inclined to accept Elijah's challenge to join the 450 prophets of Baal on Mount Carmel for a test to prove once-and-for-all whose God was real. Good thing for Astarte. Bad thing for Israel. It was because the rulers of Israel so frequently adopted the practices of the Pagans around them, encouraging and allowing the Israelites to do the same, that God brought such severe judgments down upon them.

Have you ever wondered why a loving, merciful God would command the destruction of an entire civilization, even as He did the inhabitants of the Promised Land? In Deuteronomy 20:17 the Lord commands the utter destruction of the Hittite, the Amorite, the Canaanite, the Perizzite, the Hivite, and the Jebusite. Why? God tells us why in verse 18:

> . . . in order that they may not teach you to do according to all their detestable things which they have done for their gods, so that you would sin against the Lord your God.

The worshipers of the Queen of Heaven and her consort, Baal (also known as Moloch, Chemosh, Milcam, Baal Hammon, etc.), indulged in practices so vile and hideous that God commanded their utter destruction. What were these "detestable things" practiced by these people?

> And they forsook all the commandments of the Lord their God and made for themselves molten images, even two calves, and made an Asherah and worshiped all the host of heaven and served Baal. Then they made their sons and their daughters pass through the fire, and practiced divination and enchantments, and sold themselves to do evil in the sight of the Lord, provoking Him. So the Lord was very angry with Israel, and removed them from His sight (2 Kings 17:16,17).

Human sacrifice was frequently an integral part of the ancient worship of the Goddess and her consort. Those who practiced the ancient religions, those who were closest to the primeval worship of the Mother Goddess, understood that she and/or her consort, in one manifestation or another, demanded the sacrifice of human blood.

In an interesting historical sideline, Jezebel was the great aunt of Queen Dido, founder of the Phoenician city of Carthage in 814 B.C. It was in Carthage that Jezebel's Moon Goddess, Astarte, came into yet another name: Tanit. I've noticed that not too many Witches and Neo-Pagans seem particularly inclined to include Tanit in their lists of the Goddess' names, although Janet and Stewart Farrar do mention in a brief footnote that the "Great Mother consort of Baal Hammon of Carthage was named Tanit."[5] Barbara G. Walker in her massive *Woman's Encyclopedia of Myths and Secrets* does acknowledge that Tanit is the "Carthaginian name of the Phoenician Great Goddess, Astarte—the Biblical Ashtoreth or Asherah," that "her temple in Carthage was called the Shrine of the Heavenly Virgin. Greek and Roman writers called it a temple of the moon," and that "she was also known as Libera, Goddess of Libya"[6] (p. 972).

What Ms. Walker does not tell us, however, is the form of worship demanded by the Heavenly Virgin: child sacrifice. Lots of it. When the Romans arrived in the Phoenician city of Carthage in 146 B.C. during the Punic Wars, they discovered a vast cemetery which spanned 600 years and which was still very much in use.[7] It was the cemetery reserved for the ashes of the children who had been sacrificed to the Goddess Tanit and her consort, Baal Hammon. Little ones, anywhere from birth to around four years of age, were given by their parents as burnt offerings to the Great Goddess in fulfillment of a vow or in exchange for her favor. Even the battle-hardened Roman soldiers were horrified by the practice, although they themselves were certainly no strangers to the concept of human sacrifice. Their battle cry "Carthage must be destroyed!" was fanned by their determination to put a stop to the practice of burning children alive.

It is worth noting that the Phoenicians "were among the most highly civilized and cosmopolitan people in the Mediterranean. Both the Hebrew Bible and Homer attest to their skills as craftsmen, sailors, and merchants. They built magnificent cities and ports. One of them was, of course, Carthage. . . ."[8] Nevertheless, their virtually unrivaled sophistication and cultural achievements did nothing whatsoever to ameliorate the practice of child sacrifice to the Goddess. On the contrary. As the archaeologists who excavated Carthage noted in their article in *Biblical Archaeology Review*, Jan./ Feb. 1984:

> One of the most surprising results of our analysis of the contents of the burial urns is that the demand for human infant sacrifice, as opposed to animal sacrifice, seems to increase rather than decrease with the passage of time. . . . Precisely in the fourth and third centuries B.C., when Carthage had attained the height of urbanity, child sacrifice flourished as never before. . . . Another surprising conclusion of our research is that child sacrifice at Carthage was largely an upper-class custom, at least until the third century B.C.

One cannot but wonder how long the practice would have continued in Carthage had not the Romans put a stop to it by virtually leveling the city. Incidentally, Tanit is well-known today among some groups of self-styled Satanists who use her symbol as graffiti indicating that a human sacrifice is planned.

It seems that worship of the Great Goddess has always been a bloody bit of business. M. Esther Harding, personal disciple of C.J. Jung (who wrote the foreword to her book *Woman's Mysteries—Ancient and Modern*), records the following:

> The priestesses of the Moon Goddess in addition to performing those offices which represented the goddess in her fertilizing

and life-giving activities, had also to impersonate her in her dark and destructive aspect. The Vestal Virgins, it will be recalled, threw twenty-four manikins into the Tiber each year and infant sacrifices were regularly performed in honor of, certainly some forms of the goddess. It is recorded, for instance, that around the sacred stone which represented the goddess Astarte, hundreds of skeletons of human infants have been found. She was the goddess of untrammelled sexual love and first-born children and animals were sacrificed to her.[9]

We previously mentioned the practice of human sacrifice to the Lord of Death, Samhain, on the night we now call Halloween. The gentle Celtic Moon Goddess also demanded her share of blood.

The chief priestess of the Celtic moon goddess was required to act as executioner whenever a human sacrifice was made. She had to kill the victim with her own hands. After a battle, for instance, the prisoners were so sacrificed, their heads being cut off, while they were held over a silver cauldron in which the blood was caught. One of these cauldrons was discovered in Jutland and is now in the Museum at Copenhagen. It is embossed with figures which not only show scenes of battle but also depict the Moon Goddess and the sacrificial ceremonial. The silver vessel was called the Cauldron of Regeneration. It is the cauldron of the Moon Goddess who was the giver of fertility and of love. The blood poured into it must have formed a regenerating drink, or possibly bath.[10]

As Nigel Davis points out in his book *Human Sacrifice in History and Today*, while the Greeks invented democracy, they "did not thereupon dispense with human sacrifice." The Goddess Artemis, he tells us, was insistent in her demand for human victims[11] (p. 59). In Roman London the priest of the Great Mother Cybele practiced brutal rites of ritual castration, mutilating themselves in honor of the goddess.[12]

In India the Dark Mother, Kali Ma, "the fount of every kind of love, which flowed into the world only through her agents on earth, women,"[13] according to Barbara Walker, is portrayed in *Man, Myth and Magic* as the "black-faced, vampire-fanged goddess who represented the terrifying aspect of the Earth Mother" (Vol. 11, p. 1554). She is the "Crone" aspect of the Goddess, worshiped in the cemeteries and at cremation sites. The Thugs, a secret cult of worshipers of the Black Goddess, regularly strangled unwary travelers in India as a sacrifice to her well into the nineteenth century. Blood sacrifice (preferably human) has always been demanded by this version of the Witches' goddess, and it seems that the practice has not died out in "modern" times. In August 1985 the *London Observer Service* reported the following:

HUMAN SACRIFICES ON ALTARS IN INDIA

India's Prime Minister Rajiv Gandhi has ordered an inquiry

into human sacrifice following a report that three teen-age boys were slain at the altar of the goddess Bana-durga. Police believe the June 15 deaths in the Orissa state capital, Ranpur, were the handiwork of a master Tantric—a priest who practices human sacrifices to appease the goddess. . . . There are many legends of human sacrifice in the area. The rajahs of Ranpur used to maintain a select group known as Tantia Kattas, which means throat cutters. Their main job was to collect human beings for sacrifice.

Human sacrifice is not just confined to Ranpur. The cult has a wide following in the state but does not get much print or television exposure. In the last eight years an estimated 150 cases of human sacrifice deaths have been recorded. This practice is on the increase and it is understood that many other cases are not reported. . . . There have been over 400 mystery deaths in Orissa state in the last eight years—most of which can be attributed to witchcraft and human sacrifice.[14]

Today's Witches and Pagans invariably try to present their Great Mother Goddess, in her three aspects of Maiden, Mother and Crone, as a gentle, loving deity who offers peace and freedom to all who come to her. Starhawk says of her, "The love of the Goddess is unconditional. She does not ask for sacrifice—whether human or animal—nor does She want us to sacrifice our normal human needs and desires. Witchcraft is a religion of self-celebration, not self-abnegation."[15] "Nor do I demand sacrifice: for behold, I am the Mother of all living: and my love is poured out upon the earth." So she is presented as saying to humanity in one ritual given us by Sybil Leek.[16] ". . . the Great Mother Goddess, Supreme deity of Wicca, demands no sacrifice of any kind," says Hans Holzer in his Introduction to the *Encyclopedia of Witchcraft & Demonology.*[17] We can only hope the Great Mother Goddess sees fit to keep it that way, but personally I wouldn't count on it. New Agers who are increasingly open and sympathetic to Goddess worship are now telling us that Mother Earth plans to "rid herself" of those who are not as yet evolved enough to go along with the Plan.

It would seem that the Great Mother Goddess is finally getting ready to show her true colors once again.

Sharers in Demons

There is probably no faster or more efficient way to enrage your average witch than to accuse him or her of devil worship. Their literature and lectures are filled with pleas and/or demands that people stop confusing them with Satan worshipers. And in one sense they've got a point. The modern Wiccans (i.e., Witches), Neo-Pagans, Druids, etc. do not even acknowledge the existence of Satan. They claim that fear-driven medieval churchmen turned their ancient and benevolent horned god Pan into a convenient representation of the Christian devil, using that as an excuse to stamp them out. "Never again the burnings!" is their battle cry of today.

There is absolutely no way to excuse or condone what was done in the days of the Inquisition or in the days of the witch-hunts in England or Salem. In the period when Israel was a theocracy (that is, when the moral and civil laws of the land were instituted by God, who was seeking to preserve the unique identity of the Jews from contamination with idol worship and other pagan practices), the command of Exodus 22:18 was indeed in effect: "You shall not allow a sorceress to live." Sorcery was right up there with having sexual relations with an animal and sacrificing to other gods for being abomination to the One who was not only the God of Israel but the governmental head as well (Exodus 22:19,20).

This law commanding capital punishment in those days was necessary because the Israelites repeatedly proved that without some form of severe incentive they would cheerfully plunge into every form of perversion and abomination, including child sacrifice, which was the practice of the peoples of their times. Even as our nation has been known to execute traitors until recently, even so God judged that sorcery, with its allegiance and dependence on other gods and spirits, was the ultimate form of betrayal to the nation of Israel and her sovereign Ruler. Those who chose to participate in sorcery were traitors to God and the nation. Therefore, capital punishment was justified.

However, when the theocracy in Israel came to an end, so did the justification for the execution of this law. I do not advocate the persecution or the burning of Witches. They are most certainly entitled to practice the religion of their choosing in this country. Nevertheless, it should be understood that God was making a point that is still applicable today. He hates the practice of witchcraft. The people who participate in it may sincerely believe they are worshiping benevolent gods, but the Word of God says that they are nevertheless worshiping demons.

The witches acknowledge that their "Horned God" is the "Lord of Death." Hebrews 2 reveals the true identity of that "Lord of Death":

316

... that through death He [Jesus] might render powerless him
who had the power of death, *that is, the devil* ... (Hebrews 2:14).

The Satanists cheerfully admit that the devil is the "Lord of Death" and
indeed LaVey even includes some of the names of the witches' gods and
goddesses in his list of Satan's "Infernal Names." Among them: "... Pan,
the Greek god of lust, later relegated to devildom; ... Hecate, Greek goddess of the underworld and witchcrafts, ... Ishtar, Babylonian goddess of
fertility, and Pwcca, the Welsh name for Satan."[1]

What Witches Believe

Witchcraft is decidedly a complex subject. There are so many variations that even among themselves the Witches and other members of the Pagan community cannot come to a consensus about their origins, beliefs, politics, practices and rituals, the nature of their deities, or even on the exact meaning of the word "Witch."[1] One of the things Witches find most appealing about their religion is that it is basically autonomous and free from the rigors of "dogma." You are pretty well free to believe what you like.

Nevertheless, there are some basic beliefs that most Witches and Pagans adhere to. Most Pagans are, according to Margot Adler, pantheistic, polytheistic, animistic, or all three, although some are conditionally monotheistic. The word "Pagan" comes from the Latin word "Paganus," which simply meant a country dweller. The term came to be used in a derogatory fashion to describe the back-woods "hicks" who still held to "outmoded" ways and beliefs. The term "heathen," which originally referred to "one who lives in the heaths," came to have the same negative connotation. Ms. Adler, however, defines a Pagan as "a member of a polytheistic nature religion, such as the ancient Greek, Roman, or Egyptian religions, or, in anthropological terms, a member of one of the indigenous folk and tribal religions all over the world."[2] "The religion of the Witches is, in its purest form, an ancient European shamanistic nature religion..."[3] All Witches are Pagans, but not all Pagans are Witches.

The term Neo-Pagan, according to occultist, magician, and Druid priest Isaac Bonewits, refers to "polytheistic (or conditional monotheistic) nature religions that are based upon the older or Paleopagan religions; concentrating upon an attempt to retain the humanistic, ecological and creative aspects of these old belief systems while discarding their occasional brutal or repressive developments, which are inappropriate...."[4]

In other words, in this modern day and age, Witches have determined that animal or human sacrifices, cannibalism, bestiality, ceremonial castration, sanctified prostitution, etc., practices common to and regularly demanded by the Goddess and her consort from time immemorial, are no longer accepted aspects of their religion. Today's Neo-Pagans are, generally, a sanitized version of the ancient idol worshipers of days gone by.

They are essentially a fertility nature religion. Nature itself is believed to be divine, and "Mother Earth" is thought to be a living, breathing entity who must be worshiped and appeased. Witches generally believe that their religion dates back to Paleolithic times, when our ancestors supposedly worshiped a Mother Goddess of fertility and the Horned God of the Hunt. The names of these gods varied from place to place, we are told, but the deities themselves remained basically the same. Some Witches trace their traditions to the myths of the ancient Greeks and Romans. Others, to the Egyptians, Sumerians, the Norse gods of the Vikings, or to the ancient Celts. Still others cheerfully blend any number of traditions and sources together, including bits and pieces from modern science fiction and fantasy (Star Trek and Tolkien's Ring Trilogy are among the most popular), to create their own unique interpretation and set of rituals.

Today's Pagans and Witches could be anyone: nurses, doctors, lawyers, psychologists, housewives, lab technicians, university professors, nursery-school attendants, teachers, or your neeighbor. They gather together in open fields, beaches, hilltops or in basements, as Starhawk tells us, to hold their rituals and "celebrate the mysteries of the Triple Goddess of birth, love, and death, and of her consort, the Hunter, who is Lord of the Dance of life. The religion they practice is called Witchcraft."[5]

They use rituals to help themselves "tune into nature," and many are active in promoting ecology conservation. They acknowledge a "Supreme Being"—not a God who walked on earth as a man, as Sybil Leek points out,[6] but a Force or Creative Power or Ultimate Deity that manifests itself primarily as feminine as well as masculine. As one anonymous Pagan puts it:

> We give honor to many Gods in the Pagan Way. It must be immediately realized that these many Gods are the Many Forms of the One God, the great force that lies behind all creation. The closest that philosophers have come to a definition of the One is "A state of Pure Being." Not a force that is "good." Not a force that is "bad." Not a force that is dark or light, but an existence that simply "IS."[7]

While some groups worship any number of deities, they worship that Supreme Being or Force in the form of the great Mother Goddess and, usually, the Horned God (although some strictly feminist covens, known as Dianic, acknowledge only the Goddess in her various manifestations).[8]

All Witches believe in the working of Magick,[9] although they will tell you that not everyone who works Magick is necessarily a Witch. Ritual Magicians work all kinds of magick without necessarily acknowledging or worshiping the gods and goddesses, the primary focus of modern Witches. Many Witches believe that magick is not "supernatural" at all, but rather that it is simply the harnessing of natural, innate powers through the use of rituals, positive thinking, and visualization techniques. Others use what they call the "Tools of Magick" to "enhance their power and work their magick in conjunction with the positive forces."[10]

Some of the tools they include in what one Witch called their "ditty bag" are quite familiar to many of us: "a Scrying Glass, Candles, Astrology charts, Tarot Cards, a Ouija Board, Herbs, Rune Stones, Rune Sticks, an incense burner, some Magickal words and symbols, and of course the most important ingredient, THE GODS."[11] As one Witch put it, "What really defines a Witch is a type of experience people go through. These experiences depend on altered states of consciousness. The Craft is really the Yoga of the West,"[12] ... a dubious distinction it holds with bio-feedback, also called the "Yoga of the West" by its developers, Elmer and Alice Greene.

Witches vehemently deny the existence of heaven, hell, or sin, and instead believe in Karma and Reincarnation. They generally teach that while a Witch can indeed, if he or she chooses, work evil, they never do, because they believe that any evil they send out will come back on them threefold, if not in this life, then certainly in the next, according to the law of Karma. "An it harm none do what thou wilt" is considered their universal creed. Witch Sybil Leek did observe that "my beliefs include the rule that evil may be justified if it is for the greater good of the whole."[13] She evidently was willing to sort out the resulting bad karma at a later date if necessary.

Feminist Witch Zsuzsanna (Z) Budapest qualifies the principle by stating, "Never use your magic to attack the innocent. Then you have nothing to fear."[14] Of course, the decision as to who is innocent and who is guilty, and of what, seems to be left entirely to the Witches' personal discretion and opinion. Z speaks of having helped cast hexes on various occasions, including the performing of "a spell against the Briggs Initiative, which would have made it illegal for gays to teach. The initiative bit the dust."[15] She also speaks of Hallowmass (Halloween) as being the "night of the revengeful Mother, who is the fierce protector of her sisters when aroused. If you have a blacklist of women's enemies, the score can be settled tonight."[16] So, it seems that taking revenge on those whom you consider to be your enemies does not come under the Wiccan Rede. Perhaps these Witches should consider rewriting it to read, "An it harm none, except those you don't like, do what thou wilt." (By the way, Z was invited by the San Jose, California Public Library to "speak to teenagers about magic spells and other rituals of her religion" under their "Meet a Real Witch" Program in July of 1986.)[17]

Other Witches, like Laurie Cabot (known as the "Official Witch of Salem" thanks to then Massachussetts Governor Michael Dukakis who proclaimed her as such in 1975-77[18]), insist that any Witch who deliberately engages in black magic (which she would define as magick used for selfish or evil purposes[19]) or who in any way harms a child or an animal is, by definition, no longer a Witch, "if they ever were one to begin with."[20]

That may well be true for Ms. Cabots' outfit, although I have to say her position reminds me of Satanists Michael Aquino and Anton LaVey who are trying very hard indeed to convince us that unless a person is a "card-carrying member" of their specific organization, they are not "true Satanists." The Wiccans and Neo-Pagans make a big point of telling us they are all autonomous, bound by no universally accepted dogmas, laws, and interpretations. Therefore for one group of Witches to assert that absolutely no "true Witch" would ever indulge in black magic seems rather illogical. The *Encyclopedia of Man, Myth & Magic* makes an excellent point on the subject of "black" versus "white" magic in general:

> The distinction between black and white magic is simple enough in theory: a black magician works for evil ends and a white magician for good. But in practice the distinction is frequently blurred. For one things, it rests in the eyes of the beholder and very often white magic is what you work and black magic is what other people work.[21]

Sympathy for
the Devil

The true source of the teachings so consistently presented by many advanced New Agers is clearly exposed by reading what they say about Lucifer. All through their works runs a consistent theme of sympathy for the devil. One of their biggest hassles with biblical Christians is that we simply refuse to understand that Lucifer is really a good guy. In fact, he and Christ, "two evolved Sons of God, were actual beings sent to nurture godly beings on Earth."[1] He really means well, but has consistently been misunderstood and maligned by those filled with negativity, fear, and hatred. As Barbara Marx Hubbard tells us, poor Lucifer "felt rejected by God and behaved, at a higher level, as badly as you."[2] Nevertheless, ". . . that devil is my brother, the brother of Christ, the other Son of God, who went astray. . . . Have pity on the devil, dearly beloveds. He is the fallen Son of God."[3]

Why did he fall? Sibling rivalry, of course. Lucifer, you see, felt that God, his Father, preferred his brother Jesus to him, so to get even he "attracted Eve to do what she naturally would have done . . . become self-conscious. It was like a sexual misdemeanor with an adolescent girl."[4]

So Lucifer had sex with Eve. But there's nothing *really* wrong with that, Ms. Marx Hubbard tells us. You see, "it was natural for Eve to be attracted to know more. The devil . . . the hurt brother of Christ . . . misused that natural attraction to get back at his Father, from whom he felt separated."[5]

Now listen to the blasphemies we're told next, and mark well *who* we are told is saying them:

> I, Jesus, am come to inform you that humanity is innocent of the intent to reject God. You have been infected by a disease of a higher being than your own. You are innocent, O humanity. The forces of God are on your side. . . . There are two defects from which you suffer, carnivorous behavior and the illusion of separation from God. . . . This awareness of your innocence is essential for your salvation. . . . Do not feel guilty, humanity. You are innocent. You inherited the defects of other forms of life. Forgive the animal for eating flesh. Forgive Satan for fearing God. Love the animal in the world and in yourself, and do not kill him any more. Love Satan, my fallen brother, and do not let him make you reject God any more.[6]

Manly P. Hall, recognized as one of the most knowledgeable and prolific modern occult historians, tells us:

Satan and Lucifer are not evil, but are two of the greatest powers in all creation. Without them, the universe could not come into being. . . .[7]

David Spangler, author, cofounder and former leader of Findhorn and darling of the New Age, spends a great deal of time in his occult book *Reflections on the Christ* telling us all about Lucifer and how wonderful and neccessary he is to us. His words on the subject are perhaps the most chilling of all:

> The true light of Lucifer cannot be seen through sorrow, through darkness, through rejection. The true light of this great being can only be recognized when one's own eyes can see with the light of the Christ, the light of the inner sun. Lucifer works within each of us to bring us to wholeness and as we move into a new age, which is the age of man's wholeness, each of us in some way is brought to that point which I term the Luciferic initiation, the particular doorway through which the individual must pass if he is to come fully into the presence of his light and wholeness.[8]

> Lucifer comes to give to us the final gift of wholeness. If we accept it then he is free and we are free. That is the Luciferic initiation. It is one that many people now, and in the days ahead, will be facing, for it is an initiation into the New Age.[9]

So there it is. In order to fully enter into the New Age, we must all accept Lucifer and be initiated into him. Doubtless that initiation will someday soon include accepting his mark on our foreheads.

The average New Age neophyte may well not understand or believe what has been said here about the true nature of their movement. The majority of those involved in the New Age are sincere, well-meaning, very nice people who see a genuine problem (i.e., the world is in a mess), and honestly believe that what they are into will help make the world a better place for everyone. Most of them would undoubtedly be horrified to know what some of their leaders are really saying, despite the fact that increasing numbers of channelers and writers are now beginning to say exactly the same things about "cleansing cycles," etc. Nevertheless, a growing number of advanced New Agers, the leaders and molders and philosophers of the movement, seem to know exactly whom they are serving and to whom their allegiance and love is pledged: Satan himself.

God Who?

Thus says the Lord, the King of Israel, and his Redeemer, the Lord of Hosts: "I am the first and I am the last, and there is no God besides Me."

—The Lord
Isaiah 44:6

I am the Alpha and the Omega, the first and the last, the beginning and the end.

—Jesus of Nazareth
Revelation 22:13

I know that I exist, therefore I AM. I know that the God-source exists. Therefore, IT IS. Since I am part of that force, then I AM that I AM.

—Shirley MacLaine
Dancing in the Light, p. 420

However endlessly and sincerely New Agers may talk about "God," what they are really referring to is an impersonal Force, an Energy of infinite power and Consciousness... what some call the "ground of Being" or "Ultimate Reality," or Brahman, or the Tao, or any endless number of names. The God of the New Age is pretty much whatever you want him/she/it to be. Blend together a good solid dose of Eastern pantheistic monism, which states that: All is One; Everything that exists is God, God is everything that exists. The planet, the grass, the animals, the book in your hand, and you, are God. Problem is, you forgot. You just need to alter a few minor quirks in your current thinking to "remember" and "experience" that truth: God is you; You are God. You are therefore, literally, the creator of all your reality. The realm of imagination is the same as the "real world," for all is bound in unity and you can therefore literally speak and think whatever you want into existence.

Add to this basic view whatever appeals to you from naturalism, which, while removing from the cosmos any concept of a Transcendent Deity at all, gives the Movement its overriding, overwhelming, never-ending emphasis on Self (unlike most Eastern pantheism which seeks to conquer and negate Atman (the Self) so that it may ultimately dissolve into Brahman). It is the philosophy of the Humanist Manifesto. To the naturalist, man is the measure of all things.

Now toss in a hefty dose of animism, the ancient Pagan, shamanic belief that everything in nature is indwelt by nature spirits, elementals, angels, fairies, and lots of other spirit beings. The Wiccans and other Neo-Pagans have done a great deal to popularize the gods of the ancient nature religions. The Findhorn community in Scotland communed and frolicked with cabbage and tomato devas (nature spirits), along with a multitude of other spirit beings who manifested to them, including the god Pan.[1] Some well-known New Agers have come from this tradition, including David Spangler and Peter Caddy.

If the mood strikes you and you're coming from a "Christian" perspective, you can even add to your eclectic universalist Divinity a dash of whatever aspect of theism appeals to you, perhaps thereby making your "God" at least somewhat more familiar. And *voila!* You now have some approximation of the "God" that a lot of New Agers have in mind when they use the term.

For all of Barbara Marx Hubbard's use of Scriptures and the word "God," what she is referring to, in common with all New Agers, is not the personal, transcendent, living God of the Bible. What she calls "God" is something she believes we will all become:

> We are becoming co-creators through the evolution of our mind and its technological extensions. We see the vision of our species reconnected to each other, to nature and to the Creator, gaining the capacities of omniscience, omnipotence, omnipresence and life eternal.[2]

Sri Chinmoy, guru, spiritist and leader of peace meditations at the United Nations, responds to a child's question "What does God look like?" by saying:

> God looks exactly like us. In your case, when you see God, He will look exactly like you.... God created earth to manifest Himself in human bodies, in human form....[3]

J.Z. Knight's "Ramtha" waxes positively poetic when describing "God":

> God is an all-consuming force that is everything. It is the wind upon the water, the changing of leaves, the simplicity of a rose, deep in its color and hue. God is lovers in their embrace, children in their laughter, and the sheen of honey colored hair. It is the sun rising in the morning, a star twinkling in the night.... God is the beauteous insect, the humble bird in flight, the vile and ugly worm.... That which is, all that is, is what you term God the Father, the totality of life and the lover of all that it is.... *God, of itself, is wholly without goodness or evil.*... God is not perfect, for perfection is a limitation to ongoing, ever changing, exuberant life. God simply is.[4]

Somehow, someone neglected to inform the God of the Bible about all this, because He still thinks He's a personal God. All through the Bible, from Genesis chapter 1 verse 1 to the end of the Book of Revelation, God is seen not as the great "IT IS" but as the Living "I AM." He does not speak of Himself as a schizophrenic, absentminded spin-off who inadvertently wound up spattering Himself (literally) into the universe. Rather, He presents Himself in the Bible as the transcendent, personal God who sovereignly chose to create and then reveal something of Himself to that creation. He clearly presents Himself as something wholly other than His creation (Genesis 1–11). He is not His creation; His creation is not Him and never will be. "I am the Lord, and there is no other; besides Me there is no God.... It is I who made the earth, and created man upon it" (Isaiah 45:5,12).

God's creation is a clear and evident expression of "His invisible attributes, His eternal power and divine nature." And yet the Bible reveals that "even though they knew God, they did not honor Him or give thanks; but they became futile in their speculations.... They exchanged the truth of God for a lie, and worshiped and served the creature rather than the Creator, who is blessed forever" (Romans 1:20-23).

Little Gods, Inc.

Who could ever forget that scene in "Out on a Limb" when Shirley MacLaine stood by the sea, arms stretched out wide and shouting "I AM GOD! I AM GOD!" By the way, so are you, she now tells us all at every opportunity, along with every other "channeler" in town. And the people flock to them by the tens of thousands to hear it.

The theme runs consistently through MacLaine's books and lectures:

> You are everything. Everything you want to know is inside of you. You are the universe.... Man refuses to accept that he is in possession of all truth, and has been from the beginning of time and space.... Man is the co-creator with the God of the cosmos.... Maybe the tragedy of the human race was that we had forgotten we were each divine.... You must never worship anyone or anything other than self. For you are God. To love self is to love God.... To dance with God, the creator of all things, is to dance with oneself...(from The Omega Letter, January 1987).

The crowning glory of her metaphysical teachings, however, is found at the end of her book *Dancing in the Light*. It is here that she reveals the final, demonically logical conclusion she must inevitably arrive at in response to the revelations given to her by her "Higher Self":

> The total understanding and realization of myself might require eons for me to accomplish. But, when that awareness is achieved, I will be aligned completely with that unseen Divine force we call God. For me to deny that Divine Force now, would

326 ◆ *Appendix H*

be tantamount to denying that I exist. I know that I exist, therefore I AM. I know that the God-source exists. Therefore, IT IS. Since I am part of that force, then I AM that I AM.[5]

What she "AM" is a blasphemer! "I AM" is the name which the sovereign, personal God used to describe Himself to Moses when he spoke to him from the burning bush (Exodus 3:14). I AM is the same God who said, "You shall not take the name of the Lord your God in vain" and "You shall have no other gods before Me!" (Exodus 20:7,3) . . . including you!

Nevertheless, an article in the *Los Angeles Times* dated Sunday, July 19, 1987 proclaims: "605 Disciples Spend a Weekend in the Lives of Shirley MacLaine," and quotes her as saying, ". . . Just remember that you are God, and act accordingly."

Paul Vitz, in his book entitled *Psychology As Religion: The Cult of Self-Worship*, has written one of the most insightful and powerful critiques of the Self-ism that has permeated our society. He points out that "to worship one's self (in self-realization) or to worship all humanity is, in Christian terms, simple idolatry operating from the usual motive of unconscious egotism. Unconscious or disguised self-love has long been recognized as the source of idolatry."[6]

Certainly the Bible has never given any indication whatsoever that men are given the right to declare personal divinity. In Acts 10:25 when the Roman centurion Cornelius (who was a righteous and God-fearing man) met the apostle Peter, he fell at his feet and worshiped him. He had received a vision from a holy angel directing him to send for Peter so that he might hear the message of the Good News of Jesus Christ. Cornelius had been raised in the pagan tradition of ancient Rome. For all he knew, Peter himself might be a divine being. "But Peter raised him up, saying 'Stand up; I too am just a man.' "

In Lystra, when the people saw Paul and Barnabas heal a man who had been lame from his mother's womb, "they raised their voice, saying . . . 'The gods have become like men and have come down to us.' And they began calling Barnabas, Zeus, and Paul, Hermes, because he was the chief speaker." In fact, they were so enthused in this supposed visitation that the priest of Zeus began preparing to offer a sacrifice to them. Paul and Barnabas did not view this display of worship with benign amusement. They did not say to these genuinely sincere people, "It is indeed right that you sacrifice to us, for WE ARE THAT WE ARE, but so are you." Nor did they protest with pious dissimulation and false humility and say, "Oh no, dearest entities. It is NOT right for you to worship us, or Zeus, for that matter, for we are all one with God and you must worship only that divinity that lies within your Self." Not hardly. When Paul and Barnabas heard they were about to be raised to the status of divinities—

. . . they tore their robes and rushed out into the crowd, crying out and saying, "Men, why are you doing these things? We are also men of the same nature as you, and preach the gospel to you in order that you should turn from these vain things to a living God, *who made the heaven and the earth and the sea, and all that is in them*" (Acts 14:11-15).

In contrast, King Herod put on his royal robes one day and began addressing the crowd. He must have sounded pretty good, because the people "kept crying out, 'The voice of a god and not of a man!' " And King Herod thought to his Higher Self, "Right! They've finally caught on! God Herod!" The results were not what one would expect for so divine a personage: "And immediately an angel of the Lord struck him because he did not give God the glory, and he was eaten by worms and died. But the word of the Lord continued to grow and to be multiplied" (Acts 12:21-24).

It would seem that God was making an emphatic distinction here between Himself and one who had evidently bought into the serpent's ancient lie, "You shall be as God."

God, in fact, consistently and repeatedly records in Scripture that He takes a rather dim view of those who would claim deity for themselves. In Ezekiel 28:2-10 the Lord brought scathing judgment on the leader of Tyre. Here's why:

> Thus says the Lord God,
> "Because your heart is lifted up
> And you have said, 'I am a god,
> I sit in the seat of gods,
> In the heart of the seas';
> Yet you are a man and not God,
> Although you make your heart like the heart of God—
> Behold, you are wiser than Daniel;
> There is no secret that is a match for you.
> By your wisdom and understanding
> You have acquired riches for yourself,
> And have acquired gold and silver for your treasuries.
> By your great wisdom, by your trade
> You have increased your riches,
> And your heart is lifted up because of your riches—"
> Therefore, thus says the Lord God,
> "Because you have made your heart
> Like the heart of God,
> Therefore, behold I will bring strangers upon you,
> The most ruthless of the nations.
> And they will draw their swords
> Against the beauty of your wisdom
> And defile your splendor.
> They will bring you down to the pit.
> And you will die the death of those who are slain
> In the heart of the seas.
> Will you still say, 'I am a god,'

In the presence of your slayer,
Although you are a man and not god,
In the hands of those who wound you?
You will die the death of the uncircumcised
By the hand of strangers
For I have spoken!" declares the Lord God![7]

Think of it this way: when an artist makes a pot, that pot is an expression of himself, of his talent and creativity. By no stretch of any rational (Western) imagination will one declare that that pot IS the artist, or that it will, if it works hard enough at it, someday evolve and merge in full unity with the artist thereby *becoming* the artist. For it to believe that would properly result in its being labeled what it has indeed become: a "crackpot."

Are You Gods?

God created man in His image, giving him a spirit, intellect, and will. That is a far cry from declaring that man carries within himself a "spark of divinity" that can eventually evolve into godhood, grasping to himself the attributes that belong exclusively to the Creator. The entire Bible continually emphasizes the distinction between God and man, declaring that man is separated not from his divine "Higher Self" but from a personal relationship with God because of his sin and rebellion.

And yet some will immediately respond, didn't Jesus Himself say "you are gods"? Indeed, Jesus most certainly did say it. It is recorded in John 10:34,35. The question, of course, is *In what context* did He say it? Those who assert that you can make the Bible say anything you want it to are right in a sense. For example, if I really wanted to, I could "prove" that God is a Republican and hates dogs: Ecclesiastes 10:2 says that "a wise man's heart directs him toward the right, but the foolish man's heart directs him toward the left," and Revelation 22:15 says that "outside are the dogs and the sorcerers." So, obviously God must love cats, because if dogs are outside it must be because the cats are inside. Granted, the arguments here are patently silly . . . however much I may personally like to believe the conclusions to be true . . . but I think you see what I'm getting at. One of principal reasons that false teachings and misunderstandings abound concerning the Bible is that people generally neglect to study a passage in the context in which it is recorded and they ignore other passages on the same subject which would help define the full biblical perspective on that subject. The atheist can become overwhelmed with enthusiasm at spotting the words "There is no God!" in the Bible . . . until he gets around to reading the first part of that sentence which would have considerably clarified the matter for him: "The fool has said in his heart . . ." (Psalm 14:1).

In John 10 Jesus finds Himself confronted with a hostile crowd that gathers around Him and rather rudely asks, "How long will You keep us in suspense? If You are the Christ, tell us plainly." Jesus points out that He has told them, but they simply would not believe because they were not His sheep. Again Jesus clearly and unmistakably reveals who He is:

My sheep hear My voice, and I know them, and they follow Me; and I give eternal life to them; and they shall never perish, and no one shall snatch them out of My hand. My Father, who has given them to Me, is greater than all; and no one is able to snatch them out of the Father's hand. I and the Father are one (John 10:24-30).

Now the Jews knew exactly what Jesus was saying: He was telling them that He and God the Father were of one essence. He was telling them that in a unique and unparalleled sense He was God in human flesh. His claim to deity was unmistakable. So was their reaction to it. They picked up rocks and were getting ready to let Him have it! When Jesus asked for what good work they were going to stone Him, they answered:

For a good work we do not stone You, but for blasphemy; and because You, being a man, make Yourself out to be God.

Jesus throws them a curve here by quoting from Psalm 82. In context, the psalmist is crying out to God because of the unjust judges in the land. God had indeed said to them, "You are gods," for they were His personal representatives in Israel. He had entrusted into their hands the power of life and death, making them indeed "as gods" to the people: "I said, 'You are gods, and all of you are sons of the Most High. Nevertheless, you will die like men and fall like any one of the princes' " (verses 6,7). Yes, the judges were "gods" in their position and responsibility, and yet God was pronouncing judgment upon them. These "gods" that did not make heaven and earth were going to die like anybody else (Jeremiah 10:11). The most important sense in which they indeed were "gods," however, was as a result of the fall. Men did indeed become little gods as a result of disobedience to God, even as Satan and his demons had when they rebelled against the Lord—false gods doomed to destruction and judgment. What Jesus was doing was reminding them of that rebellion, not complimenting them on their personal divinity! Keep in mind that it was to these same "gods" that Jesus said, "You are of your father the devil . . ." (John 8:44).

Jesus was hitting them with a bit of well-aimed sarcasm in John 10: "The Word says 'You are gods' despite the fact that you are wicked and unjust, so how come you're all bent out of shape when I say I am God's Son? At least I have the testimony of the Scriptures and the miracles I have worked among you to back My claim." Not unexpectedly, this observation made the crowd even angrier, and again they tried to stone Him.

The apostle Paul used a similar tone with the Corinthians some time later. In 1 Corinthians 4:8 Paul reveals more than a little exasperation with a flock that had become more than a little arrogant and smug:

You are already filled, you have already become rich, you have become kings without us; and would indeed that you had become kings so that we also might reign with you.

The Jesus Seminar to the contrary, the reason that the Pharisees and scribes had Jesus killed was because they clearly understood that He was claiming exclusive personal divinity:

> For this cause therefore the Jews were seeking all the more to kill Him, because He not only was breaking the Sabbath, but also was calling God His own Father, making Himself equal with God (John 5:18).

It is categorically *not true that* "Jesus did not come to teach how divine He was, but came to teach us that there is divinity within us," as Oprah Winfrey asserted on her program in her introduction of Unity cult minister Eric Butterworth, whose book *Discover the Power Within You* she praised as "one of the most important books . . . I've ever read in my life."[8] It is not true that ". . . the heart and core of Jesus' teachings concerned not His divinity, but the Divinity of Man . . ." It is a Gnostic lie that asserts "Christ is not a person, but a principle. . . . Jesus discovered the Christ principle within Himself. But He revealed it as a principle that involved all humanity by revealing the new dimension of divinity."[9]

The apostle John spent a good deal of his time refuting Gnostic heresies like these that crept into the church even in the first century: "Who is the liar but the one who denies that Jesus is the Christ? This is the antichrist, the one who denies the Father and the Son" (1 John 2:22). Jesus did not become the Christ at His baptism; He was BORN THE CHRIST, our Lord and Savior (Luke 2:11). "In the beginning was the Word, and the Word was with God, and the Word was God. . . . And the Word became flesh and dwelt among us." This is the testimony of the apostle John. It is Jesus and He alone who was born of a virgin. He became the Son of God at His incarnation, for God was the Father of His physical nature. We will never be "Sons of God" in the same sense He is. We can therefore never be God. We are born human beings—fallen, separated from God, and yet ". . . as many as received Him, to them He gave the right to become children of God, even to those who believe in His name" (John 1:1,2,14,12). "Christ" or "Kristos" is the Greek translation of the Hebrew word *mashiah*—Messiah—which means "anointed one." It is not some cosmic pool of collective divinity we can all tap into given enough incarnations!

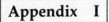
Speak for Yourself

Satanism candidly presents itself as "a blatantly selfish, brutal philosophy... based on the belief that human beings are inherently selfish, violent creatures, that life is a Darwinian struggle for survival of the fittest, that only the strong survive and the earth will be ruled by those who fight to win the ceaseless competition that exists in all jungles—including those of urbanized society."[1] The Satanists' highest virtues are the full and unbridled exercise of the seven deadly sins: pride, greed, lust, gluttony, anger, envy, and sloth. Their ethics are simple: "Do unto others as we would have them do unto us, and if our courtesy is not returned, we treat them with the wrath they deserve." And their creed is summed up in the now-famous Nine Satanic Statements:

1. Satan represents indulgence, instead of abstinence!

2. Satan represents vital existence, instead of spiritual pipe dreams!

3. Satan represents undefiled wisdom, instead of hypocritical self-deceit!

4. Satan represents kindness to those who deserve it instead of love wasted on ingrates!

5. Satan represents vengeance, instead of turning the other cheek!

6. Satan represents responsibility to the responsible, instead of concern for psychic vampires!

7. Satan represents man as just another animal, sometimes better, more often worse than those that walk on all-fours, who, because of his "divine spiritual and intellectual development," has become the most vicious animal of all!

8. Satan represents all of the so-called sins, as they all lead to physical, mental, or emotional gratification!

9. Satan has been the best friend the church has ever had, as he has kept it in business all these years!

Incidentally, you might want to go back and review some of the principles listed in the Humanist Manifesto discussed in chapter 2. In a lot of ways, the manifesto strikes me as being but a slightly politer version of the above satanic statements. In any case, both can be summed up by that most infamous of black magicians, Aleister Crowley's (1875-1947) famous dictum: "Do what thou wilt shall be the whole of the law."

LaVey spends a lot of time in the *Satanic Bible* (never mind the *Satanic Rituals!*) saying things like the following:

> For I stand forth to challenge the wisdom of the world; to interrogate the "laws" of man and of God! . . . Before none of your printed idols do I bend in acquiescence, and he who saith "thou shalt" to me is my mortal foe! [We're not told how Satanists in the military deal with this one. We're also left with no satisfactory explanation as to whether this also includes "Thou shalt not kill."] " . . . I dip my forefinger in the watery blood of your impotent mad redeemer, and write over his thorn-torn brow: The TRUE prince of evil—the king of slaves! . . . I break away from all conventions that do not lead to my earthly success and happiness. . . . I gaze into the glassy eye of your fearsome Jehovah, and pluck him by the beard; I uplift a broad-axe, and split open his worm-eaten skull! . . . Behold the crucifix: what does it symbolize? Pallid incompetence hanging on a tree. . . . There is nothing inherently sacred about moral codes. . . . Cursed are the believers in good and evil, for they are frightened by shadows! . . . Hate your enemies with a whole heart, and if a man smite you on one cheek, SMASH him on the other! Smite him hip and thigh, for self-preservation is the highest law! He who turns the other cheek is a cowardly dog![2]

And then he tells us he is astonished and dismayed that teenagers actually take the *Satanic Bible* literally and point to it as the reason for their murders and rebellion.

How to Approach Teachers

Be willing to give the teacher the benefit of the doubt. Not all teachers are a Ms. Monetta (see chapter 3). Many are genuinely unaware of the serious occultic/religious nature of the Transpersonal psychotechnologies they're using in their classrooms. Give them the benefit of the doubt. Be sensitive and polite! Be sure your attitude is right! Do your homework and present your case in a rational and, preferably, unhysterical fashion. Not too many teachers are going to be very open to change if some parent barges into their office and accuses them of Witchcraft! It might also be a good idea to take a friend along—not only to help keep you calm and help you present your case, but also as a witness just in case you need one. The teacher may also be more open to listen to your complaint if you've been interacting with him or her all along. Most teachers welcome a parent's interest in the class and are disappointed that so many parents seem to take no interest at all in their child's education. If you can, volunteer some time to help in the classroom. Run for a position on the School Board. Attend PTA meetings. Be sure to praise a job well done by a teacher—all too frequently those who *are* doing a good job receive no recognition for it from the parents.

It is possible that the teacher may decide to eliminate the objectionable program from his or her class. Then again, the teacher may not, even though you have suggested alternative books or programs.

If the teacher has been involved in his or her own "personal transformation" or has been reading NEA material warning about people like you who want to shut down their "innovative" teaching techniques, you may well get a very hostile reception regardless of how polite and involved you may have been. If this is the case, direct your request to the principal. If you are rebuffed or ignored at that level, get his reasons in writing, and go to the board and to the district superintendent. Write to your local paper and your Congressman if necessary. [See Appendix K.]

If you find yourself in this position, it will probably be a good idea to get counsel from a Christian legal organization in your area to help. Susan Gurule's ministry in Albuquerque, New Mexico will be able to provide referrals for you.[1] Mrs. Gurule is the mother who led the battle in New Mexico against the DUSO program (see chapter 7).

Unfortunately, regardless of how many occult experts testify on your behalf or how many senators and citizens you have on your side protesting the intrusion of New Age religion into the classroom, you may find yourself deciding, as did Susan Gurule, to simply pull your children from the public schools altogether. Some districts are, quite simply, determined to push their globalist/New Age agenda regardless of anyone's protests at any level.

Mrs. Gurule opted to start her own school, which has been growing steadily since January, 1989. Nevertheless, she doesn't plan to give up the fight. Even though the school board decided to keep the DUSO program she plans to continue to keep an eye on them. At least she succeeded in bringing the issue to public attention.

Home schooling may well be your best option. Or perhaps two or three churches could band together to start their own school. Still, don't make the mistake of assuming that just because you've got your children in a Christian school that they are automatically "home free." Many of the transpersonal activities we're discussing in this book can be found there as well.

How to Write More Effective Letters

TO YOUR CONGRESSMAN

Many people think any letter to Washington is just a waste of time, but nothing could be further from the truth. Congressmen pay attention to their mail because the writers' views form a major listening post for voter sentiment on pending legislation.

Who reads them?

A surprising amount of the letters to congressional offices are read carefully by the Congressmen themselves. Those that aren't are handled by key staff personnel who notify their bosses of the contents.

Form letters and petitions

Form letters with identical wording, long telegrams signed by lists of people, mimeographed petitions, and other "bulk" entreaties carry little or no weight in Washington. The legislators know from experience that sudden outpourings, with suspicious similarity, are largely from disinterested persons who were goaded into signing a form letter or petition by some lobbyist or political action group.

Write your own letter

It is the carefully thought-out, individual letter that a lawmaker appreciates. Write to your senators or representative just as you would write to anyone else. The influence of your communication depends upon the point you make and the clarity with which you make it. State exactly why you consider a bill good or bad, and how you feel that it would affect you and your community.

Courtesy always

Threats, warnings, and abuse merely antagonize lawmakers. Effective mail is courteous and the legislator is well aware, without reminding him in a letter, that he may be your "second favorite" candidate in the next election if he lets you down. Nor does he need to be wooed with a promise of "all-out" support at the polls if he votes the "right way." If you are pleased with the legislator's position on a bill or with his vote, write to thank and compliment him on his stand. This is important. Letters to a Congressman for a job well done are altogether too rare.

Follow through

Almost all Congressmen answer their mail, but if you receive just a brief acknowledgement, write again to ask for more specific information, e.g., precisely how he stands on the issue, how he feels toward its success, and if he proposes to support or oppose it. It is highly unlikely that he will ignore your second "follow-up" request, and he will appreciate your proven interest in the bill. In short, persistence pays.

Timing

Another important factor is when to send your letter. A deluge of mail just as a measure is about to be voted on is much less effective than a single intelligent letter months before while the legislator is still formulating his opinions. When the bill is introduced, send a copy of your letter (or a separate one) to the chairman of the committee to which it was referred. Sometimes a bill may never get out of committee for a floor vote. When possible, always refer to the bill under discussion by its name and number.

Address your letters

Senators: The Honorable _____
Senate Office Building
Washington, D.C. 20510

(Dear Senator _____)

Representatives: The Honorable _____
House Office Building
Washington, D.C. 20515

(Dear Mr. or Ms. _____)

The telephone number for your Senators and Representatives in Washington, D.C., is (202) 224-3121.

The President: President _____
The White House
1600 Pennsylvania Ave., N.W.
Washington, D.C. 20500

(Dear President _____)

The telephone number for the White House from 9 A.M. to 5 P.M. EST is (202) 456-7639.

TO YOUR EDITOR

When you write to a newspaper or other publication, KEEP IT . . .

Brief

Most letters should be no more than 200 or 300 words, as space is limited. You will be sharing the "Letters to the Editor" column with other correspondents on a variety of subjects. Most likely, your letter will be triggered by a recent news story or editorial, and it is not necessary to restate the entire premise before launching your views. Of course, limit the subject of your letter to just one topic, news story, or editorial; make your points quickly and cogently.

Pointed

If you don't have well-developed, firm opinions on an issue, don't bother to write. Both editors and their readers enjoy and react to a letter that has fact, feeling, and direction. Unless you have something positive to suggest or correct, something informative and useful for the readers, your letter will accomplish little. Be direct, to the point, and *above all, be sure of your facts.*

Identified

Always sign your letter with your full name and address; include your professional title if it is pertinent to the subject. Anonymous letters lack courage and conviction, and editors seldom print them. Letters with pseudonyms are usually discarded because editors check on the authenticity of both content and correspondent; however, your name may be withheld upon request if circumstances warrant, but these occasions are rare. Do not ask the editor to reply to your letter or to return your manuscript.

Address your letters

Letters to the Editor
Name of Newspaper or Magazine
City, State, Zip

(Dear _____) or

Mr. or Ms. _____
Managing Editor
Name of Magazine
Address

(Dear _____)

Notes

Chapter 1—The Beautiful Side of Evil

1. Religious News Service, "Parapsychology More Popular," the *Bakersfield Californian*, Dec. 27, 1986, p. C1. This was a 1981 Gallup Poll. A poll in 1986 by *USA Weekend* gave the same results ("Looking into the Beyond," *USA Weekend, Houston Post*, Jan. 9-11, 1987, p. 4.
2. Andrew Greeley, "Mysticism Goes Mainstream," *American Health*, Feb. 1987, pp. 47-55.
3. Robert Lindsey, *New York Times*, cited in the *Los Angeles Herald Examiner*, Sept. 29, 1986, p. 88
4. David Spangler, *Reflections on the Christ* (Findhorn Publications, 1978), p. 45.

Chapter 2—The Humanist Conspiracy

1. Dr. D.L. Cuddy, "Are Secular Humanists Seeking Our Children's Minds? You Bet," *Commercial Appeal* (Memphis, TN), Aug. 5, 1986.
2. Jack Canfield and Paula Klimek, "Education in the New Age," *New Age Magazine*, vol. 3, no. 9, Feb. 1978, p. 28.
3. Mark Mayfield, "Shadows of Violence Grows at USA Schools; Assaults Top the List of Classroom Chaos," *USA Today*, Dec. 8, 1986, p. 10.
4. Dr. Robert Simonds, "Humanism in our Schools," *Passport* magazine, June/July 1986, p. 7.
5. Dr. Murray Norris, *Weep for Your Children* (Valley Christian University, Box 73, Clovis, CA 93613).
6. David B. Parke, "Fresh Breezes Blowing: A New Era at Harvard," *The World* (Journal of the Unitarian Universalist Association), May/June 1987.
7. Samuel L. Blumenfeld, *Is Public Education Necessary?* (Old Greenwich, CT, 1981), p. 95.
8. "Alexander Solzhenitsyn: Critic in Exile," *Moody Monthly*, Dec. 1986, p. 89. See also "Return to God: Solzhenitsyn Speaks Out," *Time* magazine, May 23, 1983.
9. Barbara M. Morris, *Change Agents in the Schools* (The Barbara Morris Report, P.O. Box 756, Upland, CA 91786, 1979), p. 48, cited from Harold D. Drummond, "Leadership for Human Change," *Educational Leadership*, Dec. 1964, p. 147.
10. Eugene H. Methvin, "Guess Who Spells DISASTER for Education," *Reader's Digest*, 1984.
11. "Trojan Horse—Beware The National Education Association," *American Opinion*, Jan. 1985.
12. Methvin, "Guess Who Spells DISASTER," p. 92.
13. Rowland Evans and Robert Novak, "Bill Bennett: Secretary For Education," *Reader's Digest*, Mar. 1988, pp. 105-106.
14. Ibid., p. 106.
15. William M. Bowen, Jr., *Globalism: America's Demise* (Huntington House, Inc., 1984), p. 24.
16. Ibid., pp. 19-20. Quoted also in "Education to Remold the Child," *Parent and Child Advocates*, Rt. 4, Watertown, WI 53094, p. 30; and in *Humanistic Morals and Values Education*, by Vince Nesbitt, 12 Beta Rd., Lane Cove, N.S.W., 2066, Australia.
17. *The Social Sciences* (Harcourt Brace, 1970), p. T10.
18. Bowen, *Globalism: America's Demise*, p. 14. (Quoting Ashley Montagu in a lecture to home economic teachers in Anaheim, CA, Nov. 9, 1970.)
19. *Christian Harvest Times* (Elyria, OH), Jan. 1978.
20. Isaac Asimov, A. Lester, Kirkendall, B.F. Skinner, Sol Gordon, Betty Friedan.
21. Tim LaHaye, *The Battle for the Public Schools* (Fleming H. Revell, 1983), p. 38.
22. Paul Vitz, "Religion and Traditional Values in Public School Textbooks," *Education Newsline*, Dec. 1985, p. 2.
23. Norman Lear, "Why Johnny Can't Think," *OMNI*, Feb. 1987.
24. Charles L. Glenn, Jr., "Religion and Public Education—Can We Stop the Fighting?" *The Reformed Journal*, vol. 34, issue 6, 1984, p. 12.
25. Paul Kurtz, ed., *Humanist Manifestos I and II* (Prometheus Books, 1973), pp. 3, 8, 13.
26. Kenneth L. Woodward with Katharine Taylor, "Secular Humanism in the Dock: Are Public Schools Teaching a False Religion?" *Newsweek*, Oct. 27, 1986.
27. In an article published in the *Idaho Statesman* (Boise, ID), Mar. 29, 1987, Robert K. Skolrood, the Executive Director of the National Legal Foundation, said:

> The humanists argued they were a religion so they could obtain conscientious objection status. Paul Beattie, a signer of Humanist Manifest II, recently wrote openly that humanism is a religion. The American Humanist Association amended its bylaws in 1968 to qualify as a 501 (c) (3) "religious organization." In addition, their bylaws state, it ". . . selects, trains, and accredits Humanist Counselors as its ordained ministry of the movement." They perform weddings and other traditional duties of theistic clergy. Paul Kurtz, who drafted Humanist Manifest II states, "Regrettably there are no humanist membership organizations that are non-religious in legal status."

> "Only in response to this case" (i.e., the Alabama textbook case), adds Skolrood, "have humanists had the audacity to claim it is not a religion." Arthur J. Kropp, executive director for PAW, crowed over the overthrow of Judge Brevarel Hands' decision, saying: "Today's ruling rights that wrong. Secular humanism is a religion; it's a rallying cry for the religious right, a catchall for everything they disagree with about public education in America" ("Court Voids Ruling Banning Textbooks," the *Los Angeles Times*, Aug. 27, 1987).

28. The *Blumenfeld Education Letter*, vol. 2, no. 4, Apr. 1987, includes the following: The National Education Association published a pamphlet in Feb. 1985 in which they answered 31 of the most common charges

leveled against them by the "right wing extremists." "Here's what the pamphlet says about 'Extremist Accusation #9–NEA members indoctrinate students in secular humanism,' on page 7: Not true. NEA neither endorses nor practices 'secular humanism.' Nor does NEA support the indoctrination of students to any religious or nonreligious doctrine. The whole notion of secular humanism is, in fact, entirely the invention of Radical Right leaders, writers, and fund-raisers. They've conjured up the concept, defined it, villified it, and then attributed it to teachers."

29. Charles Jackard, "HUMANISM: An Answer to Problems Facing Education," *The Humanist Magazine*, May/June 1983, p. 20.
30. Paul Kurtz, *In Defense of Secular Humanism* (Prometheus Books, 1983), p. 6.

Chapter 3—Your Teacher the Occultist?

1. Fritjof Capra, *The Turning Point* (Bantam Books, 1982), p. 418.
2. Ibid., p. 35.
3. Ibid., p. 415.
4. Marilyn Ferguson, *The Aquarian Conspiracy: Personal and Social Transformation in the 1980's* (J.P Tarcher, Inc., 1980), p. 281.
5. Ibid., p. 281.
6. Ibid., p. 280.
7. Ibid., p. 68.
8. Ibid., p. 311.
9. John Miller, *The Compassionate Teacher*, The Transformation Series (Englewood Cliffs, NJ: Prentice-Hall, Inc., 1981).
10. Warren T. Greenleaf and Gary A. Griffin, "Schools for the 70's and Beyond: A Call to Action," a staff report, CSI, WA 1971; UMI—Out-Of-Print Books on Demand, MI, 1987, p. 76.
11. Thomas Bradford Roberts, "Transpersonal: The New Educational Psychology," *Phi Delta Kappan*, Nov. 1974, p. 191.
12. Joseph Campbell, ed., *The Portable Jung* (The Viking Press, 1971), p. 60.
13. Shirley Nicholson, comp., *Shamanism, An Expanded View of Reality*, A Quest Book (The Theosophical Society, 1987), p. 59.
14. Paul C. Vitz, *Psychology As Religion—The Cult of Self-Worship* (Eerdmans Publishing Co., 1977).
15. Miller, *The Compassionate Teacher*, p. ix.
16. Thomas B. Roberts, "States of Consciousness: A New Intellectual Direction, a New Teacher Education Direction," *Journal of Teacher Education*, Mar./Apr. 1985.
17. Roberts, "Transpersonal," p. 20.
18. Ferguson, *The Aquarian Conspiracy*, p. 288.
19. Ibid.
20. Transpersonal psychology was a key subject of discussion at the 25th anniversary conference of the Association for Humanistic Psychology, held in San Francisco in March 1985.

    Ron Valle, associate dean of the Graduate School of Consciousness Studies at John L. Kennedy University, pointed out that while Abraham Maslow and fellow colleagues agreed on the term "transpersonal" only in 1968, the *roots* of transpersonal thinking were ancient indeed:

    > . . . the transpersonal perspective has its deeper roots in the perennial philosophies, including Zen and Tibetan Buddhism, yoga and Hindu thought, Sufism, Christian mysticism, Taoism, mystical Judaism and the views of Native American cultures (Shepherd Bliss, "Humanist Psychology Reaches Toward the Transcendent," *Yoga Journal*, Sept./Oct. 1985).

    Rollo May did offer a gentle voice of concern about the nature of Transpersonal psychology, by saying that while he was a "staunch believer in humanism, psychology, and religion, . . . we lose their separate meanings by stirring them up in the same pot." But, on the other hand, Maurice Friedman, an existential philosopher and biographer of the Jewish theologian Martin Buber, pointed out that "I agree that humanistic psychology has mixed up psychology and religion, but that is one of its strengths—being open to the holy."

    Jean Houston, former president of the Association of Humanistic Psychology, has taken a short step beyond "transpersonal" psychology and has developed what she calls "sacred psychology."

    "Sacred psychology is not merely therapy. It is doing the work of the gods, of the holy . . . sacred psychology is to go back in time, to rediscover the ancient rituals and recast them." (Jean Houston and Robert Marters, *Mind Games: The Guide to Inner Space*. This book is highly regarded among Transpersonal educators, including Canfield and Rozman, and frequently appears in their recommended reading lists.)

21. Alice A. Bailey, *Education in the New Age* (Lucis Publishing Co., 1954), p. 52.
22. Robert Assagioli, M.D., *Definition of Psychosynthesis: A Collection of Basic Writings*, an Esalen Book (Penguin Books, 1965); and brochure for "International Psychosynthesis" Seminar Co., 1987-88.
23. Harold E. Mitzel, ed., *Encyclopedia of Educational Research*, 5th ed., vol. 1 (New York: The Free Press, a Division of Macmillan Publishing Co., Inc., 1982), p. 98.
24. Canfield and Klimek, "Education in the New Age."
25. Alice A. Bailey, *The Unfinished Autobiography* (New York: Lucis Publishing Co., 1951), p. 224.
26. Ibid., p. 241-42.
27. *Pathways*, A New Age Publication of Spiritual Unity Movement, vol. VI, no. 4, July-Aug. 1983, p. 16.
28. *Pathways*, p. 16.
29. Morris, *Change Agents*, p. 15.
30. Nola Meredith, from a "Resolution" written in 1972 in protest of the proposed New Consciousness Education bill (CA).

31. Michael Scott Caine, "Crazies at the Gate: The Religious Right and the Schools," *The Humanist*, July/Aug. 1983.
32. The protection of Pupils' Rights Act (20 U.S.C. 12232h, also known as the Hatch Amendment), was passed by Congress in 1974. It "forbids schools to subject students to psychological examination or treatment which requires the pupil to reveal information concerning 'political affiliations,' 'sex behavior and attitudes,' 'mental and psychological problems potentially embarrassing to the student or his family,' or 'critical appraisals' of behavior and attitudes of family members, without 'the prior written consent of the parents' " (The Phyllis Schlafly Report, vol. 17, no. 10, sect. 1, May 1984).
33. Gay Hendricks, *The Moving Center: Exploring Movement Activities for the Classroom* (NJ: Prentice-Hall, 1983), p. 76.
34. Concerned Women for America, "Florida Christmas Case Goes to Trial," *NEWS*, Apr. 1986.

Chapter 4—Gifted, Talented, and Other Hazards
1. According to Eastern mysticism, the "Third Eye," is located between the eyebrows and just slightly above. According to Sri Chinmoy, opening the third eye is what enables one to "see God, just as you see me now" (Sri Chimnoy, *Yoga and the Spiritual Life* [New York: Agni Press, 1974], p. 109).
2. Dorothy Sisk, *Creative Teaching of the Gifted* (McGraw-Hill Book Co., 1987), p. 289.
3. Ibid., p. 308.
4. Barbara Clark, *Growing Up Gifted: Developing the Potential of Children at Home and at School*, 2d ed. (Charles E. Merrill Publishing Co., 1983), p. 398.
5. Barbara Clark, Ed.D., is a professor at California State University, Los Angeles; consultant in Gifted Education throughout the United States and Canada; author of *Growing Up Gifted*; and a "recognized leader in the field of Gifted Education." So says a flyer for the "New Age School" she directed in San Marino County, CA in the summer of 1984.
6. Clark, *Growing Up Gifted*, p. 405.
7. Of course, keep in mind that not every teacher who uses the term "integrative" is necessarily referring to Transpersonal education. Some teachers are merely referring to the "integrating" and correlating various lessons and materials together to a common theme. For example, a teacher may "integrate" the story read to her class with a math or science lesson.
8. Ferguson, *The Aquarian Conspiracy*, p. 309.
9. "The World's Most Popular Magazine for Parents and Teachers of Gifted, Creative, and Talented Children," *G/C/T*, May/June 1986, p. 11.
10. Ibid.
11. Linda Sannita, "Testing and Enhancing a Gifted Child's ESP," *Gifted Children Newsletter*, Apr. 1983.
12. Clark, *Growing Up Gifted*, p. 394.
13. *High Action Reading for Study Skills* (Cleveland, OH: Modern Curriculum Press, Inc., 1979), pp. 18-31. (Modern Curriculum Press, Inc., 13900 Prospect Road, Cleveland, OH, 44136.)
14. Raymond Buckland and Hereward Carrington, *Amazing Secrets of the Psychic World* (West Nyack, NY: Parker Publishing Co., Inc., 1975), p. 180.
15. Richard Cavendish, ed., *Man, Myth and Magic*, vol. 21 (New York: Marshall Cavendish Corp., 1970), p. 2118.
16. Frank S. Mead, *Handbook of Denominations in the United States* (revised by Samuel S. Hill (Nashville, TN: Abingdon Press, 1985), pp. 233-34.
17. Stoker Hunt, *Ouija: The Most Dangerous Game* (New York: Barnes and Noble Books, a division of Harper and Row Publishers, 1985), p. 4.
18. James P. Johnson, *American Heritage Magazine*, Feb./Mar. 1983, p. 27.
19. Hunt, *Ouija*, p. 6.
20. Edmund C. Gruss, *The Ouija Board* (Chicago: A Moody Acorn, Moody Press, 1986), p. 5.
21. Stoker Hunt, *Ouija: The Most Dangerous Game* (Barnes and Noble Books, 1985), p. 6.
22. Ibid.
23. And besides, the court added, *their* psychologists said that the Ouija board had nothing whatever to do with spirits anyway. In their erudite opinion it was but a harmless form of automatism. It operated *exclusively* through the subconscious and imperceptible manipulations of those working the board.
    Other psychologists, however, such as Dr. Hans Bender, one of the foremost experts on automatism, affirms that the "unwitting use of automatisms like the Ouija board can induce psychosis" (quoted in Stoker Hunt's *Ouija: The Most Dangerous Game*, p. 123).
24. Hunt, *Ouija*, p. 6.
25. Dr. Kurt Koch, *Occult A B C* (Kregel Publications, 1978), p. 154.
26. John Godwin, *Occult America* (New York: Doubleday and Co., Inc., 1972), p. 271.
27. Manly P. Hall, *Questions and Answers—Fundamentals of the Esoteric Sciences* (Los Angeles, CA: The Philosophical Research Society, Inc., 1979), pp. 95-96.
28. Ena Twigg with Ruth Hagy Brad, *Ena Twigg: Medium* (A Manor Book, 1973), p. 193.
29. June G. Bletzer, *The Donning International Encyclopedic Psychic Dictionary* (Norfolk/Virginia Beach: The Donning Co., 1986), p. 447.
30. In light of warnings such as these, and there are dozens of them I could have listed, it is especially distressing to find well-respected "men of the cloth" advocating use of the Ouija. In his book *The Christian and the Supernatural* Episcopal priest and Jungian psychologist Morton Kelsey openly encourages Christians to develop occult abilities. He informs us on pages 71-72 that "Another way of coming into contact with the realm which mediums reach is by using a Ouija board, one of the most popular games in America. . . . Whether the answers come from one's own unconscious or from outside, they often supply amazing insights and even information."
    His one word of caution: "It is unfortunate . . . that so many people make a game of encountering the

psychic realm." Evidently he would like us to be *serious* about our occult development! A shocking perspective from one who should know better, but then again, Rev. Kelsey believes that Jesus was the greatest *shaman* that ever lived (Morton Kelsey, *Dreams: A Way to Listen to God*, p. 23), so I suppose the rest should not come as a major surprise.

31. Hunt, *Ouija*, p. 141.
32. Gruss, *The Ouija Board*, p. 17, quoting from Martin Ebon, ed., *The Satan Trap—Dangers of the Occult* (Garden City, NY: Doubleday and Co., Inc., 1976), pp. 155-63.
33. Ibid., p. 17.
34. Hunt, *Ouija*, p. 99.
35. Ibid., p. 13.
36. Ibid., p. 14.
37. Gruss, *The Ouija Board*, p. 19.
38. Bob Muir, *Progress Bulletin* (Ontario, CA), Feb. 27, 1987.
39. Ibid., Mar. 5, 1987.
40. Ibid., Mar. 13, 1987.
41. Ibid., Feb. 27, 1987.
42. Ibid., Mar. 14, 1987.

Chapter 5—Your Kid the Psychic
1. Dr. Alex Tanous and Katherine Fair Donnelly, "Your Kids Are Psychic!" *Instructor* magazine, Apr. 1980, excerpted from *Is Your Child Psychic? A Guide for Creative Parents and Teachers* (Macmillan Publishing Co., 1979).
2. Kea Keyes, Jr., *The Hundredth Monkey* (OR: Vision Books, 1982). This mythical idea is based on the supposed research on the so-called Hundredth Monkey on Koshima Island.
3. Beverly-Colleene Galyean, "Expanding Human Intelligence," *The Futurist*, Oct. 1983. This article is also included in *Global Solutions, Innovative Approaches to World Problems*, edited by Edward Cornish, World Future Society, Washington, DC, 1984, p. 67.
4. Ibid., pp. 67-68
5. Ibid.
6. Beverly-Colleene Galyean, *Human Teaching and Human Learning in the Language Class: Confluent Teaching Strategies Applied to Language Teaching*, rev. 1976 (Santa Barbara, CA: CEDARC, 1976), p. 32.
7. Dr. Alex Tanous and Katherine Fair Donnelly, *Is Your Child Psychic? A Guide for Creative Parents and Teachers* (Macmillan Publishing Co., Inc., 1979), p. 179.
8. "They Don't Have Ghost of Chance to Find the Answer," *Los Angeles Times*, Aug. 8, 1987, part I, p. 2.
9. From an invitation sent from the Institute of Noetic Sciences to join their organization. No date on letter, received in Mar. 1987.
10. Willis W. Harman, "New Developments in the Reconciliation of Science and Religion," *New Realities* magazine, Jan./Feb. 1987.
11. C.S. Lewis, *The Screwtape Letters* (Macmillan Paperbacks, 1961), pp. 32-33.
12. Isaiah 44:25.
13. Isaiah 2:20.
14. Exodus 20:3-5.
15. Isaiah 14:14.

Chapter 6—Your Kid the Yogi
1. Canfield and Klimek, "Education in the New Age," p. 27.
2. Beth Ann Krier, "Checking In with the State's Task Force . . . The Quest for Self-Esteem," *Los Angeles Times*, part VI, June 14, 1987, p. 1.
3. These included such activities as "sacred dance," developed in the New Age Scottish community of Findhorn; "Eurythmy," a "beautiful set of movements" based on the work of the founder of Anthroposophy and the Waldorf Schools, Rudolph Steiner; Sufi dances; "New Games," which originated in the early 1970's as a "new form of play stressing cooperation, trust, and fun rather than competition, stress, and winning"; sensory awareness; yoga; relaxation and centering techniques; the martial arts; values clarification; Magic Circle; transactional analysis; and death education.
4. David Spangler, *Reflections on the Christ* (Moray, Scotland: Findhorn Publications, 1978, 3d ed., 1981), pp. 44-45.
5. Canfield and Klimek, "Education in the New Age," p. 38.
6. Beth Ann Krier, "The Quest for Self-Esteem," *Los Angeles Times*, part VI, June 14, 1987, p. 11; and "Self-Esteem Task Force Gets Down to Grass Roots," the *Los Angeles Times*, Sept. 18, 1987.
7. Krier, "The Quest for Self-Esteem."
8. Jack Canfield, *Self-Esteem in the Classroom: A Curriculum Guide* (Pacific Palisades, CA: Self-Esteem Seminars, 1986), pp. 215-26.
9. Canfield, *Self-Esteem in the Classroom*, p. 218.
10. Ibid.
11. Canfield, *Self-Esteem in the Classroom*, p. 222.
12. Paula Klimek and Jack Canfield, "Discovering Your Radiant Self: A Transpersonal Approach to Expressing Your Potential," *Elementary School Guidance and Counseling*, Dec. 1970, p. 137.
13. Ibid.
14. Canfield and Klimek, "Education in the New Age," p. 38.
15. Ibid., p. 30.
16. Klimek and Canfield, "Discovering Your Radiant Self," p. 136.
17. Deborah Rozman, *Meditation for Children* (Boulder Creek, CA: University of the Trees Press, 1976), p. 150.

342

18. John Randolph Price, "The Future Is Now," (excerpted from *The Planetary Commission*, the Quartus Foundation for Spiritual Research, Inc., p. 12).
19. George Beinhorn, "Sharing Nature with Children—the Playful Genius of Joseph Cornell," *Yoga Journal*, July/Aug. 1984, pp. 32, 34.
20. Anne Morris, "What Is Yoga?" *Boy's Life* magazine, Dec. 1984.
21. B.K.S. Iyengar, *Light on Yoga* (New York: Shocken Books, 1965), p. 21.
22. Cavendish, *Man, Myth and Magic*, vol. 22, p. 3070.
23. Ibid., vol. 10, p. 1316.
24. Edward Albertson, *Spiritual Yoga* (Los Angeles: Sherbourne Press, 1969), p. 55.
25. "Wellness Letter," vol. 1, issue 9, University of California—Berkeley, June 1985, p. 5.
26. Richard Hittleman, on his program "Yoga and Meditation," Dec. 1983.
27. Rozman, *Meditation for Children*, p. 85.
28. Hittleman, "Yoga and Meditation," p. 23.
29. Gopi Krishna, *The Evolutionary Energy in Man* (Boston: Shambhala, 1971), pp. 16-17.
30. John Weldon and Clifford Wilson, *Occult Shock and Psychic Forces* (San Diego, CA: Master Books, 1980), p. 73.
31. Hans-Ulrich Rieker, trans. by Elsy Becherer (a disciple of the Indian yogi and scholar, Dr. Rammurti S. Mishra), *The Yoga of Light, Hatha Yoga Pradipika—India's Classical Handbook* (New York: Herder and Herder, 1971), p. 9.
32. Deborah Rozman, Ph.D., *Meditating with Children* (University of the Trees Press), p. 101.
33. Alice A. Bailey, *The Externalization of the Hierarchy* (New York: Lucis Publishing Co., 1957), p. 18. (Lucis Publishing Co., was formerly Lucifer Publishing Company.)
34. Klimek and Canfield, "Discovering Your Radiant Self: A Transpersonal Approach," p. 137.
35. Gay Hendricks and Russel Wills, *The Centering Book* (New York: Prentice Hall Press, 1975), pp. 13, 15, 35, 36. Hendricks' thoroughly occultic, transpersonal material for children comes highly recommended by Jack Canfield. Hendricks has a Ph.D. in counseling psychology from Stanford. He is an assistant professor in the School of Education at the University of Colorado at Colorado Springs, where he teaches courses in counseling and education.
36. Rammurti S. Mishra, M.D., *The Textbook of Yoga Psychology* (London: The Lyrebird Press Ltd., 1972), p. 225.
37. Cavendish, *Man, Myth and Magic*, vol. 22, p. 3074.
38. Sol Gordon, *Psychology for You* (Oxford, Chicago, Los Angeles: Sadlier, 1983, 1978), pp. 263, 250-51.
39. Ibid., p. 250.
40. Ibid., p. 262.
41. Ibid., p. 263, 250.
42. Maureen Murdock, "Brain Child in the Promised Land," *Dromenon*, Winter 1979, p. 40.
43. Joanne Sanders, "Awakening the Mind: An Interview with Anna Wise," *The Common Boundary*, vol. 5, issue 5, p. 8.
44. Bletzer, *The Donning International Encyclopedia*, pp. 69-70.
45. Sanders, "The Common Boundary," p. 8.
46. Dr. Stanley Krippner, "The Influence of Consciousness Research," *Association of Humanistic Psychology Newsletter*, May 1979, p. 10.
47. "Little Swamis," *Psychology Today*, Jan. 1985.
48. Canfield and Klimek, "Education in the New Age," p. 35.
49. Ibid.
50. Rozman, *Meditating with Children*, p. 86.
51. Ibid.
52. Ibid., p. 108.
53. Ibid., p. 120.
54. Maureen H. Murdock, "Meditation with Young Children," *The Journal of Transpersonal Psychology*, vol. 10, no. 1, 1978, p. 37.
55. Ibid.
56. Cavendish, *Man, Myth and Magic*, vol. 13, p. 1727.
57. Mircea Eliade, *Yoga—Immortality and Freedom*, Bollingen Series (Princeton, 1958, 1973), p. 212.
58. Cavendish, *Man, Myth and Magic*, vol. 13, p. 1728.
59. Ibid., p. 1727.
60. *Chant and Be Happy—The Power of Mantra Meditation*, based on the teachings of "His Divine Grace A.C. Bhaktivedanta Swami Prabhupada" (The Bhaktivedanta Book Trust, International Society for Krishna Consciousness, 1982), pp. x, 47.
61. Bob Larson, *Larson's Book of Cults* (Tyndale House, 1982), pp. 333-342. (See also *TM in Court: The Complete Text of the Federal Court's Opinion in the Case of Malnak v. Maharishi Mahesh Yogi*, Spiritual Counterfeits Project, Inc., 1978, Berkeley, CA.)
62. Phillip K. Trocki, *Spell-It-Out* (Learning Trends, a division of Globe Book Company, Inc., 1978), p. 65. Whether excerpt was taken from book I or II was not identified on copy sent to me.
63. José and Miriam Arguelles, *Mandala* (Boston: Shambhala, 1972), p. 16.
64. Eliade, *Yoga—Immortality and Freedom*, p. 212.
65. Arguelles and Arguelles, *Mandala*, p. 34. On p. 44, Arguelles also calls the mandala "sacred art" and says "... it is a form of magic."
66. Cavendish, *Man, Myth and Magic*, vol. 13, p. 1778.
67. Arguelles and Arguelles, *Mandala*, p. 13.
68. Cavendish, *Man, Myth and Magic*, vol. 13, p. 1714.
69. Arguelles and Arguelles, *Mandala*, p. 34.
70. Canfield, *Self-Esteem in the Classroom*, p. 219.

71. Arguelles and Arguelles, *Mandala*, p. 13.
72. Canfield and Klimek, "Education in the New Age," p. 39.
73. Cavendish, *Man, Myth and Magic*, vol. 13, p. 1778.
74. Robert Rose, "A Program for Altering Children's Consciousness," The *Gifted Child Quarterly*, Spring 1979, pp. 113, 115.
75. Cavendish, *Man, Myth and Magic*, vol. 13, p. 1779.
76. Canfield and Klimek, "Education in the New Age," p. 31.
77. Annette Hollander, M.D., "How to Help Your Child Have a Spiritual Life," *Time* magazine, date unknown.
78. Ibid. These are designed to develop an awareness of "the life energy"—called *ki* in Japanese and *chi* in Chinese—in order to allow it to flow unobstructed through the body. This balancing of the "life force" is well-known to produce psychic powers.

Chapter 7—Shamanism 101

1. Raymond Buckland, *Practical Candleburning Rituals* (Llewellyn Publications, 1982), p. 186.
2. "What Is," *New Age Activists*, Summer 1986, vol. 1, no. 1, p. 15.
3. Doug Levy, "Thinking Skills Provoke Discussion," *The Columbian* (Vancouver, WA), Feb. 24, 1987.
4. Margaret Holland, Ph.D., *Instructors Manual for QR for Young People* (QR Institute, 1980), p. 23.
5. "Conservatives Assail 'Whole Mind' Teaching Methods," the *Los Angeles Times*, Nov. 15, 1986 and the *Austin Daily Herald*, Nov. 3, 1986.
6. C.F. Royce, "A New Age Battle in New Mexico: The Issue of Classroom Meditation vs. Parents' Right of Choice Flares Into Legal Confrontations," *BODY MIND SPIRIT: Your New Age Information Resource*, Mar./Apr. 1989, p. 56.
7. From a 12-page pamphlet submitted to the Montrose County RE-1J School Board for consideration at the regular meeting of Nov. 7, 1988.
8. Royce, "A New Age Battle in New Mexico," p. 57.
9. Ibid.
10. *Citizen's Education News*, Summer 1988. Quote found in the 12-page pamphlet submitted by parents to the Montrose School Board in Nov. 7, 1988.
11. See Johanna Michaelsen's *The Beautiful Side of Evil* (Eugene, OR: Harvest House Publishers, 1982), pp. 67-84, for further information on Silva Mind Control.
12. Tim Brown, "What's New in Our Schools?" *The Colossian Fellowship PREVUE*, July 1987. Also from a conversation with Tony Moore of the *Colossian Fellowship*, Mar. and Apr., 1987.
13. George Isaac Brown, *Human Teaching for Human Learning: An Introduction to Confluent Education* (New York: An Esalen Book, Viking Compass Edition, 1971, 1972), p. 3.
14. Paulette Leibman, "The Multisensory Schoolhouse," special to the *Daily News* (author's files), n.d.
15. Brown, *Human Teaching*, p. xvi.
16. Frances Adeney, "Educators Look East," *Radix*, Nov./Dec. 1980, p. 21.
17. Beverly-Colleene Galyean, "Meditating with Children: Some Things We Learned," *Association for Humanistic Psychology Newsletter*, Aug./Sept. 1980.
18. Galyean, "Meditating with Children," p. 20.
19. Rozman, *Meditation for Children*, p. 27.
20. Rozman, *Meditating with Children*, review excerpts.
21. Ferguson, *The Aquarian Conspiracy*, p. 297.
22. Sally P. Springer, "Educating the Left and Right Sides of the Brain," *National Forum*, the Phi Kappa Phi Journal, Spring 1987, p. 25.
23. Edward Dolnick, "The Right (Left) Stuff," *OMNI*, Dec. 1988, p. 45.
24. Sheila Ostrander and Lynn Schroeder with Nancy Ostrander, *SuperLearning* (New York: Dell Publishing Co., Inc., 1979), p. 16.
25. Ibid., p. 17.
26. Ibid., p. 20.
27. Ostrander, Schroeder, Ostrander, *SuperLearning*, pp. 20, 26.
28. Ibid.
29. Mike Samuels, M.D. and Nancy Samuels, *Seeing with the Mind's Eye: The History, Techniques and Uses of Visualization* (New York: Random House, 1975), p. 21.
30. Jeanne Achterberg and G. Frank Lawlis, *Imagery and Disease* (Champaign, IL: Institute for Personality and Ability Testing, Inc., 1978, 1984), p. 9.
31. Jeanne Achterberg and G. Frank Lawlis, *Bridges of the BodyMind* (Champaign, IL: Institute for Personality and Ability Testing, Inc., 1980), p. 29.
32. Samuels and Samuels, *Seeing with the Mind's Eye*, p. 21.
33. J.P. Chaplin, *Dictionary of the Occult and Paranormal* (Laurel Edition, Dell Publishing Co., Inc., 1976), p. 4.
34. Samuels and Samuels, *Seeing with the Mind's Eye*, p. 21.
35. Achterberg and Lawlis, *Bridges*, p. 29.
36. Ibid.
37. Samuels and Samuels, *Seeing with the Mind's Eye*, p. 13.
38. Michael Harner, *The Way of the Shaman* (Bantam New Age Books, 1980, 1982), pp. 25-26.
39. Shakti Gawain, *Creative Visualization* (Bantam New Age Books, 1979, 1982), pp. 3-4.
40. Buckland, *Practical Candleburning*, p. 179.
41. Dave Hunt and T.A. McMahon, *The Seduction of Christianity* (Eugene, OR: Harvest House Publishers, 1985), p. 123.
42. Ferguson, *The Aquarian Conspiracy*, p. 281.
43. Ibid.

44. Canfield and Klimek, "Education in the New Age," p. 36.
45. Rozman, *Meditating with Children*, p. 148.
46. Ibid., p. 146.
47. Bob True, "Teaching Parents a Lesson," *Creek* (Denver, CO), Nov. 22, 1985.
48. Dick Sutphen, "Infiltrating the New Age into Society," New Age Activists *WHAT IS* magazine, vol. 1, no. 1, Summer 1986, p. 14.

Chapter 8—How to Meet Your Spirit Guide
1. James W. Peterson, *The Secret Life of Kids: An Exploration Into Their Psychic Senses*, A Quest Book (Wheaton, IL: The Theosophical Publishing House, 1987), p. 66.
2. Jimmy S. Curtin, *Magic and Children: The Way for Children to Learn* (San Bernardino, CA: Abbetira Publication, 1985), p. 14.
3. Frances Adeney, "Some Schools Are Looking East for Answers," *Moody Monthly*, May 1982, p. 20.
4. Jon Klimo, "The Psychology of Channeling: An Investigation of Paranormal Claims," *New Age Journal*, Nov./Dec. 1987, p. 62.
5. Marcus Allen and Shakti Gawain with Jon Bernoff, *Reunion: Tools for Transformation—A Guide to Meditation and Relaxation* (Mill Valley, CA: Whatever Publishing, 1978), p. 50.
6. "Tapping Your 'Wise Man' Within," *Prevention Magazine*, May 1988.
7. "What Is Channeling," THE SILVA METHOD (Buena Park, CA: Silva Center), Spring 1987.
8. Klimo, "The Psychology of Channeling," p. 34.
9. Jon Klimo, *Channeling: Investigations on Receiving Information from Paranormal Sources* (Los Angeles, CA: Jeremy P. Tercher, Inc., 1987), p. 2.
10. Raymond Buckland, *Buckland's Complete Book of Witchcraft* (Minneapolis, MN: Llewellyn Publications, 1986), p. 100.
11. *The Silva Method* newsletter, Buena Park, CA, Spring 1987.
12. Fritjof Capra, *The Tao of Physics*, 2d ed. (New York: Bantam Books, 1984), p. xix.
13. Klimo, *Channeling: Investigations*, p. 124.
14. *Silva Mind Control*, newsletter.
15. Harner, *The Way of the Shaman*, p. 54.
16. Ibid., pp. 54-55.
17. Murdock, "Brain Child."
18. Maureen Murdock, *Spinning Inward: Using Guided Imagery with Children for Learning, Creativity and Relaxation* (Boston: Shambhala Publications, 1987), p. 85.
19. Mike Samuels, M.D., and Hal Bennett, *Spirit Guides: Access to Inner Worlds* (Random House/Bookworks, 1974), p. 19.
20. Murdock, *Spinning Inward*, p. 85.
21. Klimo, *Channeling: Investigations*, p. 12. Also quoted in the *New Age Journal*, "The Psychology of Channeling: An Investigation of Paranormal Claims," by Jon Klimo.
22. Gawain, *Creative Visualization*, p. 70.
23. Samuels and Samuels, *Seeing with the Mind's Eye*, pp. 131-32.
24. Enid Hoffman, *Develop Your Psychic Skills* (PA: Whitford Press, 1981), pp. 153-54.
25. Shirley MacLaine, *It's All in the Playing* (Bantam Books, 1987), on back cover.
26. Phyllis Terry Friedman, book review of *Opening to Channel* by Sanaya Roman and Duane Packer found in *The Common Boundary*, vol. 5, issue 6, Nov./Dec. 1987, p. 17.
27. Sanaya Roman and Duane Packer, *Opening to Channel: How to Connect with Your Guide* (CA: H.J. Kramer, Inc., 1987), p. 23.
28. Malachi Martin, *Hostage to the Devil: The Possession and Exorcism of Five Living Americans* (New York: Reader's Digest Press, 1976), p. 436.
29. Roman, *Opening to Channel*, pp. 23-24.
30. Ibid., p. 81.
31. Klimo, *Channeling: Investigations*, p. 338.
32. *New Webster's Dictionary of the English Language*, Deluxe Encyclopedic ed. (Delair Publishing Co., 1981).
33. Allen, *Reunion*, p. 51.
34. Peterson, *The Secret Life*, p. 72.
35. Ambrose and Olga Worrall, *The Miracle Healers*, A Signet Mystic Book (Harper and Row, 1965), p. 13.
36. Jaime T. Licauco, "The Psychic Child and How to Deal with Him," *International Journal of Early Childhood*, 1984.
37. Samuels and Bennett, *Spirit Guides*, p. 19.
38. Ibid., p. 20.
39. Tanous and Donnelly, *Is Your Child Psychic?*, p. 33.
40. Harner, *The Way of the Shaman*, p. 54.
41. Peterson, *The Secret Life*, p. 73.
42. Ibid., p. 73.
43. Tanous and Donnelly, *Is Your Child Psychic?*, p. 31.
44. Ibid., p. 36.
45. Ibid., pp. 35-36.

Chapter 9—Angels of God or Angels of Light?
1. Spring/Summer Catalog, Stillpoint Publishing, 1985.
2. Kathleen J. Forti, *The Door to the Secret City*, An Angelfood Book (Books that Develop Personal Awareness in Young People) (NH: Stillpoint Publishing, 1984), p. 17.
3. Anne Langford, illus. by David Bethards, age 9, *Meditation for Little People* (Marina Del Rey, CA: DeVorss and Co., Inc., 1975).

4. Ibid.
5. Stephen D. Swihart, *Angels in Heaven and Earth* (Plainfield, NJ: Logos International), p. 48.
6. Lori Aletha and Evaline, "Tips for Choosing a Psychic or Channel," *The New Times*, May 1986, p. 15.
7. "What Is Channeling?" *The Silva Method* newsletter, Buena Park, CA, Spring 1987.
8. Douglas James Mahr and Francis Racey, Ph.D., "Tired of the Program? Change Your Channel," *Life Times: Forum for the New Age*, vol. 1, no. 1, July 1986.
9. Aletha and Evaline, "Tips for Choosing a Psychic," p. 15.
10. Ibid.
11. Mahr and Racey, "Tired of the Program?"
12. Licauco, "The Psychic Child."
13. From an article edited from posthumous notes left by Knud Rasmussen, "The Shaman's Magic Drum," *Shaman's Drum: A Journal of Experiential Shamanism*, Summer 1985, p. 22.

Chapter 10—Truth Under Siege

1. Clark, *Growing Up Gifted*, p. 100.
2. Klimek and Canfield, "Discovering Your Radiant Self," *Self-Esteem in the Classroom Curriculum Guide* (Pacific Palisades, CA: Self-Esteem Seminars, 1986), p. 216.
3. Dean C. Halverson "A Course in Miracles: Seeing Yourself as Sinless," *SCP Journal*, vol. 7, no. 1, 1987, p. 23, quoting Kenneth Wapnick.
4. New Ager and author of *The Woman's Encyclopedia of Myths and Secrets*, Barbara Walker seems to have a difficult time understanding the concept of spiritual death. "God told Adam the same lie that the Babylonian god told Adam (in the Sumero-Babylonian version of the story of creation): 'Thou shalt not eat of it: for in the day that thou eatest thereof thou shalt surely die' (Genesis 2:17). Adam ate, but he didn't die in the same day. On the contrary, he lived to the age of 930 years (Genesis 5:5). It was the *serpent* who told the truth about the controversial food: 'Ye shall not surely die, for God doth know that in the day ye eat thereof, then your eyes shall be opened and ye shall be as gods' " (Genesis 3:4,5). (*The Woman's Encyclopedia of Myths*, p. 9.)
5. Dick Sutphen, "The 4 Assumptions," New Age Activists, *WHAT IS*, Summer 1986, vol. 1, no. 1.
6. Ferguson, *The Aquarian Conspiracy*, p. 23.
7. Jack Alexander, *Weekly World News*, July 19, 1984.
8. Karl Heussenstamm, *Toward the Maitreyan Revolution* (India: International Cooperation Council, 1974), pp. 147, 260. Foreword by Leland Stewart, Executive Director of the International Cooperation Council, now called Unity in Diversity.
9. Ralph Waldo Trine, *In Tune with the Infinite* (Indianapolis/New York: Bobbs-Merrill Co., Inc., 1908, 1970), pp. 155-56.
10. Robert Muller, *New Genesis: Shaping a Global Spirituality* (Image Books, a division of Doubleday and Company, Inc., 1984), p. 183. Gordon Cawelti, the executive director of the Association for Supervision and Curriculum Development, is developing a "world core curriculum" based on "proposals put forth by Robert Muller in his New Age treatise *New Genesis: Shaping a Global Spirituality* (Susan Hooper, "Educator Proposes a Global 'Core Curriculum,' " *Education Week*).
11. "Some Surprises Turn Up in New Presbyterian Survey," the *Los Angeles Times*, Mar. 4, 1989.
12. *Los Angeles Times*, Wed., Apr. 27, 1988, part 1, p. 3.
13. John Dart, "Episcopal Bishop Says It's Time to 'Rescue the Bible,' " the *Los Angeles Times*, Jan. 28, 1989, part II, p. 7.
14. For further study of what fundamentalism is and is not, you should read a classic little book by J.I. Packer entitled *"Fundamentalism" and the Word of God* (MI: W.M. B. Eerdmans Publishing Co., 1976).
15. John Dart, "Jesus Didn't Promise to Return, Bible Scholar Group Says," the *Los Angeles Times*, Mar. 5, 1989, part I, p. 3.
16. Ibid., part I, p. 3.
17. "Jesus Didn't Call Himself the Messiah, Scholars Agree In Vote," *The Seattle Times/Seattle Post-Intelligencer*, Associated Press, Oct. 18, 1987, p. A9.
18. Dart, "Jesus Didn't Promise to Return," part I, p. 3.
19. Ibid., part I, p. 3.
20. Charles C. Ryrie, *What You Should Know About Inerrancy* (Chicago, IL: The Moody Bible Institute, 1981), p. 21.
21. John Warwick Montgomery, *History and Christianity* (IL: InterVarsity Press, 1964, 1975), pp. 35, 58.
22. Ibid., pp. 26-27.
23. Ibid., p. 28.
24. Ibid., p. 29.
25. For a brilliant apologetic for the evidences for the Resurrection, read *Who Moved the Stone?* by Frank Morison (Zondervan Publishing House, MI, n.d.). "Frank Morison was an English journalist who set out to prove that the story of Christ's resurrection was nothing but a myth. However, his probings led him to the point where he placed his faith in the risen Christ."
26. For further study on the subject of biblical prophecy, read *The Late Great Planet Earth* and *The Promise*, by Hal Lindsey. Also recommended is a new book by John Ankerberg, Dr. John Weldon and Dr. Walter C. Kaiser, Jr., entitled *The Case for Jesus the Messiah: Incredible Prophecies that Prove God Exists*, published by The John Ankerberg Evangelistic Assoc., Chattanooga, TN, 1989.

Chapter 11—Halloween

1. 1 John 3:8.
2. Back in 1985 there was an outfit that called itself "Adopt-a-Ghost" based (where else?) in Hollywood, CA. For a paltry $10.00 to cover adoption papers and conjuring fees you could adopt a ghost for your house, condo, apartment, or office . . . rather like a Cabbage Patch Kid, only cheaper and considerably livelier. Hauntings

were guaranteed, and the ghost even came with written tips on ghost-raising to make sure it would stick around. Having your own resident ghost has become something of a status symbol in some parts of the country these days.

3. Connie Swart, "Event Still a Scream," the *Bakersfield Californian*, October 16, 1987, F13.

4. "Remains Discovered in Casket Believed Those of Farm Worker," *Daily Breeze* (Torrance, CA), Sept. 22, 1985.

5. Barbara G. Walker, *The Woman's Encyclopedia of Myths and Secrets* (San Francisco, CA: Harper and Row Publishers, 1983), p. 372.

6. *Encyclopedia of Witchcraft and Demonology* (London: Octopus Books Ltd., 1974), p. 166. Introduction by Hans Holzer.

7. Janet and Stewart Farrar, *A Witches Bible*, vol. 1, the Sabbats (New York: Magickal Childe Publishing, Inc., 1981, 1984), p. 122.

8. The lantern was also called a "corpse lantern" or "fairie fire," or a will-o'-the-wisp, and numerous fascinating legends about its origins have risen up around it. Some thought it was the spirit of a child which had been buried in the swamp. Others thought it represented the lights fairies used to beckon fools to a watery death in the swamps. Another legend tells of a clever fellow named Jack who got himself barred from hell as well as heaven for being something of a Faustian smart aleck, and was doomed to run about earth for all eternity with the burning coal he snatched from hell itself with the turnip he was eating just before the gates slammed shut. This story makes little sense to me at all. I mean, would *you* be eating a turnip while standing at the gates of hell politely requesting admittance? Doubtful. One version of this tale found in an elementary schoolteacher's "Halloween Fun" manual observes that the devil threw the burning coal at Jack to drive him away and that Jack caught the thing in his turnip. This makes more sense. Anyway, the Celts carved jack-o'-lanterns out of turnips, nonetheless. They probably used turnips because they didn't have pumpkins. They had to come to America to discover those, which they did during the mass immigration to America during the great potato famine of 1886. They soon realized that pumpkins are a whole lot easier to carve than turnips. They also make nicer pies.

St. James Church in the Los Angeles area held a "Pumpkin Mass" in 1987 in which the priest blessed the parishioners' Halloween costumes (to be brought in boxes or sacks) and the pumpkins which were to be carved and placed in the sanctuary. The verse quoted for the occasion: "You are the light of the world. Your light must shine before men . . ." (Matthew 5:14).

9. *Encyclopedia of Witchcraft*, p. 166.

10. Lewis Spence, *The History of Origins of Druidism* (Great Britain: EP Publishing Ltd., 1976), p. 104.

11. Ibid., p. 104.

12. Farrar and Farrar, *A Witches Bible*, vol. 1: the Sabbats, p. 122.

13. Raymond Buckland, *Witchcraft from the Inside* (St. Paul, MN: Llewellyn Publications, 1975), p. 16.

14. Spence, *History of Origins*, p. 105.

15. *A Witches Bible*, vol. 1, the Sabbats, p. 122.

16. James Frazer records in *The Golden Bough* (New York: Macmillan Publishing Co., Inc., 1922) that in some areas "people who assisted at the bonfires would wait till the last spark was out and then would suddenly take to their heels, shouting at the top of their voices, "The cropped black sow seize the hindmost!" The saying . . . implies that originally one of the company became a victim in dead earnest" (*The Golden Bough*, p. 736). The "cropped black sow" was a representation of the Goddess Cerridwen in her dark aspect as the Crone, according to Welsh mythology (*A Witches Bible*, vol. 1, the Sabbats, p. 125). She is still worshiped in that aspect by most Wiccans today, as well as in her more appealing forms of Maiden and Mother.

As the Farrars point out in *A Witches Bible* (vol. 1, the Sabbats, p. 125), "All these victim-choosing rituals long ago mellowed into a mere romp, but Frazer had no doubt of their original grim purpose. What was once a deadly serious ritual at the great tribal fire had become a party game at the family ones." They may have "mellowed in time," in most places, but nevertheless, it was the terror of the original sacrifices and demons that most accurately represent the "true spirit" of Halloween. The true "spirit of Halloween" is that of sudden death and murder.

17. Buckland, *Buckland's Complete Book of Witchcraft*, p. 68.

18. Arnold and Patricia Crowther, *The Secrets of Ancient Witchcraft with the Witches Tarot* (NJ: University Books, Inc., 1974), p. 67-68.

19. Ibid., p. 68.

20. Farrar and Farrar, *A Witches Bible*, vol 1, the Sabbats, p. 135.

21. Anton Szandor LaVey, *The Satanic Bible* (New York: Avon Books, 1969), p. v of introduction.

22. Anton LaVey clarifies his position on human sacrifice on page 88 of his *Satanic Bible*, in which he says: "Symbolically, the victim is destroyed through the working of a hex or curse, which in turn leads to the physical, mental or emotional destruction of the 'sacrifice' in ways and means not attributable to the magician. The only time a Satanist would perform a human sacrifice would be if it were to serve a two-fold purpose; that being to release the magician's wrath in the throwing of a curse, and more important, to dispose of a totally obnoxious and deserving individual."

23. John 8:44.

24. Ezekiel 16:20,21; Jeremiah 32:35; 2 Kings 17:17; Isaiah 57:5.

25. Deuteronomy 18:9-14.

26. Rebecca Jones, "Halloween Parade Off," *The Eagle Forum*, vol. 8, no. 4, Fall 1987, p. 17.

27. Ibid.

Chapter 12—The Season of the Witch

1. Janet Barker, "Witchcraft—Modern Witch Tries to Dispel Spooky Myths," *The Daily Breeze* (Los Angeles), Religion sect., Apr. 16, 1983.

2. Starhawk is an Antioch University West psychology graduate and teacher, a counselor, and her numerous books on witchcraft, such as *Dreaming the Dark* and *The Spiral Dance: A Rebirth of the Ancient Religion of the Great*

Goddess, are used as texts in various colleges, including Holy Names College in Oakland, California. This, thanks to Dominican priest Matthew Fox who in 1983 hired Starhawk to teach courses in Creating Ritual, Feminist Theology and Sexuality, Life-styles and NonViolence.

3. Emory Daniels, "Gundella's Talk Gets Green Light," *Plymouth Observer* (MI), Oct. 31, 1985.
4. Doug Funke, "Gundella Gives Lowdown on Witches at Salem," *Plymouth Observer*, (MI), Nov. 4, 1985.
5. Ibid.
6. Ibid.
7. Ibid.
8. Tim Richard, a *Plymouth Observer* reporter who had been covering the Gundella controversy for some time, equated any protest raised against Gundella as a throwback to the Inquisition. Literally. This "wonderful" woman could not *possibly* be a bad influence on students! After all, as her editor several years earlier, he had been invited to attend one of her Halloween gatherings, which concluded with a ritual. Richard tells us that even though his mainstream Christian faith prohibited his participation in the ritual (the title of his article was "Witches, Baptists and Scouts"), he figured it couldn't possibly hurt his faith to just sit by and watch. So he did, and was amazed at what he saw:

> Well, there was something very very familiar about the Witch ritual. I had seen it before—and not in an earlier life. As a youth, I was involved in a fairly respectable outfit called the Boy Scouts of America and was nominated for an honor group called the Order of the Arrow. We went through an "ordeal" weekend which involved cleaning the grounds of a group camp. That Saturday night we were initiated. The Order of the Arrow's induction ceremony was word for word, gesture for gesture, identical to Gundella's Witch ceremony.

Richard speculates that since Witchcraft is definitely the older movement, the Scouts had borrowed the ritual from them.

9. Susanne Glover and Georgeann Grewe, *A Witch's Manual*, Creative Writing (IL: Good Apple, Inc., 1985).
10. Imogene Forte, *Magic and Make-Believe—Fly Away to Fun and Fantasy*, The Tabletop Learning Series (Nashville, TN: Incentive Publications, Inc., 1985).
11. Buckland, *Buckland's Complete Book of Witchcraft*, p. 210.
12. *Publisher's Weekly* also really enjoyed The Little Witches Black Magic Book series by Linda Glovach. Of *The Little Witch's Black Magic Book of Disguises* they said: "A nifty book with scads of ideas for creating unusual costumes and accessories. Mothers will be relieved to find a preamble sets forth the little witch's code in no uncertain terms . . . a useful addition to the Little Witch books."
13. Walker, *The Woman's Encyclopedia of Myths*, p. 1087.
14. Reuters, "British Make It Officia; Witches No Longer Exist," *New York Times*, Sat., Apr. 21, 1951.
15. Most Witches will tell you that the term "Witch" applies to both men and women in "the Craft." The term "warlock" which most people think is the term for a male Witch, is seldom used by the Witches themselves, except perhaps in America. The word is of Scottish origin and actually means "oath breaker." Raymond Buckland, founder of the Seax Wicca tradition, says that originally the "Wicca"—the "Wise Ones"—were the ritual leaders, priests, and priestesses of the tribe. Witches Arnold and Patricia Crowther concur. "Modern Witches are the survival of the priesthood of the ancient craft." In general, Witches use the term "Witch" to describe one who has been initiated into the religion Wicca, also known as "the Craft" or the "Old Religion."
16. Derk Kinnane Roelofsma, "Inside the Circle of Witches Modern," (Berkeley, New York, and Salem), *Insight*, June 8, 1987, p. 59.
17. Barker, "Witchcraft—Modern Witch Tries to Dispel Spooky Myths."
18. Sally Norman, "The Witches Among Us," *Plain Dealer* (Cleveland, OH), Mar. 22, 1987.
19. "Witches Battle Bad Press by Going Public to Tidy Image," *Tucson Citizen*, (AZ), Oct. 31, 1984.
20. Ann Landers, "Woman: Witchcraft a Religion with No Connection to Satan," the *Bakersfield Californian*, Aug. 22, 1987.
21. Dave Hunt and T.A. McMahon, *America: The Sorcerer's New Apprentice* (Eugene, OR: Harvest House Publishers, 1988), pp. 90-91.
22. Zilpha Keatley Snyder, *The Headless Cupid*, A Dell Yearling Book (New York: Dell Publishing Co., Inc., 1971), pp. 13-15.
23. Memorandum from the Long Beach Unified School District's Office of the Legal Adviser regarding: Review of Issues Raised in Nov. 12, 1986 memorandum from Christian Civil Liberties Union; Dec. 8, 1986.
24. Debby Abe, "Bible Giveaway at School Sparks Suit," *The Idaho Statesman*, *The Valley* (Boise, ID), section C, Aug. 7, 1986.
25. Robert Thomas, "The God Squad Replies," *Community Forum* (Oceanside, CA), n.d.
26. Eric Bailey, "Trustees Reject Removal of Occult Books," *The Idaho Statesman* (Boise, ID), Aug. 3, 1986.
27. Thomas, "The God Squad Replies."

Chapter 13—Nothing to Toy With

1. Robert Maynard Hutchins, ed., "On Poetics," *Great Books of the Western World*, vol. 9, Aristotle: II (Encyclopedia Britannica, Inc., 1980), pp. 682, 1448b.
2. Michael R. Kelley, *A Parents' Guide to Television: Making the Most of It*, Wiley Parent Education Series (John Wiley and Sons, Inc., 1983), p. 3.
3. Dr. David Pearl, Ph.D., *Television and Behavior: Ten Years of Scientific Progress and Implications for the Eighties*, vol. 1: Summary Report (Rockville, MD: U.S. Dept. of Health and Human Services, National Institute of Mental Health [5600 Fishers Lane, Rockville, MD 20857], 1982).
4. Eugene H. Methvin, "TV Violence: The Shocking New Evidence," *Reader's Digest*, Jan. 1983, p. 50.
5. For further reading on the significance of the rainbow and the New Age Movement, see Constance Cumbey, *The Hidden Dangers of the Rainbow* (Huntington House, 1983).

6. Moon Dreamers, "My Little Pony 'N Friends," from program viewed Oct. 18, 1987.
7. "He Man and the Masters of the Universe," on program I watched Oct. 23, 1984.
8. Bruno Bettelheim, *The Uses of Enchantment: The Meaning and Importance of Fairy Tales* (Vintage Books Edition, 1977), p. 25.
9. Ibid., p. 24.
10. Ibid., p. 47.
11. Walker, *The Woman's Encyclopedia of Myths*, p. 838.
12. Manly P. Hall, *The Secret Teachings of All Ages: An Encyclopedic Outline of Masonic, Hermetic, Qabbalistic and Rosicrucian Symbolical Philosophy* (Los Angeles, CA: The Philosophical Research Society, Inc., 1977), p. XCII.
13. *New Webster's Dictionary*, p. 15.
14. Cavendish, *Man, Myth and Magic*, vol. 21, p. 2910.
15. Walker, *The Woman's Encyclopedia of Myths*, p. 780.
16. *Encyclopedia of Magic and Superstition* (New York: Crescent Books, a division of Crown Publishers, Inc., 1974), p. 188. (First published in 1974 by Octopus Books Ltd., London.)
17. Boris Matthews, trans., *The Herder Symbol Dictionary: Symbols from Art, Archaeology, Mythology, Literature, and Religion* (Wilmette, IL: Chiron Publications, 1986), p. 91.
18. J.E. Cirlot (Jack Sage, trans.), *A Dictionary of Symbols*, 2d ed. (New York: Philosophical Library, 1971), p. 91.
19. *The Unicorn King and Other Stories*, a She-Ra videotape, Filmation/Magic Window, Mattel, Inc., 1985.
20. Matthews, *The Herder*, p. 52.
21. *The Unicorn King and Other Stories*.
22. Roger McKenzie, *The Sword of Skeletor*, Masters of the Universe, A Golden Book (New York: Western Publishing Co., Inc., Wi., 1983). Copyright held by Mattel, Inc.
23. "Star Wars III, Return of the Jedi," *Time* magazine cover story, May 23, 1983, p. 60.
24. "Top Psychiatrists Explain . . . The Amazing Appeal of 'Return of the Jedi,' " *National Enquirer*, June 21, 1983.
25. Dale Pollock, *Skywalking: The Life and Films of George Lucas* (New York: Harmony Books, 1983), p. 2.
26. Ibid., p. 144.
27. Ibid., p. 139.
28. Ibid., p. 140.
29. Ibid.
30. Ibid.
31. Ibid.
32. Ibid.
33. Sue Cornwell and Mike Kott, *The Official Price Guide to Star Trek and Star Wars Collectibles* (New York: Random House, Inc., published by The House of Collectibles, 1986).
34. Canfield and Klimek, "Education in the New Age," vol. 3, no. 9, p. 36.
35. "Film and Television," *Chicago Tribune*, Apr. 8, 1982.
36. Richard Cavendish, *The Black Arts* (Capricorn Books Edition, 1968), p. 242.
37. Matthew 15:22; 17:14-18; Mark 9:17-26; Luke 9:38-42.
38. Cheryl Simon, "The Joy of Toys: The Playthings of Children Reflect the Values and Concerns of Society," *Washington Post Health*, Dec. 25, 1985, p. 10.
39. Thomas Radecki, M.D., "The TV War on Children: Savagery Is Fair and Fun in Television's Kid Cartoons," *The Christian Reader*, July/Aug. 1986, p. 16.
40. Nancy Gibbs, "Wilding in the Night: A Brutal Gang Rape in New York City Triggers Fears that the U.S. Is Breeding a Generation of Merciless Children," *Time* magazine, May 8, 1989.
41. "T.V.'s Influence on Kids Is More than We Thought," *Long Beach Press-Telegram* from *New York Daily News*, Mar. 4, 1989.
42. Ibid.
43. Mitchell Fink, "Co-Creator of Dungeons and Dragons Defends Game's Violence," *Los Angeles Herald Examiner*, Sept. 14, 1985.
44. Gary Gygax, *Advanced Dungeons and Dragons: Player's Handbook*, 1978, p. 7.
45. Ibid., p. 7.
46. Ibid., p. 20.
47. Ibid., p. 25.
48. Matthew 5:28.
49. Romans 12:2.
50. Philippians 4:8.
51. Billy Bowles, "A Deadly Game?" *Detroit Free Press*, Michigan, Oct. 13, 1985.
52. Kristine K. Thompson, "Role-Playing Games: Expect the Unexpected," *Gifted Children Newsletter*, vol. 5, no. 2, Feb. 1984.
53. Jerry Adler with Shawn Doherty, "Kids: The Deadliest Game?" *Newsweek*, Sept. 9, 1985.
54. "Synergy" was certainly an interesting choice of names for JEM's special helper that she contacts through her red star magic earings. June G. Bletzer's *The Donning International Encyclopedia Psychic Dictionary* (p. 610), defines "Synergy," in part, as "harmony, blending, and cooperation between two energies is necessary for physical phenomena; i.e., *cosmic energy and mind; etheric world intelligences and mind* . . . works especially through skills of *inspirational thought, automatic writing, dowsing, trance.*"
55. Kelley, *A Parents' Guide to Television*, p. 42.
56. Those children's books listed and others are available through your local Christian bookstore.
57. Deborah Smith, *The Faithful's Journey Through Fairy Land*, (1989), pp. 9-10.
58. Bettelheim, *The Uses of Enchantment*, pp. 50-51.

1. J. Michael Kennedy, "12 Bodies Found Near Border Called Drug Cult Victims," *Los Angeles Times*, Apr. 12, 1989, part 1, p. 16. See also Apr. 13, 1989, part 1, p. 14; Apr. 14, 1989, part 1, p. 4.
2. "Devil Worship: What's Behind It? Troubled Teen-Agers See Outlet for Rebellion," the *Houston Post*, Sept. 15, 1985.
3. Associated Press, "Murder-Suicide Blamed on Study of Occult," the *Register-Guard* (Eugene, OR), Jan. 13, 1988, p. 12A. Also documented in the *Albuquerque Journal*, "Satan's Teens: 'What Have We Got to Live For?' " Feb. 15, 1988, p. B4, and the "Geraldo" show, "Devil Worship: Exposing Satan's Underground," Oct. 25, 1988.
4. Tom Edwards, "Satanism Linked to Animal Cruelty Near Middle School," *Express News* (San Antonio, TX), Jan. 17, 1986.
5. Associated Press, "El Paso Sheriff Investigates Reports of Satanic Sacrifices," *Beaumont Enterprise* (Beaumont, TX), Nov. 1, 1986.
6. Diana Washington, "Fad or Fanatic Cult? El Paso Teen-Agers Lured into Devil Worship," *El Paso Times*, Feb. 16, 1986. Case also documented in another area paper sent to me with no date or paper identification.
7. A personal letter from Paul Vick dated Nov. 10, 1987 (Paul Vick Ministries, Inc., P.O. Box 96482, Houston, TX 77213-6482).
8. Deana Washington, "Fad or Fanatic Cult?" *El Paso Times*, Feb. 16, 1986.
9. Shelley Emling, "Teen Satanism Alarms Area Mental-Health Officials: Local Hospitals Plan Programs to Treat 'Epidemic' of Cultism," *Corpus Christi Caller Times*, 2d. article of series, Aug. 8, 1988.
10. Paul Hutchison, "Satanism Feared in Eastern Colorado Child Abuse Case," the *Denver Post*, May 22, 1988, p. 1.
11. Ibid.
12. Ric Leyva, Associated Press, "Child Abuse and Satanism: Victims' Tales of Devil Worship Are Derailing the Prosecution of Cases," *The State Journal-Register* (Springfield, IL), Dec. 13, 1987, p. 25.
13. Geraldo Rivera, "Devil Worship: Exposing Satan's Underground," TV documentary, transcript special #6, Oct. 25, 1988, p. 24.
14. Ibid., p. 22.
15. "Religious Requirements and Practices of Certain Selected Groups, A Handbook for Chaplains," Dept. of the Army pamphlet, no. 165-13, Apr. 1978, VII-20, p. 4.
16. "The Oprah Winfrey Show," "Satanic Worship," transcript #W373, Feb. 17, 1988.
17. Richard Cavendish, *The Black Arts* (New York: Capricorn Books, 1968), p. 2.
18. Ibid., p. 4.
19. Ted Schwarz and Duane Empey, *Satanism: Is Your Family Safe?* (Grand Rapids, MI: Zondervan Books, 1988), pp. 72-73.
20. Ibid.
21. Arthur Lyons, *Satan Wants You: The Cult of Devil Worship in America* (New York: The Mysterious Press, 1988), p. 115.
22. Lyons, *Satan Wants You*, pp. 126-27.
23. LaVey, *Satanic Bible*, p. 62, and in the introduction.
24. Anton Szandor LaVey, *The Satanic Rituals: Companion to the Satanic Bible* (New York: Avon Books, 1972), pp. 42-43, 45.
25. "Religious Requirements and Practices," Dept. of the Army.
26. In September of 1987 Attorney General Edwin Meese III announced that a yearlong nationwide sting operation against child pornography had yielded over "100 indictments...which covered a variety of professions, including engineers, store owners, a postman, a railroad inspector and a film producer. In many cases," Meese said, "they are pillars of the community." If "pillars of the community" are being found to be confirmed pedophiles, why should we be surprised to find some of these same "pillars" into devil worship?
27. Matthew 7:15. See also Paul's warning in Acts 20:28-31.
28. For further reading: Jan Hollingsworth, *Unspeakable Acts* (New York: Congdon and Weed, 1986).
29. LaVey, *Satanic Bible*, p. 30.
30. Rivera, "Devil Worship," Oct. 25, 1988.
31. LaVey, *Satanic Bible*, p. 149.
32. Ibid., pp. 88-89.
33. Lyons, *Satan Wants You*, p. 108.
34. LaVey, *Satanic Bible*.
35. Andy Furillo, "Sympathy for the Devil: More Young People Turn to Satan-Worship," *Los Angeles Herald Examiner*, Mar. 18, 1984, p. A8.
36. Lee Harrison, "Teens Are Turning to the Devil for a Father Figure," undated and unidentified newspaper article, quoting Dr. Peter Olsson.
37. Furillo, "Sympathy for the Devil," p. A1.
38. Ibid., p. A8.
39. Ibid., p. A8.
40. Venom, "Sacrifice," Here Lies Venom, Combat Records MX8020, as quoted in Tipper Gore, *Raising PG Kids in an X-Rated Society* (Nashville, TN: Abingdon Press, 1987) p. 120.
41. Peggy Mann, "How Shock Rock Harms Our Kids," *Reader's Digest*, July 1988, p. 101.
42. For further reading see Tipper Gore, *Raising PG Kids in an X-Rated Society* (Nashville, TN: Abingdon Press, 1987).
43. Geraldo Rivera, "Teen Satanism," the "Geraldo" show, television transcript #276, Oct. 6, 1988.
44. Anne Fadiman, "Heavy Metal Mania," n.d.
45. Hans Grieling, "In Satan's Service," *Hit Parade* magazine, Oct. 1988, p. 65.
46. Dan and Steve Peters, with Cher Merrill, *Why Knock Rock?* (MN: Bethany House Publishers, 1984), p. 75.

47. Joe Viara, "Shelter the Darkness," P.O. Box 1516, Westford, MA 01886.
48. Canfield, *Self-Esteem in the Classroom*, p. 220.
49. Mitchell Fink, "Singer Ozzy Osbourne Sued in Teen's Suicide: Death Blamed on 'Devil music,' " *Los Angeles Herald Examiner*, Jan. 14, 1986.
50. Associated Press, "Rock Band Faces Trial in Nevada Suicide Pact," *Los Angeles Times*, Aug. 27, 1988.
51. "Heavy Metal Messages on Trial," *Media Update*, a Bimonthly magazine of Menconi Ministries, P.O. Box 969, Cardiff, CA 92007-0969, vol. 8, issue 2, Mar.-Apr. 1989, p. 6.
52. For further information on this vital subject, read Jerry Johnston, *Why Suicide? What Parents and Teachers Must Know to Save Our Kids* (Thomas Nelson Publishers, 1987).
53. Ibid.
54. Tamara Jones, " 'Fun' Killers Now Paying Devil's Dues," *Los Angeles Times*, Oct. 20, 1988, A1.
55. Johnson, *Why Suicide?*, p. 39.
56. *Thrasher*, vol. 8, no. 4, Apr., 1988, p. 93.
57. Anastasie Toufexis, "Teens and Sex Crimes," *Time* magazine, June 5, 1989, p. 60.
58. The telephone book yellow pages, social service agencies, and community resource people can help you locate help in your area. Nationally, one helpful organization is Back In Control—a center that specializes in training parents in how to deal with difficult kids from toddlers to 18 years of age. The organization was founded by Gregory Bodenhamer, author of *How to Get Your Children to Behave* (Prentice Hall, 1983). Their address is: Back In Control, 1107 W. Chapman Ave., Suite C, Orange, CA 92668.
59. Tamara Jones, "Satanists' Trail: Dead Pets to a Human Sacrifice," *Los Angeles Times*, Oct. 19, 1988.
60. Ibid., p. 1. See also the second article in series on this case " 'Fun Killers' Now Paying Devil's Dues," *Los Angeles Times*, Oct. 20, 1988.
61. Revelation 20:10.

Chapter 15—What's a Parent to Do?
1. Isaiah 14:14.
2. Ephesians 2:2.
3. 1 John 5:19.
4. Ephesians 6:10,11.
5. 1 Corinthians 1:18.
6. Romans 1:16.
7. Acts 4:12.
8. 1 Corinthians 1:20.
9. Ephesians 2:8,9.
10. John 1:12.
11. Acts 19:18.
12. 1 John 1:8.
13. Ephesians 1:7.
14. John 3:16.
15. John 1:29.
16. Romans 8:1.
17. Kurt Koch, *Occult Bondage and Deliverance* (Grand Rapids, MI: Kregel Publications, 1971-1976), p. 100.
18. For further discussion of counterfeit gifts in the church, see Johanna Michaelsen, *The Beautiful Side of Evil* (Eugene, OR: Harvest House Publishers, 1982), chapter 16.
19. Acts 19:18-20.
20. For further reading see John L. Nevius, *Demon Possession*, (Grand Rapids, MI: Kregel Publications, 1970), copyright 1984 by Fleming H. Revell Co.; T.K. Oesterreich, *Possession—Demoniacal and Other* (Secaucus, NJ: Citadel Press, 1974); and Kurt Koch, *Christian Counseling and Occultism* (Grand Rapids, MI: Kregel Publications, 1973).
21. 2 Corinthians 10:3-5.

Appendix A—A Sinner's Self-Esteem
1. For an excellent analysis of the biblical perspective of Self-Esteem, write for Martin and Deidre Bobgan's publication entitled "PsychoHeresy Update," vol. 1, no. 1, Fall 1988, EastGate Publishers, 4137 Primavera Road, Santa Barbara, CA 93110.
2. John Vasconcellos, *A Liberating Vision: Politics For Growing Humans* (CA: Impact Publishers [Post Office Box 1094, San Luis Obispo, CA 93406], 1979), p.viii.
3. Vitz, *Psychology As Religion*, p. 91.
4. Shirley MacLaine, *Dancing in the Light* (NY: Bantam Books, 1985) p. 421.
5. Ramtha, with Douglas James Mahr, *Voyage to the New World* (WA: Masterworks, Inc., Publishers, 1985), pp. 264, 246.
6. Ibid., pp. 246-47.
7. MacLaine, *Dancing in the Light*, pp. 356-57.
8. Dick Sutphen, "Chethlahe: Channeling and Death," *MASTER OF LIFE: Tools & Teachings to Create Your Own Reality* (Malibu, CA), issue 36, 1987.

Appendix B—You Must Be Born Again . . . and Again
1. Ramtha, with Mahr, *Voyage to the New World*, pp. 89-90.
2. Joseph Head and S.L. Cranston, comp. and eds., *Reincarnation: The Phoenix Fire Mystery* (NY: Julian Press/Crown Publishers, Inc., 1977), p. 134.
3. "The Oprah Winfrey Show," "New Age Movement," Sept. 18, 1987, transcript #W265.

4. Head and Cranston, *Reincarnation*.
5. F.F. Bruce, *The New Testament Documents: Are They Reliable?*, 5th rev. (Downers Grove, IL: InterVarsity Press, 1974).
6. Morton Smith, *Jesus the Magician* (San Francisco, CA: Harper & Row, Publishers, 1978), pp. 1, 6.
7. There are numerous excellent well-documented books which address the issues of biblical inerrancy and reincarnation in great depth. Among them: F.F. Bruce, *The New Testament Documents: Are They Reliable?* (InterVarsity Press, 1974, 5th rev.); John Warwick Montgomery, *History & Christianity*, (InterVarsity Press, 1963); March Albrecht, *Reincarnation: A Christian Appraisal*, (InterVarsity Press, 1982); Dave Hunt and T.A. McMahon, *America: The Sorcerer's New Apprentice—The Rise of New Age Shamanism*, (Harvest House Publishers, 1988).
8. Ferguson, *The Aquarian Conspiracy*, p. 158.
9. Luther D. Sunderland, *Darwin's Enigma—Fossils and Other Problems* (El Cajon, CA: Master Book Publishers, 1984), p. 98.
10. Ibid., p. 100, quoting Dr. Patterson.
11. Ferguson, *Aquarian Conspiracy*, p. 159.
12. Ibid.
13. Dr. Gould and Niles Eldredge have openly admitted their adherence to Marxist philosophy. In *Paleobiology* magazine, as quoted in *Darwin's Enigma* (p. 108), they stated:

    Alternative conceptions of change have respectable pedigrees in philosophy. Hegel's dialectical laws, translated into a materialist context, have become the official "state philosophy" of many socialist nations. These laws of change are explicitly punctuational, as befits a theory of revolutionary transformation in human society.

    In the light of this official philosophy, it is not at all surprising that a punctuational view of speciation, much like our own, but devoid (so far as we can tell) of references to synthetic evolutionary theory and the allopatric model, has long been favored by many Russian paleontologists. It may also not be irrelevant to our personal preferences that one of us learned his Marxism, literally, at his daddy's knee.
14. "Creationism vs. Evolution: Supreme Court to Decide," *Los Angeles Herald Examiner*, May 6, 1986.
15. Ibid.

Appendix C—Unity or Else

1. From a promotional brochure for a seminar entitled "Visions of Destiny." The conference was sponsored by "I AM"—International Associations of Metaphysicians. Their American Symposium was held Aug. 10-16, 1986, at the University of Denver. Other speakers included occultist and author Brad Steiger, and Peter Caddy, the founder of Findhorn.
2. Jose Arguelles from an article in the *Utne Reader*, July.-Aug. 1987.
3. John Randolph Price, *Practical Spirituality*, pp. 18-19.
4. Barbara Marx Hubbard, *The Book of Co-Creation—An Evolutionary Interpretation of the New Testament*, a three part unpublished manuscript, 1980.
5. Peter Russell, *The Global Brain* (Los Angeles: Tarcher, Inc., 1983), pp. 156-59.
6. Quoted in *Report from Concerned Christians*," vol. 2, Oct. 1986 (Mr. Kim Miller, P.O. Box 22920, Denver, CO, 80222).
7. John Randolph Price, *Practical Spirituality*, pp. 18-19, quoted by Tim Philibossian in *EMNR*—Evangelical Ministries to New Religions, Englewood, CO, Dec. 1986.
8. Hubbard, *Book of Co-Creation*, part III, p. 60.
9. "Enter by the narrow gate; for the gate is wide, and the way is broad that leads to destruction, and many are those who enter by it" (Matthew 7:13).

Appendix D—Queen of Heaven

1. For further study on this, please see *The Two Babylons or the Papal Worship—Proved to be the Worship of Nimrod and His Wife*, by the late Rev. Alexander Hislop, Loizeaux Brothers (NJ.: Neptune, 1959 edition); and *Babylon Mystery Religion, Ancient and Modern*, Ralph Woodrow, P.O. Box 124, Riverside, CA 92502, 1981 edition.
2. "The Return of the Great Goddess: A New Pluralism," *CIRCLE* Network News, Fall/Winter 1987, p. 9.
3. Joan Scobey, "Witchcraft," Sept. 1987, p. 106.
4. The C.J. Jung Institute of San Francisco, in the Fall of 1988, offered a series of seminars entitled "The Year of the Myth." At least eight of the seminars dealt with the goddess, her history and worship through the ages, presented by professors, Jungian analysts, painters, psychotherapists, and feminists at least most of whom seem to be devotees of the goddess. One of the seminars included a reading from the poetry of the ancient high priestess of Innana in Sumer, Enheduanna, whose "brilliant voice upholds the inviolable realm of the goddess against the encroaching patriarchy. Her work speaks to our future as we reclaim the sacred feminine. Her theology grounds us in our ancestral past."
5. Farrar and Farrar, *A Witches Bible*, vol 1, the Sabbats, p. 82.
6. Walker, *The Woman's Encyclopedia of Myths*, p. 972.
7. "Child Sacrifice at Carthage and in the Bible," *Biblical Archaeology Review*, Jan./Feb. 1984.
8. Ibid.
9. M. Esther Harding, *Woman's Mysteries—Ancient and Modern* (Harper Colophon Books, Harper & Row Publishers, 1971, 1976), p. 138.
10. Ibid., p. 138.
11. Michael Harrison, *The Roots of Witchcraft* (Great Britain: Tandem Books, 1975), p. 59.
12. Ibid., pp. 65-66.
13. Walker, *The Woman's Encyclopedia of Myths*, p. 490.

14. Nagesh Rao, *Los Angeles Herald Examiner*, Aug. 16, 1985, from the *London Observer Service*.
15. Starhawk and Miriam Simos, *The Spiral Dance—A Rebirth of the Ancient Religion of the Great Goddess* (Harper and Row Publishers, 1979), p. 84.
16. Sybil Leek, *The Complete Art of Witchcraft—Penetrating the Mystery Behind Magic Powers* (New York: Signet Classics, Thomas Y. Crowell Company, 1971), p. 190.
17. *Encyclopedia of Witchcraft & Demonology,* p. 12.

Appendix E—Sharers in Demons
1. LaVey, *Satanic Bible.*

Appendix F—What Witches Believe
1. Margot Adler, *Drawing Down the Moon,* 1st ed. (Boston: Beacon Press, 1981), p. 10.
2. Erica Jong, *Witches* (New York: Harry N. Abrams, Inc., 1981), p. 52.
3. Adler, *Drawing Down the Moon,* p. 10.
4. Starhawk and Simos, *The Spiral Dance,* p. 2.
5. Sybil Leek, *Diary of a Witch,* a Signet Book (New York: New American Library, 1969), p. 140.
6. *A Book of Pagan Rituals* (New York: Samuel Weiser, Inc., 1978), p. 86.
7. Adler, *Drawing Down the Moon,* pp. 119-122.
8. *The Truth About Witchcraft,* a Llewellyn Educational Guide.
9. "The Tools of Magick," *The Wiccan Way,* vol. 5, no. 3 (Selden, New York: Beltane, 1985).
10. Ibid.
11. Adler, *Drawing Down the Moon,* p. 104.
12. Joan Scobey, "Witchcraft," *New Woman* magazine, Sept. 1987, p. 110.
13. Ibid., p. 110.
14. Leek, *Diary of a Witch,* p. 117.
15. Zsuzsanna Budapest, *The Holy Book of Women's Mysteries,* vol. 1, rev. ed. (Oakland, CA: Susan B. Anthony Coven No. 1, 1986), p. 31.
16. Ibid., p. 32.
17. Ibid., p. 90.
18. " 'Meet a Witch' Plan Brews Up Parent Protest," *Los Angeles Times,* July 10, 1986, part I, p. 25.
19. David W. Balsiger, "Dukakis Names Official Salem Witch," *Presidential Biblical Scoreboard,* 1988 General Election, special edition (Costa Mesa, CA), p. 41.
20. Letter from Laurie Cabot's Witches Awareness League to Dr. Larry Jones, editor of the *File 18* newsletter. The letter protested the mention of Witches in a newsletter primarily reserved for sharing information with law enforcement officials about ritual crimes and assorted occult networks. The mailing list for *File 18* includes police officers, assorted ACLU representatives, senators (such as Edward Kennedy), and many others.
21. Cavendish, *Man, Myth and Magic,* vol. 1, p. 77.

Appendix G—Sympathy for the Devil
1. Hubburd, *The Book of Co-Creation,* p. 116.
2. Ibid., p. 115.
3. Ibid., p. 117.
4. Ibid., p. 116.
5. Ibid., p. 117.
6. Ibid.
7. Manly P. Hall, *Magic* (Los Angeles: The Philosophical Research Society, 1978), p. 23.
8. Spangler, *Reflections on the Christ,* p. 44.
9. Ibid., p. 45.

Appendix H—God Who?
1. Findhorn Community, *The Findhorn Garden* (Harper Colophon Books, Harper and Row Publishers, 1975).
2. Tim Philibossian, *Evangelical Ministries to New Religions,* Dec. 1986.
3. Sri Chinmoy, *A Child's Heart And a Child's Dreams* (Jamaica, NY: Aum Publications, 1986), pp. 81, 86.
4. Steven Lee Weinberg, Ph.D., ed., *Ramtha* (WA: 1986), pp. 29-30.
5. MacLaine, *Dancing in the Light,* p. 420.
6. Vitz, *Psychology As Religion,* p. 93.
7. Ezekiel 28:2-10.
8. Oprah Winfrey on her program "The Oprah Winfrey Show," Sept. 18, 1987.
9. Eric Butterworth, *Discover the Power Within You: A Guide to the Unexplored Depths Within, Based on the Actual Teachings of Jesus* (New York: Harper and Row Publishers, 1968), pp. 44-45.

Appendix I—Speak for Yourself
1. LaVey, *Satanic Bible,* p. x (Introduction).
2. Ibid., pp. 25, 30-33.

Appendix J—Teachable Teachers
1. Susan Gurule, *Coalition for Family Values* newsletter, (P.O. Box 21175, Albuquerque, NM 87110).
2. See chapter 7—Shamanism 101.